Justice and Leadership in Early Islamic Courts

Islamic Legal Studies Program: SHARIAsource
Harvard Series in Islamic Law, VII

Justice and Leadership
in
Early Islamic Courts

Edited by Intisar A. Rabb and Abigail Krasner Balbale

Published by the
Islamic Legal Studies Program, Harvard Law School
Distributed by Harvard University Press
Cambridge, Massachusetts
2017

Library of Congress Control Number:
2017948414

Printed in the United States of America
ISBN 9780674984219

CONTENTS

ACKNOWLEDGEMENTS

This volume would not have been possible without the hard work of many—from the contributors who moved their articles through several stages of review rapidly and the anonymous peer reviewers who provided critical and timely feedback, to the research assistants who worked late into the night copyediting and tracking down references. Our desire to bring this volume to press soon after Roy Mottahedeh's retirement created a tighter timeline than most academic books have, and we are grateful to our contributors and to all who helped make this happen.

We gratefully acknowledge the contributions of Roy Mottahedeh's friends, colleagues, and students to this volume. Hossein Modarressi and Fred Donner graciously agreed to interviews about Roy for our introduction to the volume and offered their memories of Roy as a friend, colleague, and mentor dating back forty-odd years. Cemal Kafadar introduced Roy's publications with reflections on his colleague as a scholar and a friend. Michael Cook and William Graham wrote introductions for sections of the book, relating the subjects of the chapters to Roy's work. Other colleagues and friends served as session moderators and presenters at the conference that preceded the book: Abbas Amanat, William Granara, and Baber Johansen. Sarah Bowen Savant and Kristen Stilt organized a wonderful celebration for Roy in 2012, and their work gave rise to the Tabula Gratulatoria included here.

We would like to express special thanks to Sharon Tai, whose assistance through every stage of this book's planning, execution, and publication was singularly important. From helping to plan the conference that led to this volume to typesetting its pages and coordinating an online companion for the book, Sharon's indefatigable energy and consistently cheerful demeanor made this project possible.

Many others at Harvard also helped facilitate the production of this book and the conference that preceded it, including Ashley Davis, Ceallaigh Reddy, and S. Darrick Northington at the Islamic Legal Studies Program. For the conference, Halah Ahmad, Faiq Habash, Sarah Mokh, and Anwar Omeish helped with research and logistics. As we moved through the various stages of the book's production, research assistants Janan Delgado, Yusuf Lenfest, Ari Schriber, and Lispeth Tibbits-Nutt helped with copy-editing, bibliographic work, and more.

Thank you to Steven Moore for rapid and fastidious indexing, to our anonymous reviewers for critical feedback on the volume and on individual chapters, to Alma Giese for assistance in securing some permissions, and of course to Patricia Mottahedeh for all of her help and support.

The papers in this volume largely arise out of proceedings from a conference organized in honor of Professor Roy Mottahedeh upon the occasion of his retirement. The conference was organized by the Islamic Legal Studies Program and SHARIAsource at Harvard Law School, with support from the Luce and MacArthur Foundations. The conference was co-sponsored by the Center for Middle Eastern Studies, the Prince Alwaleed bin Talal Islamic Studies Program, and the Department of History, and had support from the Radcliffe Institute for Advanced Study at Harvard. We are grateful to each for their institutional support.

Most of all, we wish to thank Roy Mottahedeh for his mentorship and advising, and for his friendship and intellectual inspiration. As he has said to each of us many, many, times: Flourish! Onward!

Roy Parviz Mottahedeh. Photo credit: Stephanie Mitchell/Harvard News Office. Special thanks to the *Harvard Gazette*.

Roy Parviz Mottahedeh and some of the authors of this volume at the *Courts and Judicial Procedure in Early Islamic Law Conference* at Harvard Law School in May 2016. Photo credit: Sharon Tai/ILSP.

INTRODUCTION

New York and Kashan meet elegantly in the person of Roy Mottahedeh, who in turn meets scores of students, colleagues, and casual readers from everywhere with insights that are clear and eloquent, critical and colorful. He has always approached the study of Islamic social and administrative-legal history with a method that vividly brings the sources, and those who produced them, to life.[1] In honor of the man and his method, this volume brings together a few of the many who have learned from him, as well as his admirers and colleagues, to add texture to the early social and legal history of courts and judicial procedure in Islamic law.

ON ROY

Roy Parviz Mottahedeh was born in 1940 in New York City to a Kashani father and New Jersey-born mother, who built a family business by importing Iranian arts and crafts and later by reproducing Chinese export porcelain. Despite his many accomplishments, ever the modest scholar, he insists that his friends and intellectual interlocutors call him Roy.

Roy entered Harvard College at sixteen and graduated with a degree in history, *magna cum laude,* in 1960. He spent the next several years traveling in the Middle East and Europe, earning a second bachelor's degree in Persian and Arabic at Cambridge University in the United Kingdom, where he won the E.G. Browne Prize. Returning to Cambridge, Massachusetts, he began his doctoral studies in History under the tutelage of H.A.R. Gibb, Robert Lee Wolff, and Richard Frye, with a dissertation on Buyid administration. After a Junior Fellowship at the Harvard Society of

1 Cemal Kafadar's introduction to the list of publications is so on-point that it bears telegraphing up front: Roy Mottahedeh "has made the best of his background in being a New Yorker and a son of a Kashani mercantile family from two places known for their intellectual sophistication and down-to-earth worldliness at the same time. It may be that mercantile background of his family that gives him a particular perspective on the world of scholars, poets, and scribes, all of whom he knows how to appreciate but also to observe with an ethnographer's eye to see into all their bizarre ways and follies, their accomplishments and pretensions...." (Cemal Kafadar, "Reading with Roy" 173–74, this volume).

Fellows, he received his PhD in 1970. He was immediately appointed as Assistant Professor in Near Eastern Studies at Princeton, where he would remain for the next sixteen years.

Fred Donner arrived at Princeton soon after as Roy's first doctoral student. Roy's unique approach inspired his students to apply the new approaches of social history to Islamic history. As Donner put it:

> Early in my time at Princeton, he decided to offer a class on medieval Islamic social history, which had never been offered before. Social history was still new in the United States. He had us read a book by [George] Rudé called *The Crowd in History* [1964], which was about the French Revolution. The point was to think about how this person was doing history and to inquire whether we could ask the same kinds of questions of Islamic history. It was really very stimulating in encouraging us to think more broadly than the scholarly world in Islamic history was doing. He was blowing the walls off and forcing us to look far beyond Islamic history to think about how to do history.

Years later, in 1977, Roy attended a historical meeting in Hamadan, where some of the most prominent scholars of Islamic and Iranian studies from his generation and the preceding one would gather in a single conference—many of whom would become fast friends: Richard Bulliet, Anne Lambton, Wilferd Madelung, and Hossein Modarressi, to name a few. Roy's presence and the enduring friendships that emerged were not accidental. He had already distinguished himself as a thoughtful historian of the Islamic world, having written an erudite dissertation on the local histories of Qum, Qazwin, and Rayy, and having distinguished himself as teacher and scholar at Princeton. True to form, he immediately impressed the scholars there. As Hossein Modarressi put it:

> As soon as we started to speak to each other it was apparent that he was a very learned person, that he carried deep knowledge of global history and other subjects, such as Greek philosophy. He had clearly read a lot, he followed the discussions, and he contributed to each.

After the Hamadan conference, an intrepid group ventured together on visits to the grave of Avicenna and to a system of water caves, which—though they appeared unassuming—were in fact the largest network of such caves in the world. These caves had long provided a home to hidden treasures of ancient artwork, jugs, and other artifacts, some dating back twelve thousand years. Like these caves, Roy's unassuming face belies the depth and breadth of his curiosity, interest, and eloquent expertise. Those lucky enough to enter his space and call themselves colleagues or friends—who are many—encounter the treasures of his cavernous mind and stores of generosity, thought, and exchange.

One notable example is the generous friendship and intellectual exchanges that developed between Roy Mottahedeh and Hossein Modarressi over the years. After Modarressi moved to Oxford in 1979, the two visited each other—Roy visited his friend at Oxford, and his friend visited him at Princeton. Roy would play a role in inviting Modarressi to Princeton as a visiting professor for the 1982-1983 academic year—which he accepted in Spring 1983 and which would turn permanent three years later. Roy wrote The *Mantle of the Prophet* during these years, returning regularly to Oxford to visit various friends there and think through the book. On one impromptu visit, he walked and talked with friends for some three hours. It seems that the basic planning of the work was done—the skeletal text sketched—that day through that conversation. Roy would often stop as he toured Oxford's grounds, take out his pencil, and jot down notes. His initial idea, to write a book about the making of an ayatollah, would become a book that examined the far-ranging history of not only the institutions and social history that shaped the clerics and society of modern Iran, but of the centuries and major events that led to its Revolution.

Since then, Roy has transformed the field through the generations of scholars he has trained, the hundreds of students he has exposed to Islamic history, and the myriad scholarly networks he has constructed. In the forty-six years that he taught at Princeton and later at Harvard before retiring in 2016, he mentored dozens of doctoral students who would go on to establish Islamic social, cultural, and intellectual history at universities around the country and the world. In the History Department at Harvard, his teaching helped cement the pre-modern Islamic world as a field that could be examined within the confines of history rather than the more philological discipline of Near Eastern Languages and Civilizations, though he always maintained strong connections with his philologist colleagues. And as the director of the Center for Middle Eastern Studies (CMES) and later as the founding director of the Islamic Studies Program at Harvard, he developed academic centers that welcomed colleagues from disparate geographic and political backgrounds. CMES, for example, provided a haven from the political maelstroms that wracked Islamic studies more generally in the 1980s and 1990s, offered a home to displaced scholars from the Middle East, and fostered international cooperation. To all, he brought and cultivated the same infectious curiosity and critical insight that permeates his own work.

Roy's books, especially *Loyalty and Leadership in an Early Islamic Society* (1980) and *The Mantle of the Prophet* (1985), brought the new questions that emerged with social history to bear on Islamic historical sources ranging from chronicles and administrative records to literary and scriptural texts. His approach married a philologist's ability to read closely with a social historian's desire to illuminate the lives of people and institutions from a long-ago past. His books changed the way scholars understood Islamic history and approached the sources. His works also won accolades in both scholarly journals and newspapers, and were translated into multiple languages. His lucid writing, grasp of a wide range of sources, and imaginative approach won him support from public service-oriented foundations such as Guggenheim and MacArthur, and from the scholarly community writ large.

Loyalty and Leadership was the first of many projects that built upon and developed the work that Roy began as an undergraduate and graduate student in new directions. He had initially become interested in questions of social history from reading the letters of al-Ṣāḥib b. ʿAbbād (d. 385/995)—the celebrated vizier of the Buyids of Rayy—while writing his undergraduate thesis. In those documents, he noticed letters addressed to the governors of Qum and Rayy. One of those letters was a letter appointing the prominent Muʿtazilī theologian, ʿAbd al-Jabbār, as chief judge of the Buyid kingdom of Rayy. This letter in particular became something of a curiosity and obsession for Roy. In his initial reading of it, Roy found it surprising that the document instructed the judge to consider sources of law that include the opinions of the best scholars as well as *ijtihād*, or legal interpretation through analogical reasoning. He also found it fascinating that the letter also mentions the judge's duties with respect to several other court officials and roles that one might not ordinarily associate with regular judicial practice. While reading the sources early on, Roy also noticed that *Ta'rīkh Bayhaqī* provides descriptions of just how things were done back then: descriptions of the court(s), how the king sits, what people surround him.

Roy knew the value of the sources. The sources gave fodder for the idea behind *Loyalty and Leadership*—guiding his reading of documents, histories, and even Qur'ānic quotes about how key matters were conceptualized early on, how dynasties were formed, and how they managed to work through social realities. This same method underlay his other projects: the article on *shuʿūbiyya*, on how the *kharāj* tax was administered, and many more. His works all point to the same thing:

documents and local histories provide the raw material around which he is able to illuminate social, legal, and administrative histories of the Islamic world.[2] In the spirit of this method and of al-Ṣāhib's letter, and Roy's now lifelong interest in it, we convened a conference on the theme of courts and judicial procedure in early Islamic law in May 2016.

The conference brought together several of Roy's students and colleagues who work on questions related to judicial procedure, as well as some scholars who had not worked with him but were inspired by his approach. Roy's famous modesty had made him resistant to a traditional Festschrift, but the idea of a substantive conference and volume on a subject of close interest that would aim to make a scholarly contribution was acceptable. This volume is thus an untraditional tribute to Roy, designed to cohere around a single theme that animated his initial forays into the field and that honor his continued attention to and interests in this line of scholarship. In focusing on courts and judicial procedure in early Islamic law and society, this book places theory alongside practice in ways that concern events of legal history-as-social history to reflect the mark that Roy left on the field. We offer the following essays in appreciation for Roy's generosity, kindness, and brilliance, with the hope that they may offer food for thought, which he has so often offered to all of us.

ON THIS VOLUME

In most studies that examine the early history of Islamic law, the primary focus has been on the origins, authenticity, and authority of particular legal institutions and rulings. In recent years, focus has turned increasingly to the social contexts of the scholars elaborating the law. But many of these histories tend to take legal literature as the main source for analysis, sometimes supplemented with historical chronicles and biographical dictionaries. And many of them tend to shy away from close studies of early courts. With recent exceptions, in fact notable for their recentness, the common wisdom seems to be that the available sources—given an absence of court records as verbatim transcripts—do not allow for robust histories of early courts.[3] Roy has shown us otherwise.

This volume broadens the sources and areas of focus for the early history of Islamic law by examining the workings of courts and judicial

2 For a full list of his publications, see *Roy Mottahedeh's List of Publications* (this volume).

3 The most prominent exception to this attitude is Mathieu Tillier, whose scholarship illuminates the workings of early Islamic courts. Along with dozens of articles and translations, see especially his *Les cadis d'Iraq et l'État abbasside (132/750-334/945)* (Damascus: IFPO, 2009), and more recently, *L'invention du cadi. La justice des musulmans, des juifs et des chrétiens aux premiers siècles de l'Islam* (Paris: Publications de la Sorbonne, 2017).

procedure in early Islamic law, 632–1250. The contributing authors approach questions of early Islamic law with an eye on the social logic of judicial actors and judicial procedure, and with attention to both *how* and *why* the courts and the people associated with them functioned in early Islamic societies. Each author draws on diverse sources for judicial practice and procedure that reveal a broader and deeper vision of law and society in early Islam than self-consciously produced law books alone can provide. For this reason, the sources in this volume go well beyond the traditional sources of legal literature to also include historical chronicles, biographical dictionaries, legal canons, exegetical works, theological and eschatological sources, and mirrors for princes. These essays simultaneously illuminate the varied legal landscapes stretching across early Islam, and map new approaches to interdisciplinary legal history.

The chapters that follow fall into three temporally and geographically defined sections. The first section, "**Judicial Procedure and Practice during the Founding Period of Islamic Law**," illustrates some of the defining issues of Islam's early founding period, from roughly 632 until 750. The four essays that make up this section center on questions of how social and pragmatic factors shaped judicial discretion to determine the admissibility of evidence from non-Muslims and professional witnesses, to mediate relations between *qāḍīs* and *muftīs*, and to strategically deploy or avoid the political use of evidence and legal canons in court proceedings.

The second section, "**Concepts of Justice in the ʿAbbāsid East**," follows many of the themes that emerged from the early founding period and extended well into the ʿAbbāsid period, which began in 750 and lasted until 1258. The three essays in this section reflect the increasingly cosmopolitan and dynamic context of an expanding Islamic empire. Again, with attention to changing social and pragmatic factors, the authors reflect on how scholars from this period attempted to integrate changing legal and political ideals of justice. These chapters also reveal how new concepts of justice evolved among varied groups of scholars, judges, and the general populace in exegetical, eschatological, and political works.

The third and final section, "**Judges and Judicial Practice in the Islamic West**," examines developments parallel to those in the eastern Islamic world in a pair of essays that focus on al-Andalus and the Maghrib, or Islamic Spain, Portugal, and North Africa through the twelfth century. These chapters highlight tensions between idealized legal concepts elaborated in legal treatises and actual legal practices and norms as they played out in courts—each as reflected in chronicles, biographical dictionaries, and other literature.

All of the chapters comprising this volume—each of which is profiled in the relevant section's introduction—bring legal texts into conversation with legal practice relevant to early Islamic courts. They illuminate the diverse actors involved in constructing legal processes throughout the long founding period of Islamic law. And they go beyond the common sources of legal literature to provide a powerful overture that suggests far-ranging possibilities for broader studies in early Islamic legal history, which include the dynamic social and political history of courts and judicial procedure.

Hossein Modarressi sums up Roy—the man and the method—this way:

> It may appear odd to the eye, but Roy was, in a way, like *sharīʿa*. The jurists against analogical reasoning used to say that [interpretation involves] *jamʿ al-mutafariqāt wa-majmaʿ al-mutaḍādāt*: bringing together varied elements and opposing ideas. Roy was like that. He brought together people who you could not otherwise imagine gathering under the same ceiling. But he was friends with all of them. And they all owed him a debt of gratitude and friendship reflected in their scholarship and good humor when it came to Roy.

That debt and spirit is reflected in the pages that follow.

~Abigail Krasner Balbale (New York),
Hossein Modarressi (Princeton),
& Intisar A. Rabb (Cambridge)

PART ONE:
Section Introduction

Judicial Procedure and Practice during the Founding Period of Islamic Law

William Graham
Harvard University

Roy Mottahedeh has distinguished himself over his career by his interest in a range of Islamic phenomena from law to Qurʾānic interpretation to government to educational systems to communal norms, as well as by placing whatever he studies historically in terms that go beyond its literary or theoretical manifestation to encompass, even preeminently, its social and practical context. Thus it is fitting that the first four contributions to the present volume should shed interesting light on important developments in, and the crystallization of, Islamic legal procedures and practices, focusing on both practice and theory employed or created in the course of the late Umayyad and early ʿAbbāsid periods. These studies probe fundamental developments and issues that proved consequential for the eventual shape of classical Islamic legal institutions: witness qualification, disqualification, and certification; *qāḍī* discretion and the role of jurisconsults (*muftī*s); types, usage, and legal status of evidence; judges' negotiation of political and social pressures and constraints; and the early development of juristic consultation (*mushāwara*) together with its role in actual adjudication.

In the four essays in this section, it is not difficult to see affinities with Roy Mottahedeh's interests: in the relation of practice and theory, the social roles of Islamic (legal or other) institutions, the tension between government and various social and professional groups, and the ways in which history offers a window into the development and inculcation of Muslim societal and personal norms.

When Ahmed El Shamsy focuses on the second/eighth-century

development of criteria for exclusion or inclusion of legal witnesses in early *qāḍī* courts, he shows how judicial guidelines regarding acceptable witnesses shifted and changed through Umayyad and early ʿAbbāsid times, especially in terms of the treatment of minorities, both religious and social in the Islamic heartlands. Here we can see the kind of reconstruction of actual practices in the courts regarding different classes of persons that gives us a window into the social history of the Umayyad and early ʿAbbāsid eras.

Hossein Modarressi's treatment of key procedural differences regarding evidence that supposedly distinguished criminal, or *maẓālim,* courts from ordinary courts in ʿAbbāsid times shows how gradually, in practice, the theoretical limitations of *qāḍī* procedures to oral testimony and oaths were expanded to include circumstantial evidence or a judge's personal knowledge of such evidence. Again, actual practices are shown to have been informed by social history.

In Intisar Rabb's close analysis of one historical property case, she demonstrates how an early *qāḍī* managed to tread a fine line between political, legal, and socio-religious interests and pressures to resolve the case judiciously. Rabb probes the political and juristic roles of procedure and legal canons exemplified in this case as crucial to the development of Islamic law in the second/eighth century. In showing how the judge proceeded to resolve the property dispute in this case, she shows how the procedures he relied on were shaped by the social and political history of the time.

In her article, Nahed Samour looks at issues of authority and adjudication in second/eighth- and third/ninth-century courts in which judges turned to the institution of *mushāwara,* or judicial "consultation" with one or more expert jurists (*muftīs*). Her core argument is that "the relationship of judge and jurisconsult was one of cooperation, confrontation, and cooptation." Reviewing both critics and advocates of such consultations, she also shows a connection between legal and social history in arguing that the consultations gave scholars a say in actual legal adjudication, producing collaborative institutional practice in the courts.

In these four varied contributions, we find differing but telling evidence of the formative period of creation and crystallization of theory and practice for adjudication in the developing legal system in the early Islamic centuries. In significant ways, all of these essays intersect with Roy Mottahedeh's work in this dual practice-and-theory focus and in their strong emphasis on the social working-out of formal principles, rules, and institutions under the historical and contextual forces of the respective problems with which they deal.

Chapter One

The Logic of Excluding Testimony in Early Islam

Ahmed El Shamsy
University of Chicago

Testimony is arguably the central element of Islamic judicial practice. Determining what testimony is acceptable and what is not is consequently an important task, with repercussions for the very identity of the Islamic court system. In this paper, I examine the issue of the exclusion of potential witnesses in the second *hijrī* century—the earliest period for which sources exist—in order to provide a tentative sketch of changes in this aspect of judicial practice over the course of that century. I pay particular attention to the treatment of potential non-Muslim witnesses and the changing rationales given for their admission to, or exclusion from, Muslim courts. My analysis reveals shifts and interconnections along two axes: between communal and individual criteria of witness acceptability, and between considerations applying to Muslim witnesses and those applying to non-Muslim ones.

CONFLICTING EARLY OPINIONS

For the earliest sources on the exclusion of potential witnesses, we must look to collections of prophetic and post-prophetic reports compiled in the second and third *hijrī* centuries (eighth and ninth centuries CE), because legal treatises proper began to be authored only in the second half of the second/eighth century. The material preserved on the topic in these collections—the most important of which are the compilations of ʿAbd al-Razzāq al-Ṣanʿānī (d. 211/827) and Ibn Abī Shayba (d. 235/849)—is dominated by early second/eighth-century reports. Ibn Abī Shayba cites no prophetic *ḥadīth* concerning the exclusion of potential witnesses, and Ṣanʿānī cites just one report, according to which the Prophet Muḥammad said: "No community may testify against another, except the community of Muḥammad."[1] The legal import of this statement, if indeed it has any,[2] is ambiguous; it seems to speak to the question of testimony across confessional lines, but is silent on the acceptance of non-Muslim testimony *per se*. More importantly, this *ḥadīth* was never picked up by jurists and was largely ignored even by *ḥadīth* scholars, who deemed its transmission history weak.[3]

There are episodes in the Prophet's biography that could have served as evidence for constructing a law of non-Muslim testimony—one instance in particular in which Muḥammad appears to have accepted the testimony of Jewish witnesses against a Jewish couple accused of adultery—but, apart from Isḥāq b. Rāhawayh (d. 238/853), no jurist seems to have considered this case as Sunnaic proof of the permissibility of such testimony.[4] In sum, on the important question of the admissibility of non-Muslim witnesses' statements in a Muslim court, early authorities such as Ṣanʿānī and Ibn Abī Shayba do not cite prophetic *ḥadīth*, but instead provide a great number of later reports, starting with the second generation of Muslims.

As is often the case, interpretation of these later reports is hampered by the fragmentary form in which they have been transmitted and the scarcity of historical data by which to contextualize them. A basic ambiguity that already struck *ḥadīth* collectors such as Ṣanʿānī lies in the phrase "the testimony of scripturalists (or 'people of the book') against each other: *shahādat ahl al-kitāb baʿḍuhum ʿalā baʿḍ*."[5] This phrase appears frequently in reports relevant to the potential exclusion of non-Muslim witnesses, but it is not intuitively clear whether the phrase refers to *all scripturalists* as a single, undifferentiated group whose members may or may not testify against each other, or whether it should be understood as applying only to members of individual confessional groups testifying against *members of the same group*.

The collectors made what sense they could of their material. Ṣanʿānī transmits two opinions from early second/eighth-century authorities. On the one hand, he cites a report in which his teacher Maʿmar b. Rāshid

1 ʿAbd al-Razzāq al-Ṣanʿānī, *Muṣannaf*, ed. Ḥabīb al-Raḥmān Aʿẓamī (Beirut: al-Majlis al-ʿIlmī, 1970), 8:356, no. 15525.

2 The statement could be related to Qurʾān 2:143, which does not seem to address testimony in court but rather refers to ethical witnessing, either in this world or in the hereafter.

3 Abū Bakr al-Bayhaqī (d. 458/1066), *Maʿrifat al-sunan waʾl-āthār*, ed. ʿAbd al-Muʿṭī Amīn Qalʿahjī (Aleppo: Dār al-Waʿī, 1991), 14:282.

4 Isḥāq b. Manṣūr al-Kawsaj al-Marwazī (comp.), *Masāʾil al-Imām Aḥmad b. Ḥanbal wa-Isḥāq b. Rāhawayh* (Medina: Islamic University, 2002), 8:4096–97.

5 The question of which faiths, precisely, are included in the category "scripturalist" (*ahl al-kitāb*) lies beyond the scope of this discussion, but Christians and Jews were usually the archetypal referents.

(d. 153/770) asks Ibn Shihāb al-Zuhrī (d. 124/742) about "the testimony of scripturalists against each other" and receives the response: "It is permissible." Ṣanʿānī follows this report with another that he heard from Maʿmar regarding a statement by Qatāda b. Diʿāma (d. 117/735) and Rabīʿa b. Abī ʿAbd al-Raḥmān Farrūkh (d. 130/747 or 136/753) to the effect that "The testimony of a Jew against a Christian or of a Christian against a Jew is not permissible." Ṣanʿānī comments: "I consider this to be an explanation of the report by Maʿmar from Zuhrī." In other words, Ṣanʿānī believed that Zuhrī also considered the testimony of adherents of *different* scriptural faiths against each other inadmissible, in contrast to testimony by members of the same community. But, on the other hand, another report preserved by Ṣanʿānī claims that Caliph ʿUmar II (ʿUmar b. ʿAbd al-ʿAzīz, d. 101/720) allowed a Zoroastrian to testify against a Christian, and that his judge in Kūfa, ʿĀmir b. Sharāḥīl al-Shaʿbī (d. after 100/718), permitted the testimony of a Christian against a Jew.[6] Both scenarios permit non-Muslims to testify against other non-Muslims in a Muslim court, but they differ on whether such testimony is possible across confessional lines or whether it is limited to testimony against litigants within a single religious community.

Although the dearth of sources on this issue makes any theory conjectural, I propose that there may be a historical explanation for the difference between the two opinions. Maʿmar b. Rāshid, who transmitted the report from Zuhrī, studied with the latter at the court of the Umayyad caliph Hishām (r. 105–125/724–743) in Ruṣāfa.[7] This means that Zuhrī's opinion, which prohibits cross-confessional testimony, postdates that of ʿUmar II and Shaʿbī, which permits it. Why did the acceptability of non-Muslim testimony come to be limited to cases involving coreligionists? The first clue lies in another statement transmitted from Zuhrī on the matter: "The testimony of a Jew against a Christian or of a Christian against a Jew is not permitted given the enmity (*ʿadāwa*) between them that God mentions, saying, 'We have placed enmity between them until the day of resurrection.'"[8] This report is significant because it proposes an explicit reason for the impermissibility of cross-confessional testimony—namely,

6 See, e.g., Ṣanʿānī, *Muṣannaf*, 6:129, no. 10232. Bukhārī claims that Shaʿbī held the opposite opinion, but he gives no *isnād* for this claim. See his chapter "Bāb lā yus'al ahl al-shirk ʿan al-shahāda wa-ghayrihā," in his *Jāmiʿ al-ṣaḥīḥ*, ed. Muḥammad Zuhayr al-Nāṣir (Beirut: Dār Ṭawq al-Najāh, 2001), 3:181. A Christian source claims that ʿUmar II forbade the testimony of Christians against Muslims, suggesting that such testimony had not been unheard of previously. See Luke Yarbrough, "Did ʿUmar b. ʿAbd al-ʿAzīz Issue an Edict Concerning Non-Muslim Officials?," in *Christians and Others in the Umayyad State*, ed. Antoine Borrut and Fred M. Donner (Chicago: Oriental Institute, 2016), 173–206, esp. 180.

7 See the introduction to Maʿmar b. Rāshid (d. 153/770), *The Expeditions: An Early Biography of Muḥammad*, trans. Sean Anthony (New York: New York University Press, 2014), xxiv–xxv.

8 Ṣanʿānī, *Muṣannaf*, no. 15526. The quoted verse is Q. 5:64.

communal enmity or bias. Ibn Wahb (d. 197/813, an Egyptian student of Mālik (d. 179/795), picked up this motif of communal bias among Jews and Christians, and cited it explicitly as the reason for prohibiting the sale of Jewish slaves to Christians or of Christian slaves to Jews. It likewise provided the rationale for his view that Jews and Christians could not testify against one another.[9] Ibn Rushd II (d. 595/1198) would later argue that this prohibition was particular to Jews and Christians because of the historical rivalry between these two communities, and thus that it did not apply to Zoroastrians.[10]

The same logic seems to be at work in another instance of excluded testimony, this time in an intra-Muslim context: Tawba b. Namir, who served as a judge in Egypt between 115/733 and 120/738, prohibited the testimony of Qaysī Arabs against Yamanī Arabs and vice versa.[11] No explicit reason for the exclusion is given, but most likely the escalating conflicts between the two tribal groups, which had plagued and weakened Umayyad rule in the first decades of the second Islamic century, had begun to also affect the judicial process, with tribesmen seeking to co-opt the courts and concomitant state power in the service of their own side in the conflicts.[12] Tawba's response was to refer any disputes between Qaysīs and Yamanīs to out-of-court arbitration (*ṣulḥ*) between the disputing parties' tribes.

The appearance of a connection between intra-Muslim rifts and the perception of tensions among non-Muslim communities is strengthened by the fact that the same scholars who transmit reports in which enmity (*ʿadāwa*) among non-Muslims is described as a reason to exclude non-Muslim testimony also transmit reports that thematize enmity among Muslims. One such report depicts Caliph ʿUmar I (d. 23/644) breaking into tears when the riches of the conquered territories are brought into his presence. When he is asked why such a joyous occasion makes him cry, he exclaims: "Nay; when such opulence besets a people, God casts enmity

9 Ibn Abī Zayd al-Qayrawānī (d. 386/996), *al-Nawādir wa'l-ziyādāt ʿalā mā fī al-Mudawwana min ghayrihā min al-ummahāt*, ed. ʿAbd al-Fattāḥ al-Ḥulw et al. (Beirut: Dār al-Gharb al-Islāmī, 1999), 6:183.

10 Ibn Rushd, *al-Bayān wa'l-taḥṣīl wa'l-sharḥ wa'l-tawjīh wa'l-taʿlīl fī masā'il al-Mustakhraja* (Beirut: Dār al-Gharb al-Islāmī, 1984), 7:511.

11 Muḥammad b. Yūsuf al-Kindī (d. 350/961), *The Governors and Judges of Egypt, or Kitāb el umarā' (el wulāh) wa Kitāb el quḍāh of el Kindī*, ed. Rhuvon Guest (Leiden: Brill, 1912), 346.

12 The tensions persisted even after the downfall of the Umayyads: when the governor of Basra ʿUqba b. Salm (in office 149–50/766–67) was threatened by the judge Sawār b. ʿAbd Allāh b. Qudāma (in office 138–56/755–73) to release an unjustly imprisoned man, the governor was advised not to pick a fight with Sawār, since the latter was from Muḍar (i.e., a Qaysī) while the governor from Yaman, which lacked strong support in Basra. See Muḥammad b. Khalaf al-Wakīʿ (d. 306/918), *Akhbār al-quḍāt*, ed. ʿAbd al-ʿAzīz al-Marāghī (Cairo: al-Maktaba al-Tijāriyya al-Kubrā, 1947), 2:59.

and hatred in their midst!"[13] Such reports provided an explanation for the disintegration of the close-knit community of Muslims in the post-conquest era and a justification for the progressive limitation of the right to give testimony, culminating in the establishment of a category of professional witnesses.[14]

THE CLASSICAL POSITIONS EMERGE

Over the course of the second *hijrī* century, the "enmity" rationale for excluding testimony underwent a significant transformation. Most importantly, it was divorced from the communal context and came to be applied to individuals, rather than groups. The first to take this step appears to have been the aforementioned Medinan jurist Rabīʿa b. Abī ʿAbd al-Raḥmān, who was a contemporary of Zuhrī and Tawba. Rabīʿa argued that individual bias (again using the term *ʿadāwa*) on the part of a potential witness against any of the parties to a lawsuit constituted grounds to reject the testimony of that witness.[15] But changes in the theorization of bias and non-Muslim testimony alike are most evident in the detailed and systematic treatment of the various issues surrounding the exclusion of testimony in the *Kitāb al-Umm* of Muḥammad b. Idrīs al-Shāfiʿī (d. 204/820), which was composed around the year 200 AH.

As a general rule, Shāfiʿī asserts that "We do not permit the testimony of an enemy against his enemy: *lā nujīz shahādat ʿaduww ʿalā ʿaduwwih*."[16] He does not mention the specific case of Qays vs. Yaman—understandably, since by his time the conflict had long ago lost its political explosiveness. But he does discuss factionalism (*ʿaṣabiyya*) among Muslims as a cause for excluding testimony. According to Shāfiʿī, although it is not blameworthy to be more attached to one's own people than to others, hating others solely on the basis of their tribal affiliations constitutes unacceptable factionalism, even if it does not translate into actually fighting those others. Shāfiʿī gives the example of someone saying of another person, "I hate him because he is from the clan of so-and-so: *abghaḍuh li-annah min banī fulān*," as a

13 See, for example, Maʿmar b. Rāshid, *al-Jāmiʿ* (addendum to ʿAbd al-Razzāq al-Ṣanʿānī's *Muṣannaf*), 11:99, no. 20036.

14 Limiting the right to give testimony to pre-certified witnesses was a judicial innovation that was not, to my knowledge, theorized or discussed in legal writings of this period. See Émile Tyan, *Le notariat et le régime de la preuve par écrit dans la pratique du droit musulman*, 2nd ed. (Harissa, Lebanon: Saint Paul, 1959); and Ahmed El Shamsy, *The Canonization of Islamic Law: A Social and Intellectual History* (New York: Cambridge University Press, 2013), 106–07.

15 On *shahādat al-ʿaduww*, see ʿAbd al-Salām b. Saʿīd Saḥnūn (d. 240/854) (comp.), *Mudawwana* (Riyadh: Wizārat al-Awqāf, n.d.; reprint of Cairo: Maṭbaʿat al-Saʿāda, 1906), 13:52.

16 Shāfiʿī, *Kitāb al-Umm*, ed. Rifʿat Fawzī ʿAbd al-Muṭṭalib (Mansura: Dār al-Wafāʾ, 2001), 6:746.

statement that renders the speaker ineligible to testify. He derives the justification for such exclusion from the principle, articulated in both the Qurʾān and the *Sunna*, that the believers are brothers to one another. Factionalism thus constitutes open disobedience to God and therefore disqualifies the disobedient person from giving witness testimony, even in cases that have nothing to do with the hated group.

Besides tribal bias, Shāfiʿī also mentions theologically grounded bias. In his discussion of the testimony of heretical Muslims, Shāfiʿī distinguishes between heretics whose opinions have no precedent and are not based on any possible interpretation of revelation—and whose testimony is consequently rejected—and heretics whose views are based on a possible, even if extreme, interpretation (*yaḥtamil al-taʾwīl*) and whose testimony remains *prima facie* acceptable. By recognizing gradations of heresy with differing implications for the acceptability of the heretic's testimony, Shāfiʿī largely agrees with the Ḥanafī position and diverges from that of his teacher Mālik, who rejected the testimony of heretics without qualification.[17] Shāfiʿī outlines two further categories of people whose testimony ought to be excluded on the basis of theological convictions: individuals who believe false testimony to be permissible and those whose theological differences with their opponents have turned into enmity, rendering them ineligible to give testimony with regard to their opponents. In contrast to tribal affiliation-related factionalism, which undermines a potential witness's uprightness (*ʿadāla*) and precludes the acceptance of any testimony from that person, bias rooted in theological differences bars only testimony specifically against the target of the bias.

This approach to defining the grounds for excluding witness testimony focuses on the individual rather than the community: it evaluates potential witnesses on a case-by-case basis and disqualifies them only if they display traits that make them unfit to provide testimony. This can be the case when their testimony is epistemologically suspect, such as when they are biased against a particular party; or when they consider lying permissible; or when their uprightness (*ʿadāla*) is compromised, either in general or with regard to specific (groups of) individuals. For Shāfiʿī, the same reasoning applies to other questionable categories of potential witnesses, including poets and people obsessed with playing games such as chess or backgammon. His explicit discussion of these two groups suggests that he was arguing against a proposal to bar poets and game-players from giving testimony altogether. His own position is that neither group is categorically unfit to testify; however, certain actions can preclude

17 Abū Bakr al-Jaṣṣāṣ (d. 370/980) and Abū Jaʿfar al-Ṭaḥāwī (d. 321/933), *Mukhtaṣar Ikhtilāf al-ʿulamāʾ*, ed. ʿAbd Allāh Nadhīr (Beirut: Dār al-Bashāʾir al-Islāmiyya, 1996), 3:334.

individual members of the two groups from serving as witnesses. A poet may be excluded as a witness if he is an exaggerating sycophant, a liar, or a proponent of factionalism; and a chess player is disqualified if his passion for the game leads him to neglect the obligatory prayers.[18]

In all of these cases, Shāfiʿī argues against the wholesale exclusion of entire groups of people from the category of acceptable witnesses. However, in the case of non-Muslims' testimony, he takes a diametrically opposed stance, arguing not only that they cannot testify against members of other religious communities, but that they are excluded from giving witness testimony under any circumstances. In his defense of this position, Shāfiʿī ignores the statements of previous jurists on the issue and, given the absence of reliable *ḥadīth* reports on the topic, relies exclusively on two Qurʾānic verses that address the issue of witnesses. Verse 2:282 calls on the parties to a contract or a dispute to choose "from those you approve as witnesses," while verse 65:2 refers to "upright witnesses from among you." Neither of these verses actually deals with court procedure; rather, both relate to private documents and contracts—namely, the recording of a debt and the resolution of a marital dispute, respectively. Shāfiʿī nonetheless finds it acceptable to use these verses to set standards for judicial testimony, even though this extension is conceptually problematic.[19] Take the first verse that refers to "those you approve": in the context of two individuals recording a private debt, it seems plausible to read this phrase as stipulating the parties' mutual agreement on a witness to the contract. For Shāfiʿī, by contrast, the category of "those you approve/are content with" (*mimman tarḍawna*) necessarily excludes non-Muslims, since their denial of Islam precludes them from being approved by Muslims. Shāfiʿī thus extends the meaning of "approval" from a practical sense to a doctrinal one. As for the second verse, in Shāfiʿī's reading, the "you" to whom the verse is addressed and among whom upright witnesses are to be sought refers to the community of Muslims, rather than to the families of the quarrelling partners.[20]

Shāfiʿī's final argument for barring non-Muslim testimony takes an *a fortiori* approach against his interlocutor Muḥammad b. al-Ḥasan al-Shaybānī (d. 189/804–5), who endorsed the acceptability of testimony from non-Muslims who belonged to scriptural religions on the grounds that it was necessary for maintaining their legal rights. In his challenge to

18 Shāfiʿī, *Umm*, 7:513–16.

19 See Ibn Taymiyya's (d. 728/1328) critique of this extension in Mohammad Fadel, "Two Women, One Man: Knowledge, Power, and Gender in Medieval Sunni Legal Thought," *International Journal of Middle East Studies* 29, no. 2 (1997): 185–204.

20 Shāfiʿī, *Umm*, 7:573–74.

Shaybānī's position, Shāfiʿī first asks rhetorically why the right to testify should be granted to scripturalists but withheld from non-Muslims without a revealed scripture, even though the latter, unlike scripturalists, have not falsified their scripture and should thus be considered more trustworthy. Second, he queries, why does Shaybānī not show equal concern for guaranteeing the legal rights of Muslims whom both Shāfiʿī and Shaybānī consider unacceptable witnesses, such as slaves or such as Bedouins and seafarers, whose uprightness (*ʿadāla*) cannot be ascertained?[21]

Shāfiʿī's arguments on the issue of excluding testimony are consistent with his overall legal approach, which granted decisive authority to scripture. For Shāfiʿī, the opinions of legal authorities belonging to the *tābiʿūn* and subsequent generations no longer constituted authoritative precedents. The criteria for valid testimony were now sought in the Qurʾān, and earlier approaches that had focused on the classification of entire groups, such as the wholesale exclusion of those embroiled in tribal animosities, were reduced to individualized tests of factionalism. For Shāfiʿī, factionalism was defined as a contravention of the divine law that entailed a loss of uprightness (*ʿadāla*), which was a prerequisite for witness eligibility. Shāfiʿī justified the exclusion of testimony by non-Muslims both through an interpretation of Qurʾānic verses relating to testimony and by pointing out what he saw as an inconsistency inherent to the acceptance of witness statements from scripturalist non-Muslims, but not from pagans or from Muslims whose uprightness was either compromised or could not be ascertained.

Of the three other schools of Sunnī law, the Ḥanbalīs followed the Shāfiʿī position quite closely,[22] with one exception. In contrast to Shāfiʿī, Aḥmad b. Ḥanbal (d. 241/855) granted the opinions of post-prophetic legal authorities some probative weight. He thus permitted a non-Muslim to testify in a Muslim court for the specific purpose of confirming the otherwise unattested testamentary wishes of a Muslim who dies while traveling. This position was based on a Qurʾānic verse (Q. 5:106), supported by the reported practice of the Companion Abū Mūsā al-Ashʿarī (d. between 42/662 and 53/673), and was widely adopted among early jurists.[23]

21 Shāfiʿī, *Umm*, 8:40.

22 Interestingly, Isḥāq b. Rāhawayh disagreed with Aḥmad Ibn Ḥanbal and maintained the opinion of earlier jurists that the testimony of scripturalists is acceptable; however, he excluded testimony across communal boundaries. See Marwazī (comp.), *Masāʾil al-Imām Aḥmad*, 8:4096–97.

23 Abū Dāwūd al-Sijistānī (d. 275/888), *Sunan Abī Dāwūd*, ed. Muḥammad Muḥyī al-Dīn ʿAbd al-Ḥamīd (Beirut: al-Maktaba al-ʿAṣriyya, n.d.), 3:307, under the heading "Bāb shahādat ahl al-dhimma wa-fī al-waṣiyya fī al-safar"; Aḥmad b. Muḥammad al-Khallāl (d. 311/923), *Aḥkām ahl al-milal min al-jāmiʿ li-masāʾil al-Imām Aḥmad b. Ḥanbal*, ed. Sayyid Kasrawī Ḥasan (Beirut: Dār al-Kutub al-ʿIlmiyya, 1994), 128 and 134; and Bayhaqī, *al-Sunan al-kubrā*, ed. ʿAbd al-Raḥmān al-Muʿallimī (Hyderabad: Majlis Dāʾirat al-Maʿārif al-Niẓāmiyya, 1925–37), 10:165–66.

The early Mālikī opinion on non-Muslim testimony is unclear. Mālik b. Anas (d. 179/795) does not address the issue in his own work, the *Muwaṭṭaʾ*, but the third/ninth-century compilation of his opinions, the *Mudawwana*, claims that Mālik did not accept witness testimony by non-Muslims in any situation, even in the case of a Muslim traveler's last testament. However, the *Mudawwana* offers as evidence the earlier opinions that bar non-Muslims only from testifying against members of other religious communities and against Muslims, leaving open the obvious question of why the testimony of non-Muslims against their own coreligionists should be disallowed.[24]

The Ḥanafī position diverges significantly from that of the other schools by allowing any non-Muslim to give testimony against any other non-Muslim, regardless of the particular faith of either party. The Ḥanafīs rooted their position explicitly in earlier juristic precedent. The imperial grand judge Yaḥyā b. Aktham (d. 242/857) claimed that "consulting the opinions of the earliest jurists, I have found no one forbidding the testimony of the protected people, except two [conflicting] opinions attributed to Rabīʿa."[25] The Ḥanafīs appealed to the precedent set by the report about ʿUmar II and Shaʿbī, which has a continuous history of transmission and use in early Ḥanafī law. By the second half of the second *hijrī* century, the argument from precedent had been joined to a sophisticated theoretical justification. This new argument relied on the legal canon "Unbelief constitutes a single community: *al-kufr milla wāḥida*," which has diverse applications in various areas of the law but had originally been extracted from a statement attributed to the caliph ʿUmar I on the topic of inheritance: "All of unbelief is one community; neither do we inherit from them, nor they from us."[26] Based on this statement, Ḥammād b. Salama al-Baṣrī (d. 167/784) concluded that "all of the idolators may testify against each other;" Sufyān al-Thawrī (d. 161/778) proclaimed that "Islam is a community and unbelief is a community, and testimony within them is permitted;" and Abū Ḥanīfa's student Abū Yūsuf (d. 182/798) stated that "testimony of the protected people against each other is permissible, even if they are from different communities, for unbelief is a single community."[27]

24 Saḥnūn, *Mudawwana*, 6:44, 12:132.

25 Shams al-Aʾimma al-Sarakhsī (d. 483/1090), *Mabsūṭ*, ed. Khalīl al-Mays (Beirut: Dār al-Fikr, 2000), 16:135.

26 Abū Yūsuf, *Kitāb al-Āthār*, ed. Abū al-Wafāʾ al-Afghānī (Hyderabad: Lajnat Iḥyāʾ al-Maʿārif al-Nuʿmāniyya, 1355/1936), 171.

27 Ibn Abī Shayba, *Muṣannaf*, 4:532, nos. 22873, 22874; Muḥammad b. al-Ḥasan al-Shaybānī (d. 189/804-5), *Aṣl*, ed. Mehmet Boynukalın (Qatar: Wizārat al-Awqāf and Beirut: Dār Ibn Ḥazm, 2012), 11:516.

Already in Abū Yūsuf's discussion, cited by Shaybānī, the rules of testimony are placed in a hierarchical order: a non-Muslim foreigner cannot bear witness against a protected (i.e., resident) non-Muslim, and a protected non-Muslim may not bear witness against a Muslim. Within this hierarchy, one can testify against individuals of equal or lower social status, but not against one's superiors.[28] By the time of Shams al-Aʾimma al-Sarakhsī (d. *ca.* 490/1096), if not earlier, this notion of hierarchy came to be theorized with reference to the concept of legal authority (*wilāya*). This concept represented an acknowledgment that testimony was not just about the imparting of information and the concomitant efforts to ascertain whether this information could be trusted; rather, it involved an exercise of power by the witness over the parties in the case. The debate over the categorical exclusion of testimony was therefore a debate about which groups could legitimately exercise such power, and under what circumstances.[29]

In the Ḥanafī scheme, non-Muslims did possess some legal authority—in the first instance over themselves, but also potentially over others, such as their children. The Ḥanafī hierarchy differentiated not only between members of different religious communities but also between insiders and outsiders (*dhimmī* vs. *ḥarbī*), men and women, adults and children, and free individuals and slaves. On the axis of religion, non-Muslims of *dhimmī* status could testify against each other and against non-Muslim foreigners (*ḥarbī*s), but not against Muslims, whereas non-Muslim foreigners could not testify against *dhimmī* non-Muslims owing to the latter's superior status.[30] So while Shāfiʿī applied purely individual criteria to evaluate the testimony of Muslim witnesses, while dismissing non-Muslim testimony on purely communal grounds, the Ḥanafīs placed both Muslims and non-Muslims within a hierarchical framework defined, *inter alia*, by community affiliation. Although the Ḥanafīs, too, required potential witnesses to display individual uprightness, this individual criterion was subordinated to the rules imposed by the communal hierarchy.

One of the challenges facing such a hierarchical view of testimony was the existence of the Qurʾānic verse 5:106, which appears to permit non-Muslim testimony in the affairs of Muslims in the particular circumstance, mentioned earlier, of the testament of a Muslim who dies while away from home. The verse states: "O you who believe: when death approaches you, let two upright men from among you act as witnesses to the setting down of a bequest, or two men from another people if you are traveling when

28 On social hierarchies in the classical period, see Louise Marlow, *Hierarchy and Egalitarianism in Islamic Thought* (New York: Cambridge University Press, 1997).

29 Fadel, "Two Women, One Man," 195–98.

30 Sarakhsī, *Mabsūṭ*, 5:44.

death approaches." The phrase "from another people" could reasonably be understood to refer to non-Muslims, and it had been so understood in a case brought before the Companion Abū Mūsā al-Ashʿarī. As noted earlier, Aḥmad Ibn Ḥanbal permitted non-Muslim testimony in this particular situation as an exception to his general position, but the Iraqi jurist and foundational forebear of the Ḥanafī school Ibrāhīm al-Nakhaʿī (d. 96/715) declared the verse to have been abrogated by a later verse (Q. 65:2).[31] The latter view was also adopted by the early Mālikī jurist Ibn al-Qāsim (d. 191/806).[32] Shāfiʿī, too, held the verse to have been abrogated; as an alternative argument, he denied that "from another people" necessarily referred to non-Muslims, claiming that it had also been glossed as members of other tribes. He thus refused to grant an exception to his general rule to accommodate this scenario.[33]

For those Muslim jurists who did, in principle, accept the testimony of non-Muslims in a Muslim court, evaluating the individual reliability of potential non-Muslim witnesses posed a challenge. The Egyptian *ḥadīth* scholar and judge Khayr Ibn Nuʿaym (in office 120–27/738–45), who allowed non-Muslims to testify against their coreligionists, ascertained the probity of non-Muslim witnesses by making inquiries regarding their uprightness among other members of their religious community (*yasʾal ʿan ʿadālatihim fī ahl dīnihim*).[34] His contemporary, the Iraqi jurist and teacher of Abū Ḥanīfa, Ḥammād b. Sulaymān (d. 120/737), also maintained a notion of non-Muslim uprightness, but he went further than Ibn Nuʿaym by also permitting cross-confessional testimony by non-Muslims.[35] Importantly, he specified that his criterion for potential witnesses was "uprightness in *their* religion," acknowledging that behavior that would have clearly undermined a witness's uprightness according to Muslim standards, such as nonperformance of obligatory Muslim rituals or consumption of forbidden foods, did not compromise the acceptability of non-Muslims who belonged to communities according to whose norms these behaviors were licit.

A century later, Aḥmad Ibn Ḥanbal rejected this idea of non-Muslim uprightness, asking, "Who examines the *dhimmī*: *man yuzakkī al-dhimmī*?" He dismissed the claim that a culturally relative definition of uprightness could suffice to establish a witness's reliability, arguing of non-Muslims that "only their own community declares them upright" and that "even the

31 Abū Yūsuf, *Āthār*, 166.

32 Ibn Abī Zayd, *Nawādir*, 8:425.

33 Shāfiʿī, *Umm*, 7:358.

34 Kindī, *Governors and Judges*, 351.

35 Ṣanʿānī, *Muṣannaf*, 8:357, no. 15530 (*tajūz shahādatuhum baʿḍuhum ʿalā baʿḍ idhā kānū ʿudūlan fī dīnihim*).

best of them drink wine and eat pork, so who can declare them upright?"[36] For Aḥmad, uprightness as a guarantor of acceptable testimony was not predicated on the standards of the relevant community, but rather was an exclusive characteristic of Muslims.

Differing prerequisites for testimony also determined the exclusion or inclusion of other groups, such as slaves. Shāfiʿī tentatively sided with his teacher Mālik in disqualifying slaves from giving testimony, arguing that their lack of freedom necessarily compromised their uprightness as witnesses. But he admitted that he was not certain of this position, given that it had no clear scriptural foundation.[37] Aḥmad Ibn Ḥanbal, on the other hand, did not consider slave status to undermine uprightness, and therefore accepted the testimony of slaves.[38] Ḥanafīs, meanwhile, disallowed the testimony of slaves on grounds that had nothing to do with uprightness, but rather were based on the distinctly Ḥanafī concept of authority (*wilāya*): unlike non-Muslims, who possessed limited legal authority and thus qualified as witnesses in certain circumstances, slaves lacked any authority, even over their own selves.[39]

CONCLUSION

Let me summarize the overall developments that can be detected in the material I have discussed, fragmentary though it is. In the early second/eighth century, the acceptability of non-Muslims as witnesses in Islamic court proceedings appears to have been narrowed by the application of a notion of communal bias between different confessional groups. Concurrently, judges placed restrictions on intra-Muslim testimony on the same basis. It seems likely that both of these efforts to bar cross-communal testimony were motivated by a desire to rein in real or perceived communal animosities among Muslim factions and across religious communities alike. Over the course of the second/eighth century, the rationales for admitting or excluding witness testimony changed. Shāfiʿī, guided by his strictly scripturalist legal theory, transformed the notion of bias into an individualized test for Muslim witnesses, while disqualifying non-Muslims wholesale from giving testimony in Muslim court cases. At the other end of the spectrum, the Ḥanafīs upheld the early precedent of permitting non-Muslims to testify against other non-Muslims, regardless

36 Khallāl, *Aḥkām ahl al-milal*, 128–30.

37 Shāfiʿī, *Umm*, 8:134–35.

38 Marwazī (comp.), *Masāʾil al-Imām Aḥmad*, 8:4104.

39 Sarakhsī, *Mabsūṭ*, 16:135.

of confessional differences among them. But they placed such testimony within a multidimensional hierarchy of legal authority, which regulated the admissibility of witness testimony on the grounds of religion, *dhimma*, gender, and free or slave status.[40]

The formalistic criteria for excluding testimony developed in the second/eighth century by Ḥanafī jurists and Shāfiʿī would remain influential but not unchallenged over the ensuing decades and centuries. The most significant dissent came from jurists who considered the heart of the judicial process to consist not of the production of valid testimony but rather of efforts to convince the judge of one's claim beyond a reasonable doubt (the so-called *qaḍāʾ bi-ʿilm al-qāḍī* doctrine).[41] From such a perspective, any testimony that could shed light on the issue at hand was potentially valuable. The differences between these two judicial models remain largely unexplored, however, and a full consideration of their respective implications for the acceptance of particular types of witness testimony must await further study.

40 On the Ḥanafī conception of the legal authority of women (not discussed in this paper), see Sarakhsī, *Mabṣūṭ*, 16:113.

41 See "Qaḍāʾ al-qāḍī bi-ʿilmih," in *MF*, 1:244; Muḥammad Raʾfat ʿUthmān, *al-Niẓām al-qaḍāʾī fī al-fiqh al-islāmī* (Beirut: Dār al-Bayrūt, 1994), 501–14; Mohammad Fadel, "Two Women, One Man," 197–99. Shāfiʿī famously believed in the *qaḍāʾ bi-ʿilm al-qāḍī* doctrine in theory, but he would not espouse it in practice out of fear of corrupt judges. See Tāj al-Dīn al-Subkī, *Ṭabaqāt al-Shāfiʿiyya al-kubrā*, ed. Maḥmūd al-Ṭanāḥī and ʿAbd al-Fattāḥ al-Ḥulw (Cairo: Maṭbaʿat ʿĪsā al-Ḥalabī, 1964), 6:251.

Chapter Two

Circumstantial Evidence in the Administration of Islamic Justice

Hossein Modarressi
Princeton University

In a decree that the ʿAbbāsid caliph al-Ṭāʾiʿ li-Allāh (r. 974–991) issued for the position of *ṣāḥib al-maẓālim*, an office in the Islamic judicial system with the authority to use executive power that was set up to investigate complaints of injustice where the intervention of the executive power was deemed necessary,[1] it is stated:

> The jurisdictions of the judge and the officer in charge of the *maẓālim* are the same, except that the judge is bound by solid and plain evidence, while the officer in charge of the *maẓālim* looks for types of evidence that are obscure and concealed.[2]

In a similar way, the mid-eleventh-century chief judge of the ʿAbbāsid caliphate Abū al-Ḥasan al-Māwardī (d. 450/1058) explains in his manual of Islamic administrative practice that:

> The officer in charge of the *maẓālim* uses extra [means of] intimidation and looks for clues through indications and circumstantial evidence (*al-amārāt al-dālla wa-shawāhid al-aḥwāl*)—means that are not available to judges.[3]

These statements accurately, even if briefly, define a main difference between the two juridical institutions: Ordinary courts acted strictly on the

1 The office could also investigate complaints of unfair treatment by branches of the administration, similar to Star Chamber in the English justice system from the late 15th to mid-17th centuries (with many thanks to Intisar Rabb for bringing this parallel to my attention).

2 Aḥmad b. ʿAlī al-Qalqashandī (d. 821/1418), *Ṣubḥ al-aʿshā* (Cairo: Dār al-Kutub al-Khidīwiyya, 1913-1922), 10:252.

3 Abū al-Ḥasan al-Māwardī (d. 450/1058), *al-Aḥkām al-sulṭāniyya waʾl-wilāyāt al-dīniyya* (Cairo: al-Maktaba al-Tawfīqiyya, 1978), 93.

basis of oral testimony (including voluntary confession) and oath, and were not supposed to use any other evidence. However, *maẓālim* courts would examine a case in its proper context and seriously consider all internal and external indications for resolving that case, including circumstantial evidence.

Ignoring the internal and external evidence pertaining to a case in traditional Islamic courts would, at times, impose major costs on the judiciary, as the system often could not function with oral testimony alone.[4] Examples of such situations are abundantly cited in pre-modern Islamic sources. Jalāl al-Dīn al-Dawānī's description of how the court functioned in his time should suffice as a case in point.[5] He writes:

> As a matter of fact, the absence of *maẓālim* courts caused many rights of Muslims to be wasted, and allowed the wicked and deceitful to dominate and seize people's property. (In cases like this) when the victim goes to court, first the *ʿudūl* (that is, close aides to the judge who function like court clerks) dally and scruple as to how to draft the petition. This process could take considerable time, and could delay the presentation of the petition for a long period by employing various kinds of tricks deliberately used to postpone [a decision].
>
> Next, when the petition is submitted and the witnesses give their testimony, the *ʿudūl* start finding fault with the wording that the witnesses used in their statements, and go around and ask the jurists whether that specific wording can be valid, and thus delay the [operation of] procedural due process in the case for an even longer period.
>
> Next comes the stage [in which the judge is] to review the trustworthiness of the witnesses through character witnesses who will be asked to certify that they know the [testimonial] witnesses to be righteous and reliable. This will take considerably more time, especially as the *ʿudūl* continue to scruple as to the wording of the certifications of the character witnesses to make sure that they satisfy the rules.

4 For reports of an eyewitness to examples of this phenomenon, see Jalāl al-Dīn al-Dawānī (d. 908/1502-3), *Dīwān-i Maẓālim*, ed. Hossein Modarressi in *Farhang-i Irānzamīn* 27 (1987), 98–119.

5 Jalāl al-Dīn al-Dawānī was a respected late-9th/15th century Iranian philosopher and author of a celebrated work on ethics called *Akhlāq-i Jalālī*. He served as the chief judge of the southern Iranian province of Fars during one period of his life. See Ann K.S. Lambton, "al-Dawānī," *EI²*, 2:174; and Andrew J. Newman, "Davānī, Jalāl al-Dīn Moḥammad," *Encyclopaedia Iranica*, 7:132–33.

> Then comes the turn of the other party to contest the reliability of the witnesses by presenting affidavits of parallel character witnesses to certify the untrustworthiness of the witnesses for the petitioner. This process, in turn, has to go through the scrutiny of the religious character of the character witnesses who contest the reliability of the witnesses, and so on and so forth.
>
> At times, a small petition lingers around in court for such a long time that the parties get fed up with the process. And when the case is a criminal case, the purpose is completely lost.[6]

Nevertheless, traditional Islamic legal procedures did not permit judges to go beyond the use of testimony and oaths as evidence, and would not allow any modification or reform.

There were two exceptions to that general rule: First, an old opinion among some Sunnī[7] and Shīʿī[8] jurists allowed judges to act according to their own *personal knowledge*. The concept of knowledge in this context was conventionally[9] understood to refer to instances in which the judge had personally witnessed an event, such as the murder of the victim by the killer or the utterance of the formula of divorce by the husband.[10] Among those who allowed judges to use their personal knowledge, there were considerable differences of opinion, often along the lines of differences between various schools and scholars. That is, some allowed the judges to use their personal knowledge, with certain constraints surrounding the context in which this knowledge could be obtained and the context to which

6 Dawānī, *Dīwān-i Maẓālim*, in *Farhang-i Irānzamīn* 27:115.

7 These Sunnī jurists included most of the Ḥanafīs, as well as Ibn Ḥazm (d. 456/1064) of the Ẓāhirī school. See Ibn Ḥazm, *al-Muḥallā* (Cairo: Idārat al-Ṭibāʿa al-Munīriyya, 1929-1934), 9:370. The early Shāfiʿīs agreed with this opinion in principle, but ruled against its application in practice in order to hold judges accountable for their decisions. They did so "because of the corruption of the court in their times." See Muwaffaq al-Dīn Ibn Qudāma (d. 620/1223), *al-Mughnī* (Cairo: Dār Hajar, 1986-1990), 14:31. See also ʿAbd al-Karīm Zaydān, *Niẓām al-qaḍāʾ fī al-sharīʿa al-Islāmiyya* (Baghdad: Maṭbaʿat al-ʿĀnī, 1984), 211–15 and the sources cited therein.

8 See their opinions as quoted in Muḥammad Jawād b. Muḥammad al-ʿĀmilī (d. 1226/1811), *Miftāḥ al-karāma fī sharḥ Qawāʿid al-ʿAllāma* (Qum: Muʾassasat al-Nashr al-Islāmī, 1999), 25:94 and the sources quoted in the footnotes. Two of the earliest examples are al-Sharīf al-Murtaḍā (d. 436/1044), *al-Intiṣār* (Najaf: Manshūrāt al-Maṭbaʿa al-Ḥaydariyya, 1971), 237; and Shaykh al-Ṭāʾifa Muḥammad b. al-Ḥasan al-Ṭūsī (d. 460/1067), *Kitāb al-Khilāf* (Qum: Muʾassasat al-Nashr al-Islāmī, 1987–1996), 6:242. One of the most recent is Ayatollah Khomeini, *Taḥrīr al-Wasīla* (Najaf: Maṭbaʿat al-Ādāb, 1387/1967), 2:539.

9 There are other definitions as well. Some authors make a distinction between knowledge acquired by the senses (*ʿilm ḥissī*) and knowledge acquired by "guessing" (*ʿilm ḥadsī*), the latter further defined as knowledge obtained through all types of indications, including circumstantial evidence.

10 See, for instance, Abū al-Ḥasan al-Māwardī, *Adab al-qāḍī* (Baghdad: Dīwān al-Awqāf, 1972) 2:375.

it could be applied.[11] Nevertheless, the opinion permitting decisions based on the personal knowledge of the judge had the potential to substantially expand the jurisdiction of a judge and his ability to go beyond the traditional framework of an Islamic court.[12]

Second, a number of prominent medieval Sunnī jurists from various schools,[13] some of whom served as judges in different parts of the Muslim world, required the judge to consider all kinds of internal and external evidence, including circumstantial evidence (*qarāʾin*) in his decision-making. The most outspoken among these jurists was Ibn Qayyim al-Jawziyya (d. 751/1350), or Ibn al-Qayyim as he is commonly known, who wrote a special book dedicated to arguing for the importance of judges using all kinds of evidence in their process of adjudication.[14] Both in this book and in his other works, he advocated for the position that limiting legal evidence to verbal testimony and oaths, while ignoring other internal and external types of evidence,

> has caused many rights to be wasted and laws to be stalled; has emboldened the vicious and depicted the *sharīʿa* as a system that cannot function; and has deprived judges of so many essential means by which to distinguish truth from falsehood. Ignoring this host of evidence has, in fact, made the Islamic court non-functional. Everyone knows for certain that these types of evidence are right and essential, but most think that their use is against the accepted canon. This assumption, a major fault in understanding the *sharīʿa*, persuaded the rulers to take matters into their own hands and create administrative rules to bring the situation under some kind of control. The combination of the fault

11 A major point of disagreement was whether the judge could rule according to his personal knowledge only in civil suits (*ḥuqūq, ḥuqūq al-nās*), as advocated by most Sunnī and Shīʿī jurists who allowed the judge to use his personal knowledge, or whether he could use it in criminal justice (*ḥudūd, ḥuqūq Allāh*) as well.

12 In practice, however, it seems that this potential was never actualized. As a contemporary writer on the topic concluded, "whoever does thorough research on this topic will become certain that the personal knowledge of the judge was never used in an Islamic court as an acceptable basis for adjudicating legal disputes." See Maḥmūd al-Hāshimī, "Ḥukm al-qāḍī bi-ʿilmih," *Fiqh Ahl al-Bayt* 16 (1420/2000), 11–84.

13 They included such prominent scholars as the Shāfiʿīs Ibn Abī al-Dam (d. 642/1244), judge of Hama in west-central Syria, and al-ʿIzz b. ʿAbd al-Salām (d. 660/1262), who later in life served as the judge of Cairo; the Ḥanbalī Ibn Qayyim al-Jawziyya (d. 751/1350); the Mālikīs Ibn Juzayy (d. 741/1340) of Granada and Ibn Farḥūn (d. 799/1397), judge of Medina; and the Ḥanafīs ʿAlāʾ al-Dīn al-Ṭarābulusī (d. 844/1440), judge of Jerusalem, Ibn al-Ghars (d. 894/1489), Ibn Nujaym (d. 970/1563), and more recently Ibn ʿĀbidīn (d. 1252/1836). For the viewpoints of these jurists, see ʿAbd Allāh al-ʿAjlān, *al-Qaḍāʾ biʾl-qarāʾin al-muʿāṣira* (Riyadh: Jāmiʿat al-Imām Muḥammad b. Saʿūd al-Islāmiyya, 2006), 1:31–32 and the sources cited therein.

14 Ibn al-Qayyim, *al-Ṭuruq al-ḥukmiyya fī al-siyāsa al-sharʿiyya*, ed. Nāyif b. Aḥmad al-Ḥamad (Mecca: Dār ʿĀlam al-Fawāʾid, 2007). This work is available in a number of other editions.

> which prevented Islamic courts from functioning and the introduction of these man-made rules and institutions led to persistent evil and widespread corruption, to the extent that matters have gotten out of hand.[15]

To support his argument, Ibn al-Qayyim relied on a passage from the Qurʾān stating that God sent His messengers and scriptures to establish the rule of justice.[16] The logical conclusion is that when one clearly observes the signs of fairness or justice, *that* is the law of God and His religion, regardless of how one reaches that observation. God did not strictly define the indications and signs of fairness or justice. So, to limit them to a couple of types of evidence, while leaving out similar or stronger types of evidence, is incoherent. After all, God made clear that his purpose was the establishment of the rule of justice and, as such, whatever can fulfill that purpose is what the religion requires.[17]

Furthermore, Ibn al-Qayyim maintained that judges and other early Muslim authorities never limited themselves to verbal testimony and oaths for distinguishing right from wrong in legal cases,[18] and that the validity of all kinds of evidence and indications is the basis for many rules in various chapters of Islamic law.[19] He argues these points by means of stories quoted in biographical sources and anthologies in which judges in different parts of the Muslim world and in various periods of Islamic history went well beyond the traditional bipartite procedures that Islamic law formally recognized, and used all sorts of techniques to discover the truth.[20]

Most of those examples are, however, anecdotal, representing the legal wit and wisdom of the judges[21] in cases where they smelled a rat, so

15 Ibn al-Qayyim, *Badāʾiʿ al-fawāʾid* (Mecca: Dār ʿĀlam al-Fawāʾid, 2004), 3:1088–89.

16 Q. 57:25.

17 Ibn al-Qayyim, *Badāʾiʿ al-fawāʾid*, 3:1089.

18 Ibn al-Qayyim, *al-Ṭuruq al-ḥukmiyya*, 1:10–48.

19 Ibid., 1:48–64 and passim.

20 Ibid., 1:65–67.

21 Ibn al-Qayyim suggests that this wisdom was sanctioned by the caliph ʿUmar in his alleged letter to the judge whom he assigned to Basra, Abū Mūsā al-Ashʿarī, a letter in which he urged judges to be savvy (*al-fahm! al-fahm!*). See Ibn al-Qayyim, *Iʿlām al-muwaqqiʿīn ʿan Rabb al-ʿĀlamīn* (Beirut: Dār al-Kutub al-ʿIlmiyya, 1991), 1:69. The text of this letter is included at pages 67–68,

to speak, and suspected that something was wrong.[22] The judges thus tried various means by which to find indications that one or the other party to a conflict was being dishonest in his or her claim. In most of these instances, the case would abruptly terminate due to a confession on the part of the culprit. As such—that is to say, because the conclusion of these cases depended on a type of oral testimony—these instances should not actually be considered exceptions to the traditional procedures that Islamic law advocated.

There were certainly examples in which the judge decided the merits of the case on the basis of a piece of evidence that showed the falsity of the petitioner or defendant's claim, but in these cases too the decision would occur before the official procedural due process began. Here is an example: A petitioner once brought a charge to a judge claiming that he trusted someone and left his money with him, but that the trustee now denied having accepted that trusteeship. The judge asked *where* the petitioner had entrusted the other man with the money. The petitioner named a mosque far away from the town, and the defendant pretended not to know where that mosque was. The judge then asked the petitioner to go to the mosque immediately and to bring back a copy of the Qurʾān so that the judge could make the defendant take the oath with the Qurʾān from that specific mosque. The man left to retrieve the Qurʾān, while the judge held the defendant in the court, keeping himself busy with other cases. After some time had passed, the judge, complaining about how much time bringing a copy of the Qurʾān should require, turned to the defendant and asked if he thought that

---

and can also be found in many early collections of Sunnī *ḥadīth.* Ibn Ḥazm identifies this text as fake, and most of its chains of transmission do not meet the required standards for authenticated documents. See Ibn Ḥazm, *al-Muḥallā*, 1:590; and his *al-Iḥkām fī uṣūl al-aḥkām* (Cairo: Dār al-Ḥadīth, 1984), 2:443. However, Ibn al-Qayyim and others accept its authority as "a historical document which has received acceptance from many of the scholars of the previous generations," a genre of religious reports known in the Shīʿī tradition as "widely accepted reports" (*maqbūla*). Using the terminology of the science of *ḥadīth*, later Sunnī scholars defined the document in question as a reliable text received by *wijāda*—a term used when a written text is found with no dependable chain of transmission. See Ibn Kathīr (d. 774/1373), *Musnad al-Fārūq* (Manṣūra: Dār al-Wafāʾ, 1991), 2:546–48; and Muḥammad Nāṣir al-Dīn al-Albānī, *Irwāʾ al-ghalīl*, 2nd ed. (Beirut: al-Maktab al-Islāmī, 1985), 8:241.

22 Iyās b. Muʿāwiya, the judge of Basra in the early 2nd/8th century, was clearly referring to this ability of a judge to guess that something is amiss when he stated that "judgment is nothing to be taught; it is rather an acumen" in response to a request to teach someone the art of judgment. See Ibn ʿAsākir (d. 571/1176), *Taʾrīkh madīnat Dimashq* (Beirut: Dār al-Fikr, 1995), 10:30. See also al-Khaṭīb al-Baghdādī (d. 463/1071), *Taʾrīkh Madīnat al-Salām wa-akhbār muḥaddithīhā* = *Taʾrīkh Baghdād* (Beirut: Dār al-Gharb al-Islāmī, 2001), 12:242–43 (whence Ibn al-Qayyim, *al-Ṭuruq al-ḥukmiyya*, 1:70–72), where Abū Khāzim al-Qāḍī speaks about his own experience with this acumen. This man, Abū Khāzim ʿAbd al-Ḥamīd b. ʿAbd al-ʿAzīz al-Baṣrī al-Ḥanafī (d. 292/905), was a former judge of Syria and Kūfa who was appointed in 283/896 by the ʿAbbāsid caliph al-Muʿtaḍid (r. 279-89/892-902) as judge of the eastern section of Baghdad, a position that he held until the end of his life.

the petitioner might have already reached the mosque. The man, who had originally pretended not to know where the mosque was, answered "not yet." That was enough evidence for the judge to decide that the defendant was deceitful and charge him with paying the money back to the petitioner.[23]

23 Ibn al-Jawzī (d. 597/1201), *al-Adhkiyāʾ* (Beirut: al-Maktab al-Tijārī, 1966), 66–67 (whence Ibn al-Qayyim, *al-Ṭuruq al-ḥukmiyya*, 1:70). Ibn al-Jawzī quotes other witty stories of the early judges. Here is an example reported by a mid-4th/10th century jurist: A person commonly known as reliable used to frequent the court of the judge of Hamadān. It happened that, one day, the judge summoned him to the court to give testimony, but when he arrived and gave his testimony, the judge rejected it. When asked why, he answered that he had discovered that the man was a hypocrite (murāʾī), saying: "I counted his steps everyday from the moment he arrived at the court to the point when he sat down close to me. This time when I called him to come and give testimony, it took him three or four more steps to reach the same point, indicating that he walked slower to feign dignity. I therefore decided that he was a hypocrite." See Ibn al-Jawzī, *al-Adhkiyāʾ*, 68–69, (whence Ibn al-Qayyim, *al-Ṭuruq al-ḥukmiyya*, 1:72–73).

Chapter Three

The Curious Case of Bughaybigha, 661–883: Land and Leadership in Early Islamic Societies

Intisar Rabb*

Harvard Law School

> *Mūsā b. Isḥāq b. ʿAmmāra said: We passed by Bughaybigha, which was flourishing, with Muḥammad b. ʿAbd Allāh b. al-Ḥasan. He remarked: Do you ever wonder at that? By God, you will continue to die until nothing green remains in it. You will [simply] live and die.*[1]

The calm that preceded Islam's first Civil War in the seventh century found ʿAlī b. Abī Ṭālib—soon-to-be caliph—tending to his land on a fertile farm

---

* This paper was inspired by a course that I co-taught with Roy Mottahedeh in 2014 on ʿAbbāsid-era courts, influenced by the impression his method in *Loyalty and Leadership* (1980) and his prose from *The Mantle of the Prophet* (1985) left on me for my own work (at least, such is my aspiration), and improved by his reading of the case under discussion in this essay with me. The paper could not have been written without the generous help of Hossein Modarressi in figuring out what this case was about, energetically discussing and debating both my questions and answers, and pointing me to several unknown sources and unconsidered ideas. It also benefitted from comments and sources shared by Hassan Ansari, Abigail Balbale, Aslı Bâli, Elizabeth Papp Kamali, Ella Landau-Tasseron, Máximo Langer, Behnam Sadeghi, Asma Sayeed, Adnan Zulfiqar, and participants of the 2016 conference on "Courts and Judicial Procedure in Early Islamic Law" at Harvard Law School, where this paper was first presented, as well as the attendees of a talk at UCLA Law School presented 1336 years to the day after the events of October 10, 680 that gave rise to the major controversy surrounding this case. It was completed at the Radcliffe Institute for Advanced Study, with appreciation to Susan and Kenneth Wallach for generous fellowship funding and friendship.

1 Abū ʿUbayd al-Bakrī al-Andalusī (d. 487/1094), *Muʿjam mā ʾstuʿjim min asmāʾ al-bilād waʾl-mawāḍiʿ*, ed. Jamāl Ṭulba (Beirut: Dār al-Kutub al-ʿIlmiyya, 1998), 2:253: *Mararnā biʾl-Bughaybigha maʿa Muḥammad b. ʿAbd Allāh b. Ḥasan, wa-hiya ʿāmira, fa-qāla: a-taʿjabūna lahā, wallāh la-tamūtunna ḥattā lā yabqā fīhā khaḍrāʾ thumma la-taʿīshunna thumma la-tamūtunna.* See also Muḥammad b. Muḥammad b. ʿAbd Allāh al-Ḥimyarī (d. ca. 9th/15th c.), *al-Rawḍ al-miʿṭār fī khabar al-aqṭār*, ed. Iḥsān ʿAbbās (Beirut: Maktabat Lubnān, 1975), 112. Bakrī and Ḥimyarī are quoting a report from the leader of an ʿAlid rebellion who intended to reclaim the land and leadership of the young Muslim community, on whom see Amikam Elad, *The Rebellion of Muḥammad al-Nafs al-Zakiyya in 145/762: Ṭālibids and Early ʿAbbāsids in Conflict* (Leiden: Brill, 2015).

called Yanbuʿ to the west and slightly north of Medina.[2] Curiously, a spring emerged—curious as no one had expected a rushing spring to bubble up on the farm. Curious, too, was the name he gave to the spring: "Bughaybigha"—an onomatopoeia meant to mimic the *bagh-bagh* sound of gurgling water. ʿAlī immediately turned the spring and its surrounding land into a charitable endowment to serve the poor, travelers, and members of his family in need, and he placed the endowment in the charge of his sons Ḥasan and Ḥusayn.

What happened next is even curiouser than the name or origins of Bughaybigha. ʿAlī had moved to Kūfa, but retained the land at Yanbuʿ. Not long after his death in 661 and right at the start of Islam's expansion, a generations-long battle over Bughaybigha ensued. The battle began after Ḥasan's death in 670 with a series of attempts by the first Umayyad caliph to take the land from ʿAlī's remaining son, Ḥusayn. The battle for control over Bughaybigha continued in a series of takings and "givings" by subsequent caliphs over the course of some one and a half centuries.[3] Having started off in ʿAlid hands, by the mid-eighth century, control over Bughaybigha had shifted to Umayyad hands.[4] But the ʿAlids continued to assert rights to the land, which made the Umayyad caliph Walīd II keen to put an end to the dispute when he assumed the caliphate in 743. He appointed one of his agents to represent his interests—in court if need be. So it was that, almost a century after ʿAlī first discovered the spring, the struggle over Bughaybigha landed in court.

2 Aḥmad b. Yaḥyā al-Balādhurī (d. 279/896), *Jumal min Ansāb al-ashrāf*, ed. Suhayl Zakkār and Riyāḍ al-Ziriklī (Beirut: Dār al-Fikr, 1996), 3:7, reporting on the location of the estate as four *farsakhs* north of Medina.

3 I borrow this term from the concept developed in American law to describe government distributions of property, rather than seizures of it as defined by common notions of takings. See Abraham Bell and Gideon Parchomovsky, "Givings," *The Yale Law Journal* 111, no. 3 (2001): 547–618.

4 The caliph Yazīd b. ʿAbd al-Mālik (Yazīd II) had seized the land as soon as he assumed the caliphate in 720. See Ibn Saʿd (d. 230/844-5), *al-Ṭabaqāt al-kubrā*, ed. ʿAlī Muḥammad ʿUmar (Cairo: Maktabat al-Khānjī, 2001), 6:414–15.

THE CASE OF BUGHAYBIGHA[5]

The Case

ʿAlī's great-grandson ʿAbd Allāh b. al-Ḥasan was tending to Bughaybigha, "cultivating a reed bed fed by a spring of his in the farmlands of Yanbuʿ." Claiming the land for the caliph, Walīd II's agent tried to stop ʿAbd Allāh, but to no avail. The agent then entered a claim in court presumably asserting that the caliph had rights to the entire valley of Yanbuʿ.

The court was in Medina, which had jurisdiction over nearby Bughaybigha, and the presiding judge was Saʿd b. Ibrāhīm (d. 127/745-6).[6] The agent made an appearance in court on behalf of the caliph, as the petitioner, lodging a claim against ʿAbd Allāh, as the respondent. Judge Saʿd b. Ibrāhīm asked the agent to produce evidence of his claim—namely, that the caliph owned the land that ʿAbd Allāh was working. But the agent failed to do so before the requisite time expired. The judge then turned to ʿAbd Allāh, and the following dialogue ensued:

Judge:	Do you agree to having me [resolve the matter and to the idea that I may] authorize you to work only the land that you have cultivated? If I find that you have worked land to which you are entitled, then you may continue to work that land as you have been doing. But if I find that you have worked land to which you are not entitled, then you

5 This narrative is a stylized account of the case reported in Muḥammad b. Khalaf Wakīʿ (d. 306/917), *Akhbār al-quḍāt*, ed. Saʿīd Muḥammad al-Laḥḥām (Beirut: ʿĀlam al-Kutub, 2001), 102–03. The first paragraph, giving background, draws from the account in Ibn Saʿd, *al-Ṭabaqāt al-kubrā*, 6:414–15. On the early history of the case—beginning with Muʿāwiya's initial seizure of Bughaybigha—see ʿUmar Ibn Shabba (d. 262/876), *Taʾrīkh al-Madīna al-Munawwara*, ed. Fahīm Muḥammad Shaltūt (Beirut: Dār al-Turāth, 1990), 1:222; and ʿAlī b. ʿAbd Allāh al-Samhūdī (d. 911/1506), *Wafāʾ al-wafā bi-akhbār dār al-Muṣṭafā*, ed. Qāsim al-Sāmmarāʾī (London: Muʾassasat al-Furqān, 2001), 4:164–66.

6 Saʿd b. Ibrāhīm b. ʿAbd al-Raḥmān b. ʿAwf al-Zuhrī (d. 127/745-6) was appointed by ʿAbd al-Wāḥid b. ʿAbd Allāh b. Qanīʿ al-Naḍrī, governor of the Ḥijāz district that encompassed Medina, Mecca, and Ṭāʾif, who himself was appointed by the caliph Yazīd b. ʿAbd al-Mālik (Yazīd II) during his reign (102–105/720–724). Typically, judicial appointments run with the nomination or confirmation by a new governor, but it is not clear when Saʿd b. Ibrāhīm was first appointed as there is a blank in the edition of Wakīʿ's *Akhbār al-quḍāt* where the appointment year of the governor would be (p. 102). Although Wakīʿ's narrator suggests that it may have been the judge immediately before Saʿd b. Ibrāhīm who heard the case (see Wakīʿ, *Akhbār al-quḍāt*, 103), the timing accords with the judge being Saʿd himself. That is, if the case occurred during Walīd II's reign (125–126/743–744), which lasted only two years, it would have occurred toward the end of Saʿd's judgeship and at least a year before his death in 127/745-6—that is, in 743 or 744.

	must enter a contract [with the owner governing the future use of the land].[7]
ʿAbd Allāh:	Agreed.
Judge:	I authorize you to continue to cultivate only the reed bed.[8]

At this point, the caliph's agent stormed out of court, shouting to anyone who would listen that he was *not* in fact representing the caliph:

Agent:	To all the people gathered here, I hereby swear by God and to all of you: I am neither the representative, nor the petitioner! The petitioner is the caliph, al-Walīd b. Yazīd (Walīd II).

This comment was a move to render the judge's decision invalid, on a common procedural rule governing the courts—namely, that a judge could not enter a decision against a petitioner who was not present in person or by representation.[9] The judge dismissed this move as without merit, and explained that the case could have gone another way had he used a different procedure: judging on the basis of his knowledge rather than the evidence, which was lacking. He responded as follows:

Judge:	You already testified that you are indeed the caliph's representative and agent. But when faced with the decision going against him, you *now* say that you are neither the representative nor the petitioner. By God, had I judged by my own knowledge about Bughaybigha, I would have judged differently.

7 Wakīʿ, *Akhbār al-quḍāt*, 103: *A-tarḍā an nukhallī baynak wa-bayna ʿamalik? Fa-in kunta ʿamilta fī ḥaqqik [fa-]kamā ʿamilta; wa-in kunta ʿamilta fī ghayr ḥaqqik, ʿuqida ʿalayk.* This exchange suggests that the judge would not give the land to ʿAbd Allāh outright and without condition, such that if it proved to be under the caliph's actual authority, ʿAbd Allāh would have to enter a contract with him to gain permission to work the land and remit to the owner some portion of the proceeds from it.

8 See ibid., 103–04, mentioning the reed bed that ʿAbd Allāh had been cultivating.

9 The rule was not universal, but common enough to have borne mention in reports about early judges. Following it, for example, the Kūfan and Baṣran Judge Shurayḥ b. al-Ḥārith al-Kindī—who was first appointed by ʿUmar and confirmed by ʿUthmān, ʿAlī, and Muʿāwiya—did not rule against absent litigants. See ibid., 357–472, esp. 414. On this judge, who judged for several decades and occupies the longest entry in Wakīʿ's collection, see Etan Kohlberg, "Shurayḥ," *EI*[2], 9:508–09.

> At this stage, the narrator, a Baṣran man named Juwayriya b. Asmāʾ (d. 173/789-90) (who originally narrated the case to one of Ibn Saʿd's informants), sought to place the judge's final statement in context. He asked someone who had also witnessed the episode: "What does he know? What is this knowledge?" The fellow attendee explained that *everyone knew* that Bughaybigha was a charitable endowment established by ʿAlī b. Abī Ṭālib and entrusted to his children and their descendants, but that it was seized by Yazīd b. Muʿāwiya (r. 60–64/680–683) and contested by the Umayyads ever since. He then narrated the rest of the story of Bughaybigha that he and everyone else in that early community—including the judge—*knew*, even generations later. This narrative suggested that ʿAlī and his descendants were the proper stewards of the land, but that no evidence was available to prove it.[10]

This case vividly displays the extent to which discretionary use of judicial procedure drove substantive outcomes in ways little-recognized by conventional accounts of early Islamic law. The implication of the judge's final statement was that, had he ruled according to his own knowledge, the caliph would have lost control over even more land. But instead of resolving the major issues in the case by appealing to judicial knowledge, or to other procedural tools available when evidence was lacking on both sides, the judge chose to avoid a full resolution that might entail a total win for one side or the other. The outcome was thus a compromise-settlement of sorts: a partial win for the caliph, who would keep most of the contested valley, and a partial win for the ʿAlids, who retained the land of the smaller tract within it called Bughaybigha. Likely in view of the lack of evidence, the judge found himself unable or unwilling to fully resolve the case.

At one level, this case presents a competition between procedures for addressing major disputes in court. The judge here was conflicted. He had to choose between the prevailing procedural rule requiring petitioners to produce clear and convincing evidence, usually in the form of witness testimony (the "evidence canon": *al-bayyina ʿalā al-muddaʿī*), and another disfavored rule permitting a judge to decide cases according to his own knowledge (the "judicial knowledge" norm: *ʿilm al-qāḍī*). The first canon

10 Wakīʿ, *Akhbār al-quḍāt*, 103–04.

followed the famous statement—attributed to the Prophet Muḥammad in a *ḥadīth*—that "the petitioner bears the burden of proof." This rule was the more widespread and robust norm, as a popular procedural rule known to bind judicial (but not caliphal) courts.[11] The second rule is often attributed to practices of the Prophet and leaders of his early community. However, by the time of this case in the eighth century, although judicial knowledge was acceptable in the caliphal courts, it was controversial in judicial courts.

There was a third rule, in the shadow of which the judge orchestrated his settlement.[12] Another legal canon stipulated that *continuous land possession and use gives a presumption of authorized use, if not ownership* (the "possession canon": *qāʿidat al-yad* or *istiṣḥāb al-yad*). This canon was once a presumption commonly used to establish land entitlements in the absence of evidence. Had the judge applied it to the ʿAlid cultivation of the reed bed to demonstrate the respondent's rights to the entire valley—on the notion that the valley represented a single, indivisible land tract—the caliph also would have lost, just as he would have lost if the judge had appealed to his own knowledge about who had rights to the valley. On either notion, the judge could have given the entire farmland to ʿAbd Allāh b. al-Ḥasan outright. But that conclusion would have been politically very tricky and therefore potentially unenforceable. Apparently, in the judge's estimation, resolution of the larger question was not necessary. The scope of the present case allowed him to safely punt that larger question by resolving the narrower matter at hand.[13]

At a deeper level, I argue that the dispute over Bughaybigha, together with the dueling canons attached to it, demonstrates how *procedure* came

11 Caliphal courts were not bound by this rule. Consider the early case in which the ʿAbbāsid caliph Hārūn al-Rashīd (r. 170-93/786-809) felt obliged to rely on his knowledge that his son, the prince, was guilty of sexual misconduct and must be punished. He was relieved when the soon-to-be-chief judge Abū Yūsuf (d. 182/798) invoked the *doubt canon*—requiring judges to avoid criminal punishments in cases of doubt—to sidestep punishment, on the grounds that a judge's knowledge was insufficient to prove the crime. For a discussion of this case, see my *Doubt in Islamic Law* (Cambridge: Cambridge University Press, 2015), 90–92, which cites medieval literary and historical reports of this episode from Qāḍī al-Tanūkhī's (d. 384/994) *Nishwār al-muḥāḍara*; Ibn Khallikān's (d. 681/1282) *Wafayāt al-aʿyān*; Ibn al-Wardī's (d. 749/1349) *Taʾrīkh*; and Abū ʿAbd Allāh al-Yāfiʿī's (d. 768/1366-7) *Mirʾāt al-jinān*. See also Maribel Fierro, "*Idraʾū al-Ḥudūd bi-al-Shubuhāt*: When Lawful Violence Meets Doubt," *Hawwa* 5, nos. 2–3 (2007): 208–38; and Christian Lange, *Justice, Punishment and the Medieval Muslim Imagination* (Cambridge: Cambridge University Press, 2008), 192.

12 This concept draws on the idea of settlements as bargains devised "in the shadow of the law." See Robert Mnookin and Lewis Kornhauser, "Bargaining in the Shadow of the Law: The Case of Divorce," *Yale Law Journal* 88, no. 5 (1979): 950–97.

13 Indeed, the larger question involved stakes so high that it became a matter not just of political or religious conflict, but of armed conflict, with ʿAbd Allāh b. al-Ḥasan eventually encouraging people to swear allegiance to his son, Muḥammad al-Nafs al-Zakiyya, who staged a rebellion against the caliph (see above, note 1). See Abū al-Faraj al-Iṣbahānī, *Maqātil al-Ṭālibiyyīn* ([Najaf]: Maktabat al-Ḥaydariyya, 1423/[2002-3]), 224–25.

to play a critical role in the development of early Islamic law. Procedure also intervened in questions of legitimacy on disputes of land and leadership in that period. Conventional accounts of Islamic law tend to discount the role of procedure and inflate the importance of a symbiotic relationship between caliphs and jurists. However, the relationship between caliphs and jurists was often mediated through courts—courts laden with procedure. No account of early Islamic law so far shows the centrality of procedure to producing this symbiosis; and no account charts how and why judges may have helped mediate the jurist-caliph relationship or what significance it had for questions of legitimacy, land, and leadership.

I use this case as an example with which to begin filling that gap. The dispute over Bughaybigha highlights how conflicting theories of religious authority and political legitimacy could be litigated in courts; it indicates the legitimacy-conferring dominance of procedure—later encapsulated in the form of legal canons—in those courts; and it shows how both courts and judicial procedure could be used politically—precisely because of the legal legitimacy that the courts and procedure together conferred. To understand the dispute over Bughaybigha is to better understand the development and role of judicial procedure in resolving major questions at the core of Islamic law during its "founding period," from the seventh to eleventh centuries.[14]

This essay explores the history and procedures of this case. Following this basic recitation of the case, the next section traces the making and taking of Bughaybigha, and the third part assesses the procedures relied on to resolve the dispute in court. In the end, the judge decided the case without explicit *citation* of procedures or legal canons. Yet it is clear that both were very much in play, as signaled by the judge's own final comments quoted above to explain his choice to pursue a narrow course of action. The perception and use of procedure in the *Case of Bughaybigha* illustrate how ordinary disputes over land reflected extraordinary dynamics of political leadership, judicial independence, and questions related to legitimacy that accompany each. More specifically, this case is important because it shows how judges—even when a political authority attempts to place him in the service of politics—could use legal canons to thread the needle of power, here as between ʿAlid claims of right and Umayyad might.[15]

14 For more on my use of this term for periodization in Islamic legal history, see my *Doubt in Islamic law*, 8–9.

15 While the fuller operation and development of legal canons require further study, my treatment of the legal canons involved in this case methodologically draws on Roy Mottahedeh's ascription of verisimilitude to various anecdotes from early Islamic sources to analyze prevalent attitudes that buoyed leadership networks under Būyid rule. In my treatment, I similarly take judicial references to various legal canons in anecdotal cases (even where they are not historical court records) to have verisimilitude to the social-legal workings of courts sufficient to reflect prevalent understandings of and attitudes toward judicial procedures as they intersected with

THE MAKING AND TAKING OF BUGHAYBIGHA

The struggle for Bughaybigha was no ordinary dispute. More than a bountiful spring or mere tract of land, Bughaybigha was located both geographically and symbolically at the center of political and religious contestations for power and legitimacy from the time of Islam's very beginnings. The spring that ʿAlī discovered fed fertile land that was geographically close to the seat of the early empire and that lay along the trade- and expansion-route from Medina to Syria. Producing dates in abundance, Bughaybigha was a source of sustenance and wealth for ʿAlī and his descendants. Moreover, it was the only portion of inheritance or legacy, according to some accounts, that ʿAlī managed to retain from the Prophet for his sons and grandsons. These features made Bughaybigha extraordinarily important, both strategically and religiously, and they explain why the land was the locus of so much controversy for such an extended period.

The Origins of Bughaybigha

Bughaybigha refers to the most prized and hotly contested part of the larger tract of farmlands in the valley called Yanbuʿ, just outside of Medina.[16] With its early history now somewhat obscured, the spring is often referred to by different names that conflate the actual spring both with others nearby and with the entire expanse of land at Yanbuʿ. Perhaps counterintuitively, this conflation actually confirms the early importance of Bughaybigha itself. Often confused in the literature,[17] a careful reading of the sources sheds

political realities of the time. See Roy Mottahedeh, *Loyalty and Leadership in an Early Islamic Society*, 2nd ed. (London: I.B. Tauris, 2001).

16 See al-Ṣāḥib Ibn ʿAbbād (d. 385/995), *al-Muḥīṭ fī al-lugha*, ed. Muḥammad Ḥasan Āl Yāsīn (Beirut: ʿĀlam al-Kutub, 1994), 4:520, defining Bughaybigha as an estate in [read: near] Medina. For additional descriptions of Bughaybigha, see ʿAlī Khān b. Aḥmad al-Madanī al-Shīrāzī, *al-Ṭirāz al-awwal wa'l-kināz li-mā ʿalayh min lughat al-ʿArab al-muʾawwal* (Mashhad: Muʾassasat Āl al-Bayt li-Iḥyāʾ al-Turāth, 2006), 7:325, noting that local mountains were sometimes ascribed to a Bughaybigha located in Yanbuʿ, near, not "in Medina." See also Muḥammad b. Muḥammad al-Murtaḍā al-Zabīdī (d. 1206/1791), *Tāj al-ʿarūs min jawāhir al-Qāmūs*, ed. ʿAlī Shīrī (Beirut: Dār al-Fikr, 1994), 6:306; and Muḥammad b. Muḥammad Ḥasan Shurrāb, *al-Maʿālim al-athīra fī al-sunna wa'l-sīra* (Damascus: Dār al-Qalam, 1991), 50, 301—both noting the same. Also compare Khalīl (d. between 160/776 and 175/791), *Kitāb al-ʿAyn* (Qum: Hijrat, 1989), 4:350, saying that Bughaybigha was assigned to Jaʿfar Dhū al-Janāḥayn—that is, to ʿAlī's brother Jaʿfar b. Abī Ṭālib; and Ibn Manẓūr (d. 711/1311), *Lisān al-ʿArab* (Beirut: Dār Ṣādir, 1997), 1:231, calling Bughaybigha an estate in Medina belonging either to the "Family of Jaʿfar" or to the Family of the Prophet.

17 The word is often vowelled Bughaybagha. See, for example, Ḥamad al-Jāsir, *Bilād Yanbuʿ: Lamaḥāt taʾrīkhiyya jughrāfiyya wa-inṭibāʿāt khāṣṣa* (Riyadh: Dār al-Yamāma, 1967). It sometimes appears as Buqaybaqa, a simple substitution of gh for q, as in ʿAbd al-Karīm Maḥmūd al-Khaṭīb, *Yanbuʿ* (Riyadh: Jāmiʿat al-Malik Saʿūd, [1993]). Other renderings include al-Bughaybigh / al-Bughaybagh, al-Bughaybiʿ / al-Bughaybaʿ, al-Baqīʿa, al-Muʿayniʿa / al-Muʿīnaʿa, and al-Mughaybigha / al-Mughībigha / al-Mughībagha. See Yāqūt b. ʿAbd Allāh al-Ḥamawī (d. 626/1229), *Muʿjam al-buldān*, ed. Muḥammad Amīn al-Khānjī ([Cairo]: Maṭbaʿat al-Saʿāda, 1323/1906);

light on the term and its history.

The proper name of the spring is Bughaybigha, "as in the diminutive form of *baghbagha*."[18] As previously noted, the onomatopoeic word refers to a rushing, gurgling sound,[19] or it may also refer to a well where water is close to the surface and easy to draw up.[20] Occasional reference in the sources to its plural form, Bughaybighāt, refers to the fact that the area actually encompassed a network of springs.[21] Both the singular and the plural also seem to refer, interchangeably, to a nearby spring otherwise called ʿAyn Abī Nayzar[22]—named after an alleged African prince and brother-like figure to ʿAlī, formally his client (or servant), who took care of Bughaybigha proper and the surrounding springs.[23] All of these springs together were

---

2:248; Yāqūt, *Muʿjam al-buldān* (Beirut: Dār Ṣādir, 1374/1955), 1:479; and the editor's note in Kulaynī (d. 329/940-1), *Kāfī*, 4th ed. (Tehran: Dār al-Kutub al-Islāmiyya, [1999]), 4:22 n. 3. The 1950 Cairo edition of Wakīʿ's *Akhbār al-quḍāt* renders it Nuʿayniʿa, a straight-forward corruption of Bughaybigha by simple transposition of the underdot of the b to an overdot to render the letter n. Asad Ahmed notes this rendering with some uncertainty about its meaning in his *The Religious Elite of the Early Islamic Ḥijāz: Five Prosopographical Case Studies* (Oxford: Unit for Prosopographical Research, 2011), 130 n. 707. To determine which variant Wakīʿ or his copyists or editors used, one would need to examine the relevant manuscript directly.

18 Bakrī, *Muʿjam mā ʾstuʿjim*, 1:241: *ʿalā lafẓ taṣghīr*; and Yāqūt, *Muʿjam al-buldān* (Beirut), 1:469–70. See also Yāqūt, *Kitāb al-Mushtarak waḍʿan waʾl-muftaraq ṣuqʿan*, published as *Jacut's Moschtarik, das ist: Lexicon geographischer Homonyme* (Bremen, Germany: Druck und Verlag der Dieterichschen Buchhandlung, 1846), 319; Yāqūt, *Marāṣid al-iṭṭilāʿ fī maʿrifat asmāʾ al-amkina waʾl-biqāʿ*, ed. Muḥammad al-Bajāwī ([Cairo]: Dār Iḥyāʾ al-Kutub al-ʿArabiyya, 1954), 1:210; Ibn Manẓūr, *Lisān al-ʿArab*, 1:231; and Samhūdī, *Wafāʾ al-wafā*, 4:164–65.

19 Bakrī, *Muʿjam mā ʾstuʿjim*, 1:241: as in the saying *al-biʾr baghbagh*; and Yāqūt, *Marāṣid al-iṭṭilāʿ*, 1:210.

20 Bakrī, *Muʿjam mā ʾstuʿjim*, 1:241: *māʾ bughaybagh ayy qarīb al-rishāʾ*; Yāqūt, *Muʿjam al-buldān* (Beirut), 1:469: *al-biʾr al-qarībat al-rishāʾ*; Yāqūt, *Marāṣid al-iṭṭilāʿ*, 1:210; and Shurrāb, *al-Maʿālim al-athīra*, 50.

21 Ibn Shabba, *Taʾrīkh al-Madīna*, 1:222, naming three springs collectively referred to as Bughaybighāt: Khayf al-Arāk, Khayf Laylā, and Khayf Basṭās; and Samhūdī, *Wafāʾ al-wafā*, 4:165, quoting Ibn Shabba. For notes on the total number of springs surrounding Bughaybigha, see below, note 29.

22 See Mubarrad (d. 286/900), *al-Kāmil fī al-lugha waʾl-adab*, Muḥammad Abū al-Faḍl Ibrāhīm, 3rd ed. (Cairo: Dār al-Fikr al-ʿArabī, 1417/1997), 3:153, mentioning this spring along with Bughaybigha; ʿAbd al-Raḥmān b. ʿAbd Allāh al-Suhaylī (d. 581/1185), *al-Rawḍ al-unuf fī sharḥ al-Sīra al-Nabawiyya li-Ibn Hishām*, ed. ʿAbd al-Raḥmān al-Wakīl ([Cairo]: Dār al-Kutub al-Ḥadītha, [1967-1970]), 1:368, noting that ʿAyn Abī Nayzar is sometimes referred to as Bughaybigha; and Samhūdī, *Wafāʾ al-wafā*, 4:166, copying from Mubarrad. See also Ahmed, *Religious Elite*, 129, noting the frequent mention of the two springs together in the historical, biographical, and geographical literature.

23 Abū Nayzar—exceptionally pronounced Abū Nīzar—was called a "foreign prince," and reportedly was the son of the Negus, the Abyssinian Christian ruler who offered Muslims sanctuary when they fled persecution by Meccan leaders in response to Muḥammad's early message during the first migration (*hijra*). Abū Nayzar is said to have converted while young and—giving up future kingship—to have gone to live with the Prophet as a client (*mawlā*) under his protection in Medina, where ʿAlī was also being raised, and then to live with ʿAlī and Fāṭima upon the Prophet's death. See Ibn Isḥāq (d. 151/767), *al-Sīra al-Nabawiyya*, ed. Aḥmad Farīd al-Mazīdī (Beirut: Dār al-Kutub al-ʿIlmiyya, 2004), 254; Mubarrad, *Kāmil*, 3:153; Bakrī, *Muʿjam mā ʾstuʿjim*, 2:252; Abū

subsequently also simply called "'Alī's springs."[24] The report of the *Case of Bughaybigha* similarly simply refers to it as "a spring belonging to [an 'Alid] in Yansuʿ [sic = Yanbuʿ]."[25] Even more generally, the springs and the land surrounding them were sometimes called "the springs of Yanbuʿ," "the land in Yanbuʿ," or simply "Yanbuʿ."[26]

As for Yanbuʿ itself, this term names a vast expanse of land, covering some 150 square kilometers, located between Medina and Syria on the trade route between those two cities, for which reason it bore some mention even in pre-Islamic and early Islamic works of local history and geography.[27] It got its name from the abundance of underground springs there—*yanbūʿ* or *manbaʿ* being synonyms for the usual Arabic word for "well" or "spring."[28] One source mentions that there were over 170 springs in that region alone.[29]

Available records diverge as to how 'Alī acquired the land that was to become Bughaybigha. According to one report, the Prophet himself had given a portion of the land in Yanbuʿ to 'Alī as part of an initial land allocation.[30] According to another report, 'Alī had bought land from Kushd

---

al-Qāsim al-Zamakhsharī (d. 538/1144), *Rabīʿ al-abrār wa-nuṣūṣ al-akhyār* ([Baghdad?]: Wizārat al-Awqāf, [1976–1982?]), 5:346; and Yāqūt, *Muʿjam al-buldān* (Beirut), 1:469–70. Some sources further report that Abū Nayzar served 'Alī as a slave-servant who was later freed, as 'Alī refers to him in his last will and testament as one of three former slaves (*raqīq*) living at Yanbuʿ who had become freedmen. See Muḥammad Bāqir al-Majlisī (d. 1110/1698), *Biḥār al-anwār*, ed. Jawād al-ʿAlawī (Tehran: Dār al-Kutub al-Islāmiyya, 1376–1392/[1957–1973]), 42:72: *ʿutaqāʾ*; and Ibn Shabba, *Taʾrīkh al-Madīna*, 225–26: *aʿtaqnāhum*.

24 Somewhat circularly, in the historical literature these springs (*ʿuyūn ʿAlī*) could refer to 'Ayn Abī Nayzar, 'Ayn al-Buḥayr, 'Ayn Nawlā or Bawlā (also called 'Ayn al-ʿUshayra), and 'Ayn 'Alī (probably Bughaybigha, another name for 'Ayn Abī Nayzar, and/or the spring referred to as Nawlā). See Jāsir, *Bilād Yanbuʿ*, 19.

25 Wakīʿ, *Akhbār al-quḍāt*, 103.

26 Jāsir, *Bilād Yanbuʿ*, 28–29, reporting on fourth-, sixth-, and seventh-century descriptions by travelers and geographers. Some also referred to Yanbuʿ as Jabal Juhayna, named for the tribe that first populated the area and the mountain under whose shadow the valley lay. See Iṣbahānī, *Maqātil al-Ṭālibiyyīn*, 337. While later descriptions divide Yanbuʿ into Yanbuʿ al-Nakhl, for the date palm orchards, and Yanbuʿ al-Baḥr, for the port city, the historical Yanbuʿ corresponds to Yanbuʿ al-Nakhl. See Jāsir, *Bilād Yanbuʿ*, 28–29; Shurrāb, *Maʿālim al-athīra*, 301. See further E. van Donzel, "Yanbuʿ," *EI*², 11:281, who also observes that Sharm Yanbuʿ is another name for the modern port city.

27 Jāsir, *Bilād Yanbuʿ*, 7–9, 11.

28 Ibid., 11.

29 The larger surrounding area in Yanbuʿ contained perhaps well over 100 springs, many of which were said to be discovered and endowed by 'Alī. See Ibn Shahrāshūb (d. 588/1192), *Manāqib Āl Abī Ṭālib* (Qum: n.p., 1379/[1959]), 2:122: putting the number of springs at 100; Bakrī, *Muʿjam mā ʾs-tuʿjim*, 2:251, putting the number of springs at 99, according to Muḥammad b. 'Abd al-Majīd b. al-Ṣabāḥ; Muḥammad b. Yaʿqūb al-Fīrūzābādī (d. 823/1415), *al-Maghānim al-Muṭāba fī maʿālim Ṭāba*, ed. Ḥamad al-Jāsir (Riyadh: Dār al-Yamāma, 1969), 440, putting the number of springs at 170, according to al-Sharīf Ibn Salama b. 'Ayyāsh al-Yanbuʿī.

30 Ibn Shabba, *Taʾrīkh al-Madīna*, 1:220.

for some unspecified price.[31] According to a third, it was ʿUmar who, upon assuming the caliphate, gave land from Yanbuʿ to ʿAlī at his request.[32]

Combining all three of these reports, "ʿAmmār b. Yasār explained that the Prophet gave ʿUshayra [a tract in Yanbuʿ] to ʿAlī, ʿUmar then gave him a portion of Yanbuʿ after he assumed the caliphate, and ʿAlī purchased a portion."[33] Without resolving exactly how ʿAlī acquired land at Yanbuʿ, the upshot of these reports is that they confirm his acquisition of land there. They underscore that some portion of Yanbuʿ may have been conferred on him by the Prophet himself, and that, even if not, ʿAlī's rights over this land at Yanbuʿ was completely beyond dispute.

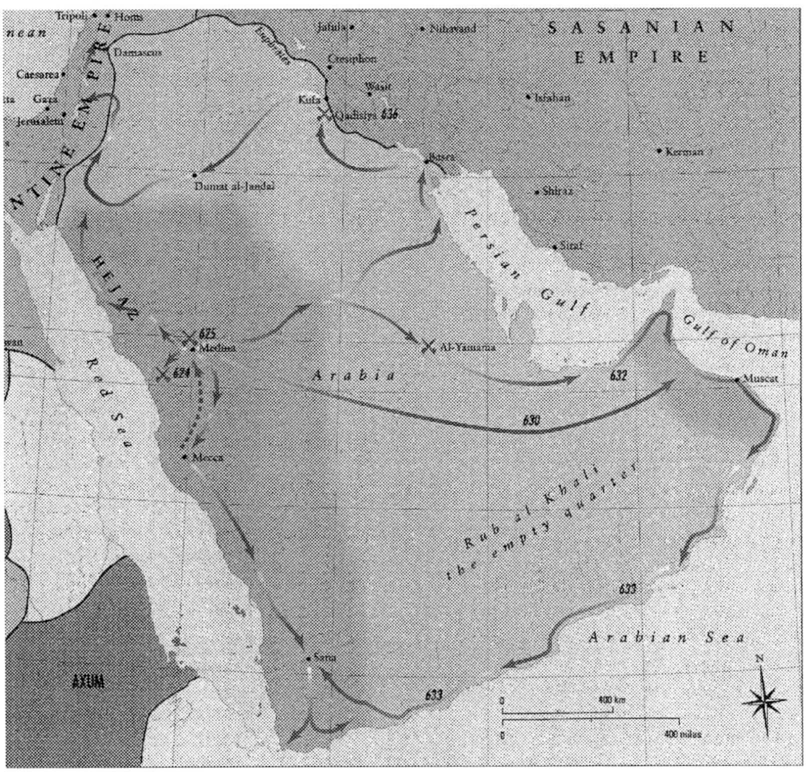

Figure 1. "Muḥammad's Missions and Campaigns to 632." Source: Malise Ruthven, *Historical Atlas of Islam* (Cambridge: Harvard University Press, 2004), 27.[34]

31 Ibid., 1:219, noting that ʿAlī bought it *biʾl-thaman.*

32 Yaḥyā b. Ādam al-Qurashī (d. 203/818), *Kitāb al-Kharāj*, ed. Aḥmad Muḥammad Shākir (Cairo: al-Maṭbaʿa al-Salafiyya, 1347/[1929]), 78; and Ibn Shabba, *Taʾrīkh al-Madīna,* 1:220.

33 Ibn Shabba, *Taʾrīkh al-Madīna*, 1:220.

34 For a modern-day map depicting the location of historical Yanbuʿ (now called Yanbuʿ al-Nakhl) and its sister-city Yanbuʿ al-Baḥr (now called Yanbuʿ), see Khaṭīb, *Yanbuʿ*, 24. Modifications are based on the location of Yanbuʿ in present-day Saudi Arabia. See the German-produced Map of the World, available at http://www.posterwissen.de/maps/map.php?Saudi_Arabia&id=196&ln=en (last accessed 15 April 2016).

It was immediately after his arrival at his newly acquired land at Yanbuʿ that ʿAlī discovered the spring that he then named Bughaybigha.[35] He recognized its value immediately, exclaiming with elation: "Give my heirs the good news!"[36] He then promptly turned Bughaybigha and its surrounding lands into an endowment-trust designated for his sons Ḥasan and Ḥusayn (and their descendants).[37]

The Significance of the Contests over Bughaybigha

It is clear from the sources that Bughaybigha was extraordinarily important. But exactly *why* was it so significant? Why was control over it so contested?[38] Bughaybigha was so significant and contested because it symbolized, I argue, the last *tangible* holding by which the ʿAlids might make a claim to the prophetic legacy.[39] To be sure, their claim was less a matter of landed property than it was of religious and political leadership. Yet Bughaybigha was significant with respect to both because claims upon it invoked critical questions of leadership and legitimacy that were sometimes debated over land and that continued long after ʿAlī's death. In this case, Bughaybigha served as the site on which an Umayyad-appointed judge resolved an ʿAlid-related dispute in ways that drew upon and gave insight into early Islamic judicial procedure. Tellingly, the case went to the procedure-laden

35 Ibn Shabba, *Taʾrīkh al-Madīna*, 1:220; and Mubarrad, *Kāmil*, 3:154.

36 Ibn Shabba, *Taʾrīkh al-Madīna*, 1:220: *bashshara ʿAlī biʾl-Bughaybighāt ḥīna ẓaharat fa-qāla tasurr al-wārith*; and Samhūdī, *Wafāʾ al-wafā*, 4:165: same.

37 See Ibn Shabba, *Taʾrīkh al-Madīna*, 1:220–24, listing versions of the endowment. See also Mubarrad, *Kāmil*, 3:154, noting that ʿAlī asked Abū Nayzar to bring him ink and a writing instrument to write down the bequest himself on the spot; and Samhūdī, *Wafāʾ al-wafā*, 4:165, reporting on a different version of the endowment.

38 For a review of the endowment documents, see Ibn Shabba, *Taʾrīkh al-Madīna*, 1:220–21, 225–27; and Mubarrad, *Kāmil*, 2:172. For alternate versions in later records of them, see also Samhūdī, *Wafāʾ al-wafā*, 4:165; Abū Saʿd Manṣūr b. al-Ḥusayn al-Ābī (d. 421/1030), *Nathr al-durr fī al-muḥāḍarāt*, ed. Muḥammad ʿAlī Qurna ([Cairo]: al-Hayʾa al-Miṣriyya al-ʿĀmma lil-Kitāb, [1980-]), 1:302; Bakrī, *Muʿjam mā ʾstuʿjim*, 2:252–53; Zamakhsharī, *Rabīʿ al-abrār*, 5:346; ʿAlī b. Muḥammad al-Khuzāʿī (d. 789/1387-8), *Takhrīj al-dalālāt al-samʿiyya*, ed. Iḥsān ʿAbbās, 2nd ed. (Beirut: Dār al-Gharb al-Islāmī, 1999), 568; and Ḥimyarī, *al-Rawḍ al-miʿṭār*, 112–13. Although space here does not permit analysis of endowment documents or laws here, I plan to take up that analysis in a future publication. See ʿAlī Ḥājī Ābidī, *al-Waqf waʾl-mawqūfāt Amīr al-Muʾminīn* (Mashhad: Majmaʿ al-Buḥūth al-Islāmiyya, 1435), esp. 78–92: discussing the law of trust and ʿAlī's endowment properties at Yanbuʿ, including Bughaybigha.

39 In my usage, "ʿAlids" refers to the descendants of ʿAlī and Fāṭima through their sons, Ḥasan and Ḥusayn, rather than to the Ṭālibids or the descendants of ʿAlī's son by Khawla bt. Jaʿfar—that is, Muḥammad b. al-Ḥanafiyya and others, more than one of whom laid claim to some of the land and legacy of ʿAlī. For accounts of Muḥammad b. al-Ḥanafiyya's claim, see Ahmed, *Religious Elite*, 129–30, commenting on Muʿāwiya's attempts to forcibly marry Umm Kulthūm—the daughter of ʿAbd Allāh b. Jaʿfar b. Abī Ṭālib—to his son Yazīd, as evidence that the former was not interested in "restoring good relations," as he had claimed, but that the marriage proposal had "something to do with inheriting or acquiring Ṭālibid land in the Ḥijāz." See also generally Elad, *Rebellion of Muḥammad al-Nafs al-Zakiyya*.

judicial arena for resolution here because that arena was regarded as more objective and legitimate than the political realm.

The political and moral significance of Yanbuʿ and, later, Bughaybigha, may well have been inflated by the loss of another land tract called Fadak. As Wilferd Madelung describes in his appraisal of contestations over succession to the Prophet after his death, Fadak likewise highlighted conflicts of political and religious ambition. The caliphs immediately succeeding the Prophet determined that Fadak would *not* go to Prophet's family members, Fāṭima and ʿAbbās, who claimed rights to it, on the notion that the Prophet had instructed Abū Bakr that: "We [prophets] do not have heirs [or: leave inheritance] (*lā nūrith*). Whatever we leave is alms (*ṣadaqa*)...."[40] Symbolically, the Fadak episode epitomized a physical transfer of inheritance from the Prophet away from his Family, and with it, the transfer of religious and political leadership away from his Family as well. He who controlled and disposed of Fadak and the Prophet's other landed property determined who would control and dispose of the Prophet's legacy, materially and figuratively. Was Bughaybigha for Ḥusayn the equivalent of what Fadak meant to ʿAlī?

Having been forced to relinquish Fadak, ʿAlī (as head of the Prophet's Family) likely held onto the land at Yanbuʿ, and Bughaybigha within it, even more firmly.[41] That is, perhaps the confusion over Fadak and similarly situated lands explains the reports that ʿAlī immediately called for a scribe upon discovering Bughaybigha after acquiring the land at Yanbuʿ. By putting his intentions into writing, his idea was likely that there would be no doubt as to the intended disposition of that land as a charitable endowment placed under the charge of his sons Ḥasan and Ḥusayn. In short, Bughaybigha was not just a tract of land. It came to symbolize a familial and moral descent from the Prophet's legacy as a leader noted for a type of religious-charismatic legitimacy borne of perceptions of his piety and morality.

Despite his best efforts, ʿAlī was not entirely successful in securing the land's status as in the charge of his descendants. He was certainly successful in securing the *moral claim* to the land, as far as the communal historical memory was concerned. This much was reflected in historical records of his endowment and, as noted above, in claims of judicial knowledge given the judge's comment in this case when the issue later went to court. But the *legal claim* to the land was, as told here, another story. Bughaybigha was quickly wrested from Ḥusayn by the first Umayyad

40 Madelung, *Succession to Muḥammad*, 50–52, citing Ṭabarī and Ibn Shabba.

41 Ibid., 277, noting that, upon assuming power, ʿAlī let ʿUthmān's Fadak decision stand—that is, granting the land to Marwān—though ʿAlī sought to create an equal distribution thereafter.

caliphs, and the ʿAlids struggled to regain the land in a back-and-forth contest that lasted almost two centuries. The law did not constrain the caliphs, who episodically took the land; and it conferred only a portion of Bughaybigha to the ʿAlid descendant ʿAbd Allāh b. al-Ḥasan when the matter finally went to court.

To be sure, Bughaybigha had enormous economic value accompanying its symbolic worth. The land produced hundreds of thousands of *dīnār*s worth of dates, conferring wealth on whoever controlled it[42]—including the ʿAlid trustees.[43] ʿAlī sometimes sent dates from the abundant land to feed the needy.[44] Ḥusayn reportedly used money from the land's proceeds to satisfy debts incurred by one family member and to avoid an Umayyad forced marriage to another family member. And more generally, the economic advantages of Bughaybigha fueled ʿAlid independence and no doubt partially inspired Umayyad attempts to divest them of the land. For example, the land funded more than one ʿAlid campaign staged in an attempt to reclaim their Prophet-conferred land and legacy, to which the Umayyads responded by razing or seizing the lands.[45] The land also housed the ʿAlids, and provided respite for their descendants in times of peace and otherwise.[46] In these ways, Bughaybigha provided enormous

42 See Samhūdī, *Wafāʾ al-wafā*, 4:165, citing Wāqidī's report that the amount of date production had reached 1000 *awsāq* by the time of ʿAlī, where a single *wasq* is approximately 3 kilograms. The sources are unclear, but presumably this amount was the yearly output. To truly determine the value of the produce would require determining the value of a *wasq* of dates on the market at the time.

43 Although they would not own the land, they could freely use its proceeds, as the terms of ʿAlī's trust designated use for members of the family, and otherwise the poor and the needy. See, e.g., Ibn Shabba, *Taʾrīkh al-Madīna*, 1:225–27, recording a copy of the endowment designating "all of the water resources and the lands surrounding them that are known to be in my possession at Yanbuʿ ... to be held in trust (*ṣadaqa*)," for Ḥasan and Ḥusayn, who were to use "what is customary and spend[] according to God's guidance as to permissible acts, without restriction" and specifying that "no part of this land is to be sold, gifted, or inherited." Compare, Mubarrad, *Kāmil*, 2:172, quoting the text of the endowment to include the stipulation that the lands be used "for the poor of Medina and for those who fight in the way of God" and that "these lands are not to be sold or inherited until God bequeaths them, for He is the best of those who bequeath, unless Ḥasan and Ḥusayn need them—in which case they are for their sole, unfettered use."

44 See Kulaynī, *Kāfī*, 4:22–23, reporting on ʿAlī's gift of some five *awsāq* of dates—approximately 15 kilograms—to a poor man whose custom was not to ask for handouts. See also Ibn Bābawayh (d. 381/991-2), *Kitāb Man lā yaḥduruh al-faqīh*, 2nd ed. (Qum: Daftar-i Intishārāt-i Islāmī, 1413/[1992]), 2:72, no. 1762; and Fakhr al-Dīn al-Ṭurayḥī (d. 1085/1674), *Majmaʿ al-baḥrayn* (Tehran: Murtaḍā, 1375/[1960]), 5:5—both reporting the same *ḥadīth*.

45 On the rebellions, see Elad, *Rebellion of Muḥammad al-Nafs al-Zakiyya*; and Jāsir, *Bilād Yanbuʿ*, 24–25, detailing, in addition to the rebellion led by al-Nafs al-Zakiyya, the rebellion of Muḥammad b. Ṣāliḥ b. ʿAbd Allāh b. Mūsā b. ʿAbd Allāh against al-Mutawakkil in 244/858.

46 On Yanbuʿ as the dwelling place of the ʿAlids in the Ḥijāz, see Elad, *Rebellion of Muḥammad al-Nafs al-Zakiyya*, 22–23, who notes that the family of ʿAlī b. Abī Ṭālib lived on the ʿAlid estate of Suwayqa within Yanbuʿ. The sources further show that ʿAlī himself lived there. See Balādhurī, *Ansāb al-Ashrāf*, ed. Shelomo Dov F. Goitein (Jerusalem: Azriel Press, 1936), 5:77, reporting that Usāma b. Zayd b. Ḥāritha counseled ʿAlī to move there out of fear that, if he remained in Medina,

economic benefits for the ʿAlids—economic benefits that met their material needs and that, in turn, provided a basis for them to assert claims on the land.[47]

Furthermore, Bughaybigha was strategically located. It lay along the road connecting the old seat of the empire in Medina to its new seat, following the rise of the Umayyad caliphs, in Damascus. Bughaybigha and surrounding estates in Yanbuʿ were also important stops on the *ḥajj* route between these and other those cities. On one occasion, Walīd II traveled the route through Bughaybigha from Damascus to Medina—escorted by a large number of troops—in order to build a dome on top of the Prophet's mosque. The troops and the mosque construction project were a clear challenge to the judge Saʿd b. Ibrāhīm's authority as a local leader, and they were a visual assertion of the caliph's power over the region.[48] This episode reinforced the strategic significance and location of the land.

In addition, the land was of high monetary value given its economic and strategic importance. Muʿāwiya and other Umayyad caliphs offered astounding sums of money for the purchase of Bughaybigha. On one occasion, Muʿāwiya reportedly offered to buy the land for one million *dīnārs*—an enormous sum today, and much more so then.[49] When that failed, his son Yazīd seized the land after the massacre of Ḥusayn and his men at Karbalāʾ.

But ultimately—notwithstanding the ongoing economic benefits, strategic location, and lucrative offers of money—it stands to reason that Bughaybigha's primary significance still lies in the moral and legal claims

---

he would be blamed and killed for ʿUthmān's surely eminent death, even if he had nothing to do with it. The sources also feature some of the mundane affairs of ʿAlid descendants showing their use of the estate, including an episode in which al-Ḥasan b. al-Ḥasan went to Bughaybigha from Medina for a three-day period of rest. See Abū al-Faraj al-Iṣbahānī (d. 356/967), *Kitāb al-Aghānī*, ed. Dār Iḥyāʾ al-Turāth al-ʿArabī (Beirut: Dār Iḥyāʾ al-Turāth al-ʿArabī, 1994), 1:472–73; Shihāb al-Dīn al-Nuwayrī (d. 733/1333), *Nihāyat al-arab fī funūn al-adab* (Cairo: al-Muʾassasa al-Miṣriyya al-ʿĀmma, [1923-97]), 4:281–82, recounting the story from Iṣbahānī.

47 For a general overview of the land at Yanbuʿ and Fadak, the significance of the Ḥijāz to the ʿAlids and the ruling elites, and the associated rebellions through Fāṭimid times in the 6th/12th century, see Ella Landau-Tasseron, "Arabia," in *The New Cambridge History of Islam*, ed. Chase F. Robinson (Cambridge: Cambridge University Press, 2010), 1:397–447, esp. 403–13.

48 Wakīʿ, *Akhbār al-quḍāt*, 108–09.

49 See Ibn Isḥāq, *Sīra*, 252; and Ibn Saʿd, *al-Ṭabaqāt al-kubrā*, 6:414. In the latter account, Juwayriya b. Asmāʾ (the same person who narrates the *Case of Bughaybigha* recorded in Wakīʿ's accounts), reportedly told Ibn Saʿd's informant, contradictorily, that Ḥusayn both suggested to ʿAbd Allāh that his debts could be paid by the revenue from Bughaybigha and that ʿAbd Allāh nevertheless attempted to sell the estate to Muʿāwiya for this hefty sum (which Ḥusayn then blocked, saying "you know what your uncle did with this land," namely, that he converted it into a trust). The first account seems more consistent with the weight and variation of reports establishing the land as part of ʿAlī's endowments as against this single outlying report suggesting dissolution of the trust. In addition, the sale narrative only appears in some accounts that perhaps seek to establish Umayyad entitlement to the land when noting that Yazīd seized it upon Ḥusayn's death, suggesting that it was an Umayyad interpolation to justify the takings.

attached to it. Bughaybigha had become Ḥusayn's Fadak.

Over time, the taking of Bughaybigha entailed multiple episodes, involving various Umayyad and ʿAbbāsid caliphs over the course of some one hundred and fifty years.[50] The sources are confused about who had control over Bughaybigha after Ḥusayn's death, but they agree that it was taken by the Umayyads at various points during their reign, and that the land ended up back in the hands of the ʿAlids under the ʿAbbāsids. When discussing the Umayyad period, Ibn Shabba—and following him, Samhūdī—report that either the Umayyads or the Ṭālibids more generally (that is, the descendants of ʿAbd Allāh b. Jaʿfar b. Abī Ṭālib) held the land at the end of Umayyad rule, and the sources provide variant accounts of how and when control over it transferred hands thereafter.[51]

Namely, the sources describe the ʿAbbāsids as having subsequently confiscated and returned the endowment lands to the ʿAlids as *ṣawāfī*,[52] the legal status of which had long been contested among the ʿAlid leaders and the mainstream political elite. Under the Umayyads, early Sunnī law and caliphal practices adopted a definition of *ṣawāfī* that "refer[ed] to lands which the *imām* selects from the conquered lands for the treasury, with the consent of the Muslims."[53] As Hossein Modarressi further details for Sunnī law:

50 That is, from Ḥusayn's death in 61/680 through the ʿAbbāsid caliph Maʾmūn's reign that ended with his death in 218/833. For accounts of its subsequent history through the present, see Jāsir, *Bilād Yanbuʿ*, 27–43. Although mention of Bughaybigha disappears from the common ʿAbbāsid sources after the report on Maʾmūn, Jāsir's sources suggest that ʿAlī's land in Yanbuʿ remained in his descendants' hands until the ʿAbbāsid caliph al-Mutawakkil's far-ranging response to the ʿAlid rebellion against him in 244/858, when he completely razed the ʿAlid stronghold there called Suwayqa. See Jāsir, *Bilād Yanbuʿ*, 24–25, citing Iṣbahānī, *Maqātil al-Ṭālibiyyīn*, 600; and Yāqūt, *Muʿjam al-buldān* (Beirut), 4:171. Subsequent sources report that the lands remained episodically important in the *ḥajj* route from the 4th/10th century until the 14th/20th century. See Jāsir, *Bilād Yanbuʿ*, 41–43. At that point, attention shifted from the historical Yanbuʿ [now: Yanbuʿ al-Nakhl] to the nearby port city when it became the main port between the Ḥijāz and Egypt for trade. See Khaṭīb, *Yanbuʿ*, 33. Eventually, even the Port of Yanbuʿ lost its economic and geographic appeal for the *ḥajjī*s when the main port once again shifted to Jedda. See Jāsir, *Bilād Yanbuʿ*, 43.

51 For various accounts, see Mubarrad, *Kāmil*, 2:172: "This farmland remained in the hands of Banū ʿAbd Allāh b. Jaʿfar from Umm Kulthūm's side, inheriting from her until al-Maʾmūn assumed the caliphate." See also Samhūdī, *Wafāʾ al-wafā*, 4:166; and Bakrī, *Muʿjam mā ʾstuʿjim*, 2:253.

52 The *ṣawāfī* public lands that Muʿāwiya had confiscated may have originally included the seven endowments of the Prophet in and around Medina. These lands were the reason for the ʿAlid revolt against the Umayyads, fueled by the Medinans who viewed Muʿāwiya's claim to the land as unfounded and void. See M.J. Kister, "Land Property and Jihād," *Journal of the Economic and Social History of the Orient* 34, no. 3 (1991): 270–311, esp. 308–09; M. J. Kister, "The Battle of the Ḥarra: Some Socio-Economic Aspects," in *Studies in Memory of Gaston Wiet*, ed. Myriam Rosen Ayalon (Jerusalem: Hebrew University of Jerusalem, 1977), 33–49, 41–42, citing Frede Løkkegaard, *Islamic Taxation in the Classical Period* (Copenhagen: Branner and Korch, 1950), 49–51, and Saleh E. el-Ali, "Muslim Estates in the Hidjaz in the First Century AH," *Journal of the Economic and Social History of the Orient* 2 (1959): 247–61, esp. 251.

53 Modarressi, *Kharāj*, 8.

> The legal basis for this practice was laid by ʿUmar, the second caliph, who, after the defeat of the Sassanids, confiscated all lands belonging to the king, the royal family and the courtiers, including all public domain as well as all land without a known owner. These estates were, therefore, known as *ṣawāfī*: a term with a stem which means to select and later came to imply the idea of the confiscation of the land by the government.[54]

By contrast, in early Shīʿī law, *ṣawāfī* referred to "the crown property (movable and immovable) in the conquered countries.... Such land, according to Shīʿī law, belongs neither to the fighting men as does movable war booty, nor to all Muslims as do other conquered lands, but to the Imām and is considered as part of *anfāl* [war booty]."[55] Thus, Yazīd and perhaps subsequent early caliphs saw themselves as entitled to take the land under the mainstream Umayyad conception, but after the ʿAbbāsid Revolution, many of the new caliphs saw themselves as unentitled to the land, under the ʿAlid-Shīʿī conception. That is, the second set of caliphs saw restoring ʿAlid land, such as Bughaybigha, to that part of the Family as helping to build the case for their own legitimacy in assuming leadership as an extension of the ʿAlid legacy, and thus returned the land.[56]

In the long struggle over Bughaybigha, not only did control over the land episodically change hands, but legitimacy of various sorts was also episodically at play. At various points, gaining the *moral legitimacy* that alliance with the Family of the Prophet could confer made giving back the land an attractive option in caliphal courts, as explored above. At one point, a particular conception of *legal legitimacy* made referral to judicial courts an attractive option for resolving the dispute, as explored below. To

54 Ibid., 8–9 (citations omitted).

55 Ibid., 9–11. Modarressi here also details a related term and contested property law concept in Shīʿī law, which accorded with and helped underscore the view of *ṣawāfī* as a type of *anfāl* under the control of the Imām: *ṣāfī*. This type of property typically came from war booty rather than land, and was considered the "private property of the Prophet[, which] some Sunnī scholars held ... after his death should be handed over to the treasury and would belong to the Muslim community" but which Shīʿī jurists held to be "an instance of *anfāl* and belonged to the leader of the Muslims by virtue of his position. Thus it should be transferred to the successors of the Prophet in the leadership of the community"—that is, the Imāms (and here: ʿAlī and his children).

56 See Ibn Shabba, *Taʾrīkh al-Madīna*, 1:222 (*al-Bughaybighāt ... qubiḍat ḥīna malaka Banū Hāshim al-ṣawāfī*) (whence Samhūdī, *Wafāʾ al-wafā*, 4:165); and Mubarrad, *al-Kāmil*, 4:165: *fa-lam tazal hādhihi al-ḍayʿa fī aydī Banī ʿAbd Allāh b. Jaʿfar min nāḥiyat Umm Kulthūm yatawārathūnahā ḥattā malaka amīr al-muʾminīn al-Maʾmūn* (whence Samhūdī, *Wafāʾ al-wafā*, 4:166). See also Elad, *The Rebellion of Muḥammad al-Nafs al-Zakiyya*, 103–04. According to this last source, the "phrase *ṣārat fī al-ṣawāfī* means that 'a certain estate was confiscated and became included in the corpus of confiscated lands under a special *dīwān*,' and typically refers to the beginning of ʿAbbāsid rule."

unpack the latter claim, we return to examining the *Case of Bughaybigha* more closely below.

THE CASE OF BUGHAYBIGHA, REVISITED

Returning to the case as it appeared in court, records of the case first arise in the biographical dictionaries—namely, in Ibn Saʿd's account, which details the history of the case through the last Umayyad taking of Bughaybigha and ends with Walīd II's referral of the matter to court. The narrative then picks up in the only judicial "record" of it that we have from the early courts: in a collection of biographies of judges from Islam's founding period by the ninth-century judicial chronicler Wakiʿ, who reports on cases, procedures, and appointments, in addition to basic biographical data of judges.[57] Conveniently, his report of this case picks up where the more generalist biographer Ibn Saʿd had left off. That is to say, while Ibn Saʿd ended his account of the matter by merely indicating that Walīd II had referred the case to court, Wakīʿ reports on the actual case as it appeared in court.[58]

The judicial approach to the case is heavy on procedure—in contrast to the caliphal approach to the land dispute. In what follows, the aim is to give attention to key features of the judicial version of dispute resolution that point to the pull of procedure in early Islamic courts.

The Evidence Canon

Recall that upon first hearing the case, the judge asked the caliph's representative to present evidence of his claim of ownership or right to the land. In requesting proof, the judge referred directly to the *evidence canon* stipulating that the petitioner bears the burden of proof for what he claims: *al-bayyina ʿalā mā-ʾddaʿā* [sic].[59] The full canon, as recorded in later works of legal canons, states that "the petitioner bears the burden of proof, and the respondent may swear an oath of denial: *al-bayyina ʿalā al-muddaʿī, waʾl-yamīn ʿalā man ankar* (or: *ʿalā al-muddaʿā ʿalayh*)." This procedural rule means that a judge may rule in favor of the petitioner if the petitioner produces two reliable male witnesses to verify the claim and the respondent either refuses to swear an oath of denial to a colorable claim (thus confessing implicitly) or confesses explicitly by making a statement. This basic distribution of burdens of proof was straightforward, and became the consensus view among judges and jurists by the end of the founding

57 On Wakīʿ's collection, see M. Khālid Masud, "A Study of Wakīʿ's (d. 306/917) *Akhbār al-quḍāt*," in *The Law Applied: Contextualizing the Islamic Sharīʿa*, ed. Wolfhart Heinrichs et al. (London: I.B. Tauris, 2008), 116–27.

58 Wakīʿ, *Akhbār al-quḍāt*, 104–05.

59 Ibid., 103–04.

period.[60] In fact, these procedures were so often invoked in the form of a legal canon that the rule became *the* central evidentiary canon governing Islamic courts.[61]

But if probative evidence required two witnesses or a denial oath (or else, a confession), in this case, who would attest to what? The Umayyads had no evidence that they had purchased the land (despite some records in the historical sources noting attempts by Muʿāwiya to purchase it). ʿAbd Allāh b. al-Ḥasan was not required to produce evidence nor to swear an oath, given that he was not the one who had brought the claim. And he did not confess to using the land without right, as he fully believed the land to be properly under his control. Yet, were he to attempt a counter-claim in order to assert his right to the full valley encompassing Bughaybigha, he would have been hard-pressed to do so. The four witnesses who had attested to one version of ʿAlī's written endowment document, if its historicity and authenticity are to be supposed, had long since passed away. Indeed, Wakīʿ's record of the case mentions no document at all.[62] Where, as here, neither witness testimony nor a confession or oath is available, nor is there written documentation, the judge is forced to seek some other means of resolution.[63]

60 Ibn Qudāma, *Mughnī*, 11:404: *wa-lā khilāf.*

61 There were more complicated instances in which it was difficult for a judge to determine who the petitioner was—that is, who had the greater *prima facie* entitlement and thus which opponent would bear the burden of proof when there were multiple petitioners with similar claims, or when only circumstantial evidence and other types of proof were available. To address these and other issues requires a systematic study of the literature on judging Such a study would include, for example, Abū al-Ḥasan al-Māwardī (d. 450/1058), *Adab al-qāḍī*, ed. Muḥyī Hilāl al-Sarḥān (Baghdad: Maṭbaʿat al-ʿĀnī, 1972); and al-Ṣadr al-Shahīd Ibn Māzah (d. 536/1141), *Sharḥ Adab al-qāḍī* [by Aḥmad b. ʿUmar Khaṣṣāf (d. 261/ 874)], ed. Muḥyī Hilāl al-Sarḥān (Baghdad: Maṭbaʿat al-Irshād, 1977).

62 Detailed discussion of ʿAlī's endowment documents is beyond the scope of this paper, and should be taken up in future work. For sources on these early documents see Hossein Modarressi, *Tradition and Survival: A Bibliographical Survey of Early Shīʿite Literature* (Oxford: Oneworld, 2003), 2–17, 25–32.

63 See Muwaffaq al-Dīn Ibn Qudāma (d. 620/1223), *al-Mughnī ʿalā Mukhtaṣar Abī al-Qāsim al-Khiraqī*, ed. ʿAbd Allāh b. ʿAbd al-Muḥsin al-Turkī and ʿAbd al-Fattāḥ Muḥammad al-Ḥulw (Cairo: Hajar, 1986), 11:404. See also Abū al-Ḥusayn al-Qudūrī (d. 428/1037), *Tajrīd* (*al-Mawsūʿa al-fiqhiyya al-muqārana*), ed. Muḥammad Aḥmad al-Sirāj and ʿAlī Jumuʿa Muḥammad (Cairo: Dār al-Salām, 2004); 12:6548; al-Sharīf al-Murtaḍā (d. 436/1044), *Intiṣār*, ed. Muḥammad Riḍā al-Sayyid Ḥasan al-Kharsān (Najaf: al-Maṭbaʿa al-Ḥaydariyya, 1971), 236; Māwardī, *Adab al-qāḍī*, 2:370; ʿAlī b. Aḥmad Ibn Ḥazm (d. 456/1064), *al-Muḥallā bi'l-āthār*, ed. ʿAbd al-Ghaffār Sulaymān al-Bandārī (Beirut: Dār al-Kutub al-ʿIlmiyya, 1988), 9:427; Ibn Rushd II (d. 595/1198), *Bidāyat al-mujtahid*, ed. ʿAlī Muḥammad Muʿawwaḍ and ʿĀdil Aḥmad ʿAbd al-Mawjūd (Beirut: Dār al-Kutub al-ʿIlmiyya, 2000), 2:689; Abū Bakr al-Kāsānī (d. 587/1191), *Badāʾiʿ al-ṣanāʾiʿ fī tartīb al-sharāʾiʿ*, ed. Aḥmad Mukhtār ʿUthmān ([Cairo]: Zakariyyā ʿAlī Yūsuf, 1968), 9:4088.

The Judicial Knowledge Canon?

Recall that Judge Saʿd b. Ibrāhīm felt compelled to rule contrary to his own knowledge, which—like the caliphal and communal memory alike—would have led him, no doubt, to conclude that the ʿAlids were entitled to all of the land in the Yanbuʿ valley surrounding Bughaybigha. In fact, as previously noted, he said as much: "By God, if I had issued a ruling according to my own knowledge as to Bughaybigha, I would have judged differently (lit.: other than what you observe)."[64] In explaining what the judge knew and how, an informant who had attended the trial recounted the part of the narrative on which the biographers and chroniclers had agreed: that "Bughaybigha was a trust of ʿAlī b. Abī Ṭālib," which Muʿāwiya sought, unsuccessfully, to take through various machinations. The informant then referred to (without quoting) a longer version of those machinations and ended his narrative with accounts of the Umayyad takings recounted above.[65] But judicial knowledge was apparently not an acceptable procedure available to this judge.

The rules governing the use of judicial knowledge were more complicated and contested than the straightforward *evidence canon*. Whereas that canon was the universally accepted gold standard for judicial decisions, the use of judicial knowledge as a stand-in for testimonial or confessional evidence had become a contested *decision rule* among early Muslim jurists, whose conflicting views broke down into three camps: those generally against it, those generally for it (and who required it), and those who permitted it only with certain constraints. This latter camp, those who permitted it with constraints, was most prevalent.[66] They tended to allow

64 Wakīʿ, *Akhbār al-quḍāt,* 104.

65 Ibid., 104: "[Following the failed marriage proposal, although] Bughaybigha remained under Ḥusayn's control (*lam tazal fī yad Ḥusayn*) until he died, Yazīd [b. Muʿāwiya] took control of it by force. Then it passed to the control of Ibn al-Zubayr, at which time, when Medina was under his control, the Family of ʿAlī took control of it from him by force.... Then ʿAbd al-Mālik returned control of it to the Family of Muʿāwiya until ʿUmar b. ʿAbd al-ʿAzīz (ʿUmar II) came to power and returned it to the Family of ʿAlī. When Yazīd b. ʿAbd al-Malik (Yazīd II) came to power, he returned it to the Family of Muʿāwiya. For similar wording from a source that was likely the source of Wakīʿ's account, see Ibn Saʿd, *Ṭabaqāt al-kubrā*, 6:414. Wakīʿ seems unaware of the subsequent history, having reported the case and its Umayyad history from Juwayriya—who reported the events to Ibn Saʿd or his informant. The ʿAbbāsid events (reported by Ibn Shabba, from an unnamed source) would have occurred just prior to their times, as Ibn Saʿd died during the reign of al-Wāthiq (r. 227-232/842-847) and Wakīʿ during the reign of al-Muqtadir (r. 295-320/908-932).

66 Ibn Qudāma, *Mughnī*, 11:401, noting that each of the Sunnī school "founders" or their close associates took positions against the absolute use of judicial knowledge: Mālik, Abū Ḥanīfa's close associate Muḥammad al-Shaybānī and, according to some, Shāfiʿī and Aḥmad b. Ḥanbal. The Sunnī rule stood in contrast to theʿAlid-Shīʿī rule, which almost unanimously *required* the use of judicial knowledge. For a discussion, see, e.g., al-Sharīf al-Murtaḍā, *Intiṣār*, 236; and ʿAbd al-Karīm al-Mūsawī al-Ardabīlī, *Fiqh al-qaḍā'*, 2nd ed. (Qum: Mu'assasat al-Nashr li-Jāmiat Mufīd, 1423/[2002-3]), 1:290–91.

the use of judicial knowledge in private or civil cases, but bar it in public or criminal cases. By and large, the use of judicial knowledge was generally disfavored as a less-constraining and more discretion-conferring tool in public law cases, which were to be approached with caution in this strand of early Islamic law.[67] The antipathy toward the use of judicial knowledge for public law matters was on display in this case, where endowment disputes were considered a matter of public law and where judicial discretion was to be minimal even for those who accepted this procedure in other cases. The antipathy toward judicial knowledge was so marked that it prompts consideration of whether it could be considered a canon at all by the eighth century (during which this case reportedly occurred) or the ninth century (at which time this case was recorded in the sources).

At any rate, unable to use the evidence canon and unwilling to use judicial knowledge, Judge Saʿd b. Ibrāhīm was left to appeal to some other recognized procedure of law. He turned, implicitly, to a presumption encapsulated in the possession canon.

The Possession Canon

Finally, recall that ʿAbd Allāh seemed to have continuously worked the land at issue, but that the caliph's representative apparently did not contemplate this fact as leading to his continued ability to do. Instead, the agent likely thought that he would prevail in taking the entire valley, with the benefit of the anticipated judgment adding legal legitimacy to the caliph's wishes to take the land. If this is a fair interpretation of the agent's line of thought, we might conclude that the possession canon was not as well-known a feature of the courts as was the evidence canon, and that, as a result, litigants such as this agent may not have known precisely how it operated.

Deprived of the normal procedures, the judge had cleverly avoided unnecessarily deciding the major question of who had the rightful claim over the entire valley.[68] It was, in fact, the possession canon that gave him

67 For and overview of the Islamic laws of judicial knowledge and circumstantial evidence, see Hossein Modarressi, "Circumstantial Evidence in the Administration of Justice" (Chapter 2, this volume).

68 In doing so, he pursued a strategy very similar to the modern U.S. constitutional avoidance rule of statutory interpretation, also known as the constitutional doubt canon, whereby judges are to interpret statutes "in a way that avoids placing its constitutionality in doubt." See Antonin Scalia and Bryan A. Garner, *Reading Law* (St. Paul: Thompson/West, 2012), 247–51. See also William N. Eskridge, Jr., *Interpreting Law* (St. Paul: Foundation Press, 2016), 425, defining the "constitutional avoidance rule" as requiring judges to "avoid interpretations that would render a statute unconstitutional (classic avoidance) or that would raise serious constitutional difficulties (modern avoidance)." For recent cases, see *Bond v. United States*, 134 S. Ct. 2077 (2014); and *Brown v. Plata*, 131 S. Ct. 1910, 1928–29, 1937 (2011). For a critique of the rule, see Richard A. Posner, "Statutory Interpretation—In the Classroom and in the Courtroom," *University of Chicago Law Review* 50 (1983), 800–22, esp. 815–16, questioning the rule that "[s]tatutes should

the means by which to narrow the inquiry to only the issue of whether ʿAbd Allāh could continue farming a portion of the land.[69] The possession canon gave a presumption of ownership to the party with land under his or her control, which a counter-claimant could rebut only with presentation of evidence of ownership or entitlement otherwise. Here, ʿAbd Allāh's cultivation of the land amounted to a presumption of his right to it. To rebut that presumption and claim ownership over the whole valley (including that land tract), the caliph or his representative would have had to present evidence that they lacked.[70] Balancing these competing claims, the judge issued a decision apparently so unexpected that it surprised the Umayyad caliph's representative into suddenly disclaiming the authority of the court over him and the case. But when the operation of the evidence, judicial knowledge, and possession canons are put into play, the decision makes sense to the observer well-versed in this latter procedural rule of early Islamic law—which, apparently, the caliph's representative was not.

CONCLUSION: THE RETURN OF BUGHAYBIGHA

When the *Case of Bughaybigha* arose in the Medinan court in 733 or 734, everyone *knew* that the land in question was properly under ʿAlid control—a fact that remained constant in the community's early historical memory.[71] The Umayyads knew it, which is why they tried to purchase the land or obtain it through various schemes before taking it outright. The ʿAbbāsids knew it too, which is why caliphs such as Saffāḥ and Maʾmūn gave the land back. But Bughaybigha was too important to be allowed to remain in ʿAlid hands whenever the power of the caliphs was threatened or their legitimacy seemed to be waning, and whenever taking (or, for that matter, giving) the land could symbolically or materially affect those dynamics.

It is significant that each ʿAbbāsid caliph who was favorable to ʿAlid claims to Bughaybigha drew on his own knowledge of this land as a trust, if we presume them to have been aware of the wider mainstream

---

be construed not only to save them from being invalidated but to avoid even raising serious constitutional questions" on the grounds that it "leaves everything ... vague" but enlarges the reach of judicial power "to create a judge-made 'penumbra.'" While comparable, the different structural reasons for and remedies intended by "constitutional" (or major-issue) avoidance tendencies in these two different systems would be ripe for future study.

69 Wakīʿ, *Akhbār al-quḍāt*, 103–04. See discussion above, note 10 and accompanying text.

70 On the operation of and conflicts between the possession and evidence canons, see, e.g., Muḥammad Ṣidqī b. Aḥmad al-Būrnū, *Mawsūʿat al-qawāʿid al-fiqhiyya*, 3rd ed. (Beirut: Dār al-Risāla al-ʿĀlamiyya, 2015), 3:130–33; Muḥammad Ḥasan al-Bujnūrdī, *al-Qawāʿid al-fiqhiyya*, ed. Mahdī al-Mihrīzī and Muḥammad Ḥusayn al-Dirāyatī, 1424/2003-4), 3:11–14.

71 On questions of historical memory in early Islam, see Hossein Modarressi, "Facts or Fables: Muslims' Evaluation of Historical Memory" (forthcoming).

view of the land as an "endowment created by ʿAlī for the children of Fāṭima."[72] By all accounts, for caliphs or their deputies to draw on their own knowledge was a regular and quite acceptable practice, including in *maẓālim* courts and their own tribunals otherwise. In this way, the *caliphal courts* unapologetically exhibited a practice for which early Islamic *judicial courts* rather sensationally gained the infamous Weberian reputation of being arbitrary and capricious, thanks to being confused or conflated in nineteenth- and twentieth-century Islamic law scholarship.[73]

But certain rules of evidence and procedure—typically embodied in legal canons—were to bind judges, even if they did not apply to caliphs. Thus, for judges to draw on their own knowledge was an issue of great controversy and generally frowned upon in public law cases in mainstream (later, Sunnī) Islamic law of the time.[74] Judges were bound by rules of evidence and procedure, which were usually encapsulated in Islam's legal canons, which conferred a high degree of legitimacy extending from a perception of moral-religious authority to judge on the basis of certain known procedures. It was this perception of procedure-derived legal legitimacy that led to the caliph Walīd II's attempt to end the long controversy over Bughaybigha by deploying a judicial rather than caliphal court to resolve it. He may have estimated that doing so would bolster his claims to proprietary (and, more pointedly, legal) legitimacy over Bughaybigha and the ʿAlid legacy attached to it through association with the procedure-bound legitimacy conferred by the court. He resorted to seizing the land once again, like Muʿāwiya's descendants, only when the legal avenues failed.

The prehistory of the *Case of Bughaybigha* suggests that certain procedural rules prevailed in judicial courts where, by the ninth century, historical events and political influences helped regularize procedures that were both shaped by and gave shape to historical events. The unfolding of this case gives texture to my overarching claim that procedure bound judges in ways that they did not bind political authorities, regardless of

72 Yāqūt, *Marāṣid al-iṭṭilāʿ*, 1:210.

73 See Max Weber, *Economy and Society*, eds. Guenther Roth and Claus Wittich, trans. Ephraim Fischoh et al. (New York: Bedminster Press, 1968), 806 n. 40, defining *kadijustiz* as "the administration of justice which is oriented not at fixed rules of a formally rational law but at the ethical, religious, political, or otherwise expediential postulates of a substantively rational law." But see David S. Powers, "*Kadijustiz* or *Qāḍī* Justice? A Paternity Suit from Fourteenth-Century Morocco," *Islamic Law and Society* 1 (1994): 332–66, esp. 365–66, contrasting Weber's imagined notion of *kadijustiz* with notions of judicial practices and procedures drawn from historical sources). For an analysis of the origins and effects of this notion on comparative law and in U.S. courts, see my "Against *Kadijustiz*: On the Negative Citation of Foreign Law," *Suffolk University Law Review* 48 (2015): 343–78.

74 See Māwardī, *Adab al-qāḍī*, 2:368–77, noting diverse positions among early Muslim jurists on the use of judicial knowledge in judicial courts, and particularly with respect to *ḥuqūq Allāh* (public law claims)—a category under which *waqf*-endowment law would fall.

the communal memory of historical facts. It also shows that procedural constraints on judges were not absolute. That is to say, judges still exercised considerable discretion when, in the absence of evidentiary proof, they were required to choose gap-filling presumptions like the possession canon and other procedures to deploy. All told, these events powerfully illustrate how integral procedure was to the very formation and meaning of Islamic law. Procedure could serve as a check on caliphal power when judges exercised the independence that procedure could confer. Or, alternatively, procedure could legitimate raw power when used to bolster political claims. And, of course, procedure could be used to stake out a neutral position between these two options, neither checking nor legitimating political power, as unfolded in this case. Here, appeals to procedure served to mediate delicate political contests in the fraught contexts of early Islamic societies, while still reinforcing the integrity and independence of the courts themselves. It is this third option that best describes the role of procedure as navigated by the judge in the *Case of Bughaybigha*. Through procedure, he offered a portion of land and legitimacy to both sides.

POSTSCRIPT

It was not long after the events described here that the endowment of Bughaybigha was functionally dissolved. By the time the historian Samhūdī wrote in the sixteenth century, the lands were "known simply as Yanbuʿ, and in possession of people who claim[ed] ownership of them." But the *Case of Bughaybigha* reveals the colorful history of the land in the early period—its discovery, endowment, and historical memory now available only in traces, almost hidden from view, yet there beneath the surface as the many springs of Yanbuʿ used to be.[75]

75 See Samhūdī, *Wafāʾ al-wafā*, 4:166. Modern-day Yanbuʿ is a district in Saudi Arabia where mostly dates are manufactured, having revived from the 1970s, when most of the springs had dried up and the residents had moved away from the farmlands to the city. The government began to restore the land in the 1980s, spurring on a renewal of date production on the farms there. See Khaṭīb, *Yanbuʿ*, 34; and Ilhām Sirāj ʿUmar Akbar, *Bilād Yanbuʿ: Dirāsa taʾrīkhiyya ḥiḍāriyya (363-923/973-1517)* (Medina: al-Ḥumaydī, 2015).

Chapter Four

A Critique of Adjudication: Formative Moments in Early Islamic Legal History

Nahed Samour
University of Helsinki

Who dispenses justice at court? Islamic legal historians have long focused on the single judge (*qāḍī*) as the embodiment of the administration of justice.[1] The judge, however, did not act alone in dispensing justice. A judicial staff supported his work, working from a position subordinate to him.[2] In addition, evading a clearly demarcated judicial hierarchy, the jurisconsult (*muftī*) shaped adjudication in many

1 The *qāḍi*-run courts were not the only courts in early Islamic history, and control over law passed through a variety of hands. Other courts included that of the arbitrator (*ḥakam*), the court of the market inspector (*muḥtasib*), the court of appeals (*maẓālim*), the court of the police (*shurṭa*), and the court of the military judge (*qāḍī ʿaskar*). Similar to the judge, yet in contrast to the jurisconsult, these judicial figures presided over courts, were authorized to terminate cases with sanctioning and binding authority, had authority over enforcement as executive officials, and were appointees of political authorities (except for the arbitrator). Still too little is known about these figures, with the noteworthy exception of the market inspector (*muḥtasib*), about whom see Kristen Stilt, *Islamic Law in Action: Authority, Discretion, and Everyday Experiences in Mamluk Egypt* (Oxford: Oxford University Press, 2011). Erwin Gräf provides a brief overview of the various courts. See hisis "Gerichtsverfasssung und Gerichtsbarkeit im islamischen Recht," *Zeitschrift für vergleichende Rechtswissenschaft* 58 (1955): 48–78, esp. 60.

On the early Islamic judicial system generally, see Mathieu Tillier, *L'invention du cadi. La justice des musulmans, des juifs et des chrétiens aux premiers siècles de l'Islam (Paris: Publications de la Sorbonne, 2017)*; Mathieu Tillier, *Les Cadis d'Iraq et l'État Abbasside (132/750-334/945)* (Damas: Institut français du Proche-Orient, 2009); Muhammad Khalid Masud, Rudolph Peters, and David Powers, eds., *Dispensing Justice in Islam: Qadis and their Judgments* (Leiden: Brill, 2006); Wael Hallaq, *Authority, Continuity and Change in Islamic Law* (Cambridge: Cambridge University Press, 2001); Irene Schneider, *Das Bild des Richters in der "adab al-qāḍī"-Literatur* (Frankfurt: Peter Lang Verlag, 1990); and Emile Tyan, *L'Histoire de l'organisation judiciaire en pays d'Islam*, 2nd ed. (Leiden: Brill, 1960).

2 Prior to the 2nd/8th century, as Kindī notes, the judge was assisted only by his clerk (*kātib*). Yet, by the second century of Islam, a full court staff emerged, including assistants to aid the judge in a variety of ways. See Abū ʿUmar Muḥammad b. Yūsuf al-Kindī (d. 350/961), *Kitāb al-Wulāt wa-kitāb al-quḍāt*, ed. Rhuvon Guest (Leiden, Brill: 1912), 386.

distinct ways through concurring and dissenting opinions at court.[3]

This contribution focuses on two legal authorities—the *qāḍī* and the *muftī*—who cooperated or competed with each other at court. Fundamental to their relationship is the Islamic principle of *mushāwara*,[4] that is, judicial consultation of experts on legal questions.[5] Islamic legal

---

3 Khaṣṣāf employs several phrases when referring to the jurisconsult, including the "people of knowledge" (*ahl al-ʿilm)* or "people of jurisprudence" (*ahl al-fiqh).* Mostly, however, he refers to jurists (*fuqahāʾ*)—or, in the singular, jurist (*faqīh*), or a solitary legal expert (*rajul fiqhī wāḥid*)—and in one case he refers to "those who sit with me [the judge]" (*julasāʾī*). Except for the last set of terms, all of Khaṣṣāf's names refer to knowledge and, specifically, to juristic knowledge. See Aḥmad b. ʿUmar Khaṣṣāf (d. 261/874), *Adab al-qāḍī*, in Abū Bakr Aḥmad b. ʿAlī al-Jaṣṣāṣ (d. 370/980), *Sharḥ Adab al-qāḍī*, ed. Farhat Ziadeh (Cairo: American University Press:1978), 37-43, secs. 10–22. Shāfiʿī, on the other hand, speaks of a "consultant" or "jurisconsult" (*mushīr*). See Muḥammād b. Idrīs al-Shāfiʿī (d. 204/820), *Kitāb al-umm*, 2nd ed. (Beirut: Dār al-Fikr, 1983), 6:219, where he discusses judicial consultation under the heading *mushāwarat al-qāḍī*. Neither Khaṣṣāf nor Shāfiʿī use the term *muftī* or *ahl al-futyā* (legal experts who issue opinions) or *fatwā* (the non-binding legal opinion produced in response to judicial consultation requests) in their discussions of judicial consultation. This absence is at first striking given that all three terms were used during the time at which each author wrote to refer to legal experts issuing legal opinions upon request and to the legal opinions, respectively. Moreover, the *muftī* was known as the legal advisor par excellence and operated as an independent legal expert. On Shāfiʿī's use of *ahl al-futyā/muftī* in his *Risāla*, see Joseph E. Lowry, *Early Islamic Legal Theory: The Risāla of Muḥammad ibn Idrīs al-Shāfiʿī* (Leiden: Boston, 2007), 277–94; and Harald Motzki, *Die Anfänge der islamischen Jurisprudenz: ihre Entwicklung in Mekka bis zur Mitte des 2./ 8. Jahrhunderts* (Stuttgart: Franz Steiner Verlag, 1991), 257. Yet, the *fatwā* is typically produced by a *muftī* alone (without the need to be in consultation with a judge) and typically outside of a court, which issues a *ḥukm*—facts that make it unsurprising that these authors do not mention the term *fatwā*. See Shihāb al-Dīn al-Qarāfī, *al-Iḥkām fī tamyīz al-fatāwā ʿan al-aḥkām wa-taṣarrufāt al-qāḍī waʾl-imām* (Cairo: al-Maktab al-Thaqāfī, 1989), trans. Mohammed Fadel, *Criterion for Distinguishing Legal Opinions from Judicial Rulings and the Administrative Acts of Judges and Rulers* (New Haven: Yale University Press, 2017); and Sherman Jackson, *Islamic Law and the State: The Constitutional Jurisprudence of Shihāb al-Dīn al-Qarāfī* (Leiden: Brill, 1996).

However, Khaṣṣāf and Shāfiʿī do clearly refer to experts of law who are to be consulted in court cases. Both the *mushīr* and the *faqīh* provided legal advice to the judge and thereby functioned as the "*muftī* at court." The *faqīh* and the *mushīr*, accordingly, were one and the same person. In this essay, I call these actors "legal experts" or "jurists" (*faqīhs*) when they wrote about Islamic law in treatises, and jurisconsults (*muftīs*) when judges solicited their opinions or when they voiced their unsolicited opinions on particular questions of law in court cases, and in adjudication at large. Likewise, I treat their issuing legal opinions (*fatwās*) and participating in the process of judicial consultation (*mushāwara*) on questions related to adjudication as the same.

4 I employ the term *mushāwara* as it is the term that the legal scholar Shāfiʿī used as the title for his section on the judge soliciting advice from the jurisconsult. See Shāfiʿī, *Kitāb al-umm*, 6:219. Similarly, the legal experts whose opinions judges in Andalusia and the Maghreb solicited at the beginning of the 3rd/9th century were officially called *mushāwars*. See Tyan, *L'Histoire de l'organisation judiciare*, 222. The Muslim-Spanish and Maghribī consilium of jurisconsults, who sat on the bench alongside judges there, will not be discussed here as it was geographically outside of the ʿAbbāsid territory and because legal consultation was not institutionalized in Sunnī legal history outside of Muslim Spain and the Maghreb. On the consilium, see, for instance, Wael Hallaq, *The Origins and Evolution of Islamic Law* (Cambridge: Cambridge University Press, 2005), 89; and Manuela Marín, "Šūrā et ahl al-Šūrā dans al-Andalus," *Studia Islamica* 62 (1985): 25–52; Jacinto Bosch Vilá, "The Administrative History of al-Andalus: An Approach," in *Regierung und Verwaltung des Vorderen Orients in islamischer Zeit 6.5* (Leiden: Brill, 1984).

5 The principle of consultation (*mushāwara, shūra,* or *mashwara*) was reflected upon and practiced in both the legal and the political realms. See Roswitha Badry, *Die zeitgenössische*

doctrine encouraged a judge confronted with particular legal uncertainties to consult a *muftī* before issuing a judicial decision.

The related principle of *mushāwara* (consultation) is anchored in the Qur'ān.[6] The Prophet himself is urged in Qur'ānic verse 3:159 to "consult them in the matter; and when you have decided, [to] place your trust in God."[7] Many early jurists came to understand this verse to mean that the judge, even when highly qualified, should seek the advice of a jurisconsult, or legal expert, to aid in adjudication. Seeking advice was considered vital for the sake of seeking the truth.[8]

Scholar of Islamic law Hilmar Krüger calls judicial consultation "an impossibility" (*ein Unding*) from today's perspective.[9] In explaining this critical stance, he refers to the Roman legal principles of *iura novit curia* (the court knows the law)[10] and *da mihi factum, dabo tibi ius* (give me the facts, I will give you the law) as universal principles of adjudication, according to which the application of law in court is the exclusive task and obligation of the judge. A judge seeking consultation from an extrajudicial authority, according to *Krüger*, is violating these two maxims.[11] Given

---

Diskussion um den islamischen Beratungsgedanken (šūrā) unter dem besonderen Aspekt ideengeschichtlicher Kontinuitäten und Diskontinuitäten (Stuttgart: Franz Steiner Verlag, 1998), esp. 108–34, for examples and an analysis of early Prophetic consultation with the Companions over military tactics, religious rites, and legal and political-administrative concerns. See also Emile Tyan, *Institutions du droit public musulman* (Paris: Sirey 1954-1957), 1:195–98, 396–97, 490; 2:38, 47, 181, 570. Tyan gives a *tour d'horizon* of consultative committees in pre-Islamic times and during the election procedure of the first four caliphs, of scholarly writings on consultation, and of the implementation of consultation practices during later caliphates and sultanates.

For other literature on consultation, especially in the political realm, see Roy Mottahedeh, "Consultation and the Political Process in the Islamic Middle East of the 9th, 10th, and 11th centuries," in *Islam and Public Law: Classical and Contemporary Studies*, ed. Chibli Mallat (London: Graham and Trotman, 1993), 19–27; and Bernard Lewis, "Mashwara," *EI*[2], 6:724–25.

6 Q. 3:159 and 42:38.

7 Early tafsīr works do not mention adjudication in interpreting verse 3:159. Instead, their authors struggle to address the questions of why God obliged the Prophet to seek consultation, and whether consultation was obligatory or voluntary. See Badry, *Die zeitgenössische Diskussion*, 66–104.

8 Khaṣṣāf, *Adab al-qāḍī*, 40–41, sec. 13.

9 Hilmar Krüger, "Grundprobleme des islamischen Fetwa-Wesens," in *Beiträge zum islamschen Recht III*, ed. Hans-Georg Ebert and Thoralf Hanstein (Frankfurt: P. Lang, 2003), 5–32, esp. 26.

10 On the foundations of the *iura novit curia* rule in pre-modern and modern European legal history, see Peter Oestmann, "Die Grenzen richterlicher Rechtserkenntnis," in Peter Oestmann, *Aus den Akten des Reichskammergerichts: prozessrechtliche Probleme im Alten Reich* (Hamburg: Kovac, 2004), 301–44, esp. 305–31.

11 The phenomenon of judicial consultation is not as exceptional to Islamic law as Krüger suggests, but a comparative study has yet to be completed. Jewish, Roman, Italian, and German legal histories—the last even up until 1870—provide examples of judges or courts reaching out to extrajudicial legal experts. References to comparable consultative practices of courts will be made throughout the study. To mention here only a few: Eva Schumann, "Beiträge studierter Juristen und anderer Rechtsexperten zur Rezeption des gelehrten Rechts," *Jahrbuch*

Krüger's objection to the very possibility of legitimate judicial consultation, should early Islamic adjudication truly be considered a type of "consultative justice"[12] in which not only the judge but also an extrajudicial authority participated in deciding cases? Whose authority in adjudication became decisive: that of the judge or of the jurisconsult? Who ultimately dispensed justice in Islamic adjudication?

To answer these questions, I focus on the so-called "formative period" of Islamic legal history: the early ʿAbbāsid period, from the eighth to the ninth centuries.[13] This period was particularly important for two reasons: First, the judicial system under the ruling ʿAbbāsids became centralized, professionalized, and bureaucratized, thereby strengthening the authority of the office of the judge.[14] Second, legal scholars, often

---

der Akademie der Wissenschaften in Göttingen (2007), 443–61; Ulrich Falk, *Consilia: Studien zur Praxis der Rechtsgutachten in der frühen Neuzeit* (Frankfurt: Vittorio Klostermann, 2006); Julius Kirshner, "*Consilia* as Authority in Late Medieval Italy: The Case of Florence," in *Legal Consulting in the Civil Law Tradition*, ed. Mario Ascheri, Ingrid Baumgärtner, and Julius Kirshner (Berkeley: The Robbins Collection, 1999), 107–40; Michael Berger, *Rabbinic Authority* (Oxford: Oxford University Press, 1998); Kaius Tuori, "The *ius respondendi* and the Freedom of Roman Jurisprudence," *Revue internationales des droites de l'Antiquité* 51 (2004): 295–337; Andre Magdelain, "Ius respondendi," *Revue historique de droit française et étranger* 28 (1950): 1–22; and Wolfgang Kunkel, "Das Wesen des ius respondendi," *Zeitschrift der Savigny-Stiftung für Rechtsgeschichte: Romanistische Abteilung* 66 (1948): 423–57. In Germany, the procedure was called *Aktenversendung*, and, from the 16th to the 19th century, German courts were obliged to submit to the (out-of-court) law faculty of a university for the final decision regarding any case in which the principle by which it should be decided was in doubt. See Peter Oestmann, "Aktenversendung," *Handwörterbuch zur deutschen Rechtsgeschichte* (2004), 1, secs. 128–32; Gerhard Buchda, "Aktenversendung," *Handwörterbuch zur deutschen Rechtsgeschichte* (1964), 1:84–87. See also Harold J. Berman, "Religious Dimensions of the Western Legal Tradition," in *The Contentious Triangle: Church, State, and University*, ed. Rodney L. Petersen and Calvin Augustine Pater (Kirksville, Mo.: Truman State University Press, 1999), 281–94, esp. 288. For Berman, the *Aktenversendung* was a particularly striking example of the professorial character of German law. I would argue that all of these examples of judicial consultation, or extrajudicial law-making, demonstrate how scholars ensured that they had a say in adjudication.

12 Carl Heinrich Becker, *Islamstudien: vom Werden und Wesen der islamischen Welt* (Leipzig: Quelle & Meyer, 1924–1932), 2:313. Becker spoke of *Konsultativjustiz* as the *fatwā*-giving practice of the *muftīs* in general. I instead use the term to stress the consultative aspect of adjudication that allows for a built-in critique of the single-*qāḍī* court.

13 This study starts with the beginning of ʿAbbāsid rule in 132/750 and ends in 247/883-4. The year 247/883-4, which marks the end of the early ʿAbbāsid period for this study, is when the title "judge" became honorary, and thus when the role of judge was emptied of many of its competences and activities and was no longer automatically related to the function of adjudication. Instead, justice was dispensed by deputy judges (*khalīfas*), delegates of the official *qāḍī*. See Nurit Tsafrir, *The History of an Islamic School of Law: The Early Spread of Hanafism* (Cambridge: Harvard University Press, 2004), 37; and Tillier, *Les Cadis*, 124–31, 184. From this time onward, we do not know a great deal about these local judges or deputy judges, and, because no major judicial scandals were reported in the judicial chronicles, it does not seem far-fetched to assume that the local judges adjudicated in line with the locally dominant legal school and customs, and in line with the reasoning of local jurisconsults. No encounters between judge and jurisconsult for the second half of the 3rd/9th century were documented in judicial chronicles.

14 The early ʿAbbāsid judicial system became increasingly bureaucratized, featuring division of work, office hierarchy, and levels of graded authority. On ways in which the judiciary thereby

acting in their private capacities, gained increasing prestige, influence, and authority through the work of producing the body of scholarly literature needed to systematize and canonize early Islamic law. Both developments led to the rise of two competing elite personae, each of whom needed to guard his authority vis-à-vis the other. Significantly, no explicit hierarchy was established between the judge and the jurisconsult,[15] although both were already acknowledged socially and governmentally as legal authorities at that time.[16]

These two legal figures could not be more distinct from one another. What set the two apart most was that the judge, as an appointee of the ʿAbbāsid caliph, belonged to the realm of the state in which law was binding, enforceable, and final.[17] The judge acted in cases of litigation—that is to say, when litigants came before him with a request to resolve a legal dispute. The judge articulated the law through a judgment (*ḥukm*). That judgment was then enforceable through the power apparatus of the caliphate—including the police (*shurṭa*)—and was therefore coercive.[18] In contrast, the jurisconsult's articulations of law were not binding. The *muftī* usually issued legal advice when consulted by individuals or by officials of the state (although he could also issue advice without an explicit request). But those individuals or officials were not bound to follow that

enhanced its organizational authority, see Nahed Samour, *Judge and Jurisconsult—Coercive and Persuasive Authority in Islamic Law* (PhD diss., Humboldt University Berlin, Faculty of Law: 2015), 294–398.

15 Under Ottoman rule (15th-20th centuries), while some jurisconsults remained private scholars, the Ottomans introduced the position of state *muftī* (*Shaykh al-Islam*), a state-employed official who watched over the judiciary and adjudication and whose *fatwās* had a law-like effect. See, for example, Colin Imber, *Ebu'suʿud: The Islamic Legal Tradition* (Edinburgh: Edinburgh University Press, 1997); and Ronald C. Jennings, *The Judicial Registers (Şerʿi Mahkeme Sicilleri) of Kayseri (1590-1630) as a Source for Ottoman History* (PhD diss., UCLA: 1972).

16 On the history of judgeship in early Islam, see Tillier, *Les Cadis*; Paul Dannhauer, *Untersuchungen zur frühen Geschichte des Qāḍī-Amtes* (Bonn: s.n., 1975); and Hussein F. S. al-Kasassbeh, "The Office of Qāḍī in the Early ʿAbbāsid Caliphate (132–247/750–861)" (PhD diss., School of Oriental and African Studies, University of London: 1990). The latter was translated into Arabic and published as *al-Sulṭa al-qaḍāʾiyya fī ʿaṣr al-ʿAbbasī al-awwal* (al-ʿAyn, UAE: Zayed Center for Heritage and History, 2001). On the origins of the practice of issuing *fatwās*, see Harald Motzki, "Religiöse Ratgebung im Islam: Entstehung, Bedeutung und Praxis des *muftī* und der *fatwā*," *Zeitschrift für Religionwissenschaften* 2.1 (1994): 3–22, esp. 6–10.

17 As a new centralization policy of the ʿAbbāsids, the judiciary was (largely) appointed by the caliph, rather than being appointed by local governors as had been the case previously. On the ways in which the authority of the judiciary was enlarged by the ʿAbbāsids' efforts to centralize, professionalize, and bureaucratize its state officials, and how those efforts affected the rising authority of the legal scholars, see Samour, *Judge and Jurisconsult*, 294–398.

18 Max Weber, for instance, considered the order of law to be coercive "when it can be externally guaranteed by the chance of (physical or psychological) *coercion* to enforce the observance or punishment in case of violation through a *specific staff* of people" [italics original]. See Max Weber, *Wirtschaft und Gesellschaft: Grundriss der verstehenden Soziologie*, ed. Johannes Winckelmann, 5th ed. (Tübingen: Mohr Siebeck, 1980 [first published 1921–1922]), 17.

advice. Thus the jurisconsult's opinions were not backed by a compulsory enforcement mechanism. Albeit typically part of a patronage system that sometimes included state funding, the jurisconsult was largely perceived by his contemporaries as an independent legal scholar and advisor, rather than as an arm of the state.[19] The jurisconsult's authority was thus, at first glance, entirely based on the persuasiveness of his argument. That said, his persuasion-based authority carried weight because it proceeded from an epistemological exploration of how to derive a sound legal norm from the authoritative texts of Islamic revelation, and epistemic authority was key to Islamic legal legitimacy.[20]

What happened when the coercive authority of the judge encountered the persuasive authority of the jurisconsult at court? Their relationship vis-á-vis one another is barely formalized in the early *adab al-qāḍī* literature of the second/ninth-century relevant texts. Moreover, with little textual descriptions of or instructions for how the judge and jurisconsult were meant to deliberate, we can only speculate as to the form that their dialogue might have taken. Looking at the etymology of the term itself, consultation (*mushāwara*) implies a mutual or reciprocal consultative activity, one involving a joint, possibly symmetrical or bilateral exchange of ideas leading to a decision. Yet, belying this etymological expectation, there is no documentation to imply that, in practice, judicial consultation involved any such back-and-forth movement of thoughts and ideas.[21] Instead, consultation seems to have been a one-way activity: legal experts giving advice to judges, with or without their requests.

With few exceptions, both judges and jurisconsults belonged to the same class of jurists (*fuqahā᾽*) and were increasingly affiliated with a set of emerging schools of law. In fact, caliphs and their chief judges (*qāḍī al-quḍāt*) recruited and accepted recommendations for judgeship positions from among the jurists.[22] Moreover, differences in legal qualifications and in knowledge of Ḥanafī legal thought did not determine the dividing line

19 See, for example, Muḥammad Q. Zaman, *Religion and Politics Under the Early ʿAbbāsids: The Emergence of the Proto-Sunnī Elite* (Leiden: Brill, 1997), 12.

20 On epistemic authority, see Wael Hallaq, "Uṣūl al-Fiqh: Beyond Tradition," *Journal of Islamic Studies* 3, no. 2 (1992): 172–202, esp. 178; and Aron Zysow, *The Economy of Certainty, An Introduction to the Typology of Islamic Legal Theory* (Atlanta: Lockwood Press, 2013), 1.

21 Bernhard G. Weiss, "Text and Application: Hermeneutical Reflections on Islamic Legal Interpretation," in *The Law Applied: Contextualizing the Islamic Sharīʿa,* ed. Peri Bearman, Wolfhart Heinrichs, and Bernhard G. Weiss (London: I.B. Tauris, 2008), 374–96, 385.

22 On the early ʿAbbāsid preference for the Medinan school and judges, see Tillier, *Les Cadis,* 149–50; Hallaq, *Origins and Evolution*, 105–06; and Kasassbeh, "The Office of Qāḍī," 77. On the process by which the ʿAbbāsid caliphs' preference shifted to the Ḥanafī school and judiciary, see Tillier, *Les Cadis*, 186; and Tsafrir, *History of an Islamic School of Law*, 21–2, 118.

between judge and jurisconsult.[23] Most judges of the early ʿAbbāsid period, at least in Iraq, had an identifiable legal background. [24]

We therefore could not convincingly argue that the necessity for judicial consultation arose because the jurisconsults, as a class, were more learned than the judges.[25] Instead, the role of extrajudicial authority in consultation reflected an early awareness of the limits of law as text and method. In other words, judges need not have been ignorant lay-people for them to face challenges in interpreting law. In fact, the burden and responsibility of adjudicating the *ius divinum* was a much discussed topic,[26] and, perhaps consultation was thought of as a means of distributing the risks of the judicial process.

Where relationships of authority were not formalized into prescribed procedures, we must sift through and analyze more indirect markers of authority. I will attempt to address a number of questions raised by the Islamic principle of judicial consultation, the most important of which are: How did the autonomy of the judge relate to the authority of the

23 On the legal educational background of the early ʿAbbāsid judges and their training in the nascent schools of law, see Samour, *Judge and Jurisconsult*, 340–47. Others, however, argue that that the dividing line between judge and jurisconsult is, in fact, knowledge, and that the judge turned to the jurisconsult as the more knowledgeable party. See, for example, Krüger, "Grundprobleme des islamischen Fetwa-Wesens," 26; and Schneider, *Das Bild des Richters*, 108.

A study of the qualifications required for judges shows that Ḥanafīs allow for exceptions to be made for the level of legal knowledge of the judge compared to the *muftī*. Having said this, Ḥanafī legal texts of the formative period still maintain that the judge is to master the disciplines of law, and additionally require the skills of interpretive reasoning (*ijtihād*). Therefore, it cannot be said, for the formative period, that the *muftī* solved, or attempted to solve, new and difficult cases, while the *qāḍī* merely applied the solutions in his court. See Wael Hallaq, *Authority, Continuity and Change in Islamic Law* (Cambridge: Cambridge University Press, 2001), 76.

24 Josef van Ess, *Theologie und Gesellschaft im 2. und 3. Jahrhundert Hidschra. Eine Geschichte des religiösen Denkens im frühen Islam* (Berlin: W. de Gruyter, 1992), 2:124; Baber Johansen, "Wahrheit und Geltungsanspruch: Zur Begründung und Begrenzung der Autorität des Qadi-Urteils im islamischen Recht," in *La Guistizia Nell'Alto Medieovo (Secoli IX-XI)*, ed. Centro Italiano di Studi sull'Alto Medioevo (Spoledo: Presso la Sede del Centro, 1997), 988, 991. Tillier, *Les Cadis*, 191.

25 While it is correct that the ʿAbbāsid judiciary included lay-judges, they seem to have been relatively uncommon. The overwhelming majority of judges enjoyed a legal education. Biographical works and the *akhbār al-quḍāt* genre capture the educational lineage and the learned engagement of judges, along with recording significant legal questions. See, e.g., Muḥammad b. Khalaf Wakīʿ (d. 306/918), *Akhbār al-quḍāt* (Cairo: Maṭbaʿat al-Saʿāda 1947-50), 3:150, 168. Masud, Peters, and Powers confirm that there was no lack of qualified jurists for the office of judge during the early ʿAbbāsid period. See their *Dispensing Justice in Islam: Qadis and their Judgments*, 10. In contrast, on the knowledge possessed by the *qāḍīs* during the first two centuries of Islamic legal history, G.H.A. Juynboll argues that some knew the law (*fiqh*) poorly because of their minor knowledge of *ḥadīth* and instead trusted their common sense. See Gautier H. A. Juynboll, *Muslim Tradition* (Cambridge: Cambridge University Press, 1983), 94.

26 On the anxieties of adjudication, see, for example, the compilation of *ḥadīths* in Wakīʿ, *Akhbār al-quḍāt*, 7–21. See also Baber Johansen, "Truth and Validity of the Qadi's Judgment: A Legal Debate among Muslim Sunnite Jurists from the 9th to the 13th Centuries," *Recht van de Islam* 14 (1997): 1–26; and Baber Johansen, "Wahrheit und Geltungsanspruch," 975–1074, 1056–59.

jurisconsult?[27] What happened in cases of conflict, that is, when the legal reasoning of the judge diverged from that of the jurisconsult?

First, I will give a normative account of how early jurists conceptualized judicial consultation, based upon the writings of the Ḥanafī scholar Aḥmad b. ʿUmar al-Khaṣṣāf (d. 261/874) and Muḥammad b. Idrīs al-Shāfiʿī (d. 204/820), eponym of the Shāfiʿī school. Second, I will turn to the historical encounters between the judge and the jurisconsult, primarily as captured by judicial chronicles. I will then conclude by classifying the potential relationship between the judge and jurisconsult according to the categories of cooperation, confrontation, and cooptation. Overall, I argue that judicial consultation was conceptualized and practiced as a "critique of adjudication."[28] Adjudication here goes beyond the very process of dispute settlement and includes the make-up of the judicial system as a whole, including the set-up of the judiciary.

Normative Encounters: The Jurisconsult as Guide or Constraint to the Judge?

One of the first legal scholars to write on adjudication was Khaṣṣāf, whose *Adab al-qāḍī* (*Etiquette of the Judge*) can be considered the main extant source on the normativity of judicial consultation in the Ḥanafī school of law during his time.[29] Khaṣṣāf spatially described a court setting (in a mosque) and affirmed the presence of jurists placed next to the judge to advise him in complicated cases:

> On his arrival in the mosque the *qāḍī* would salute the audience, offer two or four units of prayer [*rakʿas*], and

27 The question of how autonomy and authority relate to one another still haunts today's leading legal philosophers. Wolff has prominently argued that legitimate authority and moral autonomy are logically incompatible. See Robert Paul Wolff, *In Defense of Anarchy* (New York: Harper and Row, 1970). For refutations of Wolff, see Joseph Raz, *The Authority of Law: Essays on Law and Morality*, 2nd ed. (Oxford: Oxford University Press, 2009), 26–27; and Scott J. Shapiro, "Authority," in *The Oxford Handbook of Jurisprudence and Philosophy of Law*, ed. Jules Coleman and Scott Shapiro (Oxford: Oxford University Press, 2002), 282–439, esp. 385. For an attempt to reconcile autonomy and authority see Thomas May, *Autonomy, Authority, and Moral Responsibility* (Dordrecht: Kluwer Academic Publisher, 1998), 127.

28 Duncan Kennedy, *A Critique of Adjudication: Fin de siècle* (Cambridge: Harvard University Press, 1997). Kennedy claims that an essential aspect of the practice of adjudication is the denial of choice and agency that the judge inescapably faces in reaching a decision and in crafting the reasons that support it. In contrast, early Muslim source materials show a profound awareness of the burden created by the indeterminacy of law—that is to say, the risk of making a "wrong" decision and the consequences that would ensue, in this life and in the Hereafter. Judicial consultation thus becomes an attempt to distribute the risks of judicial error.

29 Khaṣṣāf's brief passages are followed by the comments and clarifications of legal scholar Jaṣṣāṣ. I am following the careful demarcations between the two authors provided by the editor Farhat Ziadeh. Given the limitations of this study, I directly reference Jaṣṣāṣ's commentary only once here.

> ask God to grant him success and guide him towards the right path, so as to enable him to uphold the truth and save him from transgression. After that, he would sit facing the Kaʿba [in Mecca]. Court chamberlains would stand in front of him, at such a distance that they might hear the *qāḍī*'s conversation with the litigants. The *qāḍī* placed his portable archive (*qimṭar*) entailing the court files on his right-hand side. The clerk sat near him, at such a distance that the *qāḍī* could watch his performance, while the deputy judge stood in front of him and called the litigants in turn. The guard would stand near him. The *qāḍī* allowed the jurists (*fuqahā'*) [...][30] to be seated near him, so that it would be easier for him to consult them on complicated legal issues. The two litigants would sit side by side in front of them.[31]

This passage offers insight into the *who*, *when*, and *under what circumstances* of judicial consultation. The single judge was surrounded by a consilium of jurists. These jurists sat in immediate proximity to the judge in order to be consulted by him, and thus the single judge's authority encountered the collective authority of the jurists. As for *when*, consultation was performed during the course of litigation. As for *under what circumstances* consultation ought to have been performed, Khaṣṣāf adds: "If the legal scholars (*ahl al-fiqh*) are present in the city, the judge should consult them."[32] He provides no further qualification as to the facts, law, or degree of difficulty of the cases requiring consultation. The mere presence of jurisconsults in the city sufficed to require a judge to solicit their counsel. In other words, Khaṣṣāf's recommendation for consultation was not qualified, possibly because of his awareness that interpretation takes place no matter how supposedly clear or ambiguous the text or the facts.

When judge and jurisconsult concur in their reasoning, the judge should adjudicate according to the jointly established consensus.[33] However, "when they disagree in their opinions, he shall judge according to what he thinks corresponds more closely with the truth."[34] Moreover, in cases of disagreement, a judge can request advice from jurists outside of his own city:

30 Khaṣṣāf also mentions other "trustworthy persons" (*qawm min ahl al-thiqa wa'l-amāna*) sitting next to the bench. It remains unclear whether his reference is to professional witnesses (*ʿudūl*), clerks, local nobility, specially skilled experts or some other class of person. Khaṣṣāf, *Adab al-qāḍī*, 85–86, sec. 80.

31 Ibid.

32 Ibid., 42, sec. 17.

33 Jaṣṣāṣ, *Sharḥ Adab al-qāḍī*, 42, sec. 17: "When they arrive at concurring opinions, the judge shall adjudicate accordingly because judge and jurisconsults have jointly established consensus. If the problem at hand required an individual effort of legal reasoning (*ijtihād*) and consensus (*ijmāʿ*) was arrived at, the joint result shall not be violated."

34 Khaṣṣāf, *Adab al-qāḍī*, 42, sec. 18.

> If the jurists (*fuqahā'*) of the city have consensus of opinion concerning an issue and the judge has a different opinion, the judge should not hasten in making his decision. He should get the opinion of other legal scholars in writing and request their counsel. Then he should arrive at his best possible opinion and act accordingly.[35]

This passage adds additional complexity to the questions of the *who* and *when* of judicial consultation as described above. When judicial consultation required non-local legal scholars, it could be done in writing and thus would have to take place outside of both the spatial and temporal boundaries of the judicial session.

Khaṣṣāf is careful to assert the autonomy of the judge. He concedes that: "when there is a problem and he consults with one legal scholar, he can follow the scholar's opinion, in case the judge has no opinion on this matter."[36] In the absence of his own opinion, the judge should incorporate that of the jurisconsult into his judicial opinion, while still making the final decision his own. Even in cases

> when the expert he is consulting is better at legal reasoning (*afqah*) than the judge, yet the judge can discern (between the two possible positions of) the problem, he is to deliberate himself (*naẓara*) ... [and] judge according to what is closer to what is correct.[37]

Khaṣṣāf is particularly adamant about maintaining the judge's autonomy when he says: "the judge shall not issue a verdict that he considers wrong, even when the [consulted] jurists (*fuqahā'*) are of [that] opinion."[38] In other words, the arguments of the jurisconsults, no matter how persuasive, never exempt the judge from deliberating for himself as to whether those arguments are correct. The final judgment is to emanate from the judge's authority, and thus the final judgment must be his. Of course, the jurisconsult's opinion should guide the judge in his effort to "correspond more closely with the truth."[39] Joint deliberations were, after all, considered better than solitary ones,[40] and consultation thus helped ensure the quality of a decision.[41] However, extrajudicial authority was meant to remain non-binding, persuasive at most, while the judge remained fully autonomous over the decision-making process and his decisions were meant to be

35 Ibid., 42, sec. 19.

36 Ibid., 42, sec. 20.

37 Ibid., 43, sec. 21.

38 Ibid., 44, sec. 23.

39 Ibid., 42, sec. 18.

40 Ibid., 42, sec. 17.

41 The quality of the decision is measured by "coming closest to the truth." Ibid., 42, sec. 18.

binding. Ḥanafīs therefore preferred to see the jurisconsult as a guide to the judge and consultation as means of joint deliberation rather than joint decision-making.[42]

Shāfiʿī's discussions of judicial consultation in his *Kitāb al-Umm* are initially similar: The jurisconsult was to guide the judge in his adjudication; judicial autonomy permitted the judge to seek the jurisconsult's opinions; and the ultimate decision was to be made by the judge. Significantly, though, Shāfiʿī takes a more restrictive approach to the role of the jurisconsult in the adjudicative process in cases in which he feared that the judge would engage in judicial legislation. His passage "on judicial consultation" (*mushāwarat al-qāḍī*)[43] starts with the following qualifications of the judicial advisor:

> I recommend that the judge consult with someone who is knowledgeable about the Qurʾān, *Sunna*, and customary traditions (*āthār*), as well as the jurists' doctrines; someone who knows [the rules] of analogy; and someone who does not violate the text and meaning [of the Qurʾān and *Sunna*]. These criteria will only be found in someone who masters the Arabic language. Even when [an expert] combines all of these criteria, [the judge] should consult him only if he is evidently pious and [only if] he seeks the truth.[44]

According to Shāfiʿī, the extrajudicial advisor had to possess thorough knowledge in a number of subjects so that he would remain true to the wording of Islam's authoritative legal texts. He considered exhibitions of piety further confirmation that the advisor possessed the requisite level of integrity to provide opinions to judges.[45]

All these qualifications were intended to mitigate one specific fear: that anyone involved in the judicial process might "violate the text and meaning [of the Qurʾān and *Sunna*]." Any interpretive action, advice sought, or judgments made were not to violate the authoritative texts or their meaning. As Shāfiʿī reiterates:

> [The judge] should not accept (*yaqbal*) the advice of such a person in a case, unless he assures [the judge] that his advice is based on a binding transmission [of text], meaning the Qurʾān, *Sunna*, consensus, or analogy on the basis of one of the [first] two. Even then he is to accept the advice

42 Jaṣṣāṣ, *Kitāb aḥkām al-Qurʾān*, (Cairo: Salafīya, 1335/[1916-7]) 2:49–50; and Badry, *Die zeitgenössische Diskussion*, 78.

43 Shāfiʿī, *Kitāb al-umm*, 6:219.

44 Ibid.

45 Farhat Ziadeh, "Integrity (*ʿAdālah*) in Classical Islamic Law," in *Islamic Law and Jurisprudence: Studies in Honor of Farhat J. Ziadeh*, ed. Nicolas Heer (Seattle: University of Washington Press, 1990), 73–93, esp. 73.

> only when he fully comprehends it, has fully persuaded himself of it, and can follow [its reasoning].[46]

In this way, Shāfiʿī appeals to the judge's own faculties of comprehension, and cautions him to adopt the jurisconsult's opinion only when the judge himself is convinced of the sound reasoning substantiating the advice. The judge himself then decides whether to incorporate his advice.

Concerned about issues of authenticity and multiple interpretations, Shāfiʿī continues:

> Additionally, he shall, even when he has in this way understood the advice, only then adopt it when he has asked him about a further interpretation. If there is no other interpretation, or when [the juristic opinion] has to do with a tradition about whose transmission (*naql*) no disagreement exists, he shall accept the advice. If, however, the Qurʾānic text offers two interpretations, or if the tradition is transmitted in different ways, or if the wording of the *Sunna* allows for different interpretations, he should then act in accordance with one of the interpretations only after he has found evidence in the Qurʾān, *Sunna*, consensus, or analogy showing that the opinion he chose as the basis for his decision is binding and more adequate than the one he left out.[47]

Here, Shāfiʿī is cautious about the fine line between legal conformism (which he rejects) and interpretation.[48] He advises the judge to seek persuasive arguments in the legal opinions of others, presumably due to implicit acknowledgment of the epistemological challenge of "discovering" the law, encountered by even the most learned jurist. According to Shāfiʿī, the judge was required to seek legal advice *only when* he was unable to reach a decision in especially difficult cases, in particular, when authoritative sources and legal traditions offered no textual answer.[49]

Shāfiʿī then continues by extending this caution to the use of analogy:

> [The judge] should approach analogy similarly. He is to then base his decision on analogy only when it is more suitable than Qurʾān, *Sunna*, or consensus, or when it is more suitable than the opinion he left out. He is forbidden from diverting from this [method] and saying: "I consider this to be more juristically preferable (*istaḥsantu*)." Because if he dares to say, "I consider this to be more juristically

46 Shāfiʿī, *Kitāb al-umm*, 6:219.

47 Ibid.

48 Ibid.

49 See also Hallaq, *Authority*, 77.

> preferable," he will also permit himself to make religious law (*yusharriʿ fī al-dīn*).[50]

Here, Shāfiʿī, much more so than Khaṣṣāf, sets guidelines for accepting advice: Advice must be based on binding transmission; law must be derived from authenticated sources; and analogy must be based on scriptural text. (In contrast, Khaṣṣāf's description of the necessity of judicial consultation is noticeably free of such guidelines.) The primacy of text is highlighted in Shāfiʿī's understanding of the generation of law—a point that is crucial to understanding his legal methodology more generally. His emphasis on textualism over rationalism or equity (*istiḥsān*) was also a common basis of critique from Shāfiʿī and among adherents of his school against Ḥanafīs.

Significantly, Shāfiʿī insists that neither the judge nor the jurisconsult is to engage in "judicial activism"—meaning here unconstrained judicial law-making—which for him risks violating or replacing revelation. This rejection of judicial activism is in line with his understanding of legal theory, and juristic reasoning in particular, whereby he argues for a more text-based approach to law. While Shāfiʿī begins the section with "I recommend (*uḥibbu*)," he finishes it with "I require him (*amartuh*)."[51] Shāfiʿī thereby shifts from recommendation to obligation over the course of his discussion of the role of the jurisconsult.[52] More precisely, Shāfiʿī seems to be positioning the status of judicial consultation *between* recommendation and binding command. Shāfiʿī law therefore conceived of the jurisconsult not only as a guide to the judge, but also as a source of constraint upon him. Shāfiʿī feared that in cases not settled by text, consensus, or analogy, the judge himself might create religious law (or, as we saw in Shāfiʿī's formulation above, "*yusharriʿ fī al-dīn*"). The jurisconsult serves to reduce the possibility of this kind of judicial activism and can therefore be a force of judicial constraint.

Normatively, the function of judicial consultation is tightly connected to a methodology for deriving Islamic law. The methodology

---

50 Shāfiʿī, *Kitāb al-umm*, 6:219.

51 Ibid. Shāfiʿī also uses the phrase "I recommend" with reference to the Qurʾānic *shūrā* verse. See Shāfiʿī, *Kitāb al-umm*, 7:86; Badry, *Die zeitgenössische Diskussion*, 94; and Zafar Ishaq Ansari, "Islamic Juristic Theology before Šāfiʿī: A Semantic Analysis with Special Reference to Kūfa," *Arabica* 19 (1972): 255–300, 296, where Ansari refers to the pre-Shāfiʿī use of the formula *aḥabbu ilayya/ilaynā* (recommended/preferred) instead of *mandūb* (recommended).

52 Irene Schneider also argues that Shāfiʿī himself and the later Shāfiʿī jurist Māwardī (d. 450/1058) speak of consultation as partly recommended and partly obligatory; but she also notes that it was regarded exclusively as an obligation. See Schneider, *Das Bild des Richters*, 193, 223. On Shāfiʿī potentially considering consultation a recommendation only, see Badry, *Die zeitgenössische Diskussion*, 93–94. On the normative character of judicial consultation and Shāfiʿī's ambivalent wording as an example of the complex nature of authority, see generally Samour, *Judge and Jurisconsult*, 140–47, 161–64.

of Islamic jurisprudence depicts the jurisconsult as a guide or constraint on the judge.[53] The jurisconsult's role was to guide the judge (especially for Ḥanafīs), but also to restrain him given the subjectivity of adjudication (especially for Shāfiʿīs). Nevertheless, in both conceptions, the autonomy of the judge was to remain intact, despite the jurisconsult's authority. In fact, failure to consult in the process of reaching a legal decision was not a reason for revision or annulment, and a judgment issued without prior judicial consultation was still regarded as valid.[54]

Judicial Encounters: Cooperation, Confrontation, Cooptation

I will now complement the above normative constructions of judicial consultation with historical encounters between the judge and the jurisconsult. The normative discussion above highlighted the role of the jurisconsult as a guide versus as a source of constraint. In the historical discussion below, I will organize instances of encounters between judge and jurisconsult according to the themes of cooperation, confrontation, and cooptation.

Cooperation

When Bakkār b. Qutayba was appointed judge by the ʿAbbāsid caliph al-Mutawakkil in 246/860 and sent from Basra in Iraq to Egypt to become a judge there,[55] he researched potential local jurisconsults in advance by asking the following of his judicial predecessor Muḥammad b. Abī Layth:

> "I am a stranger, and you have gotten to know the lands [in Egypt], so advise me on whom I can consult (*ushāwiruh*) and whom I can trust." Muḥammad b. Abī Layth mentioned two men: Yūnus b. ʿAbd al-Aʿlā and Mūsā b. ʿAbd al-Raḥmān b. al-Qāsim.[56]

The sources record that Judge Bakkār requested both men's counsel and

53 The phrasing "guide or constraint" is taken from Duncan Kennedy, who explores the rule of law as guide for or constraint upon the contemporary American judge. He posits that the judge is, paradoxically, free and bound simultaneously. See Duncan Kennedy, "Judicial Ideology," *Utah Law Review* 3 (1996): 785–825, esp. 816; and Duncan Kennedy, "Freedom and Constraint in Adjudication: A Critical Phenomenology," *Journal of Legal Education* 36 (1986): 518–62.

54 The possibility of judicial review was contingent upon the authoritative texts being violated. See Shāfiʿī, *Kitāb al-umm*, 6:220; and, more generally, David S. Powers, "On Judicial Review in Islamic Law," *Law and Society Review* 26 (1992): 315–41.

55 Kindī, *Kitāb al-Wulāt*, 477.

56 Ibid., 506. The chronicle itself states that the authenticity of this statement is doubtful, as Muḥammad b. Abī Layth had left Egypt in 241, five years before al-Bakkār had arrived in Egypt. See ibid., 507. But whether the new and the old *qāḍī* really met in Gaza, and whether Bakkār really asked for a jurisconsult, is only of secondary importance. The fact that Yūnus did in fact advise Bakkār in ongoing litigation does not seem to be disputed.

accepted each in ongoing judicial affairs.[57]

Judge Bakkār's choice of jurisconsults seemed to have been based on whom he believed knew the local law and customs and whom he believed he could trust. In general, trust (*thiqa*) between judge and jurisconsult seems to have been an important criterion for the judge to choose the jurisconsult.[58]

Digging into the biographical, educational, and intellectual background of the persons involved, it becomes even clearer why Bakkār, who was from Iraq and a renowned scholar adhering to the Ḥanafī school, would have benefited from the advice of Yūnus b. ʿAbd al-Aʿlā and ʿAbd al-Raḥmān b. al-Qāsim in Egypt. There are three reasons: First, both were legal scholars; second, both were locals of Egypt; and third, both were particularly knowledgeable in Mālikī law and thereby represented the locally dominant legal school.[59] Judicial consultation from two Mālikī scholars would allow judge Bakkār to complement his own legal knowledge base, which was founded in Ḥanafī and Baṣran law.

Consider the following example. Cases of dispute between Ḥanafī judges and Mālikī jurisconsults show that, regarding cases of *waqf* (endowments), in particular, Ḥanafī-Mālikī differences could prove very

57 Bakkār solicited Mālikī jurisconsult Yūnus's advice in a famous inheritance case that went back and forth between Ḥanafī and Mālikī judges over generations, as well as in a number of unspecified cases. This inheritance case became known as the "house of the elephant" and is treated in part here, as well as being revisited as a case of appeal later in the text. See ibid., 472–75, 502. See also Ibn Ḥajar, *Rafʿ al-iṣr*, 124, in Kindī, *The Governors and Judges of Egypt*, ed. and trans. Rhuvon Guest (Leiden: Brill, 1912), 501–614. For a French translation of Ibn Ḥajar's treatment of this case, see Mathieu Tillier, *Vies des cadis de Miṣr, 237/851-366/976: extrait du Rafʿ al-iṣr ʿan quḍāt Miṣr d'Ibn Ḥağar al-ʿAsqalānī* (Cairo: Institut français d'archéologie orientale, 2002), 51.

58 Often, when judges arrived at a city to which they were newly appointed, they requested assistance on requesting advice from people they knew they could trust. See, for example, Wakīʿ, *Akhbār al-quḍāt*, 3:130; and Tillier, *Les Cadis*, 399–400. Later, the importance of trust as a criterion for choosing consults increased, especially in the political realm. See Badry, *Die zeitgenössische Diskussion*, 145, although she does not provide further references. It was not considered necessary for the questioner to assess a potential *muftī's* scholarly reputation himself. Instead he based his choice on publicly-available information regarding not only the individual's qualifications in terms of knowledge or teaching, but specifically regarding *fatwā*-giving. Researching and evaluating such information was not discussed as a required preparatory step before approaching a jurisconsult, since *muftī*s were typically well-known within their local communities. See Muhammad Khalid Masud, Brinckley Messick, and David S. Powers, eds., *Islamic Legal Interpretation: Muftis and their Fatwas* (Cambridge, Mass.: Harvard University Press, 1996), 21.

59 Yūnus b. ʿAbd al-Aʿlā (d. 264/879) was an expert in *ḥadīth* and a Mālikī jurist who taught Mālik's seminal legal work *al-Muwaṭṭaʾ* in Egypt. See Ibn al-Nadīm b. Isḥāq (d. ca. 380/990), *al-Fihrist* (Beirut: Dar al-Maʿrifa, 1978), 234; Nawawī (d. 676/1271), *Tahdhīb al-asmāʾ waʾl-lughāt* (Cairo: Idārat al-Ṭibāʿa al-Munīriyya, 1927), 2:284; and Christopher Melchert, *The Formation of the Sunni Schools of Law, 9th-10th Centuries C.E.* (Leiden: Brill 1997), 80–81, 191. ʿAbd al-Raḥmān b. al-Qāsim (d. 191/806) was a disciple of Mālik b. Anas who spread Mālikī teachings in Egypt and the Maghreb. See Qāḍī ʿIyāḍ (d. 544/1149), *Tartīb al-madārik wa-taqrīb al-masālik li-maʿrifat aʿlām madhhab Mālik*, ed. Aḥmad Bakīr Maḥmūd (Beirut: Maktabat al-Ḥayāt, 1967), 3:245.

sensitive.[60] After all, the law of *waqf* addressed property related to the public welfare and well-being of a city, making protest against Ḥanafī *qāḍīs* adjudicating in Mālikī Egypt common.[61] Take, for instance, judge Ismāʿīl b. al-Yasāʿ, the first Iraqi and first Ḥanafī *qāḍī* of Egypt,[62] who was reproached by the famous jurisconsult Layth b. Saʿd (d. 175/791)—a student of Mālik b. Anas—"for not protecting the property of Muslims in support of endowments,"[63] and who got the caliph to remove the judge Ismāʿīl from office in Egypt. In this case, questions of endowment property (*waqf*), law school affiliation (here, the Ḥanafī-Mālikī divide), and the dynamics between center and province (Iraq and Egypt) are key to understanding how legal personae at court constructed authority and legitimacy vis-à-vis one another.

Moreover, these same questions are key to showing how such encounters could turn into critique as Mālikī scholars in Egypt confronted Ḥanafī adjudication whenever it targeted the very foundations of the economic order. This is a critique of adjudication addressing judicial activism—meaning the willingness to change or evolve the law in ways that upset existing patterns of economic and social advantage.[64]

Judge Bakkār, in all likelihood, anticipated this kind of critique and reached out to local legal scholars to consult with them, that is, as a means to initiate and consolidate cooperation between judge and jurisconsults across acute divides of school and geography. This consultation must have led to successful adjudication, because Bakkār served as judge for twenty-four years—a long period by any standard.

Confrontation

Consultation did not always result in cooperation. Instead, it could lead to confrontation between judges and jurisconsults. The following example shows how judges and jurisconsults fought over patterns of social ordering. Judge Khālid b. Ṭāliq was appointed judge in Basra under the reign of the third ʿAbbāsid caliph, al-Mahdī.[65] This case involved a group of jurisconsults who first watched and recorded the mistakes of the judge, then collectively

60 Al-Khaṭīb al-Baghdādī, Abū Bakr Aḥmad b. ʿAlī (d. 463/1072), *Ta'rīkh Baghdād, aw Madīnat al-Salām* (Cairo: Maktabat al-Khānjī, 1931) 14:282; and Kindī, *Kitāb al-Wulāt*, 371–73, 390–92.

61 Al-Khaṭīb al-Baghdādī, *Ta'rīkh Baghdād*, 14:282; and Kindī, *Kitāb al-Wulāt*, 371–73, 390–92.

62 Kindī, *Kitāb al-Wulāt*, 371–73; see also Tsafrir, *History of an Islamic School of Law*, 96.

63 Kindī, *Kitāb al-Wulāt*, 372.

64 See Duncan Kennedy, "Toward an Historical Understanding of Legal Consciousness: The Case of Classical Legal Thought in America, 1850-1940," *Research in Law and Sociology* 3 (1980): 3–24, 5.

65 Khalīfa b. Khayyāṭ al-ʿUṣfurī (d. 240/854), *Ta'rīkh*, ed. Suhayl Zakkār (Damascus: n.p., 1967-8), 2:289; and Wakīʿ, *Akhbār al-quḍāt*, 2:123.

moved to have him removed from his position. In this case, their criticism was specifically directed at Judge Khālid's application of the law of witness testimony—namely, its application to questions of the necessary number and trustworthiness of witnesses needed to provide valid evidence or the criteria necessary for a valid agent (*wakīl*) to appear in court on behalf of a litigant in case of the latter's sickness.[66] In another case, the facts were laid out as follows:

> One of the examples they have in their records [against him] is that one known witness came to his court along with three witnesses whom he [the judge] did not know. One witness said: The one witness was considered sound, and the three [unknown] witnesses replaced one [trustworthy] witness. He [the judge] then issued the judgment based on their testimony.[67]

Although at the time this case was decided, there was still diversity and uncertainty on questions surrounding the law of testimony,[68] the jurisconsults' critique of the judge functioned as a constraint on the judiciary. Through it, they attempted to ensure the "correct" application of the Islamic law of testimony as they understood it (possibly as determined by their respective school affiliations). The jurisconsults constrained the judge through critique, that is, by "watching out for infractions and slips," and thus illustrated the rivalry and checks that could exist between local jurists and judges.[69]

The jurisconsults' opinions constituted critique because the Islamic law of testimony determined who was or was not considered a trustworthy witness, and deviations from it could target and disturb the hierarchical pattern of social relations.[70] In this case, the jurisconsults' confrontation with the judge had dire consequences for him: their critique eventually led to the caliph removing the judge from office. The jurisconsults' critique could thus become a serious threat to the position of the judge.

66 Wakīʿ, *Akhbār al-quḍāt*, 2:128.

67 Ibid., 2:127.

68 See Ibn Ḥajar, *Rafʿ al-iṣr*, 127, in Kindī, *Kitāb al-Wulāt*, 388; Wakīʿ, *Akhbār al-quḍāt*, 1:146, 293, 331; 2:11, 276, 416; 3:117; and Muhammad Khalid Masud, "A Study of Wakīʿ's (d. 306/917) *Akhbār al-Quḍāt*," in *The Law Applied: Contextualizing the Islamic Shariʿa*, eds. Peri Bearman, Wolfhart Heinrichs, and Bernhard G. Weiss (London: I.B. Tauris, 2008), 116–27, esp. 123.

69 H.A.R. Gibb and Harold Bowen, *Islamic Society and the West: Islamic Society in the Eighteenth Century*, 2nd ed. (London: Oxford University Press, 1957), 122.

70 On the case of the Ḥanafī *qāḍī* Mazrūq being criticized by Egyptian jurisconsults for introducing legal "innovations" into the field of testimony law, refusing the testimony of a person who attended an evening party where frivolous songs were sung, and thereby upsetting Egyptian nobility, see Ibn Ḥajar, *Rafʿ al-iṣr*, 127, in Kindī, *Kitāb al-Wulāt*, 388. The judge changed the laws of testimony regarding who could be a credible witness at court, thereby disrupting the local social order, and was much criticized for it by the local jurisconsults.

What emerges from these two historical cases is that judicial consultation was not only a theoretical topic in normative juristic writings, but also played a role in real struggles of authority, legitimacy, and power between legal personae. In fact, I argue that judicial consultation creates space for critique of adjudication, and that this critique could allow an extrajudicial authority to cooperate with or to confront a judge, and to complement or to criticize his findings. Where legal options were not prescribed by text, jurisconsults were willing to confront (and even threaten) a judge to have their say in adjudication.

Cooptation

To what extent did consultation-as-critique not only allow for cooperation or confrontation, but also sometimes effectively function as cooptation?

Take the example of the Medinan Abū al-Bakhtarī (d. 192/807) who, when he was appointed judge in Medina, was given a list of twenty-seven jurisconsults to assist him in adjudication.[71] It remains unclear by whom he was given the list of names. Judge Abū al-Bakhtarī requested to see all the jurisconsults (*mushīrīn*), and they came to see him. The next day, the judge chose seven of them.[72] While this is not a case of the judge having been unfamiliar with local legal knowledge (with both judge and jurisconsults from Medina), it rather suggests that cooptation worked in the following way: Jurisconsults would be incorporated into the adjudicative system and bestowed with authority over their judicial colleagues *without* even a formalized procedure.

It is important to note that courts in the eastern Islamic world were ordinarily constituted as single-*qāḍī* courts. For most of Islamic legal history, the existence of a single judge was the rule, rather than there being an institutionalized bench of judges.[73] Critique leading to cooptation

71 Wakīʿ, *Akhbār al-quḍāt*, 1:247.

72 Ibid.; Masud, "The Study of Wakīʿ's Akhbār al-Quḍāt," 121.

73 Collective consultation (or the principle of collegiality, *Kollegialitätsprinzip*) historically emerged as part of the shift from single-judge courts to judicial benches, especially with regard to criminal law. On the debate over the single-judge court versus the bench in the *Reichsjustizgesetze* in Germany, see Wilfried Küper, *Die Richteridee der Strafprozessordnung und ihre geschichtlichen Grundlagen* (Berlin: de Gruyter, 1967), 305–12. The history of judicial benches in the United States was also related to criminal offenses and started in the seventeenth century. See Susan C. Towne, "The Historical Origins of Bench Trial for Serious Crime," *The American Journal of Legal History* 26, no. 2 (1982): 123–59. On the principle of collegiality as a way to control judicial arbitrariness, see Regina Ogorek, *Richterkönig oder Subsumtionsautomat? Zur Justiztheorie im 19. Jahrhundert* (Frankfurt: V. Klostermann, 1986), reprinted in Regina Ogorek, *Aufklärung über Justiz* (Frankfurt: Klostermann, 2008) 2:153, 333–34.

On the advantages and disadvantages of the single judge versus the bench, see Heike Jung, *Richterbilder: Ein interkultureller Vergleich* (Baden-Baden: Helbing and Lichtenhahn, 2006),

would then be an outcome of the relative strength of coopting judges over a coopted group of jurisconsults. The degree of alignment of their interests in effecting adjudication was typically high, and the vigor with which the jurisconsults were prepared to pursue those interests to affect adjudication was striking, too. All this speaks for cooptation as an effect, not necessarily by design. Consultation then could be, in effect, cooptation, even though jurisconsults might not have willingly agreed to be coopted.

The relationship between judge and jurisconsult could proceed differently depending on social and institutional circumstances. On the one hand, a judge soliciting consultation could help win over the solicited jurisconsults to the judge's cause. When a judge asked a jurisconsult for advice, and, even more so, when he heeded that advice, the process could improve the social standing of the jurisconsult. On the other hand, by consulting certain jurisconsults, the judge could also shield himself from the censure of other jurisconsults who may have disagreed with his decision. This function of cooptation led to a strengthening of the role of the advice-seeking judge, and, sometimes, I argue, to a joint identity of judge and jurisconsult among the legal elite.

Advice-seeking could also be a way of calling for reliability and loyalty. Being able to rely upon the support of jurisconsults would have been particularly important to a judge when adjudicating delicate topics, as the judgment would need to be accepted by the population. Judicial consultation thus also provided extrajudicial validation of adjudication, securing legitimacy when cases were legally, or possibly politically, controversial. This broader community support, in turn, helped ensure peace through justice, which was necessary for the judge to remain in office. Yet, if a judge did not seek the advice of jurisconsults, he risked inciting their opposition, and, eventually, possibly motivating them to call for his removal, as in the case of Judge Khālid above.

The fact that judicial consultation was not institutionalized, as it was in Muslim Spain, and was instead practiced *ad hoc* actually contributed to the potential for cooptation. The choice of whom to consult was not predetermined, and therefore a large number of potential jurisconsults could be integrated into the informal system.[74] In principle, a judge could solicit the opinion of *anyone* qualified to exercise legal reasoning (*ijtihād*). In fact, the process by which judges could choose to request the advice of jurisconsults most likely to offer convenient opinions might be called

---

90; Thierry Le Bars,"Juge unique/Collégialité," in Loïc Cadiet, *Dictionnaire de la Justice* (Paris: Presses Universitaires de France, 2004), 683–85, 683; and Carl Schmitt, *Gesetz und Urteil: Eine Untersuchung zum Problem der Rechtspraxis*, 2nd ed. (Munich: Beck, 1968), 72–75.

74 Similarly, with respect to the Prophet's flexible (rather than rigid) circle of consultants, see Badry, *Die zeitgenössische Diskussion*, 72.

"jurisconsult forum shopping." Being able to request counsel at any time, rather than having to return to an always-present advisory committee, proved useful in preventing immanent dissent.[75] Instead, anyone whom the judge did not wish to have as his critic, or who could endanger the judge's socio-political position, could be incorporated into the judicial decision-making process, as the case of Judge Bakkār shows.

CONCLUSION

Judicial consultation served as a mechanism by which the authority of different legal personae at court was created, negotiated, and reinforced—as well as a mechanism by which critique was enacted or absorbed. I have argued that judicial consultation ensured that legal scholars had a say in adjudication through a framework of joint adjudication. In other words, the judge was not the only one to comment on or determine the law at court. Not only could the jurisconsults critically augment or even undermine the power of the judge, but they could also steer the course of adjudication. The jurisconsults' critique provided an important means by which to share the judge's burden of adjudication, and it was sometimes instrumental in regulating, ordering, and potentially controlling adjudication. At the very least, judicial critique through consultation ensured the existence of alternatives at court.

Ultimately, judicial consultation is a testament to the fact that judges and jurists alike, possess an acute sensitivity for uncertainty in Islamic law, and that critique of those *on* the bench by those *off* the bench was considered necessary, even as it was also feared. In response to this fear, the flexibility to choose from among a broad community of potential jurisconsults functioned as a means of integrating and binding extrajudicial legal personae to the judicial system. The texts of the early ʿAbbāsid period provide narratives on key moments in Islamic judicial history to begin building a genealogy of judicial critique for Islamic legal history.

75 Ibid., 71.

PART TWO:
Section Introduction

Concepts of Justice in the ʿAbbāsid East

Intisar A. Rabb
Harvard Law School
&
Abigail Krasner Balbale
*Bard Graduate Center**

This section explores issues of language, interpretation, and authority over early Islamic law in three chapters that address themes connecting the use of religious sources to the construction of social and political institutions, as well as to the conceptions of courts and procedures within them; and it explores how each changes over time. Roy Mottahedeh was a pioneer of this method, providing a model in his *Loyalty and Leadership* for the social-historical use of traditionally religious sources. Here, Mahmood Kooria, Christian Lange, and Louise Marlow follow that method in their discussions of the historical development of the relationship between Islamic law and courts, between Arabic and non-Arabic languages, and between political-legal and divine authority.

Mahmood Kooria begins by placing emphasis on the ways in which *language* intersects with questions of law and legal authority. He focuses on early rules governing the use of foreign languages, according to which the language of Islamic courts was restricted to Arabic. The founder of the school of law promoting this view was Muḥammad b. Idrīs al-Shāfiʿī (d. 204/820), who taught that a *qāḍī* should only accept cases presented to him in Arabic. If the plaintiff was a non-Arab and incapable of expressing himself in Arabic, then the *qāḍī* was to accept his case only if his statements

*The editors gratefully acknowledge the significant contributions that Baber Johansen made to this section introduction.

were translated into Arabic by two trustworthy witnesses. The translation was meant to ensure that any petitioner presented cases in a language whose terms and legal effects are known to the *qāḍī*. Moreover, in Shāfiʿī's view, the translation counts as testimony because it gives Arabic form and effect to legal claims.

Tellingly, Shāfiʿī's rule was not static. Kooria follows the development of the doctrine requiring translation-into-Arabic in court from third/ninth-century Egypt to fifth/eleventh-century Khurāsān and Transoxania until Imām al-Ḥaramayn al-Juwaynī (d. 478/1085), one of the most important Shāfiʿī jurists, abandoned the doctrine of his school's founder. Juwaynī rejected the notion that translation counts as testimony, or that translator is a witness. Instead, Juwaynī saw it as acceptable for a judge to interpret foreign languages according to their own knowledge. Juwaynī's position became the accepted norm among sixth/twelfth-century Shāfiʿīs—a development that Kooria tries to explain by reference to Ibn al-Muqaffaʿ's (d. *ca.* 139/757) teaching that second/eighth-century authorities accepted allegorical interpretations of Sanskrit and Persian literature translated into Arabic. It seems that the political and religious status of the Persian language in eleventh- and twelfth-century Transoxania and Khurāsān may be another explanatory factor. Likely on this basis, we see a similar discussion in the Ḥanafī literature of these regions and periods. The famous Transoxanian jurist Shams al-Dīn al-Sarakhsī (d. 483/1090) also addresses the question of the interpretation of Persian claims in legal documents. After quoting the positions of the founders of the Ḥanafī school, he rejects all of them, saying: "But we say, we know our language better than they do." He adds that Persian terms have clear meanings and legal effects, which non-Persians normally do not understand.[1] With his treatment of the varied scholar's changes to rules about language in the courts over time, Kooria comes full circle on the intersection of language and law—echoing some of the controversies that first arose in earlier *shuʿūbiyya* debates that Roy Mottahedeh colorfully discussed in another context.

Christian Lange's chapter examines the proper *interpretation* of the concept of the divine Judge who decides on the punishment or reward of acts on Judgment Day, as a model for the formalized procedures in courts presided over by ordinary judges on earth. He convincingly argues that the language of Islamic judicial procedure is integrated into God's presentation of justice on Judgment Day. All parties are present. Angels act as witnesses. The divine Judge may rule according to his own knowledge. Using references to the spoken and written word, Lange shows how the evidence that takes

1 Shams al-Aʾimma al-Sarakhsī, *Mabsūṭ*, ed. Abū ʿAbd Allāh Muḥammad Ḥasan Ismāʿīl al-Shāfiʿī (Beirut: Dār al-Kutub al-ʿIlmiyya, 2001), 4:144–45.

the form of each—together with the knowledge of the divine Judge—all occupy a place in judicial procedure, both human and divine.

Has the concept of the Day of Judgment exerted its influence on the power of the human judge to imitate the divine example? "Yes," Lange answers, even though he recognizes that the analogy is not perfect. Accordingly, Lange identifies theologically problematic aspects of the analogy that Muslim scholars themselves discussed when analogizing divine justice to human justice. He also identifies potential social and political consequences of applying divine conceptions of justice to earthly arenas. One example is the judge-defined punishment of immolation that does not normally appear in the list of divinely-ordered punishments to be imposed by the *qāḍī*. Another example is the episode in which Ibn ʿAqīl (d. 513/1119), the chief of the Ḥanbalī school in Baghdad, sentenced an Ismāʿīlī man to death and compared his decision to God's sentencing sinners to hell. In another context, Ibn ʿAqīl also invoked a religious-political model, wherein the caliph ʿAlī was reported to have burned heretics in the trenches.[2] In sum, Lange vividly describes ways in which any judge who could not base his decisions on the norms of Islamic law invoked political or divine models in order to justify their deviations from the norm.

Louise Marlow examines these same themes with "Mirrors for Princes" literature as her sources, and with a focus on the *authority* over different aspects of law. She describes how Ibn al-Muqaffaʿ, the ʿAbbāsid vizier that Kooria earlier discussed, sought to solve problems of indeterminacy and questionable legal authority by describing the structure of Islamic law as being constituted by two different spheres. The first sphere admitted no human interpretation and had norms entirely restricted to divine authority. This was the sphere for judges and jurists to preside over. The second sphere made political authorities responsible for all legally permissible interpretations of the law. Following this scheme, Ibn al-Muqaffaʿ sought to authorize the caliph to provide interpretations of Islamic law whenever needed. He clearly hoped to avoid the indeterminacies created by dissent among legal experts by assigning a clear priority for the caliph's decisions. Marlow points out that this attempt manifests reflexively in "the way in which some later mirror-writers encouraged their royal patrons to equip themselves with the knowledge necessary for intervention in the religious-legal realm."

But this concept is not static either. By the time the leading Shāfiʿī judge and jurist, Māwardī (d. 450/1058), enters the scene, he determines the ruler's main contribution to be outside of the province of defining law.

2 Georges Makdisi, *Ibn ʿAqil: Religion and Culture in Classical Islam* (Edinburgh: Edinburgh University Press, 1997), 160.

That is, he sees the political authorities' area of authority to lie not in the construction of a rational law but rather in the appointment of good judges for his subjects. This change demonstrates that, by Māwardī's time, the distance between the political and legal authority has become even more evident and even more important.

Comparing the three chapters, one sees that they all discuss how different aspects of language, interpretation, and authority in courts were key to judicial procedure and how they changed over time. Kooria shows the growing readiness of the political and legal authorities to admit a pluralism as to which *language* in political, religious, and legal institutions was acceptable. Lange compares the role of the written and the spoken word in human courts and in God's decisions on Judgment Day, showing how human imagination of law and justice are shaped by the changing role that the *qāḍī*'s changing interpretations played in Muslim courts and societies. And Marlow shows the growing distance between political and legal rulers based on changing conceptions of political and legal authority over time.

Chapter Five

Words of *ʿAjam* in the World of Arab: Translation and Translator in Early Islamic Judicial Procedure

Mahmood Kooria*
Leiden University

Within a hundred years of the death of the Prophet Muḥammad, the lands under Islamic rule had grown to triple the size of the Arabian Peninsula. The new abode of Islam, from the shorelines of the Atlantic to the Indian subcontinent, incorporated a substantial non-Arab population. Although Arabic developed as a *lingua franca* across the Islamic world, it never came to be the sole medium of communication in the everyday lives of its new subjects. This reality created a procedural predicament for Muslim jurists who had been setting new rules and regulations based on Islamic scriptures and socio-cultural norms beginning in the second/eighth century. Simultaneously, non-Arab Muslims began to rule over their own lands and they constituted the vast majority of the population under Islamic rule by the third/ninth century. Anxieties over the continued primacy of the Arabic language are rife in legal and literary sources, and yet discussions of language are rare in Islamic legal historiography.

This is not to overlook the voluminous writings on the role of non-Arabs in the development of Islamic law. Scholars have argued that non-Arab legal traditions such as Hellenistic, Roman Byzantine, provincial, and Persian Sassanian laws, together with the Jewish Talmudic and Christian canon laws, had contributed to the making of Islamic law through contributions by recent converts.[1] Ulrike Mitter and Harald Motzki questioned this long-

---

*I am thankful to Abigail Balbale (Bard Graduate Center), Gladys Frantz-Murphy (Regis University), Intisar Rabb (Harvard University), two anonymous reviewers, and participants of the conference on "Courts and Judicial Procedure in Early Islamic Law" for their comments and suggestions on earlier versions of this paper.

1 For a survey of earlier scholarship along these lines together with a new perspective, See Patricia Crone, *Roman, Provincial and Islamic Law: The Origins of the Islamic Patronate*

existing argument of non-Arab dominance and suggested that indeed the Arabs had an equal or even dominant role in the development of Islamic law.[2] The statistical analysis of Monique Bernards and John Nawas on the Arab and non-Arab ratio in biographical entries on jurists who lived up to 400/1010 also has validated this argument.[3] I do not enter into such debates, except to state that even the scholars who emphasized the non-Arab dominance or contributions in the making of Islamic law have hardly addressed the question of language as a predicament in judicial procedures as well as in legal thought. In this respect, the historiography furthermore disappoints for a very simple fact that most of the non-Arab *mawālī* about whom these scholars talk in detail were first, second, third, or even fourth generation non-Arabs who were born and brought up in such Arab regions as Mecca, Medina, and Yemen. Hence, language rarely posed a problem in their communications, and they did not have to depend on a translator for their legalistic practices or formulations.[4] This was not the case for the people who lacked in-depth knowledge of Arabic or for those who lived in a region whose majority did not speak the language.

In the long-running expansion of Islamic polities from the early seventh century until the Mongol invasions in the thirteenth century, the new converts and other new subjects in "foreign" lands expected Islamic governors and judges to arbitrate in their everyday problems, and the Muslim judges commonly did adjudicate issues relating to contracts, inheritance, and other daily disputes.[5] More expansion thus meant more people and more diverse problems for jurists to encounter. The new subjects were not merely one part of the large dominion of Islam; rather

---

(Cambridge: Cambridge University Press, 1987); and Joseph Schacht, "Foreign Elements in Islamic Law," *Journal of Comparative Legislation and International Law* 32, nos. 3–4 (1950): 9–17. Neither has gone beyond the Middle East to look for the "foreign influences" on early Islamic law. Schacht's sensitivity to South Asian Islamic legal texts and translations can be found in his "On the Title of the *Fatāwā al-ʿĀlamgīriyya*," in *Iran and Islam: In Memory of the Late Vladimir Minorsky*, ed. C.E. Bosworth (Edinburgh: Edinburgh University Press, 1971), 475–78.

2 Harald Motzki, "The Role of Non-Arab Converts in the Development of Early Islamic Law," *Islamic Law and Society* 6, no. 3 (1999): 293–317; and Ulrike Mitter, "Problemen van het onderzoek naar ontleningen aan niet-Arabische rechtsstelsels in het ontstaan en de ontwikkeling van het Islamitisch recht," *Sharqiyyat* 9, no. 2 (1997): 107–23.

3 Monique Bernards and John Nawas, "The Geographical Distribution of Muslim Jurists during the First Four Centuries AH" *Islamic Law and Society* 10, no. 2 (2003): 168–81; cf. John Nawas, "The Emergence of *Fiqh* as a Distinct Discipline and the Ethnic Identity of the *Fuqahāʾ* in Early and Classical Islam," in *Studies in Arabic and Islam: Proceedings of the 19th Congress, Halle 1998*, ed. S. Leder, H. Kilpatrick, B. Martel-Thoumian and H. Schonig (Leuven: Peters, 2002), 491–99.

4 For a marginal discussion on the issue of translation in court proceedings, see Ron Shaham, *The Expert Witness in Islamic Courts: Medicine and Crafts in the Service of Law* (Chicago: University of Chicago Press, 2010), 39–40.

5 I translate the Arabic term *ʿajam* or *ʿajamī* as foreign (language or land) or foreigner (individual), by which I mean foreign to the Arabs.

they formed its majority. Even so, their access to Islamic courts was restricted through a number of different measures and regulations. From a few patchy references, we do know that even some of the non-Arab, non-Muslims preferred the Arabic-language Islamic courts over the existing local legal systems.[6]

An obvious question then is, if most Muslim judges and law-givers were Arabs, and many plaintiffs or defendants were non-Arabic speakers, did language stand as a barrier in judicial proceedings? In this chapter, I examine this problem: How did the expansion of the Islamic empire beyond the Arab realm influence Islamic judicial procedures? How did jurists address the issue of language in their discussions? To what extent did the "translator" stand as a legitimate intermediary between the Arabic-speaking judge and non-Arabic-speaking litigants? How did the notions of "translator" and "language" become more flexible in legal articulations as the lands of Islam expanded, thereby giving access to the courts to those who otherwise would have been excluded?

Since the existing historiography of Islamic law—much like the early "Arab" jurists themselves—limits itself to the juridical developments in the central Islamic lands, it tends to ignore issues relating to the non-Arab population of the peripheries. I explore how non-Arabic speech communities navigated the constraints of the new legal system by focusing on the issues of translation and language in judicial processes. Combining a host of primary sources, I show that initially Arab jurists were reluctant to allow languages other than Arabic in the court proceedings, and they theoretically denied access to non-Arabs without a Muslim free male translator. Arab jurists always stressed the primacy of Arabic (not just in its theological supremacy in Islam, but also as a valid language of law), and emphasized that the judge is obliged to initiate the proceedings only if non-Arabs come along with a translator. The debate over translation and translators spread across several generations of jurists, and the actual practices on the ground demonstrate that the translation both regulated and was shaped by judicial procedure and affected judicial outcomes.

In this regard I utilize two sorts of sources: legal manuals and non-legal historical materials. In the legal manuals, I focus on the Shāfiʿī texts as the changes of opinions found therein are very evident over time and the school had a wider appeal in the non-Arabic-speaking lands of Islam, including the Iranian, Indian, and Malay subcontinents before and after 1250 (roughly 650 AH). In the non-legal historical sources, I amass all sorts of contemporaneous sources relating to the non-Arabic lands of Islam up

6 For example, see Gladys Franz-Murphy, "The Reinstitution of Courts in Early Islamic Egypt," *Bulletin de la société archéologique d'Alexandrie* 47 (2003): 71–84.

to the end of the seventh/thirteenth century that deal with Islamic legal practices and the question of language. As the early legal histories of regions outside the central Islamic (Arab) heartlands remain largely understudied, I gather any available evidence on the theme from various languages and sources.

ONCE THE *ʿAJAM* APPEAR IN THE COURT

In the early phases of Islamic political expansion, *amīrs* (governors) appointed the *qāḍīs*. After the first century of Islam, judges were also appointed by caliphs, and by the fourth/tenth century, they served as deputies to the chief judge in Baghdad. Like the *amīrs*, the *qāḍīs* were mostly Arabs throughout much of the early history. If we look at the list of *qāḍī*-appointments in Egypt provided by Muḥammad al-Kindī (d. 350/961), all of them were Arabs and only a few non-Arab *mawālī* appear. The first *mawlā* to be appointed to the post was Isḥāq b. al-Furāt, who replaced Muḥammad b. al-Masrūq al-Kindī in 184/800 and a few more were appointed in the following decades and in the fourth/tenth century.[7] The historian Kindī prepared a book on the distinguished *mawālī* of Egypt entitled *Kitāb al-mawālī*, which itself was dedicated to Muḥammad b. Badr, a *mawlā* who held the judgeship between 324/936 and 330/942.[8] However, all these *mawālī*, as I mentioned above, were already well versed in Arabic and often knew no other languages but Arabic.

In such an Arab-dominated legal system, the functions and offices of the *qāḍī* in the newly conquered non-Arab lands often transcended boundaries of Islam and Arabic. It is beyond any doubt that the local population approached his court, despite the differences in religion, language, and/or ethnicity. We have several instances of non-Muslims and non-Arabs in the first/seventh and second/eighth centuries approaching Arabic-language Islamic courts. Non-Arabic-speaking Christians of Egypt preferred those courts over the existing local Greek and Coptic legal systems for a number of different reasons. The Islamic courts had a better enforcement mechanism than others, as we see in an episode as early as 91/709 during which the governor of Egypt, Qurra b. Sharīk, instructed the district official Zakariyā of Ishmūn to ensure justice for a Christian plaintiff

7 Abū ʿUmar Muḥammad b. Yūsuf al-Kindī, *The Governors and Judges of Egypt, or, Kitāb el-Umarāʾ (el wulāh) wa Kitāb el-Quḍāh*, trans. Arthur Rhuvon Guest (Leiden: Brill, 1912), 393. He says that even al-Shāfiʿī, whom we will meet below in detail, recommended Ibn al-Furāt to the judgeship by saying, "He chooses out of conflicting opinions, and he knows the contrarieties of earlier scholars" and "I have not seen anyone in Egypt more knowledgeable than Isḥāq b. al-Furāt on the contrarieties of people."

8 Guest, "Introduction," to Kindī, *Kitāb al-Umarāʾ*, 10.

who approached the former with a complaint of loan default by a borrower.[9]

Even so, language must have stood as a major hurdle in the proceedings as most Muslim judges were Arabs in contrast to their plaintiffs or defendants who did not know Arabic. The historiography generally is silent on this, although we have some fleeting references. In the fourth/tenth century, records of a contract of sale of residential property in which a Christian woman is involved reads that it was "read to her in Arabic and explained to her in the 'foreign' language: *quriʾa ʿalayhā biʾl-ʿArabiyya wa-fussira lahā biʾl-ʿajamiyya*."[10] The *fussira* in this sentence certainly connotes the translation process (*tarjama*) in which a certain official mediated between the two languages, and thus between the court and the litigants. In a number of Egyptian papyri documents, the plaintiffs or defendants were non-Arab non-Muslims, yet the documents themselves were written in Arabic and signed by registered Muslim witnesses from the second/eighth century onward.[11] Once we begin examining individuals who mediated between two languages and cultures, we have to deal with questions of their legal status, their religious and ethnic identity, and their involvement in the case. In most occasions, the translators were also witnesses, as we find in the papyri records.[12] Common-sense knowledge would suggest that a witness could not testify to the validity of a plaintiff's claims unless he or she knew the language. This complexity of translator-*cum*-witness lies at the heart of the Islamic juridical discussions on language and translation in courts.

But before exploring those complexities, let me take a detour to the Pancatantra stories from the Indian subcontinent, whose early renderings from Sanskrit to Pahlavi and then to Arabic offer unexpected light on the respective roles of translator and witness in early Islamic practice. The Pancatantra and its famous Arabic translation *Kalīla wa-Dimna* does not need any introduction, but to put it briefly: the text is a "mirror for princes" with moral philosophical teachings narrated through animal fables. It is known that there are many variations between the Indian and Arabic versions available today, and a major difference of interest to the present study is an interpolated section in the Arabic version on a court procedure against the protagonist Dimna (Damanaka in the Sanskrit version) for an act of treason he committed against the king and his friend.

This section is not found in the Sanskrit/Indian versions, and

9 Franz-Murphy, "The Reinstitution of Courts," 80–81.

10 Franz-Murphy, "A Comparison of Arabic and Earlier Egyptian Contract Formularies, Part I: The Arabic Contracts from Egypt (3rd/9th–5th/11th Centuries)," *Journal of Near Eastern Studies* 40, no. 3 (1981): 203–25, esp. 209–13.

11 Franz-Murphy, "A Comparison," 223; cf. Emile Tyan, *Histoire de l'organisation judicaire en pays de l'Islam* (Leiden: Brill, 1960), 236–52.

12 Franz-Murphy, "The Reinstitution of Courts;" Franz-Murphy, "A Comparison."

what is most striking to me is that its Arabic translation is done by Ibn al-Muqaffaʿ (d. *ca.* 139/757), the same scholar whom Islamic legal historians have called the first legal theorist of Islamic law.[13] A recent study has presented the translation of this part as being rather problematic, since he "confused the legal procedure" and intermixed Islamic legal concepts with Sassanian judicial practices.[14] It is quite possible that this translation reflects confusion, but the role of Ibn al-Muqaffaʿ suggests other possibilities that have been neglected. He had a distinct understanding of how Islamic law should work under the caliphal authority, believing in the discursive and interpretive components of law-making and judicial decisions, in contrast to his contemporary jurists who preferred religious law to be outside of governmental control. He emphasized these aspects in his *Risāla fī al-Ṣaḥāba*, a text that was not circulated widely in his time. Therefore, instead of seeing his potential additions to this episode of the Pancatantra as reflecting his confusion of Islamic law with Sassanian laws (such as the addition of a *qāḍī* along with an investigation committee and the king's participation in the trial), it is revealing to see them as his intentional interjections advocating for a better version of Islamic judicial procedure.

This discussion aside, what is even more interesting is a sub-story within the trial mentioned in this section, in which a foreign language and a few translators stand at the forefront. Toward the end of the legal procedure, the *qāḍī* finds himself at a crisis-point and suggests to Dimna that he could help himself by making a confession to eliminate "however small the doubt which remains in our minds" during the judicial examination.[15] Dimna refuses to do so by saying that he is surprised to see that the judge is not bound by the rules of equity and indeed that this is a trick of the judge to persecute him. He says that self-confession is disastrous to an accused person like him. In the ensuing conversation, Dimna brings in a story of a falconer who accuses his master's wife of adultery after she refused his love. To take revenge for the refusal, the falconer bought two parrots and taught one of them to say, "I saw the porter lying with my mistress in my

13 Mathieu Tillier, "Legal Knowledge and Local Practices under the Early ʿAbbāsids," in *History and Identity in the Eastern Mediterranean*, ed. Philip Wood (New York: Oxford University Press, 2013), 187–204; Joseph E. Lowry, "The First Islamic Legal Theory: Ibn al-Muqaffaʿ on Interpretation, Authority, and the Structure of the Law," *Journal of the American Oriental Society* 128, no. 1 (2008): 25–40; Charles Pellat, *Ibn al-Muqaffaʿ 'conseilleur' du calife* (Paris: G.P. Maisonneuve et Larose, 1976); and S. D. Goitein, "A Turning Point in the History of the Muslim State (Apropos of the *Kitāb al-ṣaḥāba* of Ibn al-Muqaffaʿ)," in *Studies in Islamic History and Institutions* (Leiden: Brill, 1968), 149–67.

14 Jany János, "The Origins of the Kalīlah wa-Dimnah: Reconsideration in the Light of Sasanian Legal History," *Journal of the Royal Asiatic Society* 22, no. 3–4 (2012): 505–18.

15 Bīdpāʾī, *Kalīla wa-Dimna* (Beirut: al-Maktabā al-Thaqāfiyya, n.d.), 84–85. Most of the quoted translations are from Wyndham Knatchbull, *Kalila and Dimna or the Fables of Bidpai* (Oxford: W. Baxter, 1819), 184–89.

master's bed" and the other to say, "I will not tell tales." He taught them these in a "foreign" language, that of Balkh, which could be Pashto, Bactrian, or "Indian" (as an early English translator puts it).[16] The parrots used to repeat these sentences all the time while none in the region understood it. After some months, a few friends from Balkh visited the nobleman and stayed with him. During their conversations, the talking parrots also became a point of discussion. The parrots were then brought in front of them, and the visitors were stunned to hear what the birds said. They hesitatingly translated it to their host and told him that they could not stay in such a house of ill fame. He begged them to talk more to the parrots in their language. They did so only to discover that they spoke nothing other than repeating the same sentences. Everyone was thus convinced of the wife's innocence and the trick of the falconer. The nobleman called him to give his testimonial and he confirmed what the parrots said. Upon hearing this, a hawk in his hand sprung at his face and plucked out his eyes with its claws.

This sub-story comes as a justification for Dimna to prove his point against the confession and false testimonials. What is striking to me is how a "foreign" language and its translators mediated different sets of problems, and thus cultures. This would have been a crucial point for Ibn al-Muqaffaʿ who not only was a legal theorist, but also a renowned translator of many Indian and Pahlavi texts in the early ʿAbbāsid period. In the story, the translators and witness are separate, but the whole question revolves around the correct and incorrect testimonial that a translator can verify. Immediately after the falconer's eyes were plucked out, the accused wife tells him, "You deserve this and it is a punishment from Allāh as you bore witness for what your eyes did not see." The story reflects then-contemporary conceptions of the status and functions of translators, witnesses, and judgment in eastern Islamic lands. According to this story, the translator's function paralleled that of witnesses, but it remained separate as it might in other legal traditions. This approach stands in sharp contrast to later attitudes toward the same questions. From the second/eighth to the fifth/eleventh centuries, the predominant Arab jurists' view was that translators were witnesses.

Among the Islamic legal texts written by Arab jurists on the questions of translator and language, one of the earliest direct engagements comes from Muḥammad b. Idrīs al-Shāfiʿī (d. 204/820) in his *Umm*. Although his discussion is rather short, he presents a very Arabic-centric view and presumes that the foreign complainant is familiar with the language of the *qāḍī* (which is Arabic). Even then, the judge is not obliged to listen to the litigation in un-fluent Arabic. He writes: "If a *qāḍī* is approached by an

16 Thomas North, trans., *Fables of Bidapai* (Edinburgh: Ballantyne, Hanson and Co., n.d.), 253.

ʿ*ajam* whose language is unfamiliar to him, then the foreigner's translation [into the language of the *qāḍī*] should not be accepted unless there are two trustworthy/upright (ʿ*adl*) witnesses who know that language without any doubts. If they do doubt, it should not be accepted from them either."[17] He also says that those who translate will be considered to be witnesses, and all the rules of a witness will be applied to them. The position of the translator thus becomes synonymous to a witness in his view, although he does not inform us if either of them *substitute* for the actual witnesses who otherwise are required.

In his articulation then, the actual witness does not play a role in the translation, and translators take over the role of the witnesses, whereas in the story above, Ibn al-Muqaffaʿ differentiates between the potential witness (the falconer), who is also capable of speaking the language, and the translators, who now give testimony not to what the parrots said, but to what they did not say. Ibn al-Muqaffaʿ hence does not give any credibility to the witness, and the translators become interpreters of the larger context. He does not intermix the witness with the translators; rather he questions the credibility of the witness despite him speaking the language.

Toward the end of the story it becomes clear that the witness is giving false testimony to what the "foreign plaintiffs" (the parrots) have said in accusing the wife, and his deception is exposed thanks to the translators. Through this story, Ibn al-Muqaffaʿ thus rejects the role of the witness in the translation process, in contrast to Shāfiʿī, who presumes that witnesses and translators should be identical with the same salient qualities. For Ibn al-Muqaffaʿ, the translation is more important than the witness, and he rejects the notion that the translator's qualities should be synonymous to that of a legitimate witness. The negation and differentiation of testimony from translation in ways that potentially simplify judicial procedure is crucial once we turn to later juristic positions, which also underestimate the importance of witnesses in translation. These elements also stand in opposition to Shāfiʿī's argument, in which he exhibits distrust for litigation conducted in a foreign language and for which he therefore requires additional attestations. In all these respects, the story is very enlightening even if the actual judicial procedures in formal court contexts might have been quite distinct.

We do not see Shāfiʿī's student Abū Ibrāhīm Ismāʿīl b. Yaḥyā al-Muzanī (d. 264/878) bringing in this discussion in his abridgement of the *Umm*, entitled *Mukhtaṣar al-Muzanī*. This text set the foundations for later Shāfiʿī legal discourses through a number of commentaries and super-

17 Muḥammad b. Idrīs al-Shāfiʿī, *al-Umm*, ed. Rifʿat Fawzī ʿAbd al-Muṭṭalib (Manṣūra: Dār al-Wafāʾ, 2001), 7:506.

commentaries.[18] In a way, this negligence means that Shāfiʿī's position remained unchallenged among his followers throughout the third/ninth and fourth/tenth centuries. In the fifth/eleventh century, however, we see Shāfiʿī scholars, especially the "eastern" jurists, taking up distinctive standpoints.

The approach of Shāfiʿī and the inattentive attitude of his students and followers like Muzanī for a long period must have stemmed from their Egyptian contexts between the late-second/eighth and fourth/tenth centuries. By the mid-second/eighth century, Egypt already had become largely Arabized. Kindī talks about certain processes of Arabization initiated by the earlier *qāḍīs*. ʿAbd al-Raḥmān b. ʿAbd Allāh al-ʿUmarī, who was appointed as the *qāḍī* of Egypt by Hārūn al-Rashīd in 185/801, following the aforesaid *mawlā*-judge Ibn al-Furāt, was approached by many clans asking him to recognize them as Arabs. The story of one particular clan called Ḥirs is very interesting, as they repeatedly bribed him with six thousand *dīnārs* to get their genealogy legally approved and connected to the Arab tribe of Ḥawtaka. After long negotiations, ʿUmarī approved them as Arabs—a decision that outraged many Arabs, who criticized him as a corrupt judge, since they believed that the Ḥirs were actually Coptic. But Hāshim b. Abī Bakr al-Bakrī, who took over the position from ʿUmarī, nullified this verdict by telling them, "Arabs do not need a certificate from a judge. If you were Arabs, no one would disprove you."[19] Relatedly, both ʿUmarī and Bakrī were "famous" wine-drinking *qāḍīs*, and Bakrī was known for not sitting for adjudication unless he consumed three glasses of wine. Kindī must have raised these tropes in their biographical entries to show how his informants questioned the validity of their judgments, including the one on Arab ethnicity.[20] However, these petitions reflect a larger tendency among the Egyptians of the time to claim an Arab ethnic ancestry, which would not have been possible unless they already were Arabized linguistically.

---

18 Ismāʿīl b. Yaḥyā al-Muzanī, *Mukhtaṣar al-Muzanī fī al-furūʿ al-Shāfiʿiyya*, ed. Muḥammad ʿAbd al-Qādir al-Shāhīn (Beirut: Dār al-Kutub al-ʿIlmiyya, 1998), 393–412.

19 Kindī, *Kitāb al-Umarāʾ*, 414.

20 Ibid., 416. On ʿUmarī, see ibid., 400–01. We should keep in mind that such remarks on wine-drinking before or after a judicial session reflect a common trope in judicial biographies of early Islamic history. Although such anecdotes may not have been taken literally by biographers or their informants, authors recording the stories might have used them along with remarks on bribery to impugn the decisions of such judges as non-upright. However, it also indicates that the practice of wine-drinking was widespread among Muslim scholars, intellectuals, judges and other elites of the time—contrary to what is believed generally today. For more details, see Shahab Ahmed, *What Is Islam? The Importance of Being Islamic* (Princeton: Princeton University Press, 2015), 57–71, 417–24. Also, compare this trope with discussions on having food before adjudication as good judicial etiquette, Maribel Fierro, "Joking Judges: A View from al-Andalus," Chapter 8 (this volume).

Mass conversions into Islam and the predominance of Arabic in communications had thus become the norm by the time Shāfiʿī and Muzanī wrote their works. Furthermore, in the Egyptian context *ʿajam* usually connoted a Christian population and the Coptic language—both of which had a rather limited reach by the early third/ninth century when the *Umm* by Shāfiʿī and the *Mukhtaṣar* by Muzanī were written and circulated.[21] Like the process of Islamization, the process of Arabization was both embraced and resisted by subject populations. Indeed, much of the Islamic world challenged the centrality of the Arabic language, instead of smoothly succumbing to the Arabization process as Egypt had done. Among the believing communities from al-Andalus to the Indian and Malay subcontinents, many rejected Arabic or transformed it via adaptation or vernacularization. And precisely for these reasons, the non-Arab jurists (by which I mean the jurists who were born, brought up, and/or found a successful career in foreign lands) began to play significant roles in asserting many non-Arab particularities of legal procedures, in which issues of language and translator received different treatments.[22]

TWO JURISTS AND TWO TRANSLATORS

Two Shāfiʿī authors from eleventh-century Khurāsān catch our attention with their distinctive attitudes towards "foreigners" and translators: Abū al-Ḥasan al-Māwardī (d. 450/1058) and Imām al-Ḥaramayn al-Juwaynī (d. 478/1085). The former built a successful career as a jurist and judge in Khurāsān, although he was born in Basra and grew up in Baghdad. The latter spent his entire life from childhood until death in Khurāsān, with an unexpected interruption of more than a decade when he was forced to go into exile in Mecca. Both jurists are renowned among traditional Shāfiʿīs as well as among Islamic legal historians for their wide-ranging contributions. In his *Adab al-qāḍī*, Māwardī dedicates a long discussion to the nuances of translation and translator in judicial proceedings. Citing the aforementioned standpoint of Shāfiʿī on the issue, he comes up with twenty-three multi-layered legal problems and possibilities.

He subdivides the issue into four major questions: the legal status of translation; whether the translator is a father or son of the litigant, or a woman; whether one litigant is a foreigner; and whether both plaintiff and

21 For example, see Muzanī's discussion on *ʿajamīs*' claim over the children born during their infidelity—Muzanī, *Mukhtaṣar*, 415. In addition to this, we should keep in mind that the once recurrent rebellions of the Coptic Christians were suppressed for last time in 217/832, marking thereafter the predominance of Islam in Egypt.

22 The "non-Arab jurists" here should not be confused with the existing legal historiographical identification of all *mawālī* as non-Arabs despite their birth, growth and entire life in the Arab lands.

defendant are foreigners.[23] The question of legal status—and whether the translation is witness-testimonial (*shahāda*) or a transmission (*khabar*)—is also a question of how many translators should be present if the judge does not understand the language.[24] Shāfiʿī says that translation is testimony and thus there must be two witnesses, whereas Abū Ḥanīfa (d. 150/767) says that it is only a transmission and hence one is sufficient. The latter suggests two rational justifications as evidence: first, if the transmission of *sharīʿa* by the Prophet Muḥammad is accepted despite being reported by a single person, then its translation is even more strongly regarded as acceptable; second, if the translation of a blind person is accepted but not his testimony, this norm should follow the rules of religious transmission in which his *ḥadīth*-transmission is accepted. Māwardī rebuts both of these arguments, and adds that translation, like testimony, is legitimation of an avowal (*tathbīt iqrār*) and requires independence and honesty. Thus it requires at least two people to confirm its accuracy.[25]

The next question, on the translation by blood-relatives of the litigant and by women is based on the previous argument. Hence, as the translation is testimony, Māwardī says that it will not be accepted from father or son. From women, it will be accepted only in matters in which her testimony is acceptable (such as *iqrār biʾl-amwāl* or in monetary lawsuits), and in such cases, it will be accepted from a man and two women. Although in the matters in which her testimony, and thus translation, is not accepted (such as *iqrār al-ḥudūd*, or offenses with fixed criminal penalties and marriage-related cases), there is a slightly different view that the translation can be accepted with the support of two trustworthy witnesses. However, with regard to cases of adultery, there should be four translators for each witness.[26]

If one of the two parties is a foreigner, two translators should provide their accounts in front of the judge on what she or he has said, and they should do it following the format of testimonial and not of transmission or report. Māwardī writes that some Shāfiʿīs have opined that they should give accounts in the form of a report and not as official testimony, but he refutes this view.[27] Once the account is given, "the judge should inform the Arabic-

---

23 ʿAlī b. Muḥammad al-Māwardī, *Adab al-Qāḍī*, ed. Muḥyī Hilāl al-Sarḥān (Baghdad: Maṭbaʿat al-Irshād, 1971), 1:695–700.

24 Ron Shaham, *Expert Witness*, 39–40.

25 Māwardī, *Adab al-qāḍī*, 1:695–97.

26 Ibid., 1:697–98.

27 He uses the term "some [or one] of our companions" (*baʿḍ aṣḥābinā*) and does not specify who they are. But similar discussions can be found in the work of ʿAbd al-Wāḥid b. Ismāʿīl al-Rūyānī (d. 502/1108), who also uses the phrase (*aṣḥābunā*: our companions). See his *Baḥr al-madhhab fī furūʿ madhhab al-Imām al-Shāfiʿī*, ed. Aḥmad ʿIzzū ʿInāya al-Dimashqī (Beirut: Dār Iḥyāʾ al-Turāth al-ʿArabī, 2002), 11:272.

speaking litigant [of the account] and hear his response."[28] Now, if both defendant and complainant are foreigners, can the same translators work for both parties? Māwardī relates this question to another debate among Shāfiʿīs on the permissibility of either of the two witnesses becoming an additional witness to the opposite party. He says that if it is permitted in such a case, then it would be permitted in translation too, otherwise it is not. Winding up the discussion, he says that the reverse translation—that is, translating the words of the judge—is purely a transmission and not testimony. Hence, one translator is sufficient for that purpose, even if he is a slave.[29]

Māwardī's elaborate discussions demonstrate how the issue of translation had gained central importance in his particular place and time, in contrast to Shāfiʿī, Muzanī, and the like. But was he proposing a change in Shāfiʿī's view or was he reaffirming it? To answer this, let us turn to the second jurist from Khurāsān.

In his *Nihāyat al-maṭlab*, Juwaynī engages with these same issues in detail and refutes the claim that the translator is a witness. He compares and contrasts the translator with the announcer (*musmiʿ*), whom a *qāḍī* can depend on if he is deaf or if his hearing is impaired due to distance or height from the litigants. Regarding how many of them should be present, Juwaynī rejects the differences between the announcer and translator and then argues that both of them are equal as their responsibilities are similar, for one translates the meaning while the other conveys the very words. In the following lines, he presents multiple cases in which one *or* two translators and announcers must be present.

Juwaynī's argument differentiates between those who have mastered Arabic and those who are not fluent. Consequently, if both parties know Arabic but are unable to articulate their claims meaningfully, one translator is enough (the same goes for the announcer if the judge alone is deaf while both parties can hear). If both litigants are foreigners, or if they and the judge are deaf, and if there is no one else around them, there must be two translators. If there are upright people around them who understand the language of the judge and/or of the litigants, there are different opinions. The preponderant view is that one translator and one announcer is enough. Some jurists have argued that the audience does not have any role in the procedure, thus two translators are required. But Juwaynī says that if the judge asks the upright audience to observe the process of translation (and announcement), that suffices, as they would

28 Māwardī, *Adab al-Qāḍī*, 1:698–99.

29 Ibid., 1:699–700.

report if there were any alterations.[30]

Based on all of these different opinions, Juwaynī says that the translation and announcement are not testimony and the laws of witnesses do not apply here, because "both translator and announcer are mediators between the litigant's word and the judge's grasp. That is why the discernments change according to the changes in situations as we saw above, whereas the number of witnesses does not change."[31] He continues refuting the claim that the translator is a witness and discussing the form that he or she should use (of testimony or transmission) while reporting to the judge. He remarks that he does not know anything like this [the opposite] in the *sharīʿa*. This contradicts what Māwardī classified as "some" of Shāfiʿīs' opinions.[32]

All of these arguments challenge Shāfiʿī's ruling regarding the legal status and required number of translators. While Shāfiʿī disqualified litigants who could not speak Arabic fluently, Juwaynī takes them into account. Juwaynī's rulings also incorporate many other aspects that are otherwise ignored in Māwardī's articulations. In comparing and contrasting the viewpoints of Māwardī and Juwaynī, it is very clear that the latter took a radical approach while the former restated Shāfiʿī's ruling. Māwardī's elaborate attentiveness to the issue however, in contrast to Shāfiʿī and Muzanī, only proves how the issue had become increasingly important in the non-Arabic-speaking eastern lands, though he did not depart from the view of the earlier jurists. However, Juwaynī criticized this approach outright and took a position that stood closer to the views of the Ḥanafīs and Mālikīs.

Intriguingly, Juwaynī's approach gained wider currency among Shāfiʿī scholars over the course of time, gradually becoming a majority view within the Shāfiʿī school. Juwaynī's student Abū Ḥāmid al-Ghazālī (d. 505/1111), who also hailed from Khurāsān, followed his teacher's approach to translators in his renowned law books *al-Wasīṭ* and *al-Wajīz*.[33] Writing a commentary on the latter work under the title *al-ʿAzīz*, another Persian jurist, ʿAbd al-Karīm al-Rāfiʿī (d. 623/1226) from Qazwīn, advanced this discussion and standardized the opinion that translators served as announcers, rather than as witnesses.[34] He also briefly mentioned this

30 Imām al-Ḥaramayn al-Juwaynī, *Nihāyat al-maṭlab fī dirāyat al-madhhab*, ed. ʿAbd al-ʿAẓīm Maḥmūd al-Dayyib (Jedda: Dār al-Minhāj, 2007), 18:477–78.

31 Ibid., 18:478

32 See above, note 27.

33 Abū Ḥāmid al-Ghazālī, *al-Wasīṭ fī al-madhhab*, ed. Muḥammad Muḥammad Tāmir (Cairo: Dār al-Salām, 1997), 7:299–301; and Ghazālī, *al-Wajīz fī fiqh al-Imām al-Shāfiʿī*, ed. ʿAlī Muʿawwaḍ and ʿĀdil ʿAbd al-Mawjūd (Beirut: Dār al-Arqam, 1997), 2:239.

34 ʿAbd al-Karīm al-Rāfiʿī, *al-Fatḥ al-ʿazīz fī sharḥ al-Wajīz*, ed. ʿAlī Muʿawwaḍ and ʿĀdil ʿAbd al-

position in his *al-Muḥarrar*, a text that endeavored to canonize the Shāfiʿī school of law.[35] Rectifying the lacunas of the *Muḥarrar*, Yaḥyā b. Sharaf al-Nawawī (d. 676/1277) from Damascus wrote *Minhāj al-ṭālibīn*, a text that became the canon of the school, and also reaffirmed this viewpoint.[36] How and why did this change of attitude toward translators' function in courts occur within a single school of law, especially when it clearly opposed the views of the eponymous founder?

"TRANSLATING" THE CONTEXT

It is beyond doubt that historical context plays a significant role in the various intellectual articulations discussed above, and this has been demonstrated well in the historiography of early Islamic law. Although research on the so-called post-classical phase of Islamic law (roughly after around 400/1000) in which earlier "original" and "independent" investigations were superseded by the "sterile commentarial literature" is only beginning to flourish, we know that Muslim jurists advanced legal thought from within the framework of their schools in order to address the necessities of their time and place. The existing historiography on this aspect of early Islamic law largely focused on the Mālikī and Ḥanafī traditions, whereas the Shāfiʿī one continues to be understudied. Why, then, did Juwaynī take a different stand on the issue than his predecessors in the Shāfiʿī school had? What prompted him to write a commentary on an earlier text (his *Nihāyat al-maṭlab* is a commentary on the *Mukhtaṣar* by Muzanī)? Was he responding to the particular needs of his time and place? Even if so, to what extent did he actually break away from an Arabic-centric view of law and legal procedure?

Returning to Ibn al-Muqaffaʿ's story offers insight into these questions. On the basis of the story, we explained that Ibn al-Muqaffaʿ separated the translators from witnesses although the case was already proven with the help of the translators. In the text, we saw how the nobleman required testimony from the falconer, and the wife asked him specifically, "*Did you see* what the parrots have said and informed us of?"[37] If we resituate the entire plot in a court setting: the wife is the accused, the nobleman is the inquisitorial judge, the parrots are the "foreign" plaintiffs with the accusation, the friends are the translators, and the falconer is

Mawjūd (Beirut: Dār al-Kutub al-ʿIlmiyya, 1997), 12:456–59.

35 ʿAbd al-Karīm al-Rāfiʿī, *al-Muḥarrar fī al-fiqh al-Shāfiʿī*, ed. Muḥammad Ḥasan Ismāʿīl (Beirut: Dār al-Kutub al-ʿIlmiyya, 2005), 487.

36 Yaḥyā b. Sharaf al-Nawawī, *Minhāj al-ṭālibīn wa-ʿumdat al-muftīn*, ed. Muḥammad Ṭāhir Shaʿban (Beirut: Dār al-Minhāj, 2005), 560.

37 Bīdpāʾī, *Kalīla wa-Dimna*, 85 (emphasis mine, as is the translation).

the witness. In the course of the trial, the witness becomes the culprit, in contrast to the unified position of the translator and witness in Shāfiʿī's approach. The translators inform the judge of what the "foreigners" said, and this in turn necessitates another witness, particularly because the translators are not meant to provide testimony. This is what Juwaynī also meant when he said that the translator is only a mediator between the litigants and the judge, and does not stand as a witness. I am not suggesting that Juwaynī's argument is influenced by what Ibn al-Muqaffaʿ articulated; rather both of them provide us a line of further inquiry outside the box of an Arabic-dominated Islamic legal system. Despite the long chronological gap between the two authors, they take a similar approach on issues of translation in judicial procedure.

Juwaynī affirms the centrality of the Arabic language to the functioning of a court; nevertheless, he allows non-Arabic speakers access to the court and simplifies their incorporation. Juwaynī argues that the judge must be an Arab or, at the least, fluent in Arabic. He writes: "It is unimaginable for a foreigner to be judge. It is essential for a judge that he be a *mujtahid* according to the dominant (*aṣaḥḥ*) view, as I shall explain later, God willing. To be a *mujtahid*, it is indispensable that he be well-versed in the Arabic language, as the *sharīʿa* is in Arabic."[38] This approach, in a way, demonstrates that he concurs with the notion of the centrality of Arabic in the whole Islamic legal system. Yet, he recognizes the necessity of incorporating the people who did not master the language or who did not know anything about it at all. He also simplifies the proceedings by not burdening the translator as a witness, requiring only a minimal number of them as the case and context demand, giving slaves and women a chance to be translators, and depending upon the audience—who can also contribute to the translation process and thus to the entire trial. This approach certainly is indebted to his upbringing in and around Khurāsān, where the primary medium of communication was not Arabic and many people did not master that language.

In Persia, as well as in Central, South, and Southeast Asia, Arabic was perceived as a "foreign" language by many Muslim writers and laypersons, if not by the jurists and royal elites. The historians tell us that the early Arab rulers were obliged to employ translators along with the local secretaries and civil servants to administer state affairs, that "the registers were all kept in Pahlavi until 697 in western Iran and until 742 in Khurāsān," and that "the early coins of the Arab rulers were struck with Pahlavi inscriptions."[39] Although the Umayyad Caliph ʿAbd al-Mālik b. Marwān (r. 65–86/685–705)

38 Juwaynī, *Nihāya*, 18:478.

39 A. Tafazzoli, "Iranian Languages," in *History of Civilizations of Central Asia*, ed. C.E. Bosworth and M.S. Asimov (Paris: United Nations Educational, 2000), 4:328.

attempted to replace the Sassanian, Byzantine, and other hybrid types of currency with Arabic coins and symbols, that currency did not fade away completely as we see even a gold medal struck by the Buyid *amīr* ʿAḍud al-Dawla in 359/969-70 with a Pahlavi inscription.[40]

Naturally, Arabic swept into these regions and began to be widely used in religious gatherings, inscriptions on buildings and objects, charters of charitable endowments, royal letters to Arab governors, and so forth. Yet, it never became the sole or dominant medium of communication for the inhabitants. It did generate an Arabic script-based culture in many Central, South, Southeast, and East Asian languages and literatures, including Persian, Sindhi, and Eastern Turkic. But speech culture remained dominated by the local languages. This on-the-ground reality affected legal procedures and is well reflected in Persian texts like the *Shāhnāma* of Firdawsī, written in 400/1010, the *Chachnāma* of ʿAlī b. Ḥāmid b. Abī Bakr al-Kūfī, written in 613/1216, and the Chinese account of Chau Ju-kua of the twelfth and early thirteenth centuries.

The *Chachnāma*, a text that deals with the early Arab conquests of Sind, clearly distinguished its linguistic position in the "language of the people of the ʿAjam" (*lugha-i ahl-i ʿajam*) from the "language of the Hejaz" (*lugha-i Ḥijāzī*), and across the text we see how "the Persian tongue" (*zabān-i Pahlavī*) and translation into it offer access to the "garments of exquisite language, justice, and wisdom." The very lettering of the text, or its translation from an Arabic original as it claims, is indebted to the fact that the Arabic text did not obtain currency among "the people of Fārs or other non-Arab countries," to whom that language was foreign.[41] In many legal matters too, the book states that language and translation are crucial for justice and wisdom.

For one simple example, consider the author's discussion of Muḥammad b. Qāsim's trial and treatment of a prison-warden, Qubla b. Mahtarāʾij, in Daybul, which was mediated by a translator. Muḥammad b. Qāsim had arrived in Daybul, following the command of Ḥajjāj b. Yūsuf, to

40 See Mehdi Bahrami, "A Gold Medal in the Freer Gallery of Art," in *Archaeologica Orientalia in Memoriam Ernst Herzfeld*, ed. George C. Miles (Locust Valley, New York: J.J. Augustin, 1952), 5–10.

41 The full name of the Chachnama is "*Kitāb az Hikāyat-i Rāi Dāhir b. Chach b. Silāʾij wa Halakshudan aw bidast Muḥammad Qāsim Thaqafī*: The Book of Stories of the King Dāhir b. Chach b. Silāʾij and His Death at the Hands of Muḥammad b. Qāsim Thaqafī." The edition consulted here is ʿAlī b. Ḥāmid b. Abī Bakr al-Kūfī, *Fatḥnāma-i Sind al-maʿrūf bi-Chachnāma*, ed. ʿUmar b. Muḥammad Dāʾūdpota (Hyderabad Deccan: Majlis Makhṭūṭāt-i Fārsiya, 1939), 10–11, 248. Cf. Manan Ahmed Asif, *A Book of Conquest: The* Chachnama *and Muslim Origins in South Asia* (Cambridge: Harvard University Press, 2016), 55–64; and Manan Ahmed Asif, "The Long Thirteenth Century of the *Chachnama*," *The Indian Economic and Social History Review* 49, no. 4 (2012): 467–70. Asif argues that the book is not a translation from Arabic as the would-be translator claims, and the author did so only to utilize "the prestige economy of the Arab descent" of the thirteenth century.

save a few Muslim prisoners who were captured by robbers when their ship was wrecked on the way from Ceylon to Arabia. Ḥajjāj had requested the help of the local ruler, but he refused to intervene.[42] Once Ibn Qāsim reached Daybul with his army, he broke into a temple where the prisoners were kept and saved them. He summoned Qubla, who was in charge of prisoners, and ordered that he be executed on the spot. But Qubla pleaded with Ibn Qāsim by saying, "O Amīr, first inquire of the Muslim prisoners as to how I have been treating them, and how I have been trying my utmost to console and comfort them. When your Excellency learns this, my life will be spared." Ibn Qāsim asked his dragoman to translate what he was saying. When he did so, Ibn Qāsim asked him, "Ask this man what kindness he did to the prisoners." The man replied, "Make that inquiry from the prisoners themselves so that the real state of things and the truth of my assertion may become known to His Highness." Ibn Qāsim asked the prisoners, "What kindness and sympathy has this Qubla shown to you?" They said, "We are much obliged to him. He did all he could to mitigate our misery and to comfort us. At all times he used to console us by giving us hopes of the speedy arrival of the army of Islam and of the conquest of Daybul." Thereupon the man was set free and he eventually converted to Islam. In this story, the translator comes to the rescue of the accused, just before he was about to be executed, by communicating his innocence in keeping the prisoners safe and hopeful.[43]

Similar examples of translations affecting legal procedures are plenty; the constraints of space prevent me from further elaboration. Regardless of the historicity of such stories, and whether or not they accurately depict the challenges of governing the new lands and ensuring justice in the second/eighth century, the text of *Chachnāma* reflects the seventh/thirteenth-century faith among the Muslims of South Asia in the capacity of Islamic rulers to mediate between "local" and "foreign" languages and between local subjects and universal notions of justice. This ability had increasing significance in the early seventh/thirteenth century, when Muslim rulers established new South Asian Islamic kingdoms that would rule the subcontinent for centuries. Therefore, even if the above story is not an official court procedure and the people involved are not court translators, judges, or plaintiffs, the *Chachnāma* reflects the wider attempts of the new Muslim ruling classes to negotiate with the local communities

42 For an earlier account of the episode, see Aḥmad b. Yaḥyā al-Balādhurī, *Futūḥ al-buldān*, ed. ʿAbd Allāh Anīs al-Ṭabbāʿ (Beirut: Muʾassasat al-Maʿārif, 1987), 611–12; cf. Asif, *A Book of Conquest*, 36–37.

43 Kūfī, *Fatḥnāma-i Sind*, 108–09. This translation is from *The Chachnamah: An Ancient History of Sind, Giving the Hindu Period down to the Arab Conquest*, trans. Mirza Kalichbeg Fredunbeg (Delhi: Idara-i Adabiyat-i Delli, 1979 [originally published 1900]), 84–85, with slight modifications, such as: Qubla son of Mahtarāʾij's name is given as Kublah son of Mustrayeh.

through notions of justice, good governance and building alliances.[44]

The Ghaznavid and Ghūrīd rulers who came to South Asia in this period followed Shāfiʿīsm, and many of them chose that school over other Sunnī or non-Sunnī legal traditions. For example, Maḥmūd of Ghazna (r. 388–421/998–1030) of the Ghaznavid Dynasty converted from Ḥanafīsm to Shāfiʿīsm;[45] Ghiyāth al-Dīn al-Ghūrī (r. 558–599/1163–1203) of the Ghūrīd Dynasty converted from the Karrāmiyya sect (founded in Sijistān by Abū ʿAbd Allāh Muḥammad b. Karrām, d. 255/869) to Shāfiʿīsm in 595/1199 at the hand of Qāḍī Waḥīd al-Dīn (or Wajīh al-Dīn) Muḥammad al-Marwazī or Marwarrūdī. In this last instance, he is said to have converted following both the sultan's and the *qāḍī*'s dream about Shāfiʿī, the eponymous founder of the school, on the same night. Ghiyāth al-Dīn is also said to have extended his patronage to Shāfiʿīsm against Karrāmism, and the great Shāfiʿī Fakhr al-Dīn al-Rāzī is one of the scholars who received his patronage to fight against the Karrāmi preachers in the region.[46] Although the juridical affiliation of these (or any) rulers with a school should not be taken as synonymous with their subjects without clear evidence, the rulers' conversions certainly offered their school of choice an advantage over others. Nevertheless, we need further research to get a clear picture of each school's impact in judicial procedures of these regions and of the potential influences of the school's ideas on contemporary writers like ʿAlī al-Kūfī, the author of *Chachnāma*, about whom we know very little.

Chu-fan-chï, written by the Chinese merchant Chau Ju-kua in the late twelfth and early thirteenth century presents a different picture of translation with regard to Islamic legal administration. The Islamic court that existed in Guangzhou (Canton) since the early third/ninth century, if not earlier, arbitrated civil and criminal cases and continued to function well until the seventh/thirteenth century, with a few occasional interruptions. A Chinese account of the early sixth/twelfth century informs us of how the "foreign" culprits from anywhere in the kingdom were handed over to the Muslim "foreign official" (who "wears a hat, gown, and shoes and carries a tablet just like a Chinese") in Guangzhou to execute punishments either by

44 Asif, *A Book of Conquest*, 14, 92, 119, and passim.

45 On his conversion, see Tāj al-Dīn al-Subkī, *Ṭabaqāt al-Shāfiʿīyya al-Kubrā*, ed. Maḥmūd Muḥammad al-Ṭanāḥī and ʿAbd al-Fattāḥ Muḥammad al-Ḥulw (Cairo: Maṭbaʿat ʿĪsā al-Bābī al-Ḥalabī, n.d.), 5:316. On another Ghaznavid ruler, see Muḥammad b. Sam (r. 1030–1040-41), and on his affiliation with the school, see Subkī, *Ṭabaqāt al-Shāfiʿīyya al-kubrā*, 8:60–61.

46 See Abū ʿUmar Minhāj al-Dīn ʿUthmān b. Sirāj al-Dīn Jūzjānī, *Ṭabaqāt-i Nāṣirī*, ed. W. Nassau Lees, Mawlawī Khadim Hosain and ʿAbd al-Hayy (Calcutta: College Press, 1864), 77–78. For a translation, see Jūzjānī, *Ṭabaqāt-i Nāṣirī: A General History of the Muhammadan Dynasties of Asia, Including Hindustān, from A.H. 194 (810 A.D.) to A.H. 658 (1260 A.D.) and the Irruption of the Infidel Mughals into Islām*, trans. Henry George Raverty (London: Gilbert & Rivington, 1881), 1:384–85. Cf. C. E. Bosworth, "The Rise of the Karamiyyah in Khurāsān," *The Muslim World* 50, no. 1 (1960): 5–14.

rattan-whips or banishment.[47] The legal administration in which Muslims were involved thus arguably functioned independently from the imperial courts, and the translation process was involved in the transfer of accused or convicted defendants and their adjudication. Further research into both Arabic and Chinese sources would enlighten us on more specificities of how language and translation must have been negotiated between the different legal cultures.

From South and Southeast Asia, we have interesting cases from the seventh/thirteenth century onward about the local and foreign Muslims pragmatically disentangling the linguistic complexities of their regions to ensure property rights, land acquisitions, charitable endowments, and to fight for justice. While Arabic stood as an unbreakable barrier for many, a few found more creative ways to overcome it. In some cases, Arabic was deployed alongside local languages in inscriptions, such as the bilingual inscriptions of land endowments from Somnath-Verval (Gujarat) dated 662/1264 in Arabic and Sanskrit, and from Calicut (Kerala) in Arabic and Malayalam dated in the seventh/thirteenth century. These inscriptions are pure legal documents that explained who endowed the property, as well as how, why, and when, and stated that they were exempted from taxation or secured revenue. If both of these documents are Islam-related land grants, consider the mid-ninth century copper-plates from Kollam-Terissappaḷḷi (Kerala) in which the document was drawn in Malayalam in Vaṭṭeḻuttu script, yet the witnesses undersigned their names in Kufic (fifteen people), Pahlavi (ten), and Hebrew (four), bringing together Christians, Muslims, Jews, Zorastrians, and the Hindu kings into a single micro-site of one legal document. The Terengganu Inscription (in Northeast Malaysia) from 702/1303 in Jāwī provides another fascinating example of translating Islamic criminal and civil legal procedures by a "peripheral" Muslim community, which described itself as followers of Shāfiʿī law.

In these documents we see different forms of translating Arabic, as well as Islam and its law into vernacular languages and contexts through candid interactions with particular places and periods. These materials provide us a window onto the larger worlds of Islamic legal procedure, testimony, and authentication in pluralistic legal contexts. Translators and translated documents thus formulated, transformed, and influenced judicial procedure in the wider Islamic world in which Arabic was only one among many other languages, rather than the single Arabic-focused legal

47 Chau Ju-kua, *Chu-fan-chï*, trans. Friedrich Hirth and W.W. Rockhill (St. Petersberg: Printing Office of the Imperial Academy of Sciences, 1911), 16–17, 114–19. Cf. Jean Sauvaget, *Aḫbār aṣ-Ṣīn wa l-Hind: Relation de la Chine et de l'Inde, rédigée en 851* (Paris: Belles Lettres, 1948), 7; and Eusèbe Renaudot, *Ancient Accounts of India and China by Two Mohammedan Travellers who Went to those Parts in the 9th Century* (London: S. Harding, 1733), 7–8.

world that the early Arab jurists envisioned.

CONCLUSION

Understanding the complexities of Islamic expansion and persistence across Asia, Africa, and Europe requires a deeper examination of the mediation process between law and languages in Islamic legal practices outside of the Arabian and Arabized lands. Even if the people from these lands formed the majority of the Islamic world, the early Arab jurists were theoretically reluctant to give them access to the Islamic justice system unless they brought in a trustworthy Muslim male translator. Over the course of time, however, jurists from non-Arab lands addressed the increasing need to accommodate non-Arabic speakers and resolved the related predicaments adhering to the framework of the Islamic legal tradition, as we see in the case of Māwardī, Juwaynī, and their successors. Later jurists from these regions also endeavored to institutionalize the position of the translator in the court: arranging for a translator is one of the ten good protocols (*adab*) that a judge should follow while taking office, according to Ghazālī. Some scholars even suggested that the salary for the translator should be paid from the state treasury.[48] Thus, if an early jurist like Shāfiʿī approached finding a translator as the responsibility of non-Arabic speaking litigants, later jurists made translation and translators integral parts of a good court.

The debates over translation and translators that unfolded over several generations demonstrate how translation became increasingly important for jurists from non-Arab lands who had direct engagement with non-Arabic contexts. They therefore simplified the necessary procedures for non-Arabic speakers to get access to the courts, in contrast to Shāfiʿī and Muzanī who were only familiar with Arabian and Arabized realms like those of the Ḥijāz and Egypt. Islamic law provided a platform for all of these jurists to negotiate with and reconcile the changing contexts and times. After all, it was the jurists' law, and jurists from all over the Islamic world asserted their diverse views within the framework of the tradition, as Juwaynī did by contradicting the views of Shāfiʿī, or as the Terengganu inscription did when it translated and conceived of Shāfiʿī law differently. Precisely that "logic of internal contradiction" (taking a cue from Shahab Ahmed) is what enabled the survival not only of Islam, but also of the Islamic legal system.[49]

48 Ghazālī, *Wasīṭ*, 7:300; Ghazālī, *Wajīz*, 2:239; Rāfiʿī, *al-Fatḥ al-ʿazīz*, 12: 456–57; Rāfiʿī, *al-Muḥarrar*, 487; and Nawawī, *Minhāj al-Ṭālibīn*, 560. On the detailed debates over the translator's salary, see Ghazālī, *Wasīṭ*, 7:300; Rāfiʿī, *al-Fatḥ al-ʿazīz*, 12:459; and al-Khaṭīb al-Shirbīnī, *Mughnī al-muḥtāj ilā maʿrifat maʿānī alfāẓ al-Minhāj*, ed. Muḥammad Khalīl ʿAytanī (Beirut: Dār al-Maʿrifa, 1997), 4:520.

49 Ahmed, *What Is Islam?*, 109, 233.

Chapter Six

The Judge and the judge: The Heavenly and Earthly Court of Justice in Early Islam

Christian Lange
Utrecht University

M. M. Bravmann once noted that in Qurʾānic descriptions of the divine judgment at the end of time, God is conceived in terms akin to a pre-Islamic Arab king, enjoying absolute liberty to punish or forgive.[1] The aim of the following investigation is to test the hypothesis that the Sunnī exegetes of the early centuries of Islam (second–sixth/eighth–twelfth centuries) sought to contain this issue by framing the imagery of the heavenly court in ways that made it look like an orderly courtroom on earth. That is, the early exegetes seem to have entertained, and at times even stressed, certain commonalities in the spatial and procedural protocol followed in both the heavenly and the earthly court. This, ultimately, served the dual purpose of checking the latent threat inherent in conceptualizations of both the heavenly and the earthly judge as unaccountable institutions of judicial power.

Scholars of Islamic law in the West often emphasize that Muslim thinkers of all periods were keenly aware of the fundamental incommensurability of the two systems of justice, earthly and otherworldly. Thus, in the widely cited *Encyclopedia of the Qurʾān*, one reads in the entry on "Justice and Injustice" that Islamic law "largely" maintains "a separation between divine and human justice." The entry further explains that "the Islamic judge was only to render justice on the basis of the apparent evidence, and was not responsible for the actual truth of a case, since ultimately the plaintiffs were responsible to God."[2] By contrast,

1 M. M. Bravmann, "Allah's Liberty to Punish or Forgive," *Der Islam* 47 (1971): 236–37.

2 Jonathan Brockopp, "Justice and Injustice," in *EQ*, 3:73a. For a summary of this position, see Baber Johansen, "The Muslim *Fiqh* as a Sacred Law," in *Contingency in a Sacred Law: Legal and Ethical Norms in the Muslim Fiqh* (Leiden: Brill, 1998), 1–76, esp. 23–24.

God, the ultimate Judge, renders justice on the basis of His encompassing knowledge, which ensues from from His cognizance of people's thoughts and intentions. According to the Qur'ānic verse, God is "the knower of what is hidden and what is apparent: *ʿālimu al-ghaybi wa'l-shahāda*" (Q. 59:23). The knowledge available to judges on earth, by contrast, is essentially deficient and of uncertain epistemological status. As Mathieu Tillier, in the most searching study to date of the relationship between the earthly and heavenly courtroom in early Islam, aptly puts it:

> The divine courtroom is not the mere reproduction of an earthly one. Beyond the theological reasons which could explain the absence of God's physical representation in these reports, procedures followed at the divine court are ontologically different to those prescribed by earthly courts. Whereas a Muslim judge must rely on external evidence such as testimonies and oaths that can be misleading, God's all-embracing knowledge allows him to judge rightly and immediately, without need for any further evidence.[3]

To quote a topical passage from an early Muslim source,

> the [earthly] judge judges on the basis of what he thinks and what the witnesses testify. The judge is a human being who either errs or hits the right mark (*yakhṭi'u wa-yuṣīb*). Know that the case (*khuṣūma*) of the one who was judged wrongly remains unresolved until God brings both [litigants] together on the Day of Judgment and judges in favor of the one who is right, against the one who is wrong, giving the former a bigger compensation than that received by the latter on earth.[4]

It is not difficult to list more features that distinguish the Judge from the judge. For example, the article on "Justice and Injustice" in the *Encyclopedia of the Qur'ān* asserts that "court punishments in Islam are not in lieu of eternal punishment."[5] The idea that human justice is fundamentally contingent, while divine justice is transcendent and perfect, also explains why the Judge is free to disregard evidence when He deems it appropriate, and why restrictions in this regard are imposed on the judge. God's mercy as a judge of humankind is a paramount motif in Muslim eschatological literature.

3 Mathieu Tillier, "The Qāḍī before the Judge: The Social Use of Eschatology in Muslim Courts," in *The Divine Courtroom in Comparative Perspective*, ed. Ari Mermelstein et al. (Leiden: Brill, 2014), 266.

4 Abū Jaʿfar Muḥammad b. Jarīr al-Ṭabarī, *Jāmiʿ al-bayān ʿan ta'wīl āy al-Qur'ān*, ed. ʿAlī ʿĀshūr (Beirut: Dār Iḥyā' al-Turāth al-ʿArabī, 2011), 2:221 (*ad* Q. 2:188: *wa-lā ta'kulū amwālahum baynakum bil-bāṭil* [from Qatāda]).

5 Brockopp, "Justice and Injustice," 73b.

According to the famous divine saying (*ḥadīth qudsī*), God's mercy precedes His wrath. By contrast, mercy (and for that matter, wrath), ostensibly have no place in the earthly court; the normative literature regulating the judge's etiquette (*adab*) stipulates that the *qāḍī* must show *apatheia* and keep his cool at all times.[6] One might also note that the heavenly court officials are beyond reproach. The angels who act as witnesses (*shuhūd*) in the heavenly court, as well as the two angels who write down a person's actions, clearly fulfill the condition of honesty (*ʿadāla*), and therefore God-the-judge, unlike judges on earth, does not need to make inquiries into their trustworthiness.

In sum, the differences between the Judge and the judge, and between the heavenly and the mundane court, seem abundantly clear and in fact, categorical. This does not mean, however, that it is pointless to study the commonalities and overlaps between the two courts. No attempt is made here to cast doubt on, let alone refute, scholarly assessments that highlight the heterogeneity of the divine and the earthly courtroom. What is suggested, rather, is that these differences should be considered as being generally affirmed, but not always experienced as such in people's minds or indeed acted upon in practice. This invites a certain shift of perspective. While it is no doubt true that, as Tillier affirms, "the divine courtroom is not the mere reproduction of an earthly one," it is equally correct to state that the divine courtroom is *not only and not exclusively* conceived as a transcendent institution of justice with no connection to the social imagery and judicial mores of judicial courts on earth. As this paper aims to show, in the exegetes' imagination, there was a continuum from earthly to otherworldly justice, in the sense that God did not judge in the manner of an autocratic, unaccountable absolute king, but rather followed, like the judge on earth, certain procedures and rules.

The exegetes of the period under study in this article do not make this continuum the object of their explicit deliberations. It can often appear that, if they feel at all challenged by the Qurʾānic imagery of the heavenly court, it is because of the anthropomorphism with which this imagery is replete (the "theological reasons" alluded to in Tillier's above-quoted statement). Here we face a paradox. For, while the anti-anthropomorphism prevalent in much of Muslim theology militated against descriptions of the heavenly court in terms of the earthly court, a certain conceptual and imaginary overlap between the heavenly and the earthly court, as will be shown in the following text, is in fact observable in the exegetical literature up to the sixth/twelfth century, and, as can safely be surmised, in later

6 See the examples discussed in Maribel Fierro's contribution to the present volume, Chapter 8. Cf. Irene Schneider, *Das Bild des Richters in der "adab al-qāḍī"-Literatur* (Frankfurt: Peter Lang, 1990), 138 and passim.

centuries as well.

In order to substantiate this claim, first we need a good description of the heavenly court on the Day of Judgment as it emerges from a number of sources from the second/eighth to the sixth/twelfth centuries. Although the events surrounding the resurrection (*qiyāma*), gathering (*ḥashr*), and reckoning (*ḥisāb*) constitute important chapters in works of Muslim eschatology (*ʿulūm al-ākhira*), occupying the place right between the apocalypse on the one hand and paradise and hell on the other hand, they have only been studied in perfunctory fashion by scholars of Islamic religious history.[7] Dedicated studies of the form and function of the eschatological court of justice appear altogether to be lacking. Aspects of this court that deserve study concern its spatial organization (its publicness, the position of the Judge, and other spatial coordinates), its procedural law (the questioning of the accused, the use of written evidence, as well as of witness testimony), and its personnel (the heavenly court enforcers, scribes, certified witnesses, as well as the Judge Himself).

In what follows, these elements of the heavenly court scene shall be described. The panoramic view that results from this exercise is based on two kinds of textual sources: (1) exegetical works (*tafsīrs*), written by scholars who were, for the most part, jurists as well as Qurʾān commentators, such as Ṭabarī (d. 310/923), Samarqandī (d. 373/983), Thaʿlabī (d. 427/1035), Māwardī (d. 450/1058), and Baghawī (d. 516/1122);[8] and (2) compilations of eschatological *ḥadīths* and hortatory works that include relevant sections on the events of the resurrection by the likes of Muḥāsibī (d. 243/857), Samarqandī, and Qurṭubī (d. 671/1272).[9] Next to unfolding a phenomenology of the heavenly court in early Sunnī literature, the following discussion also serves to identify salient overlaps with the representations

7 Jane Idleman Smith and Yvonne Yazbeck Haddad provide one of the most thorough overviews. See their *The Islamic Understanding of Death and Resurrection* (New York: Oxford University Press, 2002), 76–78.

8 See generally Ṭabarī, *Jāmiʿ al-bayān*; Abū al-Layth Naṣr b. Muḥammad al-Samarqandī, *Baḥr al-ʿulūm*, ed. Maḥmūd Maṭrajī (Beirut: Dār al-Fikr, n.d.); Aḥmad b. Muḥammad al-Thaʿlabī, *al-Kashf waʾl-bayān ʿan tafsīr al-Qurʾān*, ed. Abū Muḥammad b. ʿĀshūr (Beirut: Dār Iḥyāʾ al-Turāth al-ʿArabī, 2002); Abū al-Ḥasan ʿAlī b. Muḥammad al-Māwardī, *al-Nukat waʾl-ʿuyūn*, ed. Ibn ʿAbd al-Maqṣūd b. ʿAbd al-Raḥīm (Beirut: Dār al-Kutub al-ʿIlmiyya, 1992); and al-Ḥusayn b. Masʿūd al-Baghawī, *Maʿālim al-tanzīl*, ed. Muḥammd ʿAbdallāh al-Nimr et al. (Riyadh: Dār al-Ṭība, 1997).

9 See generally al-Ḥārith b. Asad al-Muḥāsibī, *al-Baʿth waʾl-nushūr*, ed. Muḥammad ʿĪd Riḍwān (Beirut: Dār al-Kutub al-ʿIlmiyya, 1406/1987); Muḥāsibī, *Kitāb al-Tawahhum*, ed. and trans. André Roman (Paris: Librairie Klincksieck, 1978); Abū al-Layth Naṣr b. Muḥammad al-Samarqandī, *Tanbīh al-ghāfilīn*, ed. Haytham Khalīfa al-Ṭuʿaymī (Beirut: al-Maktaba al-ʿAṣriyya, 1427/2006); and Muḥammad b. Aḥmad al-Qurṭubī, *al-Tadhkira fī aḥwāl al-mawtā wa-umūr al-ākhira*, ed. Yūsuf ʿAlī Badīwī (Damascus: Dār Ibn Kathīr, 1999). Gavin Picken has cast doubt on Muḥāsibī's authorship of *al-Baʿth waʾl-nushūr*, but Josef van Ess has disagreed, leaning in the direction of attributing the work to Muḥāṣibī. See van Ess, "Review Picken, *Spiritual Purification*," *Ilahiyat Studies* 2, no. 1 (2011): 126–32, esp. 131.

of earthly courts in the chronicles and legal literature of early Islam.

SPATIAL ORGANIZATION OF THE HEAVENLY COURT

After their resurrection, people are ushered to the "open grounds of the resurrection" (*ʿaraṣāt al-qiyāma*). The word *ʿaraṣa* designates any kind of publicly accessible, unroofed space used for gathering (as in a public square in the middle of a *sūq*). On the *ʿaraṣāt al-qiyāma* the first vision of God-the-judge takes place, as God manifests Himself (*yatajallā*), and the *ʿaraṣāt* "are enlightened by His light."[10] God, in other words, is fully public. The exegetical passages that detail the *ʿaraṣāt al-qiyāma* revolve around a number of verses, especially the one that states that "God will come to them in canopies of clouds (*fī ẓulalin min al-ghamām*), together with the angels" (Q. 2:210). What kind of *ẓulla* (sg. of *ẓulal*) is meant here? Ṭabarī notes the opinion that the clouds are like arches (*ṭāqāt*), and that God is "in" (*fī*) them, while being surrounded (*maḥfūf*) by angels.[11] In this view, the *ẓulla* is a kind of "canopy" or "awning." The issue here is whether God is visible or not. Anti-anthropomorphic interpretations deny this. Thus, Thaʿlabī reports the opinion that *fī ẓulal*[in] *min al-ghamām* means that God is "inside a cover (*fī sutra*) of clouds, so that the people of the earth do not look at Him"[12]—the idea being that God is shrouded in clouds, in "something like white fog."[13] Others suggest that *ẓulal* means "shadows," which serves the same idea, that is, making God invisible or barely visible. This, however, does not seem to have been the dominant position. Baghawī, the latest of the exegetes studied here, is clear in his insistence that *ẓulal* means "canopies, awnings," not "shrouds" or "shadows,"[14] and his view finds support in the classical dictionaries, which generally hold that *ẓulal* is the plural of *ẓulla* ("a thing that covers one, overhead") not of *ẓill* ("shadow," pl. *ẓilāl*).[15]

The Qurʾān announces that on the Day of Judgment, when the heaven splits asunder, "the angels will be on its borders (*ʿalā arjāʾihā*) and above them eight will carry the throne of your Lord" (Q. 69:19). The commentators elaborate that God orders the angels of the lower heaven to

---

10 Thaʿlabī, *Kashf*, 8:287 (and Q. 39:69: *ashraqati ʾl-arḍa bi-nūri rabbihā*). See also Baghawī, *Maʿālim*, *Tafsīr*, 7:132. See further Qurṭubī, *Tadhkira*, 1:384, in an explanation of the expression *yawm al-talāqī* ("Day of Meeting").

11 Ṭabarī, *Jāmiʿ*, 2:397 (from Ibn ʿAbbās).

12 Thaʿlabī, *Kashf*, 2:128 (from Ḥasan al-Baṣrī).

13 Baghawī, *Maʿālim*, 1:241: *ka-hayʾat al-ḍabāb, abyaḍ*.

14 Ibid.

15 See Edward William Lane, *Arabic-English Dictionary* (Edinburgh: Williams and Norgate, 1863), 1:1916b.

descend to the earth and surround it and all those on it, then the angels of the other heavens follow, thus creating concentric rings (*ṣaff dūna ṣaff*). "Then the Sublime King (*al-malik al-aʿlā*) descends. On his left flank is Jahannam. When the people of the earth see it, they cry out."[16] It is also related that the resurrected, terrorized by the appearance of the hell-monster Jahannam, try to flee the scene, but are repelled by the rows of angels surrounding them. Samarqandī reports that the angels of the lowest heaven surround the earth, then the angels of each successive heaven descend and form concentric rings around them, "until there are seven rows (*ṣufūf*) of angels, enclosing one another in their midst (*baʿḍuhum fī jawf baʿḍ*)."[17]

As noted above, commentators, with the exception of the literalists, are concerned with softening the anthropomorphic impression created by Qurʾānic expressions such as the one that states that God "comes to them" (Q. 2:210). By the third/ninth century, Muslim theology by and large came to settle on the position that the categories of time and space do not apply to God, who is beyond both.[18] Ṭabarī therefore raises the question whether one should understand the expression, "He comes to them," to mean that God appears in the heavenly courtroom in the same way in which an earthly judge appears to the accused. As Ṭabarī explains, this is not the case, but rather, it is as when people say: "We are afraid that the Umayyads will come to us"—that is, people do not expect the Umayyads to come in a literal sense, but only that the Umayyads' command, or judgment (*ḥukm*), will catch up with them. Another parallel, according to Ṭabarī, is "when it is said: 'The ruler (*wālī*) maimed or beat the thief,' but in reality his helpers (*aʿwānuh*) maimed him."[19] Ṭabarī thus underlines the difference between heavenly and earthly justice; however, intriguingly, he also playfully invokes an analogy between the adjudication of mundane rulers and that of the divine king.

As for the spatial organization of the earthly counterpart of the heavenly court, relatively little seems to be known about the early centuries of Islam. The *qāḍī* court, then, was an "undetermined place (*un lieu indéterminé*)."[20] Other than that the judge used to sit, and that he was encouraged to do so in an open, publicly accessible space, little can be

16 Ṭabarī, *Jāmiʿ*, 29:69 (from Ḍaḥḥāk).

17 Samarqandī, *Tanbīh*, 30.

18 For a summary of the development of this position in early Muslim theology, see Baber Johansen, "The Muslim *Fiqh* as a Sacred Law," 7–9; cf. Josef van Ess, *Theologie und Geschichte im 2. und 3. Jahrhundert Hidschra: Eine Geschichte des religiösen Denkens im Islam* (Berlin: de Gruyter, 1991-1997), 4:410. The issue of God's "aboveness" (*fawqiyya*), dear to Ḥanbalī traditionists, is discussed in a forthcoming article by Livnat Holtzman and Miriam Ovadia.

19 Ṭabarī, *Jāmiʿ*, 2:398. See also, for an extended version of this argument, Thaʿlabī, *Kashf*, 2:130.

20 Mathieu Tillier, "Un espace judiciaire entre public et privé. Audience de cadis à l'époque ʿabbāside," *Annales islamologiques* 38 (2004): 491–512, esp. 492.

gleaned from the chronicles. In the early centuries, mosques seem to have been used regularly for the séances of judges, even though the Shāfiʿīs came to condemn judges who took their seat in the mosque (out of scruples meant to avoid jeopardizing the sacredness of the space);[21] all schools of law seem to have agreed that the judge can, if he wishes, hold court even in the street. Ibn Ḥajar relates that Ibn Jabr, judge of Egypt at the beginning of the fourth/tenth century, used to convert street corners into judicial courts by simply laying out a carpet and forming a *majlis* (gathering) around it.[22] Such minimal requirements accord with the pithy data about the spatial coordinates of the heavenly court, where no more than a "canopy" (*ẓulla*) demarcates the spot where the Judge is seated. By contrast, descriptions of the audience with God in paradise, on the "Day of Surplus" (*yawm al-mazīd*), are richly detailed.[23] One may infer from this that God-the-king, in the imagination of early Muslim exegetes, is encountered on the *yawm al-mazīd*; however, on the Day of Judgment, he is first and foremost God-the-judge.

PROCEDURAL ASPECTS OF THE HEAVENLY COURT

Based on the Qurʾānic prophecy that "on that day you will be exposed (*tuʿraḍūna*); no secret of yours will be concealed" (Q. 69:18), the commentators enumerate three different instances of "exposures" or "showings" (*ʿaraḍāt*) of humankind in the heavenly court of justice. Ṭabarī relates from the Companion, ʿAbd Allāh Ibn Masʿūd (d. 32/652-3), that these three instances are (1) excuses (*maʿādhīr*), (2) arguments (*khuṣūmāt*), and (3) the flying around of the scrolls (*taṭāyur al-ṣuḥuf*). By contrast, Ḥasan al-Baṣrī (d. 110/728) is said to have spoken of (1) disputation (*jidāl*), (2) excuses, and (3) the flying around of the scrolls. Finally, from Ḍaḥḥāk (d. 117/735) a combined model is reported, according to which the three *ʿaraḍāt* are (1) arguments and excuses, (2) disputation, and (3) the flying around of the scrolls.[24] The terms *jidāl, khuṣūmāt,* and *maʿādhīr* clearly refer to the litigation between God and the resurrected, describing the trading of arguments between the plaintiff and the accused, in fact, an interrogation, such as one would habitually encounter in a judge's court on

21 Schneider, *Das Bild des Richters*, 50–60.

22 Aḥmad b. ʿAlī Ibn Ḥajar al-ʿAsqalānī, *Rafʿ al-ʿiṣr ʿan quḍāt Miṣr*, ed. ʿAlī Muḥammad ʿUmar (Cairo: Maktabat al-Khānjī, 1998), 178. See Tillier, "Espace judiciaire," 493–94; Émile Tyan, *Histoire de l'organisation judiciaire en pays d'Islam* (Leiden: Brill, 1960), 277.

23 Christian Lange, *Paradise and Hell in Islamic Traditions* (Cambridge: Cambridge University Press, 2016), 152.

24 Ṭabarī, *Jāmiʿ*, 29:71–72.

earth.[25] Samarqandī relates that the resurrected will stand before the Judge, "and you will be asked about what you did letter by letter: *tus'alūna ʿammā faʿaltum ḥarfan ḥarfan*."[26] The names (*asmāʾ*) of the Day of Resurrection reported by Samarqandī also drive home the point that a detailed verbal confrontation takes places between God-the-judge and the resurrected: Samarqandī names "The Day of Discussion" (*yawm al-munāqasha*), "The Day of Reckoning" (*yawm al-muḥāsaba*), and "The Day of Interrogation" (*yawm al-musāʾala*), among others.[27]

Again, the anthropomorphic implications of this scene motivated a number of exegetical rejoinders. Exegetes sought to soften the impression that what people will be dealing with on the Day of Judgment is some kind of accurate bookkeeper, a pedestrian judge in an ordinary court.[28] Instead, they stressed that the Judge is the almighty God, capable of forgiveness based on His encompassing knowledge. Rather worryingly, the Qurʾān states that not only those who are hell-bound but also the believers will undergo a "reckoning" (*ḥisāb*), although it will be "light" (*yasīr*) and result in the blessed's happy reunion with their families in paradise (Q. 84:7–9). A prophetic *ḥadīth* helped to alleviate any anxiety there may have been. As the Prophet supposedly explained: "This is not a reckoning, it's a [simple] exposure (*ʿarḍ*)." The blessed do not suffer interrogation because, as the *ḥadīth* continues, "[all] those who are interrogated on the Day of Resurrection will be punished."[29] Similarly, Qurṭubī comments that "the disputation (*jidāl*) [only] concerns the enemies [of God]. They dispute because they do not know their Lord. They think that they will be saved if they dispute and put up arguments."[30] The believers, by contrast, do not argue, they only plead for mercy: "The excuses (*maʿādhīr*) are [directed] to God. The Generous One forgives Adam and his progeny…."[31]

At the last exposure, written evidence comes into play, during the "flying back and forth of the scrolls" (*taṭāyur al-ṣuḥuf*). This flying of the scrolls of deeds is not a Qurʾānic motif. The Qurʾān only tells us that

25 Usually, the *khuṣūma* is the "argument" or "lawsuit" of two litigants in front of the judge. See Baber Johansen, "Wahrheit und Geltungsanspruch: Zur Begründung und Begrenzung der Autorität des Qadi-Urteils im islamischen Recht," in *La Giustizia nell'Alto Medieoevo (Secoli IX-XI)*, ed. Centro Italiano di Studi sull'Alto Medioevo (Spoleto: Presso la Sede del Centro, 1997), 975–1065, at 1013–15.

26 Samarqandī, *Tanbīh*, 33.

27 Ibid.

28 Cf. Wim Raven, "Reward and Punishment," in *EQ*, 4:451b–461a, at 457b.

29 Ṭabarī, *Jāmiʿ*, 30:143, with variants; and Qurṭubī, *Tadhkira*, 2:37: *laysa dhālika al-ḥisāb, innamā dhālika al-ʿarḍ, wa-lākin man nūqisha al-ḥisāb yawm al-qiyāma ʿudhdhiba.*

30 Qurṭubī, *Tadhkira*, 2:38.

31 Ibid.

those destined for paradise receive their scroll in the right hand, and hence are called the Companions of the Right (*aṣḥāb al-maymana*), while those destined for hell receive their scroll in the left hand, and are therefore called the Companions of the Left (*aṣḥāb al-mashʾama*, see Q. 56:41-56, 69:19, and 69:25). Like the idea of the "scrolls of deeds" (*ṣuḥuf*) itself, the flying of the scrolls is likely to have a Rabbinic background.[32] But how is one to picture the scrolls' fluttering through the air? "All the scrolls," it is explained in a tradition reported by Qurṭubī, "are [stored] under the Throne. At Judgment, God sends wind, and so they are all scattered right and left."[33] The idea here is that, underneath the Judge's seat, there is a cache in which court documents are kept, much in the manner of the *qimṭar* of a *qāḍī*, the box, or satchel, in which he archived relevant pieces of writing.

Once the scrolls are produced from underneath the Judge's throne, they are put to use as evidence. Samarqandī reports a tradition according to which God says to the resurrected: "I have given you advice (*nasaḥtu lakum*). However, [here] in your registers (*ṣuḥuf*) are [recorded] your actions. Whosoever finds a good action (*khayran*) [recorded in it], let him praise God; whosoever finds something else, let him blame noone but himself."[34] One of the most forceful illustrations of the interrogation before God-the-judge comes from Muḥāsibī:

> There you come to stand in front of a mighty, exalted, immense, and noble Lord, with a palpitating heart... in your hand a written record that leaves out no calamity you instigated, and no secret deed that you sought to hide. You read what is written in it with a weary tongue, citing pointless arguments (*ḥujja dāḥiḍa*)....[35]

Also Thaʿlabī states that God consults the scrolls and decides on the basis of what He finds in them.[36] That is to say, the eschatological judgment is the result of a forensic process in which evidence is consulted and duly weighed. God-the-judge relies on written evidence, despite His encompassing knowledge of things past and present, hidden and apparent—an obvious paradox. In sum, in Qurʾānic exegesis, written evidence, in form of the scrolls, is commonplace in the heavenly court of justice. It is interesting

32 Rabbinic literature, elaborating on Daniel 7 (which describes God sitting on His throne and judging based on books that are brought to Him), enumerates a variety of heavenly books. Cf. 2 Enoch, which includes a fully forensic scene. See Paul Volz, *Jüdische Eschatologie von Daniel bis Akiba* (Tübingen: J.C.B. Mohr, 1903), 89–95.

33 Qurṭubī, *Tadhkira*, 2:38 (from ʿUqaylī, *K. al-Ḍuʿafāʾ al-kabīr*).

34 Samarqandī, *Tanbīh*, 33.

35 Muḥāsibī, *Tawahhum*, § 61 (tr. 48).

36 Thaʿlabī, *Kashf*, 9:99.

to note that, even though written evidence was likely used from early on in mundane courts, it took some time before jurists came to agree that written documents were fully admissible evidence, and they never did so in criminal law (that is, *ḥadd* and *qiṣāṣ*).[37]

Another important procedural element that the heavenly court has in common with earthly courts is the testimony of witnesses. To begin with, there are the two angels responsible for writing up the scrolls. The exegetes connect them to two verses in particular, Q. 50:17–18 ("When the two Receivers [*al-mutalaqqiyān*] receive him, one sitting on the right, one sitting on the left. Not a word does he utter but a ready watcher is by him.") and Q. 82:11 ("Over you are guardians, noble, recording [*kātibīna*]."). These are no ordinary scribes. Ṭabarī reports that "they write down what you say and what you intend: *mā taqūlūna wa-mā taʿnūna*,"[38] a comment that makes it clear that eschatological judgment, unlike the judgment of judges on earth, takes people's intentions into account. Māwardī lists various reasons why these angels are "noble," including the view that this is so because "they do not part ways with a person except on two occasions: defecation and sexual intercourse (*ʿinda al-ghāʾiṭ wa-ʿinda al-jimāʿ*); then they withdraw. They write down what is talked about. This is why talking during defecation and sexual intercourse is abhorred." Another view holds that they are "noble" because they take punctilious notes, that is, they do not add anything or leave anything out.[39] The exegetes provide more colorful details about the two recording angels, too many to recount here.[40]

Strictly speaking, these two angels do not belong in the court scene on the Day of Judgment, as they are operative during a person's lifetime, not after death. Occasionally, however, the two recording angels accompany the dead person not only to the grave but onwards, to the Final Judgment. Thaʿlabī reports a Prophetic tradition according to which, after the death of a person, the two angels reside in the vicinity of the grave of the deceased. Then, at Judgment, God consults the person's scrolls, and if He finds a good deed at the beginning and the end of the scroll, He tells the assembly of angels to testify that He has forgiven the person.[41] This story recalls the practice of letting professional witnesses (*ʿudūl*) confirm the validity of written proof, a practice that was common in *qāḍī* courts from the late

37 Baber Johansen, "Zum Prozessrecht der *ʿuqūbāt*," *ZDMG*, Supplement III,1, XIX. Deutscher Orientalistentag (1977): 429 (on *kitāb al-qāḍī ilā al-qāḍī*).

38 Ṭabarī, *Jāmiʿ*, 30:111 (*ad* Q. 82:11, from Ayyūb). Cf. Thaʿlabī, *Kashf*, 10:148; and Baghawī, *Maʿālim*, 8:357.

39 Māwardī, *Nukat*, 6:223.

40 Ṭabarī, *Jāmiʿ*, 26:185; Thaʿlabī, *Kashf*, 9:99.

41 Thaʿlabī, *Kashf*, 9:99.

second/eighth century onward.[42]

COURT OFFICIALS IN THE HEAVENLY COURT OF JUSTICE

A number of court officials of the heavenly court of justice have already been mentioned, such as the "rows" (*ṣufūf*) of angels surrounding the Judgment scene, or the hell-monster Jahannam, which takes a seat at the left foot of God's throne, in a manner reminiscent of the executioner (*sayyāf*) standing to the left of the ruler's throne in representations of the royal court of the Islamic Middle Period.[43] Another Qurʾānic verse used by the exegetes to populate the heavenly court is Q. 50:21: "Every soul shall come, and with it a driver (*sāʾiq*) and a witness (*shahīd*)." Rather concrete, and again reminding one of mundane judicial procedure, are a number of exegetical glosses reported by Ṭabarī, specifying that the *sāʾiq* drives people to the reckoning (*ḥisāb*)[44]—which is reminiscent of the way a court sheriff, a *jilwāz*, might coerce recalcitrant litigants to appear before the judge,[45] or a judge's doorkeeper (*ḥājib*) might usher people into the presence of the judge.[46] Ṭabarī also reports the view that the *sāʾiq* is a court scribe (*kātib*),[47] a functionary who, like the *jilwāz*, was an established adjunct of the judge from as early as the end of the first century.[48]

There are also less concrete, more abstract interpretations. However, according to Baghawī, the interpretation as "scribe" and "witness" is the majority position.[49] This motivates the obvious question, raised several

42 Johansen, "Wahrheit und Geltungsanspruch," 1003. On the development of legal views of written evidence, see Baber Johansen, "Formes de langage et fonctions publiques: stéréotypes, témoins et offices dans la preuve par écrit en droit musulman," *Arabica* 44, 3 (1997): 333–76.

43 Muḥāsibī, *Baʿth*, 22. On the *sayyāf*, see Katharina Otto-Dorn, "Das seldschukische Thronbild," in *Die islamische Welt zwischen Mittelalter und Neuzeit: Festschrift für Hans Robert Roemer zum 65. Geburtstag*, ed. Ulrich Haarmann et al. (Wiesbaden: Steiner, 1979), 168.

44 Ṭabarī, *Jāmiʿ*, 26:187 (from Qatāda).

45 Wael Hallaq, *The Origins and Evolution of Islamic Law* (Cambridge: Cambridge University Press, 2005), 60, states that the *jilwāz* appears to have become "an established functionary" as early as the middle of the first century, referring to Muḥammad b. Khalaf Wakīʿ, *Akhbār al-quḍāt* (Beirut: ʿĀlam al-Kutub, 1980), 2:417. Cf. Emile Tyan, *Histoire de l'organisation judiciaire en pays d'Islam* (Leiden: Brill, 1960 [orig. publ. 1938]), 286. On court enforcers (*aʿwān, jalāwiza*), see Schneider, *Das Bild des Richters*, 41, 45.

46 While Shāfiʿī still held the opinion that the judge should not employ a *ḥājib*, lest he become inaccessible, later Shāfiʿī authors (Māwardī, Ibn Abī al-Dam) allow this, particularly in times "when people are bad." See Schneider, *Das Bild des Richters*, 32–40.

47 Ṭabarī, *Jāmiʿ*, 26:187 (from Mujāhid).

48 Hallaq, *Origins*, 60–61. Kindī first mentions a *kātib* for the year 724. See Kindī, *Akhbār quḍāt Miṣr*, ed. Richard J. H. Gottheil (Paris: P. Geuthner, 1908), 35, quoted in Johansen, "Wahrheit und Geltungsanspruch," 987 n. 22.

49 Baghawī, *Maʿālim*, 7:360.

times already in the course of this study, as to why the all-knowing Judge should need witnesses at all, angelic or otherwise, to establish a person's guilt or fidelity. Māwardī reports two alternative interpretations that appear to resolve the issue. He states that the *shahīd* is none other than the resurrected themselves, who confess their sins, presumably to exculpate themselves and thus incline the Judge toward mercy. Alternatively, the sinners' own hands and feet act as witnesses, acquiring the miraculous ability to testify against their owners.[50] Thaʿlabī reports the opinion that the *shahīd* is simply the resurrected's actions (*aʿmāl*).[51] Thus, concrete, embodied representations (reminiscent of an earthly court scene) are found next to abstract, more unreal ones; here, in the case of Q. 50:21, on balance, the latter seem to be more common than the former.[52] In addition to the figurative interpretation of *shahīd* as "actions" or "limbs of the body," it was taught that the angel drives people not toward God, but toward His command (*amr*),[53] or that the *sāʾiq* is none other than God's command itself.[54]

No description of the Islamic eschatological court of justice is complete without a mention of the pivotal role played by the Prophet Muḥammad, who acts as intercessor on behalf of Muslims. Stories about his heroic efforts to ensure the salvation of his followers abound in the eschatological literature.[55] Noteworthy is a gradual broadening over the course of the early Islamic centuries of the category of people granted the power to intercede, next to the Prophet.[56] To illustrate what *shafāʿa* meant in the early third/ninth century—a moment in Islamic religious history when intercession was still largely restricted to the Prophet—a translation of a passage from Muḥāsibī's *Kitāb al-Baʿth waʾl-nushūr* will suffice:

> A call issues from the direction of God [eulogy]: "O assembly of the Friends [of God] and of the Prophets! Make haste [towards Me] with Muḥammad [eulogy]!" And so they set out with him, he leads the way and they are behind

50 Māwardī, *Nukat*, 5:348–49.

51 Thaʿlabī, *Kashf*, 9:100 (from Abū Hurayra).

52 *Pace* Radscheit, who states that "Islamic exegesis usually takes the 'driver' to be a kind of heavenly court usher; while the 'witness' is generally understood as the angels who record the human deeds." See Radscheit, "Witnessing and Testifying," in *EQ*, 5:492a–506b, at 492b.

53 Ṭabarī, *Jāmiʿ*, 26:187 (from Mujāhid).

54 Māwardī, *Nukat*, 5:348–49 (from Ḍaḥḥāk).

55 The scholarly literature on intercession (*shafāʿa*) is not very rich. The most comprehensive study still seems to be Taede Huitema, *De voorspraak (shafaʿa) in den Islam* (Leiden: Brill, 1936). For a recent discussion, see Valerie Hofmann, "Intercession," in *EQ*, 2:551a–555b (with further bibliographical information).

56 For example, in Shīʿī sources, ʿAlī comes to play a role that is as important as that of Muḥammad in Sunnī sources.

> him, until they reach the Throne. He prostrates, and those who are behind him prostrate, too. God says: "Raise your head Muḥammad! Ask [Me a favor], and you will be given [what you ask for]! Intercede, and your intercession will be granted! Here is not a place for prayer or prostration (*sujūd*); here is a place of happiness and being (*wujūd*)!" So the Messenger says to God: "O Lord! My community! My community! Did you not promise me that You would not sadden me in regard to my community?" God [eulogy] says: "Muḥammad, these are people whom I commanded to do good, but they transgressed against Me. I forbade [certain things to] them, but they disobeyed Me. While still on earth, they did not turn towards Me to repent of [their] sins and the forbidden things [they did]. However, today I grant you the power to intercede on their behalf. Gabriel, go with Muḥammad to the keeper of hell, and say to him: 'Mālik! Let all those who have a speck of faith in their heart exit the Fire!'"[57]

Finally arriving at the figure of the heavenly Judge Himself, let us return to Bravmann's article that was mentioned at the beginning of this article. Bravmann speaks of "the early Arab idea… according to which the earthly, human ruler is conceded the choice to punish or to forgive," and he finds this idea in the Qurʾān "not applied to an earthly, human ruler, but to God himself, the king of the universe."[58] This assessment is based on a number of Qurʾānic verses, in particular Q. 5:18: "He forgives those whom He wishes, and He punishes those whom He wishes. God has sovereignty (*mulk*) over the heavens and the earth and what is between them."

As stated above, it is conceivable that early, legally trained exegetes had an interest in softening this image, by making God look more like a reasonable, accountable judge, rather than an unaccountable, almighty ruler-judge. In the examples adduced so far, fitting God-the-judge into the controlled environment of an orderly courtroom is exactly what appears to be going on. In this context, it is also relevant to note that God is not once referred to as *qāḍī* in the Qurʾān. To be precise, the verbform *qaḍā/yaqḍī* is used repeatedly: God "decides a matter" (*qaḍā/yaqḍī amr^{an}*, e.g. Q. 2:117, 3:47, 8:42, 19:45, 40:68, and passim), He "ordains a person's moment of death" (*qaḍā ajal^{an}*, e.g., Q. 6:2, *qaḍā al-mawt*, Q. 39:42), and He "passes judgment between people" on the Day of Judgment (*qaḍā baynahum bi-ḥukmih*, Q. 27:78). But God as *qāḍī* (in the nominal, not the participal sense), as the holder of *qaḍāʾ* understood as a judicial office, does not figure into the Qurʾān—which of course is not surprising, seeing that the office did

57 Muḥāsibī, *Baʿth*, 32–33.

58 Bravmann, "Allah's Liberty," 237.

not exist at the time of the Qurʾān's enunciation. In sum, in the Qurʾān, God judges, but He is no judge.

In the *tafsīrs*, by contrast, God is identified as a *qāḍī* with increasing regularity. Ṭabarī notes that certain descriptions and epithets of God in the Qurʾān, such as *al-fattāḥ* (Q. 34:27-28; see also Q. 2:117, 7:89), refer to His act of judging, and to His being a judge. Thaʿlabī repeats this information and adds further examples. As Thaʿlabī notes, the Qurʾānic epithet of God, *al-muhaymin*, is interpreted by some to mean "the judge" (*al-qāḍī*).[59] Thaʿlabī also mentions that some count *al-qāḍī* among the beautiful names of God.[60] Samarqandī, Thaʿlabī, and Baghawī paraphase the expression "Master of the Day of Judgment" (*māliki yawmi al-dīn*, Q. 1:4) plainly as "Judge on the Day of Reckoning" (*qāḍī yawm al-ḥisāb*).[61] Both Baghawī and Māwardī seem to have no scruples designating God as a judge, which may indicate that over the course of time, the appellation became rather common.

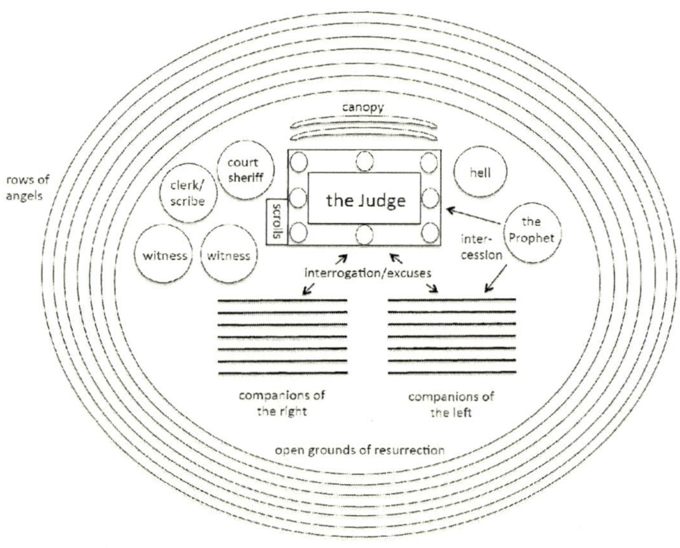

Figure 2: The heavenly court of justice on the Day of Judgment according to early Sunnī Muslim exegesis

Figure 2 attempts to visualize all the elements of the heavenly court discussed so far. It should be noted that further distinctions could be

59 See Thaʿlabī, *Kashf*, 9:287 (from Saʿīd b. al-Musayyab, d. *ca.* 94/712-3); and Baghawī, *Maʿālim*, 8:87.

60 Thaʿlabī, *Kashf*, 9:92 (from Muḥammad b. Kaʿb al-Quraẓī [Medina, middle 2nd/8th century]). This does not seem to have become standard, however, even if lists of the 99 names often include terms such as *al-fattāḥ, al-ḥakam,* or *al-muqṣit.*

61 Samarqandī, *Baḥr*, 1:42 (from Ibn ʿAbbās, Muqātil, and Suddī).

made, and more details added. For example, next to the two groups of the "companions of the right" and the "companions of the left," the Qurʾān (see Q. 56:10-11) speaks of special groups of the blessed, "those who precede" (*sābiqūn*) and "those who are brought near" (*muqarrabūn*) at the end of time. In the *ḥadīth*, these labels are identified with various groups, including the prophets, martyrs, and the underage children of Muslims, who are then declared to enter paradise without reckoning.[62] Likewise unaccounted for are the "people on *al-aʿrāf*" (see Q. 7:46-50), whom the exegetes declare to be Muslims with as many good as evil works on their account, who therefore remain in limbo, on a wall that separates paradise from hell.[63]

DIVINE JUSTICE IN HEAVEN—AND ON EARTH?

As has become clear, to imagine God as a judge, and the heavenly court in terms of an earthly court—that is, to project the mundane court onto the divine one—was a contentious exegetical move even though, from a historian's point of view, it is not particularly surprising. This concluding section asks whether the analogy could also be reversed, that is, whether the imagined overlaps between the two courts made people conceive of the court of the earthly judge as an institution that metes out otherworldly, ultimate justice.

Reading through the chronicles of early Islam, it does in fact appear that judges thought that their adjudication was divinely sanctioned and analogous to eschatological judgment, against all statements to the contrary in the theoretical literature. I suggest that this can be shown by the example of punitive immolation in early Islam, a capital punishment saturated with eschatological overtones. The Umayyad caliphs are known to have implemented the punishment, though they were probably preceded in this by the first four caliphs, the *rāshidūn*.[64] The caliph Hishām b. ʿAbd al-Malik (r. 105–25/724–43), among other Umayyad caliphs, is on record for having burned enemies publicly at the stake. It seems likely that in response to the practice, and to heap criticism on the Umayyads, a prophetic *ḥadīth* was put into circulation that stated that "only the Lord of the Fire punishes with fire: *lā yuʿadhdhib bi'l-nār illā rabb al-nār*."[65] Punishment on earth, in this view,

62 For details, see Lange, *Paradise and Hell*, 124, 195.

63 Ibid., 59–60, 199.

64 For an overview of the history of punitive burning in Islam, see now Christian Lange, "Immolation," *EI-THREE*, with further bibliographical references. In the following two paragraphs, I reproduce some of the findings of this article.

65 See Arent Jan Wensinck, *Concordance et indices de la tradition musulmane* (Leiden: Brill, 1992), 4:164a-b (s.v. ʿ*-dh-b*). Cf. G. H. A. Juynboll, *Encyclopedia of Canonical Ḥadīth* (Leiden: Brill, 2007), 280.

is unlike punishment in the hereafter, and earthly penalties, meted out by the ruler or by the judge, ought not mimic the penalties meted out by God in hell, the realm of fire.

It is not, however, as if the ʿAbbāsids put an end to punitive immolation. The crucified corpse of Ḥallāj, in 309/922, was burned in a terrible parody of what in his *Kitāb al-ṭawāsīn* he had described, longingly evoking the "annihilation" (*fanāʾ*) of the mystic in God, as the burning of the moth after circling the candle.[66] It is really in the fifth/eleventh and sixth/twelfth centuries in Iraq and Persia, however, that punitive burning hits a high, and the involvement of judges in several cases is beyond question. Many of the victims were Ismāʿīlīs, who were burned both alive and dead. This included a mass *auto-da-fé* at Isfahan in 494/1101, for which trenches were dug and filled with burning naphta, while an official, nicknamed Mālik (in reference to the angel that guards the entry to hell) oversaw proceedings. The eminent local jurist, the Shāfiʿī Abū Shujāʾ al-Iṣfahānī, explicitly encouraged this brutal course of action.[67] A striking story is related in Ibn al-Jawzī's Baghdad chronicle, according to which, in the year 530/1135-6, a woman was condemned to burning in the central mosque.[68] Such incidents seem to follow logically from the precedent set by Ibn ʿAqīl (d. 513/1119), the Ḥanbalī judge in Baghdad, who compared his sentencing to death of an Ismāʿīlī to God's sentencing sinners to hell.[69]

As some have suggested, by the end of the fifth/eleventh century, and spearheaded by figures such as Ibn ʿAqīl, "punishments formerly reserved for the hereafter were transposed into the present."[70] The notion that judges enjoyed divine authority, however, had been around much longer. According to a *ḥadīth* related on the authority of Ibn ʿAbbās, two angels descend to sit next to every judge when he adjudicates,[71] just as God is surrounded by angels when judging humankind on the Day of Judgment.

66 Annemarie Schimmel, *Mystical Dimensions of Islam* (Chapel Hill: North Carolina University Press, 1975), 70, 142.

67 ʿIzz al-Dīn b. al-Athīr, *al-Kāmil fī al-taʾrīkh*, ed. ʿUmar ʿAbd al-Salām Tadmurī (Beirut: Dār al-Kitāb al-ʿArabī, 1417/1997), 8:450.

68 Abū al-Faraj ʿAbd al-Raḥmān b. al-Jawzī, *al-Muntaẓam fī tāʾrīkh al-umam waʾl-mulūk*, ed. Muḥammad ʿAbd al-Qādir ʿAṭā et al. (Beirut: Dār al-Kutub al-ʿIlmiyya, 1412/1992), 17:310. Cf. Christian Lange, *Justice, Punishment and the Medieval Muslim Imagination* (Cambridge: Cambridge University Press, 2008), 68.

69 Frank Griffel, *Apostasie und Toleranz im Islam: Die Entwicklung zu al-Ġazālī's Urteil gegen die Philosophie und die Reaktionen der Philosophen* (Leiden: Brill, 2000), 282–83, referring to an incident in Shaʿbān 490/July 1097 reported in Ibn al-Jawzī, *Muntaẓam*.

70 Griffel, *Apostasie*, 283.

71 Muḥammad b. Khalaf Wakīʿ, *Akhbār al-quḍāt*, ed. ʿAbd al-ʿAzīz Muṣṭafā al-Marāghī (Cairo: Maṭbaʿat al-Saʿāda, 1947-50), 1:36. As Tillier notes, this tradition did not make it into the canonical collections. See Tillier, "Espace judiciaire," 499.

CONCLUSIONS

This study has sought to demonstrate that the imagery of the earthly and the divine court of justice in early Islam overlaps in significant respects, despite the great number of theological and legal scruples, voiced by exegetes and jurists alike, that militated against the confluence of these two imageries. Further, this study has suggested that there was not only an overlap, but a reciprocal influence between the two courts. This shaped how their constitutive elements were conceived and how, in the case of the earthly court, justice was meted out. Of course, it is a lot easier to claim that such a reciprocal relationship existed than to produce evidence to prove it. It appears altogether more straightforward to assume that in the early Islamic centuries, as well as in later centuries, this-worldly and otherworldly justice were two autonomous systems developing separately, with no connection whatsoever, as they reacted to different sets of challenges, such as the theological imperative to avoid anthropomorphisn in the case of the heavenly court. Yet, on the whole, it is more plausible that the two systems were in meaningful conversation. In other words, they may have been separate, but they were not independent. Their interdependency was not simply mimetic, in the sense that otherworldly justice was modeled upon earthly realities (or vice-versa); it could also be antithetic, in the sense that otherworldly justice was imagined as the exact opposite of earthly justice.

Here, a sketch has been provided of the heavenly court in some early *tafsīrs* and eschatological works, roughly from the third to the sixth century of the Islamic era. This, it is hoped, has been in itself a worthwhile exercise. One may legitimately question whether the heavenly court properly belongs to the history of the earthly court. However, it is worthwhile to remind ourselves that "a history without the imagination is an mutilated, disembodied history."[72] And, while there are significant studies of Sunnī and Shīʿī apocalypticism, the *barzakh*, as well as studies of the Muslim paradise and hell, the Day of Resurrection or Final Judgment has been written about far less frequently. The topic, and the literature in which it is given form, still await further analysis.

The analogy between the heavenly and the earthly court fulfilled a dual function in early Islam. On the one hand, in the exegetical literature, God's court of justice on the Day of Judgment is in many respects characterized in terms of an ordinary judge's court, with a certain spatial organization, procedure, and court personnel. While such characterizations may derive in part from pre-Islamic (especially Rabbinic) anthropomorphic conceptions of God-as-judge, their rise to prominence, and their persistence, in works of

72 Jacques Le Goff, "Introduction," in *The Medieval Imagination*, trans. Arthur Goldhammer (Chicago: University of Chicago Press, 1988), 1–17, esp. 5.

tafsīr indicates the exegetes' attempt to rein in the Qurʾānic notion of God as an unaccountable judge presiding over the end of time.

On the other hand, the analogy between the Judge and the judge made it possible that judges were on occasion thought to preenact God's justice on the Day of Judgment. It bears mentioning in this context that, against Brockopp's assertion that "court punishments in Islam are not in lieu of eternal punishment," *ḥadd* punishments, according to the Shāfiʿīs, are an expiation for sins (*kaffāra*), so that divine justice *is* in fact preenacted—and eschatological punishment thereby forestalled.[73] And is the mercy of the judge really something that only behooves the divine Judge, but not His earthly counterpart? "It is better to err in forgiveness than in punishment," runs a famous legal maxim.[74]

The brooding metaphysical context of the earthly court no doubt served to enhance the prestige and authority of judges. For the judges, to appear as "partners with God-the-judge, invoking God's court was a first step toward eventual judicial autonomy from the political authorities."[75] It was also, however, a step toward exposing the judicial profession to the "temptation of divinity"[76] and, as in the case of judges committing enemies of the faith to the fire, toward imagining oneself to enact ultimate, heavenly justice.

73 See the references in Lange, *Justice*, 185 n. 26.

74 See on this maxim, Intisar A. Rabb, *Doubt in Islamic Law: A History of Legal Maxims, Interpretation, and Islamic Criminal Law* (Cambridge: Cambridge University Press, 2015).

75 See Arie Mermelstein and Shalom E. Holtz, "Introduction," to *The Divine Courtroom in Comparative Perspective*, ed. Ari Mermelstein et al. (Leiden: Brill, 2014), 1–5, at 5.

76 I borrow this expression from Josef van Ess, *Chiliastische Erwartungen und die Versuchung der Göttlichkeit: Der Kalif al-Ḥākim (386-411 H.)* (Heidelberg: Carl Winter, 1977).

Chapter Seven

Justice, Judges, and Law in Three Arabic Mirrors for Princes, 8th–11th Centuries

Louise Marlow
Wellesley College

Many scholars have highlighted the centrality of the theme of justice in pre-modern Islamic political thought, and noted its especially striking prominence in "mirrors for princes."[1] The topic, often the subject of a mirror-writer's opening chapter, yields some of the mirror literature's most characteristically cited aphorisms: "The ruler is the shadow of God on earth, and in him every wronged person takes refuge;" "An hour of justice is better than sixty years of worship."[2] The prevalence and durability of these maxims did not diminish their meaning. Every repetition took place in a specific context, in which it carried immediate local significance. In his pioneering study, *Loyalty and Leadership in an Early Islamic Society*, Roy P. Mottahedeh elucidated in brilliant fashion, among other topics, the meanings that conceptions of royal justice carried for the inhabitants of the Būyid polity of

1 By "mirrors for princes," I refer to works of political advice composed for the benefit of rulers, princes, and other members of the political élites. From antiquity into the early modern period (or even later), mirrors flourished in numerous political and cultural settings, and the genre is amply represented in the Islamicate languages. The mirror literature constitutes an important vehicle for the expression of political thought. On the theme of justice in such writings, see A. K. S. Lambton, "Justice in the Medieval Persian Theory of Kingship," *Studia Islamica* 17 (1962): 91–119; Linda T. Darling, *A History of Social Justice and Political Power in the Middle East: The Circle of Justice from Mesopotamia to Globalization* (London and New York: Routledge, 2013); Linda T. Darling, "Social Cohesion (*'Asabiyya*) and Justice in the Late Medieval Middle East," *Comparative Studies in Society and History* 49 (2007): 329–57; Linda T. Darling, "'Do Justice, Do Justice, For That is Paradise': Middle Eastern Advice for Indian Muslim Rulers," *Comparative Studies of South Asia, Africa and the Middle East* 22 (2002): 3–19.

2 For examples, see Abū Ḥāmid al-Ghazālī, *Naṣīḥat al-mulūk*, ed. Jalāl al-Dīn Humā'ī (Tehran: Kitābkhāna-yi Millī, 1972), 15, 81 = F. R. C. Bagley, *Ghazālī's Book of Counsel for Kings* (London: Oxford University Press, 1964), 14, 45; cf. Lambton, "Justice in the Medieval Persian Theory," 105.

fourth/tenth- and fifth/eleventh-century Iraq and western Iran.[3] In *Loyalty and Leadership*, Mottahedeh explored a large repertoire of anecdotes, assembled from diverse sources, to evoke, with sensitivity and imagination, a society's self-understanding. In this brief essay, I shall treat the more formal literature of mirrors for princes, and attempt to link the disquisitions of the genre's learned authors to the political cultures in which they lived, with particular attention to the subject of legal justice.[4] I shall suggest that the mirror literature's underpinnings in timeless wisdom notwithstanding, the genre conveyed conceptions of justice that were complex and multiple. Not only viziers and secretaries but also jurists and judges composed mirrors for princes; having achieved high levels of accomplishment in the religious sciences and, in the case of judges, appointment to important functions within the state, these specialists in the religious law were well situated to advise the rulers whom they served.

IBN AL-MUQAFFAʿ'S *RISĀLA FĪ AL-ṢAḤĀBA*

I begin with an author who was an official secretary (*kātib*) and littérateur rather than a jurist or a judge, but who formulated what Joseph Lowry has termed "the first Islamic legal theory."[5] Ibn al-Muqaffaʿ (d. *ca.* 139/757), a major contributor to the formation of Arabic literary culture and a principal mediator into that culture of Middle Persian *andarz*, composed an advisory text known as *Risāla fī al-ṣaḥāba* ("Epistle on the Ruler's Companions"), intended, it seems, for the caliph Manṣūr (r. 136–158/754–775). Ibn al-Muqaffaʿ, Lowry asserts, confronted the "principal epistemological problem of Islamic legal theory, namely, the relationship of indeterminacy to interpretive authority within the context of a revealed law."[6] Ibn al-Muqaffaʿ, perceiving the lack of uniformity in the scholars' formulation of law, urged the caliph to review the conflicting legal rulings and adjudicate between them.[7] Under the rubrics of *dīn* (religion) and *ʿaql* (rational intellect), he distinguished between parts of the law that excluded human interpretation and parts of the law that required and permitted interpretation; in the

3 Roy P. Mottahedeh, *Loyalty and Leadership in an Early Islamic Society* (Princeton: Princeton University Press, 1980 [rev. ed., London: I. B. Tauris, 2001]), 175–90.

4 Cf. Mottahedeh's "Preface to the Second Edition," *Loyalty and Leadership*, vii–x.

5 Joseph E. Lowry, "The First Islamic Legal Theory: Ibn al-Muqaffaʿ on Interpretation, Authority, and the Structure of the Law," *Journal of the American Oriental Society* 128 (2008): 25 –40.

6 Ibid., 26.

7 Cf. Patricia Crone and Martin Hinds, *God's Caliph: Religious Authority in the First Centuries of Islam* (Cambridge: Cambridge University Press, 1986), 86 and n. 182, with reference to an example recorded in Wakīʿ, *Akhbār al-quḍāt* (Beirut: ʿĀlam al-Kutub, 1980), 3:46, in which three Kūfan authorities pronounce different legal opinions in response to a question involving the status of a sale.

latter sphere, moreover, he argued that the caliph should exercise supreme and exclusive authority. The distinction between a non-derogable sphere and a variable sphere of the law features importantly in Ibn al-Muqaffaʿ's treatment of the extent of the subjects' duty of obedience. Ibn al-Muqaffaʿ, in accepting the premise of the maxim and *ḥadīth*: "*Lā ṭāʿata li-makhlūq*^{in} *fī maʿṣiyat al-Khāliq*: There is no obligation of obedience on the part of the created being in [acts of] disobedience to the Creator," stipulates that obedience to the caliph depends on his implementation of major elements of Islamic law—such as the rules pertaining to prayer, fasting, pilgrimage, avoidance of the unlawful, and penal matters—that fell within the non-derogable sphere.

At the same time, Ibn al-Muqaffaʿ assigns to the caliph a supreme interpretive authority in matters that fall within three categories: personal judgment (*ra'y*), administration (*tadbīr*), and "the political authority (*amr*), the reins and handles of which God has put in the hands of imams."[8] By these categories Ibn al-Muqaffaʿ appears to have had in mind numerous matters, including affairs related to military strategy, the collection and distribution of war spoils, the appointment and removal of officials, legal interpretation in cases for which there is no precedent, the implementation of penal law and of legal decisions according to the Qurʾān and *Sunna*, waging war and concluding truces, and accepting and disbursing property on Muslims' behalf.[9] As Lowry points out, the ruler's upholding of the ordinances and precedents (*iqāmat al-ʿaẓāʾim waʾl-sunan*) that preclude human interpretation ensures his legitimacy and entitles him to the subjects' obedience. At the same time, the sphere of the law that entails the use of reason and in which the ruler exercises discretion also necessitates the subjects' obedience.[10] In this conception, Ibn al-Muqaffaʿ had formulated a theory of two spheres of law—one admitting no interpretation, and to the implementation of which the ruler is obligated; the other permitting and requiring rational interpretation, and the implementation of which fell largely within the ruler's discretion.

Lowry proposes that in formulating this theory of these two spheres of the law, Ibn al-Muqaffaʿ in effect anticipated later conceptualizations of

8 Lowry, "First Islamic Legal Theory," 31.

9 Ibid., 28 –34. See also Paul Heck's discussion of the "person-centered" nature of Ibn al-Muqaffaʿ's conception of law in his "Law in ʿAbbasid Political Thought from Ibn al-Muqaffaʿ (d. 139/756) to Qudāma b. Jaʿfar (d. 337/948)," in *ʿAbbasid Studies: Occasional Papers of the School of ʿAbbasid Studies, Cambridge, 6-10 July, 2002*, ed. James Montgomery (Leuven: Peeters, 2004), 83–109, at 85. See also S. D. Goitein, "A Turning Point in the History of the Muslim State," in *Studies in Islamic History and Institutions* (Leiden: Brill, 1968), 149–67, esp. 157; István T. Kristó-Nagy, *La pensée d'Ibn al-Muqaffaʿ: Un «agent double» dans le monde persan et arabe* (Paris: Éditions de Paris, 2013), 236–37.

10 Lowry, "First Islamic Legal Theory," 33.

the structure of Islamic law.[11] The largely negative response to his vision of the caliph's authority with regard to legal interpretation in the latter sphere has tended to obscure this important point.[12] Ibn al-Muqaffaʿ wrote at a time when the *madhāhib* (schools of law) were still in relatively nascent stages in their formation, and when caliphs, as Patricia Crone and Martin Hinds have asserted, perhaps possessed a credible claim to religious-legal authority.[13] Despite the divergence between Ibn al-Muqaffaʿ's vision and subsequent developments, his urging of the caliph to assume this responsibility echoes the way in which some later mirror-writers encouraged their royal patrons to equip themselves with the knowledge necessary for intervention in the religious-legal realm.

PSEUDO-MĀWARDĪ'S *NAṢĪḤAT AL-MULŪK*

Ibn al-Muqaffaʿ's distinction between the spheres of *dīn* (religious and fixed) and *ʿaql* (rational and discretionary) finds an implicit endorsement in a later Arabic mirror, the *Naṣīḥat al-mulūk* ("Counsel for Kings") of Pseudo-Māwardī, an unidentified tenth-century Muʿtazilī author schooled in the Ḥanafī tradition that predominated in the Sāmānid kingdom.[14] In keeping with the categories of juristic and theological discourse, Pseudo-Māwardī conceives of the relationship between rulers and their subjects in terms of mutual and interdependent rights and obligations (*ḥuqūq*, pl. of *ḥaqq*). Detailing the duties of the ruler in a five-part treatment of the quality of *taqwā* ("godliness," living in mindfulness of God), he lists:

> [Fourthly]: Executing God's penal laws, carrying out His ordinances among His servants, upholding equity (*qisṭ*) in His lands, exercising judgment according to that which is right (*al-ḥukm biʾl-ḥaqq*) over [the people's] lives, wealth, persons, womenfolk, and reputations; avoiding injustice

11 Ibid., 25–26; cf. Heck, "Law in ʿAbbasid Political Thought," 97 and n. 28.

12 On the apparent lack of reaction to Ibn al-Muqaffaʿ's proposals, see Goitein, "Turning Point," 166–67; Andras Hamori, "Ibn al-Muqaffaʿ," in G. Böwering, ed., *The Princeton Encyclopedia of Islamic Political Thought* (Princeton: Princeton University Press, 2013), 232–33.

13 Crone and Hinds, *God's Caliph*, 43–57, 85–87.

14 Regarding the authorship of this mirror, I follow, in the present discussion as in my *Counsel for Kings: Wisdom and Politics in Tenth-Century Iran* (Edinburgh: Edinburgh University Press, 2016), the arguments advanced by Fu'ād ʿAbd al-Munʿim Aḥmad in the introduction to his edition of *Naṣīḥat al-mulūk al-mansūb ilā Abī al-Ḥasan al-Māwardī* (Alexandria: Mu'assasat Shabāb al-Jāmiʿa, 1988), used in the preparation of this essay, entitled "Muqaddimat al-taḥqīq waʾl-dirāsa," 5–33; and in his monograph *al-Māwardī wa-kitāb Naṣīḥat al-mulūk* (Alexandria: Mu'assasat Shabāb al-Jāmiʿa, n. d.); as well as Hassan Ansari, "Yak andīshanāma-yi siyāsī-yi arzishmand-i Muʿtazilī az Khurāsān dawrān-i Sāmānīyān," *Barrasīhā-yi tārīkhī*, http://ansari.kateban.com/entryprint1951.html (last accessed June 2017). See now also the insightful discussion of Makram Abbès, *Al-Māwardī: De l'éthique du prince et du gouvernement de l'état* (Paris: Les Belles Lettres, 2015), 202–03.

> and transgression against them and partiality among them.[15]

Invoking the maxim and *ḥadīth, lā ṭāʿata* (also invoked by Ibn al-Muqaffaʿ), Pseudo-Māwardī extends the maxim's scope to subordinate the subjects' duty to obey the political authorities to the ruler's just and legitimate governance of the polity. As a premise for his argument, he affirms the king's sharing in the human condition of his subjects. He writes:

> The subjects and the ruler (*al-raʿiyya waʾl-rāʿī*) are united in closeness of kind and connectedness (*qurb al-mujānasa waʾl-munāsaba*), similarity of nature, form, and kinship (*mushākalat al-ṭabīʿa waʾl-ṣūra waʾl-ḥāma*); and connectedness (*munāsaba*) necessitates compassion and inclination. In addition, he owes them the rights (*ḥaqq*) due to the religious community (*milla*) and the covenant of protection (*dhimma*), for God has made the believers brothers, and the *dhimma* a trust (*amāna*). Obedience is incumbent on them only on condition of justice, the fulfillment of that which he has promised, compassion and mercy (*innamā yajibu ʿalayhim al-ṭāʿa bi-sharīṭat al-maʿdala waʾl-wafāʾ biʾl-ʿahd waʾl-raʾfa waʾl-raḥma*). For it is related that the Prophet said: "The Quraysh have a claim against you, to the effect that if they seek mercy they should be treated mercifully, if they submit to arbitration they should receive justice, and if they conclude pacts they should be fulfilled (*in ʿāhadū wufū*). Whoever does not act in this way, then the curse of God, the angels, and all the people will be against him; his action will not be accepted from him in any fashion." He also said: "There is no duty of obedience to the creature in disobedience to the Creator: *lā ṭāʿata li-makhlūq*^{in} *fī maʿṣiyat al-Khāliq*. And he said: "Obedience is due only in return for goodness: *innamā al-ṭāʿa fī al-maʿrūf*."[16]

The king, Pseudo-Māwardī asserts, is like his subjects in kind (*jins*) and in nature (*ṭabīʿa*), and his relationship (*munāsaba*) with them requires his sympathetic treatment of them. His debt of responsibility involves the entirety of his subjects, Muslim and non-Muslim alike. Pseudo-Māwardī cites *ḥadīth* reports that broaden the subjects' claims against the ruler to include general principles of clemency, justice, and the fulfillment of covenants. The last of these qualities, *wafāʾ* or loyalty, was essential to the maintenance of the social relationships through which the king's governance was conducted

15 Pseudo-Māwardī, *Naṣīḥat al-mulūk*, 148.

16 Ibid., 254–55. Cf. ibid., 103. For the *ḥadīth* report, see Nasāʾī, *Sunan al-Nasāʾī bi-sharḥ al-Ḥāfiẓ Jalāl al-Dīn al-Suyūṭī* (Beirut: Dār al-Fikr, 1930), 7:159–60; Ibn Mājah, *Sunan*, ed. Muḥammad Fuʾād ʿAbd al-Bāqī (Cairo: ʿĪsā al-Bābī al-Ḥalabī, 1952), 2:955–56, nos. 2863–65; and Khaled Abou El Fadl, *Rebellion and Violence in Islamic Law* (Cambridge: Cambridge University Press, 2001), 121.

and the subjects' lives rendered secure; breach of *wafā'* risked the severance of the king's bonds with the intermediaries on whose active support his governance depended.[17]

Strikingly, Pseudo-Māwardī encourages the ruler to develop a degree of expertise in the religious sciences, as well as the cultivation of personal virtues. Study of the religious laws and ordinances, he writes, is an obligation for every Muslim, but particularly necessary for kings, because they are charged with the duty to investigate the grievances of their subjects (*al-naẓar fī maẓālim al-raʿiyya wa'l-bariyya*), to listen to their claims, proofs, oaths and testimony, and to adjudicate accordingly. Pseudo-Māwardī urges the king to attain the qualifications necessary for the exercise of rational inquiry (*naẓar*) and independent reasoning (*ijtihād*) in matters pertaining to the religious law. The king may be required to lead the ritual prayer; respond to questions involving the collection of the prescribed alms and charitable donations; or adjudicate in matters concerning marriage, sale and inheritance, the division of the spoils of war, and the allocation of revenue within the kingdom. Pseudo-Māwardī impresses upon the king the desirability of limiting his dependence on specialists, such as judges, jurists and jurisconsults, for every case (*nāzila*) and eventuality (*ḥāditha*) that might occur. He adds:

> Furthermore, if the king acquires a satisfactory degree of juristic understanding, it will enable him to pursue independent reasoning (*ijtihād*) and rational enquiry (*naẓar*) in his own right. He will be equipped to seek proofs for his own reasoning, and to interpret according to his own judgments, because in his interpretation (*ta'wīl*) he will only do that which is permitted to him. A knowledge of jurisprudence will also provide the king with juridical strategies (*al-ḥiyal al-fiqhiyya*), by means of which he will be able to avoid much of what is forbidden and to follow only that which is licit (*kathīr min al-ḥarām ilā al-ḥalāl*), and to abandon the false for the true (*min al-bāṭil ilā al-ḥaqq*).[18]

In this forceful passage, Pseudo-Māwardī urges the king to cultivate juristic knowledge in order to minimize his dependence on specialists who, as he hints elsewhere, might falter in their impartiality. He envisages a minimal "sum" of beliefs to which Muslims, including the king, should subscribe, and discourages him from seeking to impose uniformity beyond

17 Cf. Mottahedeh, *Loyalty and Leadership*, 40–96 and passim; Jürgen Paul, *Lokale und imperiale Herrschaft im Iran des 12. Jahrhunderts. Herrschaftspraxis und Konzepte* (Wiesbaden: Reichert Verlag, 2016), 331–50.

18 Pseudo-Māwardī, *Naṣīḥat al-mulūk*, 159–60.

this minimum.[19] His vision of the law is of a dynamic and continually evolving phenomenon, in the continuing development and enactment of which the qualified ruler should participate.

This understanding of the ruler's qualifications to contribute in a limited fashion to the development of Islamic law finds a context in the education of the Ṭāhirid and Sāmānid *amīrs*. ʿAbd Allāh b. Ṭāhir (d. 230/845), recipient of the celebrated advisory text composed by his father, Ṭāhir,[20] was trained in *adab* and *fiqh*, literary culture and jurisprudence, and was especially noted for his poetry and prose.[21] The Sāmānid Aḥmad (I) b. Asad, governor of Samarqand until his death in 250/864, was, according to the fourth/tenth-century historian Narshakhī, "learned and pious" (*ʿālim va pārsā*), and according to Ibn al-Athīr (d. 630/1233), he was religiously observant (*dayyin*), was rationally intelligent (*ʿāqil*), and composed fine poetry in Arabic.[22] At least four of Aḥmad's sons—Naṣr (I), Isḥāq, Yaʿqūb, and Ismāʿīl—heard and transmitted *ḥadīth* reports, which they related on the authority of several transmitters, including their father.[23] They fit within a category of persons to whom Roy Mottahedeh has drawn attention: those who, while not professional scholars, devoted a portion of their time to hearing and transmitting *ḥadīth* reports. Indeed, these early Sāmānid *amīrs* provide telling examples of this perhaps "semi-professional" group.[24] Prominent among the subjects of the *ḥadīth* reports that they transmitted

---

19 Marlow, *Wisdom and Politics*, 1:218–20. Cf. Hossein Modarressi, "Essential Islam: The Minimum that a Muslim is Required to Acknowledge," in *Accusations of Unbelief in Islam: A Diachronic Perspective on Takfīr*, ed. Camilla Adang, Hassan Ansari, Maribel Fierro, and Sabine Schmidtke (Leiden: Brill, 2016), 395–412, esp. 404–408.

20 On this important Arabic work of political advice (mentioned further in what follows), see C. E. Bosworth, "An Early Arabic Mirror for Princes: Ṭāhir Dhū l-Yamīnain's Epistle to His Son ʿAbdallāh (206/821)," *Journal of Near Eastern Studies* 29 (1970): 25–41.

21 Muḥammad b. Aḥmad al-Dhahabī, *Siyar aʿlām al-nubalāʾ*, ed. Bashshār ʿAwwād Maʿrūf and Shuʿayb al-Arnaʾūṭ (Beirut: Muʾassasat al-Risāla, 2001), 10:684–85. Cf. C. E. Bosworth, "The Tahirids and Arabic Culture," *Journal of Semitic Studies* 14, (1969): 45–79, esp. 54, 58.

22 Abū Bakr Muḥammad b. Jaʿfar Narshakhī, *Tārīkh-i Bukhārā*, trans. Abū Naṣr Aḥmad b. Muḥammad b. Naṣr al-Qubāwī, summ. Muḥammad b. Zufar b. ʿUmar, ed. Mudarris Raẓavī (Tehran: Kitābfurūshī-yi Sanāʾī, 1984), 91; and the English translation by Richard N. Frye, trans., *The History of Bukhara, Translated from the Persian Abridgement of the Arabic Original by Narshakhi* (Princeton: Markus Wiener, 2007),105; Ibn al-Athīr, *al-Kāmil fī al-taʾrīkh*, ed. C. J. Tornberg, *Ibn-el-Athiri Chronicon quod perfectissimum inscribitur* (Leiden: E. J. Brill, 1862 [repr. Beirut: Dār Ṣādir, 1965-7]), 7:456.

23 Samʿānī, *al-Ansāb* (Hyderabad: Maṭbaʿat Majlis Dāʾirat al-Maʿārif al-ʿUthmāniyya, 1962–82), 7:25; Najm al-Dīn ʿUmar b. Muḥammad b. Aḥmad Nasafī, *al-Qand fī dhikr ʿulamāʾ Samarqand*, ed. Yūsuf al-Hādī (Tehran: Āʾīna-yi Mīrāth, 1999), 65, no. 60, where the author mentions the four brothers in this order, and states that all of them related *ḥadīth* (*kulluhum yuḥaddithūna*); 587–88, no. 1035.

24 Mottahedeh, *Loyalty and Leadership*, 142; W. L. Treadwell, "The Political History of the Sāmānid State" (PhD diss., University of Oxford: 1991), 99 n. 129; Samʿānī, *al-Ansāb*, 7:25; Nasafī, *al-Qand fī dhikr ʿulamāʾ Samarqand*, 65, no. 60; 587–88, no. 1035.

are the themes of *ghazw* (raiding or warfare at the frontier), justice, and respect for scholars, topics that feature prominently in mirrors for princes.[25]

Pseudo-Māwardī praised the Sāmānid *amīr* of Samarqand, Isḥāq b. Aḥmad, for his devotion to religious knowledge (*ʿilm*) and literary culture (*adab*), and for his love (*maḥabba*) for the persons who pursued these subjects, as well as his frequent and attentive contact with them.[26] The Sāmānid *amīr* Ismāʿīl b. Aḥmad (r. 279-295/892-907) likewise attained a degree of learning in both the religious and the literary branches of knowledge, specifically combining *ḥadīth* and *adab*. According to a report related on the authority of Naṣr II's vizier Abū al-Faḍl Balʿamī (d. 329/940), Ismāʿīl stated that the first book pertaining to *adab* that he had committed to memory was the *Adab al-kātib* ("Good Conduct of the Secretary") [of the littérateur Ibn Qutayba, d. 276/889], and next the *Gharīb al-ḥadīth* ("Unusual Words Used in Ḥadīth") of Abū ʿUbayd [al-Qāsim b. Sallām, d. *ca.* 224/838];[27] he then embarked on the study of *ḥadīth* and *ādāb* (pl. of *adab*). Nasafī reported further that Ismāʿīl was proficient in Arabic grammar and inflexion (*iʿrāb*), and well versed in the differences of legal interpretation (*kāna ... yaʿlamu al-ikhtilāfāt*).[28]

As detailed in the preceding discussion, Pseudo-Māwardī also mentions the types of legal issues in which the ruler might find it necessary to draw upon his religious knowledge and to exercise his rational discretion, and his observations coincide with the activities reported for the early Sāmānid *amīrs*. Their cultivation of the religious-moral style characteristic of the northeast, including their participation in religious studies, equipped them to lead the prayers at the funerals of eminent scholars.[29] They also adjudicated in matters that required a degree of juristic understanding. Naṣr (I) b. Aḥmad (r. 250–279/864–892), for example, received a document related to a *waqf*, which he was able to authenticate and implement in a beneficial manner.[30] Furthermore, the early Sāmānid *amīrs* became proverbial for their assiduous efforts to redress the grievances (*maẓālim*) of

25 Samʿānī, *al-Ansāb*, 7:24–25; Treadwell, "Political History," 99 n. 129.

26 Pseudo-Māwardī, *Naṣīḥat al-mulūk*, 107.

27 Muḥammad b. Isḥāq al-Nadīm = Ibn al-Nadīm, *Kitāb al-Fihrist*, ed. Ayman Fu'ād Sayyid (London: Al-Furqan Islamic Heritage Foundation, 2009), 1:i:237, 216, 271. Abū ʿUbayd was a grammarian, Qur'ānic scholar, and jurist; born in Herat, he was engaged as a tutor to two families in Khurāsān, enjoyed the patronage of ʿAbd Allāh b. Ṭāhir in Baghdad, and died in Mecca.

28 Nasafī, *al-Qand fī dhikr ʿulamāʾ Samarqand*, 65, no. 60.

29 Jürgen Paul, "The Histories of Samarqand," *Studia Iranica* 22 (1993): 69–92, esp. 88. On the themes that recur in the self-representation of the transmission of knowledge in the northeast, see Roy Mottahedeh, "The Transmission of Learning: The Role of the Islamic Northeast," in Nicole Grandin and Marc Gaborieau, eds., *Madrasa: La transmission du savoir dans le monde musulman* (Paris: Éditions Arguments, 1997): 61–70, esp. 61–63.

30 Nasafī, *al-Qand fī dhikr ʿulamāʾ Samarqand*, 587–88, no. 1035.

their subjects. Ismāʿīl (I) b. Aḥmad (r. 279–295/892–907) was celebrated for his regular and sustained accessibility to his subjects even at the cost of great physical hardship; according to the Ghaznavid historian Bayhaqī (d. 470/1077), Ismāʿīl I explained that if an indigent stranger (*gharībī darvīsh*) happened to wish to bring a matter to his attention and found the *amīr* unavailable, he might be moved to curse him in his prayers (*marā duʿā-yi bad gūyad*).[31]

Pseudo-Māwardī discusses the ruler's duty, as part of his upholding of justice, to "render judgment among the subjects in their grievances and their petitions (*an yaḥkuma baynahum fī maẓālimihim wa-daʿāwīhim*). He should hear their proofs and testimonies according to the Book of God and the *Sunna* of His Prophet, and that which right (the rightful claim) and the mandate of a legal judgment (*mā yūjibuh al-ḥaqq wa'l-ḥukm*)."[32]

Pseudo-Māwardī's encouragement of the ruler's individual participation in *ijtihād* and *naẓar* coincides with Muʿtazilī rejections or restrictions of *taqlīd*, the following of precedent without rational inquiry into it or its alternatives.[33] To arrive at the truth by means of *ijtihād* required exertion and effort; *naẓar* involved not merely quiet meditation but active speculation, associated with dialogue and argument.[34] Pseudo-Māwardī's exposition is somewhat reminiscent of Ibn al-Muqaffaʿ's advice to the caliph, whom the earlier writer, as noted above, exhorted to assert religious authority and adjudicate in various matters of religious law.

The appointment of judges was among the most important responsibilities of the ruler, and directly linked to his duty to uphold the law. Authors of mirrors frequently detailed the qualifications and qualities necessary in the judge, and warned their royal recipients against potential abuses of the judicial office. In his advisory testament (*waṣiyya*) to his son ʿAbd Allāh upon the latter's appointment to the governorship of Diyār Rabīʿa, Ṭāhir had emphasized the unparalleled importance of the judgeship (*qaḍāʾ*),

31 See Abū al-Faḍl al-Bayhaqī, *Tārīkh-i Bayhaqī* = *Tārīkh-i Masʿūdī*, ed. Q. Ghanī and A. A. Fayyāḍ (Tehran, 1945-6), 69. Cf. Niẓām al-Mulk, *Siyar al-mulūk (Siyāsatnāma)*, ed. H. S. G. Darke (Tehran: Bungāh-i Tarjama va Nashr-i Kitāb, 1962), 28–29; and English translation by Hubert Darke trans., *The Book of Government or Rules for Kings* (London: Routledge and Kegan Paul, 1978), 21–22; Mīrkhwānd, *Tarīkh-i rawẓat al-ṣafāʾ* (Tehran: Markazī-yi Khayyām Pīrūz, 1959-60), 4:36. Paul points out that the Sāmānids sometimes delegated the responsibility for *maẓālim* to individuals outside the dynastic family; see his *Herrscher, Gemeinwesen, Vermittler: Ostiran und Transoxanien in vormongolischer Zeit* (Beirut: Franz Steiner Verlag, Stuttgart, 1996), 151 and n. 16. On the subjects' duty to offer prayers on behalf of the ruler, see further Paul, *Herrscher, Gemeinwesen, Vermittler*, 223–32.

32 Pseudo-Māwardī, *Naṣīḥat al-mulūk*, 261.

33 Josef van Ess, *Die Erkenntnislehre des ʿAḍudaddīn al-Īcī: Übersetzung und Kommentar des ersten Buches seiner Mawāqif* (Wiesbaden: Franz Steiner Verlag, 1966), 242, 279, 303, 325–27 and passim.

34 Van Ess, *Erkenntnislehre*, 16, 20 (cf. *jadal* and *mujādala*), 303.

and described it as "God's balance, by which circumstances maintain their balance in the world: *al-qaḍāʾ … li-annah mīzān Allāh alladhī yaʿtadilu ʿalayh al-aḥwāl fī al-arḍ*."[35] In a list of the qualities necessary in judges, Pseudo-Māwardī mentions knowledge (*ʿilm*), understanding (*fiqh*), religion (*diyāna*), temperance (*ʿiffa*), trustworthiness (*amāna*), awareness (*dirāya*), integrity (*ʿadāla*), probity (*ṣiyāna*), and familiarity with the (religious) ordinances, statutory limits, precepts and stipulations (*shurūṭ*).[36] Somewhat later in his mirror, he resumes:

> The king should exert himself in the selection of judges (*ḥukkām*), and appoint only persons who are religiously observant and upright, knowledgeable and learned in jurisprudence, resourceful and trustworthy, dignified and composed.... He should direct the judge to immerse himself in investigation, rational inquiry and finding for the weak against the strong, and exhort him not to rush to judgment before the completion of the investigation and inquiry, nor to delay after the firm establishment of proof and consolidation of the evidence. For in both of those cases lie neglect and omission. The judge should not render judgment out of inclination, nor stray from the path of justice out of partiality towards the person awaiting judgment....[37]
>
> The essential prerequisite in the matter of the *qāḍī* and the *ḥākim* is that the ruler should appoint him on terms that provide him with ample and comfortable allowances, so that he has no need for, and will not covet, the possessions of the subjects; avidity for the goods of the lower world, especially in these times of ours, has become a habit among the *ʿulamāʾ*, quite contrary to what ought to be the case with them. It is related from the Prophet that he said, "Anyone who increases in knowledge and at the same time increases in cupidity for the world, increases only in distance from God, while God increases in dislike of him."[38]
>
> Aristotle summed the whole matter up when he said: "The judge (*ḥākim*) is a lord to those over whom he holds authority (*sayyid ʿalā man waliyah*), so in the judge, four qualities should come together, namely, that he be modest, scrupulous, knowledgeable, and not hasty."[39]

35 Ṭabarī, *Taʾrīkh al-Ṭabarī = Taʾrīkh al-rusul waʾl-mulūk*, ed. M. Faḍl Ibrāhīm (Cairo: Dār al-Maʿārif, 1960-77), 8:587.

36 Pseudo-Māwardī, *Naṣīḥat al-mulūk*, 240–41.

37 Ibid., 261–62.

38 Ibid., 262; cf. Manṣūr b. al-Ḥusayn al-Ābī, *Nathr al-durr* (Cairo: al-Hayʾa al-Miṣriyya al-ʿĀmma lil-Kitāb, 1980), 1:189.

39 Pseudo-Māwardī, *Naṣīḥat al-mulūk*, 262. For the Pseudo-Aristotelian citation, see also Mario Grignaschi, "La «Siyâsatu-l-ʿâmmiyya» et l'influence iranienne sur la pensée politique islamique," *Acta Iranica* VI, Deuxième Série, *Hommages et Opera Minora*, Volume III, *Monumentum H. S.*

Pseudo-Māwardī follows his citations from Pseudo-Aristotle with the full correspondence dispatched by the second Rightly Guided Caliph, ʿUmar b. al-Khaṭṭāb (r. 13–33/634–44), to Abū Mūsā al-Ashʿarī, whom ʿUmar appointed to governorships in Basra and Kufa,[40] and to Muʿāwiya b. Abī Sufyān, his governor in Damascus (later the first Umayyad caliph, r. 41–60/661–80).[41] When at a later point in the same chapter Pseudo-Māwardī turns to the ruler's redress of grievances, he again invokes the exemplary conduct of ʿUmar, and also that of the fourth Rightly Guided Caliph and, for the Shīʿa, the First Imām, ʿAlī b. Abī Ṭālib (r. 35–40/656–61):

> The king should protect the common people (*ʿāmma*) from his own injustice, and the injustice of his companions and retinue.... If the subjects oppress one another, the *sulṭān* is their place of retreat, their succor, their refuge and their source of assistance.... The king should behave in accordance with this quality—by which I mean justice (*ʿadl*)—in following the command of God and imitating Him, accustoming himself to the habits of His righteous prophets and friends, and following the path of the surpassing sages, in accordance with God's promise to the just of an ample reward and noble recompense in the afterlife, and His threat to the unjust of painful chastisement and severe punishment.
>
> The Commander of the Faithful ʿUmar brought a case before Zayd b. Thābit [d. 45/665] for judgment, swore an oath against his adversary, and they both reached agreement. The Commander of the Faithful ʿAlī brought a case before Shurayḥ b. al-Ḥārith b. Qays al-Kindī [d. *ca.* 72–99/691–718], his *qāḍī*, for judgment; Shurayḥ pronounced two decrees, and ʿAlī abided by the legal obligation placed upon him after the verdict.[42]

Nyberg (Leiden: E. J. Brill, 1975), 33–286, at 115–16; Miklós Maróth, *The Correspondence Between Aristotle and Alexander the Great: An Anonymous Greek Novel in Letters in Arabic Translation* (Piliscsaba: The Avicenna Institute of Middle Eastern Studies, 2006), 36.

40 Pseudo-Māwardī, *Naṣīḥat al-mulūk*, 263–64. Cf. Ibn Qutayba, *Kitāb ʿUyūn al-akhbār* (Cairo: Maṭbaʿat Dār al-Kutub al-Miṣriyya, 1925), 1:66; al-Jāḥiẓ, *al-Bayān wa'l-tabyīn*, ed. ʿAbd al-Salām Muḥammad Hārūn (Cairo: Maktabat al-Khānjī, 1960), 2:48–50; Māwardī, *al-Aḥkām al-sulṭāniyya wa'l-wilāyāt al-dīniyya* (Cairo: Muṣṭafā al-Bābī al-Ḥalabī, 1966), 71–72; and English translation by Wafaa H. Wahba, trans., *Al-Māwardī: The Ordinances of Government* (Reading: Garnet Publishing, 1996), 80–81.

41 Pseudo-Māwardī, *Naṣīḥat al-mulūk*, 264. Cf. Abū Yūsuf, *Kitāb al-Kharāj*, ed. Iḥsān ʿAbbās (Beirut: Dār al-Shurūq, 1975), 264–65; Jāḥiẓ, *Rasāʾil al-Jāḥiẓ*, ed. ʿAbd al-Salām Muḥammad Hārūn (Cairo: Maktabat al-Khānjī, 1964–79), 2:31.

42 Pseudo-Māwardī, *Naṣīḥat al-mulūk*, 269-70. For both individuals, the first a Companion of the Prophet, one of the Prophet's scribes and a *qāḍī* under ʿUmar and ʿUthmān, and the second a *tābiʿ*, member of the generation that followed the Prophet's Companions, and an early *qāḍī* of Kūfa, see Ṭabarī, *Taʾrīkh, sub anno* 21 = *History of al-Ṭabarī*, 14:15–16, and nn. 84 and 87. For accounts of ʿUmar's recourse to Zayd's arbitration, see Wakīʿ, *Akhbār al-quḍāt*, 1:108; for ʿAlī's consultations with Shurayḥ, see ibid., 2:194–97. Ibn Khallikān reports two incidents in which ʿAlī came before Shurayḥ in his *Wafayāt al-aʿyān wa-anbāʾ abnāʾ al-zamān*, ed. Iḥsān ʿAbbās (Beirut: Dār Ṣādir,

> The Prophet said: "Fear God in the matter of grievances (*maẓlima*), for injustice constitutes darkness on the Day of Resurrection."[43] ... We have read in the testament (*ʿahd*) of an Indian king to his son: Know that, (in the case of) the person from whom you have suffered an injustice (*maẓlima*) or against whom you have acted excessively in punishment, that which you have brought upon yourself is more severe than that which you have brought upon him. For the traces left by the injuries of this world are effaced and will disappear, whereas the injuries incurred from sins stick to (men's) souls until retribution (*qiṣāṣ*) removes them.
>
> In the same way, the resolute kings have never ceased to commend this (matter), to enjoin it in their testaments (*ʿuhūd*), to fill their books (*kutub*) with it, and to transmit it in the records (*āthār*) of their conduct (*siyar*).[44]

Pseudo-Māwardī proceeds to reproduce the full account, also reported in the ninth-century *Kitāb al-Tāj*, of the Sasanians' practices of holding *maẓālim*, followed by Pseudo-Aristotle's advice on this subject to Alexander.[45] I have cited this section at some length in order to convey Pseudo-Māwardī's underscoring of the universal nature of the imperative for royal justice, which applied to the circumstances of his particular time and space as much as it had in the societies of antiquity. He emphasizes the ruler's responsibility for ensuring equal access among the many constituencies that comprised his subjects to his fair settlement of their grievances and disputes; for upholding the law that supported the social order; and for overseeing the rightful enactment of the religious ordinances that guaranteed his legitimacy and the moral integrity of the public sphere. In a manner somewhat reminiscent of Ibn al-Muqaffaʿ, Pseudo-Māwardī urges the ruler to participate in the legal interpretation needed to achieve these ends. He also addresses certain issues of positive law, particularly in the final chapters of his book, which treat the collection and disbursement of wealth (Chapter Eight), enemies of the realm (Chapter Nine), and interpretations of controversial matters, such as listening to music and the consumption of wine, that concern kings (Chapter Ten).

1977), 2:460–63, esp. 462 no. 290.

43 Tirmidhī, *al-Jāmiʿ al-Ṣaḥīḥ wa-huwa Sunan al-Tirmidhī*, ed. Muḥammad Fuʾād ʿAbd al-Bāqī (Beirut: Dār Iḥyāʾ al-Turāth al-ʿArabī, n. d.), 3:126.

44 Pseudo-Māwardī, *Naṣīḥat al-mulūk*, 270–72.

45 Ibid., 273. Cf. *Kitāb al-Tāj fī akhlāq al-mulūk*, ed. Ahmed Zeki Pacha, *Le livre de la couronne (Kitab el Tadj)* (Cairo: Imprimerie nationale, 1914), 159–63 = Charles Pellat, *Le livre de la couronne* (Paris: Société d'Édition Les Belles Lettres, 1954), 179–82. See also Grignaschi, "La «Siyâsatu-l-ʿâmmiyya»;" Maróth, *Correspondence*, 30, 37.

AL-MĀWARDĪ'S *TASHĪL AL-NAẒAR WA-TAʿJĪL AL-ẒAFAR*

Pseudo-Māwardī, as indicated in the previous section, envisaged a sphere in which the properly qualified ruler might employ his independent legal judgment. In his urging of the ruler to devote careful attention to the appointment of judges whom he authorized to act on his behalf, Pseudo-Māwardī anticipated the concerns articulated in later mirrors, including those of the chief judge (*qāḍī al-quḍāt*), Abū al-Ḥasan ʿAlī b. Muḥammad al-Māwardī (d. 450/1058). The pre-eminent Sunnī jurist of his time, Māwardī was somewhat controversially awarded the honorific appellation supreme judge (*aqḍā al-quḍāt*) in 429/1037–8 and was involved in diplomatic as well as legal services on behalf of the ʿAbbāsid caliphs. Adviser to the caliphs al-Qādir (r. 381–422/991–1031) and al-Qāʾim (r. 422–467/1031–1074), Māwardī also enjoyed cordial relationships with the Būyid rulers (320–454/932–1062; in Iraq, 334–447/945–1055) of Iraq and western Iran. Best known for *al-Aḥkām al-sulṭāniyya* ("Governmental Ordinances"), a comprehensive treatment from a juridical point of view of political authority and the functions, rights, and duties of various governmental offices,[46] Māwardī also composed mirrors, in which he integrated his broad religious learning with his fluency in the rich Arabic literary culture (*adab*) of his time. The sense of justice displayed in his mirrors reflects and responds to the complex needs of a diverse and cosmopolitan society. Particularly telling are Māwardī's references to numerous exemplary figures, associated with a diverse array of imaginative worlds, presented as authoritative and meaningful constituents in an inclusive conceptual framework. This feature of Māwardī's writing correlates with his emphasis on the harmony that he envisages as a consequence of the diversity and multiplicity of human experience. The maintenance of this social harmony, in Māwardī's portrayal, requires the ruler's justice.[47]

Although better known for his works in the field of jurisprudence, Māwardī wrote several mirrors. They include *Qawānīn al-wizāra* ("Foundations of the Vizierate"), addressed to an unidentified vizier, and *Durar al-sulūk fī siyāsat al-mulūk* ("Pearls of Conduct in the Governance of Kings"), an abridged version, as Makram Abbès has established, of *Tashīl*

46 Written "in order that he [the addressee, 'to whom obedience is incumbent'] should know the various paths of the jurists (*madhāhib al-fuqahāʾ*) regarding his rights ... and duties." See Māwardī, *al-Aḥkām al-sulṭāniyya*, 3 = *Ordinances of Government*, 1.

47 As Heck has put it, the ruler is "the agent of political cohesion." See his "Law in ʿAbbāsid Political Thought," 87–88. On Māwardī's mirrors, see Riḍwān al-Sayyid, "Tamhīd: al-Ijtimāʿ al-basharī: Dirāsa fī ruʾyat al-Māwardī al-ijtimāʿiyya," in *Tashīl al-naẓar wa-taʿjīl al-ẓafar*, ed. Riḍwān al-Sayyid (Beirut: Dār al-ʿUlūm al-ʿArabiyya, 1987), 7–93; Abbès, *De l'éthique du prince*, 173–209; and Mohammed Arkoun, "L'Éthique musulmane d'après Māwardī," *Revue des études islamiques* 31 (1964): 1–31, reprinted in *Essais sur la pensée islamique*, Troisième edition (Paris: Maisonneuve et Larose, 1984).

al-naẓar wa-taʿjīl al-ẓafar, dedicated to the Būyid ruler of Iraq Bahāʾ al-Dawla (r. 379–403/989–1012).[48] His multi-faceted work of ethics *Adab al-dunyā waʾl-dīn* ("Rules of Conduct in Religious and Mundane Matters") and his collection *al-Amthāl waʾl-ḥikam* ("Proverbs and Wise Maxims"), both closely related to the category of *adab*, intersect with Māwardī's writings in the instructive and advisory genres.[49] The present discussion is limited to Māwardī's *Tashīl al-naẓar wa-taʿjīl al-ẓafar* ("The Facilitation of Reflection and the Hastening of Victory"), skillfully elucidated by Riḍwān al-Sayyid in the introduction to his edition of 1987, and further explored in the fine study and translation of Makram Abbès. Māwardī composed *Tashīl al-naẓar* in two parts, the first devoted to the moral dispositions of the king (*akhlāq al-malik*) and the second to the governance of the kingdom (*siyāsat al-mulk*). As Abbès has pointed out, the two parts correspond to the domains of ethics and politics respectively; the "facilitation of rational reflection" alludes to Māwardī's theoretical account of the virtues, the "hastening of victory" to their deployment in the realm of governance.[50]

Permeating his treatment of justice is Māwardī's insistence on moderation, balance and harmony, qualities in which lie the promotion of prosperity and the wellbeing of the body politic. This emphasis is apparent in his preface, which he opens with the words:

> To proceed: God, may His name be glorified, by the supreme efficacy of His wisdom (*balīgh ḥikmatih*) and the justice of His decrees (*ʿadl qaḍāʾih*), made humankind in varying categories and differing groups, in such a way that they should be kindly inclined one to another in their difference and in concord in their diversity, so that the followers and the followed among them should choose to be warmly disposed to one another, the commander and those subject to his command mutually supportive in reciprocal co-operation. [As the poet has said]:
>
> *Since of old, human beings have lived with human beings; Humanity has never lacked people whose assistance is sought, nor people who seek the assistance of their fellows.*[51]

48 Abbès, *De l'éthique du prince*, 203–09. Aḥmad, who published the edition of *Durar al-sulūk*, also concluded that it belonged to Māwardī's œuvre. See Fuʾād ʿAbd al-Munʿim Aḥmad, "Muqadimmat al-dirāsa waʾl-taḥqīq," in *Kitāb Durar al-sulūk fī siyāsat al-mulūk*, ed. Fuʾād ʿAbd al-Munʿim Aḥmad (Riyadh: Dār al-Waṭan, 1997), 7–52, at 35–40.

49 For a discussion of the likely order in which Māwardī wrote the various works relevant to political authority, see Riḍwān al-Sayyid, "Tamhīd," *Tashīl al-naẓar*, 82; Abbès, *De l'éthique du prince*, 200–09. On *Adab al-dunyā waʾl-dīn*, see Mohammed Arkoun, *Essais sur la pensée islamique*, 3rd ed. (Paris: Maisonneuve et Larose, 1984), 251–81.

50 Abbès, *De l'éthique du prince*, 211.

51 Māwardī, *Tashīl al-naẓar wa-taʿjīl al-ẓafar*, ed. Riḍwān al-Sayyid (Beirut: Dār al-ʿUlūm al-ʿArabiyya, 1987), 97 = Abbès, *De l'éthique du prince*, 239–40. The verse is by Abū Nuwās (d.

For Māwardī, as for his predecessors Ibn al-Muqaffaʿ and Pseudo-Māwardī and his contemporary the historian and polymath Miskawayh (d. 421/1030), explicating the foundations and principles of governance and sovereignty (*siyāsat al-mulk*) required attention to the wisdom and achievements of the past.[52] It was an inclusive undertaking in which humanity's collective remembered experience provided a varied and valuable repertoire of insights that coincided with the teachings of divine revelation. As Māwardī writes in his introduction:

> In this book I have treated in brief the foundations of governance and sovereignty that our predecessors have stipulated (*mā aḥkama al-mutaqaddimūn qawāʿidah*), for every religious community (*milla*) has its mode of conduct (*sīra*), and every age its distinctive character (*sarīra*). Those who came before us required some familiarity with the *sharīʿa* and the contracts it mandates, and with the contractual relationships involved in governance. Governance should at once accord with the principles of religion and correspond to the needs of the world.[53]

In the first part of *Tashīl al-naẓar*, Māwardī situates justice in the context of Platonic and Aristotelian conceptions of the virtues, of which justice represents, on the one hand, the sum and culmination of all the virtues, and on the other hand, moderation and equipoise, the mean or mid-point between extremes. Māwardī distinguishes between innate dispositions (*akhlāq al-dhāt*) and actions rooted in volition (*aʿfāl al-irāda*).[54] In his exposition of the virtues, he distinguishes between virtues that represent beginnings—primordial virtues, or means—and virtues that represent ends. The first of the virtues—the primordial virtue—is rational intellect (*ʿaql*), because it is from rational intellect that the other virtues arise and by rational intellect that the other virtues are ordered. The last of the virtues is justice (*ʿadl*), which is the result or product of all the virtues, which are bound to it. Intellect and justice are two mutually supportive and closely affiliated companions; the one necessarily stands in need of the other. The virtues that lie between the first and last occupy intermediary positions between intellect and justice, intellect being distinguished by its

between 198/813 and 200/815). See *Dīwān Abī Nuwās*, ed. al-Ḥasan b. Hāniʾ (Beirut: Dār al-Kitāb al-ʿArabī, 1982), 616.

52 See further Mohammed Arkoun, "Contribution à l'étude du lexique de l'éthique musulmane," *Bulletin d'études orientales* 22 (1969): 205–39, and "Éthique et histoire d'après les Tajarib al-Umam," *Atti del terzo Congresso di studi arabi e islamici* (Naples: Instituto Universitario Orientale, 1967): 83–112.

53 Māwardī, *Tashīl al-naẓar*, 97–98 = Abbès, *De l'éthique du prince*, 240–41.

54 Māwardī, *Tashīl al-naẓar*, 101 = Abbès, *De l'éthique du prince*, 245.

function of ordering them, justice by its function of evaluating them.[55] As Abbès points out, for Māwardī, unlike the philosophers, whether Greek or Arab, it is good government rather than happiness that constitutes the goal of the virtues.[56]

In an account reminiscent of Miskawayh's exposition of moral dispositions, Māwardī, citing "a philosopher," reports that the foundations of virtuous dispositions are four: discernment, courage, temperance, and justice; it is from these (Platonic) foundations that all of the other virtues are derived.[57] He explains further that the vices likewise have beginnings and ends; they begin with foolishness and end with ignorance.[58] The virtues lie at the praiseworthy mid-point between two blameworthy vices. By combining virtues, other virtues arise: for instance, intellect combined with courage produces patience in adversity and loyalty in fulfilling commitments.[59] If the king cultivates the virtues in accordance with balance (*taʿdīl*), he will attain just governance (*siyāsa ʿādila*) and virtuous conduct (*sīra fāḍila*); yet if he departs from moderation (*qaṣd*) and equipoise (*iʿtidāl*), he will reach one of the two blameworthy extremities.[60]

In his second section, Māwardī turns to the practical demonstration of the virtues in the ruler's governance of the kingdom. From his abstract portrayal of justice as the end and resulting product of the virtues, he addresses the enactment of justice in the political sphere. Without the ruler's authority (*sulṭān*), he writes, the subjects are incapable of defending themselves, nor can they achieve justice and equity (*tanāṣuf*) in their interactions without his kindness (*iḥsān*).[61] The subjects hold ten rightful expectations of the ruler:

(1) Ensuring their ability to dwell safely in their homes;

(2) Ensuring the security of their persons and their dwellings;

(3) Averting harm from the subjects and deterring covetousness;

(4) Exercising justice and equity with regard to them;

55 Māwardī, *Tashīl al-naẓar*, 107 = Abbès, *De l'éthique du prince*, 251.

56 Abbès, *De l'éthique du prince*, 211–12; cf. ibid., 247.

57 Cf. Arkoun, "Contribution à l'étude du lexique de l'éthique musulmane." As Abbès indicates, the assertion derives from Plato, *Republic*, Book IV. See Abbès, *De l'éthique du prince*, 252.

58 Māwardī, *Tashīl al-naẓar*, 108, 109; Abbès, *De l'éthique du prince*, 252.

59 Māwardī, *Tashīl al-naẓar*, 111, 111–13 = Abbès, *De l'éthique du prince*, 252, 255.

60 Māwardī, *Tashīl al-naẓar*, 177 = Abbès, *De l'éthique du prince*, 327. The pairing of just governance (*siyāsa ʿādila*) and virtuous conduct (*sīra fāḍila*) recur throughout *Tashīl al-naẓar*; see further below.

61 Māwardī, *Tashīl al-naẓar*, 214 = Abbès, *De l'éthique du prince*, 373.

(5) Dividing the parties to disputes among them;

(6) Urging them to follow the demands of the law (*sharʿ*) in their acts of worship and in their social transactions;

(7) Upholding the penal laws and God's claims among them;

(8) Ensuring the safety of their roads and routes;

(9) Upholding the public welfare by preserving their water supplies and maintaining their irrigation channels;

(10) Evaluating people's worth and arranging them in their stations, according to the distinguishing criteria of religion, profession, livelihood, and probity.

These ten duties, which coincide largely albeit not completely with the ten public duties listed in Māwardī's *al-Aḥkām al-sulṭāniyya*,[62] comprise just governance (*siyāsa ʿādila*) and virtuous conduct (*sīra fāḍila*), and if the ruler fulfils them, they will earn him the sincere obedience of his subjects and ensure the wellbeing of the kingdom.[63] Just governance involves, in addition to the protection of religion and the careful selection of assistants, four foundational principles: hope, fear, equity (*inṣāf*) and the rectification of inequity (*intiṣāf*).[64] Alexander, he reports, once asked the Indian philosophers which was more conducive to virtue, justice or courage? The philosophers replied, "If justice prevails, there is no need for courage!"[65]

Like other writers who combined a familiarity with and facility in Arabic literary culture with learning in jurisprudence, Māwardī, who also wrote a dedicated work *Adab al-qāḍī* ("Rules for Judges"), urges his addressee to attend carefully to the selection and oversight of judges.[66] In a section of *Tashīl al-naẓar* devoted to four categories of officials regarding whom the ruler should be particularly vigilant, he addresses as the second of these categories *quḍāt* and *ḥukkām*, judges and magistrates, of whom he writes:

> Judges and magistrates, who represent the scales of justice (*mawāzīn al-ʿadl*),[67] and to whom the ruler delegates judgment, are the guardians of the *sunna* by virtue of their following it in their judgments. By means of judges and

62 See Māwardī, *al-Aḥkām al-sulṭāniyya*, 16–17 = Wahba, *Ordinances of Government*, 16.

63 Māwardī, *Tashīl al-naẓar*, 214–15 = Abbès, *De l'éthique du prince*, 374–75.

64 Māwardī, *Tashīl al-naẓar*, 224 = Abbès, *De l'éthique du prince*, 383.

65 Māwardī, *Tashīl al-naẓar*, 225 = Abbès, *De l'éthique du prince*, 385.

66 Cf. Māwardī, *Adab al-qāḍī*, ed. Muḥyī Hilāl al-Sarḥān (Baghdad: Maṭbaʿat al-Irshād, 1971), 1:618–48.

67 Cf. Q. 21:47 (*al-mawāzīn al-qisṭ*); cf. 6:152, 11:85.

> magistrates, the aggrieved person attains justice through the rectification of his oppressor's injustice, and the weak see the fulfillment of their rightful claims against the strong. If judges and magistrates lack scruples and are much given to covetousness, they will destroy the *sunna* by innovating in their judgments, and they will undermine rightful claims by following capricious desires. Their rebuke (*qadḥ*) of religion will exceed their rebuke of the kingdom. The harm that their disregard for justice inflicts on the kingdom will exceed the harm that their negation of what is right causes plaintiffs who come before them; for it has been said: "Foolishness in judges and injustice in rulers are among the ugliest of things." Anūshīrvān [= Khusraw I, "The Immortal-Souled," r. 531–79] said: "A ruler whose judges are unjust is not just, and a ruler whose officials (*kufāt*) are corrupt is not good (*ṣāliḥ*)." In the selection of judges, after due consideration of the conditions necessary according to the *sharʿ*, good governance requires that they should be good in their outward demeanor and trustworthy in their inner selves, earnest and not given to jest, utterly scrupulous and resistant to cupidity; satisfaction averting them from entreaty, probity preventing them from greed, patience deterring them from annoyance, justice restraining them from inclination. For their knowledge they should have recourse to study, and for their comprehension they should turn to the repositories in their memory. They should be of a fine nature and excellent imagination, avoiding uncertainty and remaining distant from doubt; in obscure matters they should consult, in ambiguous matters they should proceed slowly; for the person who perfects this approach will not be diverted, and the person who deviates from it will not be sought out.[68]

At a later point in his mirror, Māwardī adds:

> A scholar said, "Justice and equity produce a period of concord (*iʾtilāf*)." ... The worst calamity that afflicts judges (*quḍāt*) is avidity, and the worst calamity that afflicts professional witnesses (*ʿudūl*) is unscrupulousness.[69]

As the previously mentioned passages from *Naṣīḥat al-mulūk* and *Tashīl al-naẓar* demonstrate, authors of mirrors frequently insisted on the ruler's conscientious attention to the selection and performance of judges. Rulers, they stipulate, should take the utmost care in their appointment of judges and provide them with generous salaries so as to protect them from

68 Māwardī, *Tashīl al-naẓar*, 239 = Abbès, *De l'éthique du prince*, 402–03. For Māwardī's treatment of doubt, see Intisar A. Rabb, *Doubt in Islamic Law: A History of Legal Maxims, Interpretation, and Islamic Criminal Law* (New York: Cambridge University Press, 2015), 36 n. 40, 183, 205, 232–33. In *al-Aḥkām al-sulṭāniyya*, Māwardī, like other Shāfiʿī jurists, employed the "doubt canon" in his treatment of criminal law. See ibid., 233 n. 15.

69 Māwardī, *Tashīl al-naẓar*, 261 = Abbès, *De l'éthique du prince*, 430.

the need to augment their earnings, especially by dishonest means. Mirrors, while warning against their frailties, also feature judges as exemplars of good conduct. Māwardī, who, reports suggest, held himself to a high standard,[70] cites the example of a judge of Ma'mūn (r. 198–218/813–33); this judge alerts the caliph to consequences and averts fiscal harm.[71]

Whereas Ibn al-Muqaffaʿ, in his category of the law that admits the use of human reason, encourages the caliph to engage in legal interpretation, and Pseudo-Māwardī urges the king to acquire the training necessary to prepare him to practice *naẓar* and *ijtihād*, Māwardī, in *Tashīl al-naẓar*, does not invite the ruler to participate through the exercise of his rational intellect in legal interpretation; rather, he limits the ruler's responsibilities to implementing the parts of the law that fall within his spheres of governance and to selecting qualified and suitably disposed judges to carry out the other facets of the *sharʿ*.

CONCLUSION

As the preceding discussion has suggested, Arabic (and Persian) mirrors for princes of the second-fifth/eighth-eleventh centuries represent a range of perspectives in their treatments of justice, judges, and the law. As Mottahedeh has described in his portrayal of the political culture of Būyid Iraq and western Iran, the ruler, by virtue of his position outside the society that he governed, was widely regarded as responsible for maintaining justice by achieving an equilibrium among the competing interests of his subjects.[72] The identification of the ruler as the subject's ultimate recourse against injustice, including and perhaps especially the injustice of his own agents, constitutes an abiding theme in the mirror literature, and numerous narratives, as well as prescriptive passages, explore the royal duty of redressing grievances in the hearing of *maẓālim*. With regard to the religious law, the three texts selected for discussion in this essay illustrate the shift from Ibn al-Muqaffaʿ's advice to the ruler that, in the face of different and conflicting legal rulings, he assert and exercise supreme interpretive authority, to Pseudo-Māwardī's assigning to the ruler the responsibility for *naẓar* and *ijtihād*, and eventually to Māwardī's limitation of the ruler's intervention in law to little more than the choice of good judges. The shift reflects the increasingly formalized location of authority for legal matters

70 See, for example, Māwardī's account of an incident in which he felt humbled by his inability to respond to a legal query in his *Adab al-dunyā wa'l-dīn*, ed. Muṣṭafā Saqqā (Cairo: Maṭbaʿat Muṣṭafā al-Bābī al-Ḥalabī, 1973), 81–82.

71 Māwardī, *Tashīl al-naẓar*, 240–42 = Abbès, *De l'éthique du prince*, 404–05, and 405 n. 8.

72 Mottahedeh, *Loyalty and Leadership*, 177–80.

in the ʿulamāʾ and the institution of the *madrasa*, and the ruler's retreat from the personal intervention that Ibn al-Muqaffaʿ, and to a degree Pseudo-Māwardī, could still envisage. The ruler remained the guarantor for upholding the religious law among the Muslim population in his kingdom and for the fulfillment of the covenant of protection extended to the non-Muslim populations. While their treatments and perspectives vary, authors of mirrors frequently emphasize the antiquity and universality of the themes of justice, redress, and law; and by their deployment of an eclectic and diverse set of authorities they make plain the rightful expectations of just governance shared by the multiple constituencies among the king's subjects. Notwithstanding the recurrence in advisory literature of well-known themes, motifs, texts, and maxims, the concept of justice is far from static in the hands of the mirror writers. It comprehends the multiple and diverse legal cultures of the particular milieux in which the authors of mirrors composed their texts, and responds to immediate and local conditions. The three texts to which I have referred chart changing political and cultural environments in which rulers situated themselves differently in relation to the religious scholars who possessed the authority to adjudicate in legal matters and in relation to the populations that constituted their subjects.

PART THREE:
Section Introduction

Judges and Judicial Practice in the Islamic West

Michael Cook
Princeton University

Shurayḥ b. al-Ḥārith al-Kindī, who died around the end of the seventh century, spent several decades sitting in judgment in Kūfa.[1] One of his cases concerned the marital affairs of a visitor from Damascus, ʿAdī b. Arṭāt al-Fazārī (d. 102/720).[2] The unfortunate Damascene found himself entrapped in the following conversation:[3]

ʿAdī:	Where are you? [meaning: Where are you at? Are you busy, or do you have a free moment for me?][4]
Shurayḥ:	Between you and the wall.
ʿAdī:	Listen to me.
Shurayḥ:	Speak, I hear you.
ʿAdī:	I'm a Syrian.
Shurayḥ:	That's a long way away.

1 Etan Kohlberg, "Shurayḥ," *EI²*, 9:508–09.

2 Jamāl al-Dīn al-Mizzī (d. 742/1341), *Tahdhīb al-kamāl fī asmāʾ al-rijāl*, ed. Bashshār ʿAwwād Maʿrūf (Beirut: Muʾassasat al-Risāla, 1985–1992), 19:520–21.

3 Ibn Khallikān (d. 681/1282), *Wafāyāt al-aʿyān wa-anbāʾ abnāʾ al-zamān*, ed. Iḥsān ʿAbbās (Beirut: Dār Ṣādir, 1971-2), 2:461. (I am not sure that my understanding of the exchange is correct at all points.) The anecdote is naturally to be found in many sources, of which the earliest known to me is ʿAbd al-Razzāq al-Ṣanʿānī (d. 211/826), *al-Muṣannaf fī al-ḥadīth*, ed. Ḥabīb al-Raḥmān al-Aʿẓamī (Beirut: Dār al-Kutub al-ʿIlmiyya, 1970-2), 6:226, no. 10,605, and cf. 226–27 no. 10,607.

4 Ḥasan al-Yūsī, *Zahr al-akam fī al-amthāl wa'l-ḥikam*, ed. Muḥammad al-Ḥajjī and Muḥammad al-Akhḍar (Casablanca: Dār al-Thaqāfa, 1981), 3:320. I owe this reference to Wasim Shiliwala.

ʿAdī:	I took a wife from among you.
Shurayḥ:	Happy marriage!
ʿAdī:	I want to take her with me [to Damascus].
Shurayḥ:	A man has a stronger right to his wife [than her family].
ʿAdī:	It was made a condition that she should remain in her abode [i.e., Kūfa].
Shurayḥ:	The condition prevails (*al-sharṭ amlak*).
ʿAdī:	So now judge between us.
Shurayḥ:	I already did.
ʿAdī:	Who did you give judgment against?
Shurayḥ:	Your mother's son.
ʿAdī:	On whose testimony?
Shurayḥ:	On the testimony of your maternal aunt's sister's son.

How much this tells us about the history of legal procedure is a question I gladly leave to Roy Mottahedeh, whose knowledge of this subject, as of so many others, is much greater than mine. But the anecdote can at least reassure us that the joking judges of Muslim Spain described by Maribel Fierro in her chapter were not guilty of the sin of innovation; as so often, the Muslims of the far west were faithfully following in the footsteps of their eastern role-models.

But none of these judges, it would seem, went so far as to make a joke about the deadly serious legal procedure of mutual cursing—whereby a husband could swear to the adulterous conduct of his wife (Q. 24:6-10)—as analyzed in the western context by Delfina Serrano in her chapter. In that respect the two chapters that make up this section do not intersect with each other except in their focus on the legal history of Muslim Spain. But thanks to Shurayḥ, there is at least an indirect connection we can make. The joking judge of Kūfa reached a decision that privileged the rights of a woman, or more precisely of her family. The jurists whose thinking is laid out by Serrano showed a similar concern. Whether it was the woman or her family that they cared about, this concern was manifestly to her advantage.

Chapter Eight

Joking Judges: A View from the Medieval Islamic West

Maribel Fierro*
Spanish High Council for Scientific Research (CSIC)

Yaḥyā b. Maʿmar (d. 229/843) held the position of judge in Cordoba, which was associated in those early times (when to be judge also implied being an Arab) with the directorship of the Friday prayer.[1] During one of the religious festivals in Cordoba, Yaḥyā b. Maʿmar went to the open air oratory (*muṣallā*) and saw that the notables (*ashrāf al-nās*) and the officials of the Umayyad administration (*khidmat al-sulṭān*) had hurried to take positions near the carpet where he was going to pray. Yaḥyā b. Maʿmar ordered his assistants to move his carpet forward, which gave the majority of people (*sawād al-nās*) the opportunity to situate themselves near him, so that those who had been the last now were the first, and those who had been the first now found themselves at the back. His action inspired admiration and was much talked about—then and afterwards—as a clever trick by which Yaḥyā b. Maʿmar outwitted the powerful in favor of the average Muslim. According to another version of this account, the trick helped him rid himself of opponents who had decided to gather around him in order to criticize his performance, instead managing to surround himself with impartial believers who were interested in the religious duty performed and not in

* This paper has been written within the research project *Practicing knowledge in Islamic societies and their neighbours*, financed by the Alexander von Humboldt Foundation (2014–2019) and it is related to my current research on the judges of al-Andalus. I wish to thank Luis Molina and Virginia Vázquez for their help.

1 On him, see PUA [Online], ID no. 11693 (last accessed March 21, 2016). The combination of the position of judge with that of director of prayer was criticized in later times: Vincent Lagardère, *Histoire et société en Occident Musulman au Moyen Âge, Analyse du Miʿyār d'al-Wanšarīsī* (Madrid, Casa de Velázquez, 1995), 7:73,129, quoting al-Wansharīsī (d. 914/1508), *al-Miʿyār al-muʿrib wa'l-jāmiʿ al-mughrib ʿan fatāwī ahl Ifrīqiya wa'l-Andalus wa'l-Maghrib* (Rabat: Wizārat al-Awqāf wa'l-Shuʾūn al-Islāmiyya, 1981), 10:77–78.

its agent.[2] If we try to visualize the scene, its comical potential is evident.[3]

Other comical scenes, as well as witty remarks and jokes, can be found in the source from which I have taken Yaḥyā b. Maʿmar's story—Ibn Ḥārith al-Khushanī's (d. 361/971) *History of the Cordoban judges* (*Kitāb quḍāt Qurṭuba*). Ibn Ḥārith al-Khushanī was a Mālikī scholar from Ifrīqiya who emigrated to al-Andalus when his homeland was under Fatimid rule.[4] He composed a number of works for the son of the Cordoban Umayyad caliph ʿAbd al-Raḥmān III (the son being the future caliph al-Ḥakam II), and among them was a history of the judges of Cordoba. In the introduction to this work, Ibn Ḥārith al-Khushanī praised the prince al-Ḥakam for fostering historical knowledge, for his efforts to preserve the genealogical lore, and for publicizing the merits of previous generations so that the memory of the past was not lost. When the prince ordered him to write a work devoted to the Cordoban judges, Ibn Ḥārith al-Khushanī approached those among his contemporaries who narrated past stories about the judges and those who had memorized their deeds (*ruwāt al-akhbār fī akhbārihim ... ahl al-ḥifẓ fī afʿālihim*). Thanks to these informants, he was able to collect edifying and delightful anecdotes about the sound intelligence of those judges, their vast knowledge, their equanimity, their refined understanding, their incisive sagacity in penetrating the interior of things, their correct firmness in making decisions coupled with their benevolent inclination to benefit everyone, their righteous administration of justice, and the probity of their behavior.[5] Looking at the biographical entries, their content is not limited to commendation: the shortcomings, mistakes, and evil deeds of some of the judges were also treated. Ibn Ḥārith al-Khushanī devoted some preliminary lines as well to reminding his readers of the seriousness of the affairs dealt with by the judges (crimes, murders, debts, slander), which could lead to

2 Ibn Ḥārith al-Khushanī, *Quḍāt Qurṭuba*, ed. and trans. Julián Ribera (Madrid: Iberica, 1914), 85 (ed.)/104–05 (trans.). In the version recorded by Qāḍī ʿIyāḍ (d. 544/1149), *Tartīb al-madārik li-maʿrifat aʿlām madhhab Mālik* (Rabat: Wizārat al-Awqāf wa'l-Shu'ūn al-Islāmiyya, 1983), 4:149, the source is Abū ʿAbd al-Malik Ibn ʿAbd al-Barr (d. 338/950), who wrote a now (lost) history of the scholars and judges of al-Andalus. In his version, instead of a carpet a staff is mentioned and those who had intentionally occupied the space closest to Yaḥyā b. Maʿmar had done that in order to criticize his sermon. By moving the staff and the ensuing change, the judge ensured that those situated near him had no ill will towards him. As a Sevillan-named judge in Cordoba and as an upright and conscientious judge, he had to face the opposition of many local jurists and notables.

3 Michael Cooperson, "Images without illustrations: The Visual Imagination in Classical Arabic Biography," in *Islamic Art and Arabic Literature: Textuality and Visuality in the Islamic World*, ed. Oleg Grabar and Cynthia Robinson (Princeton: Mark Wiener Publishers, 2001), 7–20.

4 On his biography see Jumʿa Shaykha, "Abū ʿAbd Allāh Muḥammad b. Ḥārith b. Asad al-Khushanī al-Ifrīqī al-Andalusī," *Cahiers de Tunisie* 26 (1978): 33–60; Amalia Zomeño, "Ibn Ḥāriṯ al-Jušanī, Abū ʿAbd Allāh," in *Biblioteca de al-Andalus*, vol. 3: *De Ibn al-Dabbāg a Ibn Kurz*, 290–96, no. 548; PUA [Online], ID no. 8774 (last accessed March 21, 2016); and HATA [Online], no. 6/92 (last accessed March 21, 2016).

5 Khushanī, *Quḍāt Qurṭuba*, 6–7 (ed.)/4–5 (trans.).

sentences of great gravity. Theirs was an especially imposing and complex duty, entailing consequences not only for those being judged but also for those adjudicating—to the extent that some individuals refused to become *qāḍī*s, fearing not only that a faulty performance could affect their destiny in the Other life, but that the office itself impaired their salvation and could also endanger their lives.[6] Being offered the *qāḍī*ship established the reputation of those who received the offer, while their refusal established their piety, a dynamic that had as its starting point the close connection between the judge and the ruler—the ruler being the one who named the *qāḍī*. Those who accepted the *qāḍī*ship were not only aware of its dangers, but also knew how demanding such an office was and that it required not only legal and religious knowledge and intelligence (including an understanding of human failings),[7] but also self-control and the right attitude in court.

Specific norms were established in order to teach the correct performance of judgeship, not only in terms of imparting justice, but also in terms of the judge's conduct outside of the court or courtroom during his tenure of office.[8] Those norms both reflected practice and affected it. Thus, correct behavior on the part of the judge, and his appropriate handling of verbal and physical relations with those involved in court procedures and trials, are recurring concerns in the biographies of judges without chronological restrictions. Thus, it was recorded of Abū Sulaymān b. Ḥawṭ Allāh (d. 621/1224) that, the more exalted the litigant acted, the more composed and quieter he became,[9] while Abū al-ʿAbbās b. Rashīq al-Kātib (d. 442/1050) recommended that judges give no sentence while in a

6 Ibid., 7–8 (ed.)/6–8 (trans.). On the *topos* of rejecting a nomination to the judgeship, see Noel J. Coulson, "Doctrine and Practice in Islamic law: One Aspect of the Problem," *Bulletin of the School of Oriental and African Studies* 18 (1956): 211–26. On the presence of *qāḍī*s in Hell, see Christian Lange, *Locating Hell in Islamic Traditions* (Leiden: Brill, 2015), 18, 157 (corrupt judges), 154: noting that judges who were too severe on earth would continue to rebuke the tortured in hell but are rebuked by them as well.

7 The issue of what was better, a judge with legal knowledge but no intelligence or an intelligent judge with no legal knowledge, was discussed by the Andalusī al-Bunnāhī (d. ca. 794/1391) in his work on judges and muftis, *al-Marqaba al-ʿulyā fī-man yastaḥiqqu al-qaḍāʾ waʾl-futyā, La Atalaya Suprema sobre el Cadiazgo y el muftiazgo*, ed. and trans. Arsenio Cuellas Marqués and Celia del Moral (Granada: Universidad de Granada, 2005), 12–13 (ed.)/98–99 (trans.).

8 For the case of the Mālikī legal school that prevailed in the Maghreb and al-Andalus see Alfonso Carmona, "Los *ādāb al-quḍāt* o normas de conducta del juez islámico," *Homenaje al Prof. Juan Torres Fontes*, t. I (Murcia: Universidad de Murcia, 1987), 235–43, at 241: judges should not joke; and his "Le malékisme et les conditions requises pour l'exercice de la judicature," *Islamic Law and Society* 7, no. 2 (2000): 122–57. For other schools, see Irene Schneider, *Das Bild des Richters in der "Adab al-Qāḍī" Literatur* (Frankfurt: Peter Lan, 1990).

9 Antonio Rodríguez Figueroa, "Ibn Ḥawṭ Allāh, Abū Sulaymān," *Biblioteca de al-Andalus*, 3:325–26, no. 567. He preferred that his sentences were executed far from him, with the presence of witnesses.

state of indignation and anger.[10] In an anecdote on the same theme, ʿAmr b. ʿAbd Allāh (d. 273/886) demanded that a litigant in his court give him the document (*wathīqa*) that he had presented as proof and had subsequently hidden in his sleeve. The judge had to insist several times and, eventually, the litigant, infuriated, threw the document at him, hitting his face. ʿAmr b. ʿAbd Allāh became pale and everyone in the court thought that the culprit was going to be punished, but the judge recovered his forbearance (*ḥilm*) and continued with his duty without reacting to the insult.[11] Being the first Cordoban judge of *mawlā* (loosely, non-Arab) origin and *ḥilm* being the paramount virtue of the Arabs, such a reaction proved that he was fit for the office. Judges had to control not only their reactions to the behavior of others, but their bodies in general. Thus, fearing that deprivation from food could make him harsher than needed, the judge Abū Bakr Ibn Zarb (d. 381/991) never sat in his court without having previously eaten.[12]

Many other anecdotes along the same lines could be adduced from the biographical literature devoted to judges. After all, we have here one of the discursive modes used to construct the judge's exemplarity as inscribed in social relations.[13] While positive anecdotes are to be expected in the depiction of men meant to serve as exemplars of good conduct and faultless morality—with negative anecdotes serving the inverse purpose—Ibn Ḥārith al-Khushanī also included a number of anecdotes revealing the good-humored and even jocular disposition of some Cordoban judges. In this case, and given the controversy over humor versus seriousness in the construction of exemplars in Islamic civilization, which attitude toward humor did he intend to convey? Let us first review the stories Ibn Ḥārith al-Khushanī recorded for two judges and one judge *manqué*, which represent three out of the forty-five total biographical entries included in his book.

We will deal first with the judge *manqué*. Muḥammad b. ʿĪsā al-Maʿāfirī al-Aʿshā (d. 221/836) was a scholar known for his fondness for laughter and joking, which caused serious qualms about the decision to name him judge. When approached with these qualms, al-Aʿshā made it clear that he would never accept the position, but not because he considered himself

10 Fernando N. Velázquez Basanta, "Ibn Rašīq al-Kātib, Abū l-ʿAbbās," *Biblioteca de al-Andalus*, vol. 4: *De Ibn al-Labbāna a Ibn al-Ruyūlī*, 446, 983.

11 Khushanī, *Quḍāt Qurṭuba*, 122–23 (ed.)/150 (trans.). Similar behavior is recorded of the same judge regarding the naughty behavior of some students in the mosque where he was judging.

12 Documentación, "Ibn Zarb, Abū Bakr," *Biblioteca de al-Andalus*, vol. 6: *De Ibn al-Ŷabbāb a Nubḏat al-ʿaṣr*, 256–57, no. 1431. For another example of a judge controlling his body, see Manuela Marín, "Signos visuales de la identidad andalusí," *Tejer y vestir: de la antigüedad al islam* (Madrid: Consejo Superior de Investigaciones Científicas, 2001), 137–80, at 154.

13 On such discursive modes, see Julia Bray, "Literary Approaches to Medieval and Early Modern Arabic Biography," *Journal of the Royal Asiatic Society* 20 (2010): 237–53, quoting previous studies on the topic.

unfit, only because he was concerned about his salvation, according to the well-known *topos*. He reminded those who had expressed these qualms that ʿAlī b. Abī Ṭālib never abandoned his good humor, not even when he became caliph.[14] If that was true in regard to someone as irreproachable as the Prophet's cousin and son-in-law, why would he have had to abandon his own good-humored disposition, had he accepted the position of judge?[15] Al-Aʿshā once gave testimony (*shahāda*) in front of the judge al-Aswār b. ʿUqba, who commented that, given al-Aʿshā's fondness for jesting (*hazl*), he could not determine whether his *shahāda* was serious. This comment mortified al-Aʿshā.[16] Another anecdote shows him walking in the company of the judge Muḥammad b. Ziyād (d. after 240/854) when they met a drunkard. The *qāḍī* ordered his assistants to seize that man in order to punish him. They continued walking until they reached a narrow area and the *qāḍī* went ahead, al-Aʿshā following behind with the assistants. Al-Aʿshā took the opportunity to tell those assistants that the judge had decided to set free the drunkard, which they did. When the *qāḍī* learned of this, he was not displeased with al-Aʿshā's behavior.[17]

Then we come to the men of good humor who *did* become judges. The judge Sulaymān b. Aswad al-Ghāfiqī (d. after 273/886), described as a virtuous and austere man, was famous for having been strict in making the Umayyad emir and his officials adhere to the law by submitting them to the *qāḍī*'s justice. He was also known for his jesting (*duʿāba*). A professional witness (*rajul min al-ʿudūl*) named Ibn ʿAmmār used to stand in his audience (*majlis ḥukmih*),[18] without moving, until the judge left. This Ibn ʿAmmār possessed an emaciated mule who spent the whole day at the door of the mosque. One day, a woman came before the judge and said in Romance: "Oh, judge! Look at your wretched one!" The judge answered, also in Romance: "You are not my wretched one! My wretched one is Ibn ʿAmmār's mule that spends the whole day eating away at his bit at the door of the mosque!"[19]

14 For a statement of ʿAlī that supports humor, see Franz Rosenthal, *Humor in Early Islam* (Leiden: Brill, 1956), 56.

15 Khushanī, *Quḍāt Qurṭuba*, 10–11 (ed.)/11–12 (trans.). On this scholar see also HATA [Online], no. I/5 (last accessed March 21, 2016).

16 Khushanī, *Quḍāt Qurṭuba*, 102–03 (ed.)/125–26 (trans.).

17 For the culture of leniency regarding drinking wine in al-Andalus, see below, note 64. See also Khushanī, *Quḍāt Qurṭuba*, 86 (ed.)/106 (trans.); and Maribel Fierro, "Tres familias andalusíes de época omeya apodadas Banū Ziyād," in *Estudios Onomástico-Biográficos de al-Andalus*, 12:85–142, esp. 115–18.

18 On the judge's audience and its location, mainly in the mosque during the early Islamic period, see Mathieu Tillier, "Un espace judiciaire entre public et privé: Audiences de cadis à l'époque abbaside," *Annales Islamologiques* 38 (2004): 491–512.

19 Khushanī, *Quḍāt Qurṭuba,* 138 –39 (ed.)/171 (trans.). On Sulaymān b. Aswad, see Avila (dir.), PUA [Online], ID no. 3740 (last accessed March 4, 2016).

Sulaymān b. Aswad also devised what could be considered a "practical joke", planning a mischievous trick on a man called Ibn Qulzum, causing him embarrassment and indignity. Ibn Ḥārith al-Khushanī defines the story as a *ḥikāya mustaṭrafa* or singular anecdote. Ibn Qulzum was a Cordoban who ardently desired to be named director of prayer in the Friday mosque. Knowing this, one Friday morning on which Ibn Qulzum came to visit him, Sulaymān b. Aswad told his servant to appear in front of him crying and saying that his master was dying, and then to let him into his room. Sulaymān laid down on his bed and pretended that he was at death's door. When Ibn Qulzum saw him, he started crying and lamenting his friend's state. He left shortly after and went to see the vizier Hāshim b. ʿAbd al-ʿAzīz, whom he informed that the judge was expiring and thus would be unable to direct that Friday prayer. Ibn Qulzum then exhorted the vizier to write immediately to the emir about the need to replace the dying judge. Hāshim b. ʿAbd al-ʿAzīz asked him to confirm that this was really the case, and Ibn Qulzum insisted that he had seen Sulaymān b. Aswad on his death bed with his own eyes. Hāshim b. ʿAbd al-ʿAzīz then proceeded to write to the emir describing the situation. The emir read the letter and took time to meditate about its contents: He remembered how much Ibn Qulzum wanted to be named director of prayer and that no illness was known to afflict Sulaymān b. Aswad, and he then concluded that the whole affair appeared suspicious. Thus, the emir asked one of his more trusted eunuchs to go to the judge's house and verify the situation. The eunuch found Sulaymān b. Aswad sitting and in excellent health, and they left together in the direction to the Friday mosque. The eunuch then went to the palace to inform the emir, who had a great laugh on the trick played by the judge upon Ibn Qulzum.[20]

As regards the judge Aslam b. ʿAbd al-ʿAzīz (d. 312/924), member of an important family of Umayyad *mawālī*,[21] a Christian came to him asking to be put to death. The Christian was convinced that only his likeness (*shibh*) would die, whereas his real self would directly go to heaven. The judge tried to reason with him, arguing the absurdity of his belief and

20 Khushanī, *Quḍāt Qurṭuba*, 150–51 (ed.)/186–88 (trans.). The same story is recorded by Bunnāhī, *Marqaba*, 86–87 (ed.)/217–18 (trans.). The other joking judge recorded by Bunnāhī is al-Mundhir b. Saʿīd al-Ballūṭī (265/879 or 273–355/886–966), who also has a short entry in Ibn Ḥārith al-Khushanī's work but without the joke. It tells how the judge spent one very hot summer day in the company of the caliph al-Ḥakam II and his chamberlain, the eunuch Jaʿfar al-Ṣiqlābī, who decided to swim in the pond of the garden where they were resting. The judge kept complaining about the heat but seemed reluctant to cool himself in the pool. He finally entered, but did not swim. Asked about that by the caliph, he answered that contrary to the eunuch, he had an anchor and he was afraid of drowning because of its weight. This reference to his castration deeply hurt the eunuch. See ibid., 104–05 (ed.)/240–41 (trans.).

21 He had two turns in office: 300–309/912–921 and 312–314/924–926. On him, see Maribel Fierro, "Los cadíes de Córdoba de ʿAbd al-Raḥmān III (r. 300/912-350/961)," in *Cadíes y cadiazgo en el Occidente islámico medieval*, in *Estudios Onomástico-Biográficos de al-Andalus* 18:69–98.

hoping to dissuade him of his wish to be a martyr. When the dissuasion proved unsuccessful, the judge lashed him, proving that—as he had already warned the Christian—it was his own body, and not that of his likeness, which suffered the punishment.[22] The general context of the story is the movement of the so-called voluntary martyrs—Christians who resisted the growing process of Arabization and Islamicization by publicly insulting the Muslims' Prophet and the Islamic religion in order to intentionally seek martyrdom by means of the punishment their insult invoked.[23] This case is slightly unusual, however: For one thing, this movement took place mostly between the years 235/850 and 245/859, so this case appears to be quite late. Also, in this case there is no record of the Christian having insulted Islam. The Christian's idea that only a likeness of his would die evokes the Qurʾānic conception of Jesus' death in Qurʾān 4:157,[24] suggesting a belief in the existence of "doubles." According to some Ismāʿīlī interpretations, Jesus did die on the cross, but it was only one of his natures or names,[25] which helped reassure believers in the *imāms* that their violent deaths did not affect their divine element, only their human shells (*shibh*).[26] Jessica Coope understood this case to mean that the Christian made a distinction between his body and his spirit or soul,[27] an interpretation that coincides with the Ismāʿīlī position.[28] What is of interest here is that the story is narrated in a very lively way, with the conversation between Aslam and the Christian emphasizing the stupidity and ignorance of the would-be martyr, underscored by the rationality of the judge's arguments and his condescending attitude towards the Christian—all elements that must have provoked laughter in those present at the trial.

In the other stories told of Aslam, his jokes are directed toward

---

22 Khushanī, *Quḍāt Qurṭuba*, 186–87 (ed.)/231–33 (trans.).

23 See generally Kenneth B. Wolf, *Christian Martyrs in Muslim Spain* (Cambridge: Cambridge University Press, 1988); and Jessica A. Coope, *The Martyrs of Córdoba. Community and Family Conflict in an Age of Massive Conversion* (Lincoln: Nebraska University Press, 1995).

24 See generally Todd Lawson, *The Crucifixion and the Qur'an: A Study in the History of Muslim Thought* (Oxford: Oneworld, 2009).

25 Antonella Straface, "An Ismāʿīlī interpretation of *šubbiha lahum* (Qur. IV, 157) in the *Kitāb šaǧarat al-yaqīn*," in *Authority, privacy and public order in Islam: Proceedings of the 22nd Congress of L'Union Européenne des Arabisants et Islamisants*, Orientalia Lovaniensia Analecta 148, ed. B. Michalak-Pikulska and A. Pikulski (Leuven: Peeters, 2006), 95–100.

26 Lawson, *The Crucifixion and the Qur'an*, 80. The Ikhwān al-Ṣafāʾ also accepted the death of the human nature of Jesus, see ibid., 85–89.

27 Coope, *The Martyrs of Córdoba*, 52.

28 This analysis is taken from Maribel Fierro, "Plants, Mary the Copt, Abraham, Donkeys and Knowledge: Again on Batinism during the Umayyad Caliphate in al-Andalus," *Differenz und Dynamikim Islam. Festschrift für Heinz Halm zum 70. Geburtstag/Difference and Dynamics in Islam. Festschrift for Heinz Halm on his 70th Birthday* (Würzburg: Ergon, 2012), 125–44, at 142–43.

Muslims and involve wordplay.[29] Aslam is described as a man who was able to sharply convey the truth without making much ado about it (*shadīd al-mubāyana fī al-ḥaqq qalīl al-mudārāt fīh*), sometimes revealing it with a funny remark (*lafẓ nādir*) that appeared on the surface to be merely an opinion (*ra'y*), but which conveyed another, humorous meaning (*al-nādir wa'l-fākiha*). Several examples are given. One day, the jurists Abū Ṣāliḥ Ayyūb b. Sulaymān and Saʿd b. Muʿādh entered Aslam's house and sat down.[30] Aslam looked at them and quoted the Qurʾānic verses 10:80 and 26:43, in which the prophet Moses tells the sorcerers: "Throw whatever you are going to throw: *alqū mā antum mulqūna*." Aslam astonished the two jurists with how funny the words were and how true in their meaning.[31] As with the sorcerers in the Qurʾānic story, it is implied that the jurists had come to visit him with deceiving and corrupting intentions. Another day, the jurist Muḥammad b. al-Walīd came to talk to Aslam about something he wanted to obtain from him. Aslam, instead of employing the usual formula *samʿan wa-ṭāʿatan* (I hear and I obey, i.e., I will do what you ask me), answered with the Qurʾānic verse 2:93: "We hear and we rebel: *samiʿnā wa-ʿaṣaynā*," which is what the Israelites said to Moses when he came down with the Tablets and worshipped the calf. The implication was that Aslam would not do what he wanted—as if there was something unacceptable in the request.[32] Aslam's most famous instance of verbal humor was what he told a man from the town of Niebla (Labla in Arabic). The man came to see him and asked: "Oh, judge, do you recognize me?" Aslam answered in the negative. The man then said: "I am the judge of Niebla: *anā qāḍī Labla*," and Aslam retorted that he should not disapprove of God's control over the destiny of man as he had pronounced *anā qāḍī Labla* in a way that sounded like *anā qāḍī lā bi-llāh*.[33]

The fourth and fifth examples of witticism happened when Aslam was acting as judge. Aslam was informed that one of the jurists who had to testify in his court had received a carpet as a gift from the person he would testify about. When the jurist entered his presence, taking off his boots (*akhfāf*) and walking on the carpet, the judge remarked: "Beware the carpet!" Hearing this remark, the man realized that the judge knew of his

29 For another example of a judge playing with words see Fernando N. Velázquez Basanta, "Retrato jaṭibiano del poeta y Qāḍī l-ŷamāʿa de Granada Abū Ŷaʿfar Aḥmad b. Furkūn (el abuelo)," *Revista del Centro de Estudios Históricos de Granada y su Reino* 5 (1991): 47–53.

30 On them see Manuela Marín, "*Šūrā* et *ahl al-šūrā* dans al-Andalus," *Studia Islamica* 62 (1985): 15–51.

31 Khushanī, *Quḍāt Qurṭuba*, 185 (ed.)/229 (trans.).

32 Ibid., 185–86 (ed.)/229–30 (trans.). Ibn al-Walīd retorted: *qulnā wa-iḥtasabnā.*

33 Ibid., 186 (ed.)/230–31 (trans.).

corrupt dealings, and he did not dare to testify.[34] On another occasion, a man who had a lawsuit (*khuṣūma*) came to Aslam and told him that he had brought with him a witness from Seville who would testify in his favour. The judge showed astonishment, doubtful that someone would have come from such a far place to his court. When the Sevillan witness appeared, the judge asked him: "Are you a *muḥtasib* or a *muktasib*?" (that is, someone acting with the intention to fulfill the duty of commanding good and forbidding evil, or someone acting in pursuit of something material). The Sevillan was not pleased with the remark and told him that he, as a judge, had no right to ask such questions. Aslam was in court to say what he had to say, and to listen to his testimony, and he as the judge had to make his own decision. Aslam conceded that the man's complaint was legitimate, and he listened to his declaration.[35]

This last anecdote has to do with what was and was not acceptable in the judge's dealings with those appearing before him, an issue reflected in other biographies such as that of the judge al-Naḍar b. Salama al-Kalāʿī (d. 302/914). During his time, there was in Cordoba a man called Ibn Raḥmūn, known for his love of jesting. While a lawsuit was taking place in the court, this Ibn Raḥmūn kept making jokes and funny remarks, provoking the laughter of those present. Not only did al-Naḍar not stop him, but he was also smiling. The litigant who was the object of Ibn Raḥmūn's jokes told the judge that when they were out the judge's sight, Ibn Raḥmūn did not cease to insult him and to mention his mother, and that that was what Ibn Raḥmūn did again in court, provoking the laughter of all those present with the tacit consent of the judge.[36]

Similar stories were not included in the biographical dictionary of scholars and judges of Ifrīqiya written by Abū al-ʿArab al-Tamīmī (d. 333/945) and Ibn Ḥārith al-Khushanī himself.[37] In these works, we find

34 Ibid., 186 (ed.)/231 (trans.).

35 Ibid., 185–86 (ed.)/230 (trans.).

36 Ibid., 160 (ed.)/198–99 (trans.). The precise contents of Ibn Raḥmūn's jokes are not clear, but they can be guessed. On al-Naḍar, see PUA [Online], ID no. 11243 (last accessed March 21, 2016).

37 The edition consulted is *Classes des savants de l'Ifrīqīya par Abu' l-ʿArab Moḥammed ben Aḥmed ben Tamīm et Moḥammed ben al-Ḥāriṯ ben Asad al-Ḫošanī*, ed. and trans. Mohammed Ben Cheneb (Paris: E. Leroux, 1915; Algiers: E. Leroux, 1920). The edition is based on a manuscript that belonged to the Andalusī Abū ʿUmar al-Ṭalamankī (d. 429/1038). It includes three works: 1) *Ṭabaqāt ʿulamāʾ Ifrīqiya* by Abū al-ʿArab al-Tamīmī (47 ff. in 3 parts); 2) *K. ṭabaqāt ʿulamāʾ Ifrīqiya* by Ibn Ḥārith al-Khushanī (47 ff. in 3 parts); 3) *K. ṭabaqāt ʿulamāʾ Ifrīqiya* (*Dhikr ʿulamāʾ ahl Tūnis*) (6 ffs.) by Abū l-ʿArab al-Tamīmī. In the edition, references to judges are found on pp. 79, 82, 85, 91, 94, 101, 102, 157, 158, 180, 193, 203, 211, 217, 219, 220, 225, 228, 244, 246, 247, 252, 253, 264, 266, 269, 271–72, 274, 275, 277, 280, 285, 308, 319, 320, 321, 322, 328–35, 343–44, 346. On Abū al-ʿArab, see M.J.L. Young, "Abū l-ʿArab al-Qayrawānī and his Biographical Dictionary of the Scholars of Qayrawān and Tunis," *Al-Masāq* 6 (1993): 57–75; and Fethi Bahri, "Abū l-ʿArab et al-Khuchanī, deux auteurs et une oeuvre," *IBLA* 190 (2002): 187–202.

the usual stories about scholars who refused to be judges, or who were so overwhelmed by the responsibility of the office that they never gave any sentence, and about judges who maintained their composure while being treated rudely.[38] Only of the judge Sulaymān b. ʿImrān is it reported that he made fun of people and ridiculed them, with no examples given.[39] Also, no joking judge is mentioned in al-Kindī's (d. 350/961) *Akhbār quḍāt Miṣr*,[40] whereas Wakīʿ (d. 306/918) has a number of them.[41] ʿUbayd Allāh b. al-Ḥasan al-ʿAnbarī (d. 168/785), judge of Basra, not only recited poetry while in court, but also made fun of serious affairs: after an inquiry regarding a certain man, it was revealed that the man loved young boys. The judge reacted to this by asking: "Is he the knight or the lancer?" The same judge, when dealing with a litigant from the tribe of Rabīʿa, asked him if he knew some verses that satirized his tribe, to which the litigant responded by reciting verses that denigrated the judge's tribe. The judge then acknowledged that his behavior had not been acceptable and that he had provoked the man first. The same happened when the judge joked about a woman in his audience, which led her to answer in kind, and going even further by making sexual remarks. Although ʿUbayd Allāh b. al-Ḥasan al-ʿAnbarī was generally appreciated for his performance as judge, there were some who complained to the governor about his jokes. This is what the scholar Muḥammad b. Musʿar did, reminding him that for God, mocking people was equal to ignorance.[42] Another judge, Yaḥyā b. Aktham—who started his career as judge of Basra between 202/817 and 210/825-6—was described as *kathīr al-muzāḥ* (often joking), adding that he was always trifling in his *majlis*, as was his successor Ismāʿīl b. Ḥammād b. Abī Ḥanīfa, known for his playing with words in order to mock others and for having recited in his *majlis* verses that fell into the *mujūn* category—on which more will be said later.[43]

38 Khushanī, *Classes des savants de l'Ifrīqīya*, 34–36 (ed.)/92–96 (trans.); 85 (ed.)/158–59 (trans.); 136–37 (ed.)/221 (trans.).

39 Ibid., 183 (ed.)/273 (trans.). Sulaymān b. ʿImrān followed sometimes unconventional procedures in order to give a sound judgment. For an example, see ibid., 181–82 (ed.)/271–72 (trans.).

40 Kindī, *Histoire des cadis égyptiens (Akhbār qudāt Misr)*, trans. Mathieu Tillier (Cairo: Institut Français d'Archéologie Orientale, 2012). The only case worthy of note is that of a judge who wrote a poem satirizing a governor. See ibid., 81.

41 Wakīʿ, *Akhbār quḍāt Miṣr*, ed. ʿAbd al-ʿAzīz Muṣṭafā al-Marāghī (Cairo, 1947-1950). These anecdotes have been analyzed by Tillier in his article mentioned in above, note 18, at 503–05.

42 Wakīʿ, *Akhbār quḍāt Miṣr*, 2: 112, 114–116; Tillier, "Un espace judiciaire entre public et privé," 503–05. On this same subject, see Abdullahi Ali Ibrahim, *Assaulting with Words. Popular Discourse and the Bridle of Sharīʿah* (Evanston: Northwestern University Press, 1994).

43 Wakīʿ, *Akhbār quḍāt Miṣr*, 2:166, 168; Tillier, "Un espace judiciaire entre public et privé," 503–04. On Yaḥyā b. Aktham's connection with *mujūn*, see Zoltán Szombathy, *Mujūn: Libertinism in Mediaeval Muslim Society and Literature* (Warminster: Gibb Memorial Trust, 2013), 169.

This was not behavior limited to the early period of Islam: the judge of Seville Abū Umayya b. ʿUfayr (d. 637/1239) wrote poetry while attending to the litigants and their affairs. Some of his preserved verses have a scandalous nature, among them three verses that describe a trial that allegedly took place in his court between a gazelle and a goat, with him sentencing in favor of the latter.[44]

The figure of the joking judge—of which other examples could be collected[45]—has passed into folklore. According to a widespread legend in Morocco, the stork was a judge who was bored by his job, so he put soap where the litigants had to walk. When they slipped and fell on their backs, he burst into laughter. To punish him, God transformed him into a stork: the noise of his squawk is a reminder of the judge's laughter.[46] At the same time, the *qāḍī* and the scholar also became figures of ridicule in Islamic folklore.[47] Judges were not immune from being the aim of the jokes of others[48] and especially of being satirized by poets,[49] which sometimes led to the poet being punished by the mocked judge.[50] For the early period, the Cordoban Umayyad poet al-Ghazāl (d. 250/864) considered the judge Jukhāmir b. ʿUthmān al-Shaʿbānī, known for his evil behavior towards the people, to be ignorant and foolish, and attacked him in his verses.[51] The same judge—of whom a very negative view is given—was ridiculed by another poet, Ibn al-Shamir (d. after 206/822). The judge had cards where the names of the litigants were written to be read in order to call them to appear in court. The poet put among them one card with the names of Yūnus b. Matī (Jonas) and al-Masīḥ b. Maryam (Jesus). The judge did not grasp what was going on

44 Teresa Garulo, "Notas sobre *muŷūn* en al-Andalus. El capítulo VII del *Nafḥ al-ṭīb* de al-Maqqarī," *Anaquel de Estudios Árabes* 26 (2015): 93–120, esp. 108.

45 For the Almoravid period see Alfonso Carmona, "al-Garnāṭī, Abū Isḥāq," *Biblioteca de al-Andalus*, vol. 1, *De al-ʿAbbādīya a Ibn Abyaḍ*, 396–98, no. 121.

46 Edmond Doutté, *Missions au Maroc. En tribu* (Paris: P. Geuthner, 1914), 6.

47 Ahda M'hamed, "Le droit coutumier des Ait Attad'Aoufous (Sud-Est Marocain)," *Awal. Cahiers d'Études Berbères* 24 (2001): 87–117.

48 Khushanī, *Classes des savants de l'Ifrīqīya*, 187–89 (ed.)/275–77 (trans.).

49 Antonio Rodríguez Figueroa, "al-ʿAzafī, Abū l-Qāsim Muḥammad," *Biblioteca de al-Andalus*, 1: 133–34, no. 42; Fernando N. Velázquez Basanta, "al-Basṭī, ʿAbd al-Karīm," *Biblioteca de al-Andalus*, 1:213–14, no. 65; Mayte Penelas, "al-Ilbīrī, Abū Isḥāq," *Biblioteca de al-Andalus*, 6:381–84, no. 1467; Fernando N. Velázquez Basanta, "al-Majzūmī, Abū Bakr," *Biblioteca de al-Andalus*, 6:482–86, no. 1518. For Egypt, see Kindī, *Histoire des cadis égyptiens*, 143, 163, 169, 177, 192–93.

50 Mayte Penelas, "al-Ilbīrī, Abū Isḥāq," *Biblioteca de al-Andalus*, 6:381–84, no. 1467. See also Intisar A. Rabb, "Society and Propriety: The Cultural Construction of Defamation and Blasphemy as Crimes in Islamic law," in *Accusations of Unbelief in Islam: A Diachronic Perspective on* Takfīr, ed. Camilla Adang et al. (Leiden: Brill, 2016), 434–64, for the punishment inflicted on a storeowner for making fun of a judge.

51 Khushanī, *Quḍāt Qurṭuba*, 94 (ed.)/116 (trans.). At ibid., 98–99 (ed.)/121 (trans.), the same poet ridicules the naivety of another judge.

and had them summoned, this leading to strongly-worded mocking verses on the part of the poet.[52] The judge Muḥammad b. Bashīr had had ten cards for summons with his seal (*ṭābiʿ*) prepared when he was named for the *qāḍī*ship in Cordoba and he used them until he died. Muḥammad b. ʿĪsā al-Aʿshā—the judge *manqué* already dealt with who was a man prone to jest and hyperbole (*kathīr al-nādir, kathīr al-taṭnīb*)—every time he met a friend of the judge asked him: "When are you going to meet the ten auctioneers (*dallāl*)? When are you going to visit the ten agents?" Muḥammad b. Bashīr learned of this and was displeased, and took care to warn Muḥammad b. ʿĪsā to stop saying such things.[53] Beyond their own behavior, judges could also become objects of ridicule due to the behavior of family members and relatives,[54] or due to their attire, especially when they came from the rural hinterland,[55] or, more cruelly, because of their physical appearance.[56]

We have seen that in his book on Cordoban judges, Ibn Ḥārith al-Khushanī incorporated amusing stories both about judges who were made fun of and about judges who made fun of others. Such stories do not necessarily provide a historical kernel of meaning, but—as good stories—supply a multi-faceted perspective on human behavior and choices. We know by now that "medieval Arab biographies are often less a factual record than a field of controversy," and that for many biographers, their aim was to illustrate types, not to document lives.[57] On the other hand, the joking

52 Ibid., 95–96 (ed.)/117 (trans.).

53 Ibid., 58–59 (ed.)/72 (trans.).

54 An example dealing with the wife of the judge Muḥammad b. Ziyād, that led to much gossip, is recorded at ibid., 104–05 (ed.)/129 (trans.).

55 This is what happened to Saʿīd b. Sulaymān al-Ballūṭī, who was from the rural region to the north of Cordoba known as Faḥṣ al-Ballūṭ, famous for its acorns, who dressed with a white *jubba*, a white high conical bonnet, and a white cape. When he appeared so dressed in the mosque where he adjudicated, those who worked there brought a basket full of acorn crusts and put them below the prayer carpet of the judge. Guessing that they had played the trick on him, the judge then swore that he would act with them as hard as the wood of kermes oak that cannot be broken, and forbade them from appearing in his court for a year, such that they became impoverished. See ibid., 109–10/133 (trans.).

56 ʿAmr b. ʿAbd Allāh was called al-Qubʿa (crested lark) because he was very small, so that when he was seated he was almost invisible. When he sat to judge he required the litigants to each write their names on a card, then he mixed those cards and started to call the persons there mentioned. A man asked the poet Muʾmin b. Saʿīd—who lived near the mosque where the judge acted—to write his name for him as he was illiterate, telling him that his name was ʿUqba, but Muʾmin wrote Qubʿa instead. When the judge took that card and realized what was going on, he became irate, but refrained himself from doing anything and left that card to the end. When very few people remained in the court, the judge recommended that ʿUqba—who had described to him the man who had written his name—to stay away from Muʾmin from then onward. See Khushanī, *Quḍāt Qurṭuba*, 120–21 (ed.)/147–48 (trans.). This Muʾmin—who appears as having been intimate with the judge—on another occasion made an explicit and funny reference to the judge's liking for boys.

57 Bray, "Literary Approaches," 238.

judges do not seem to be formulaic, as there are biographical dictionaries of judges that do not include any of them. Inclusion or exclusion of such stories can be understood as part of a "living chain of debate with other practitioners of biography, and perhaps even with other genres,"[58] and in this respect Ibn Ḥārith al-Khushanī's work contains a larger share of the *adab* component than similar works. Having been commissioned by the Umayyad prince al-Ḥakam to write a work devoted exclusively to Cordoban judges, as he himself states in the introduction to his book, Ibn Ḥārith al-Khushanī recorded a local memory that included amusing stories,[59] in the same way that the Iraqi Wakīʿ—who moved in literary circles—had done.[60] Making funny remarks and joking was part of the life of the cultivated elite, although it could also have dangerous consequences, as a famous trial involving a relative of the Umayyad emir ʿAbd al-Raḥmān II (r. 206–238/822–852) showed some decades before Ibn Ḥārith al-Khushanī wrote his book.[61] Restraint and restrictions in what to say and how to say it was thus also part of the cultivated elite's education. Within this context, Ibn Ḥārith al-Khushanī's biographical dictionary can be considered a work of *adab*, aiming at teaching while entertaining through a collection of stories that make for a good read and that are remembered afterwards precisely because they are appealing and offer food for thought. His work does not hide the human failings of judges, and he does not intend to portray them as models of perfection. Through their behavior and the reactions to it, his aim is to move the reader to reflect on how to decide what is right and what is wrong on the basis of religious values, never homogenous even within Islam, and even less so when other types of values were also at stake.

Ibn Ḥārith al-Khushanī started with a judge *manqué*, al-Aʿshā, whose jocular disposition was problematic from a legal point of view because it was difficult to ascertain when he was serious and when he was joking. As a witness in court, the judge did not know what to do with al-

58 See ibid., 245. See also Abdallah Cheikh-Moussa, "L'historien et la littérature arabe médiévale," *Arabica* 43 (1996): 152–88.

59 Still to explore is to what extent he supplemented and complemented that local memory.

60 Among the authors of works on judges, Wakīʿ was associated with the poet and *adīb* Abū al-Faraj al-Iṣfahānī: see his biography in A.K. Reinhart, "Wakīʿ," *EI*². Kindī, on his part, seems to have moved only in religious circles, which may explain the absence of any "joking" character in his work on Egyptian judges. A judge and literary man, Tanūkhī (d. 384/994), included judges in one of his works of *adab*. See Mathieu Tillier, "L'exemplarité chez al-Tanūḫī: les cadis dans le *Nišwār al-muḥāḍara*," *Arabica* 54 (2007): 1–24. Both Ibn Qutayba (d. 276/889) and Ibn ʿAbd Rabbihi (d. 328/940) included mention of judges in *ʿUyūn al-akhbār* and *al-ʿIqd al-farīd*, respectively.

61 The nephew of a royal concubine had been accused of blasphemy and executed, in spite of claiming that he had just talked in jest. See Maribel Fierro, *La Heterodoxia en al-Andalus durante el periodo omeya* (Madrid: Instituto Hispano-Árabe de Cultura, 1987), 57–63. (Ibn Ḥārith al-Khushanī does not include this case in his book.) For the relationship between joking and blasphemy, see also Rabb, "Society and Propriety."

Aʿshā's testimony, so what would happen if he was himself the judge? One of the stories included by Ibn Ḥārith al-Khushanī alerted the reader to the dangers of using hyperbolic language in trials: an old man had testified in front of the judge al-Ḥabīb b. Ziyād saying that he had known about the affair being judged for one hundred years. When the judge inquired about his age and he answered that he was sixty years old, the judge retorted that it was impossible for him to testify on the affair under consideration as he had been born after it had taken place. The old man apologized saying that he had spoken in a hyperbolic way (*ʿalā al-mithl*), but the judge ordered him lashed, pointing out that when giving testimony no *mithl* could be used, and he then proceeded to explain how someone had ended up being crucified for having spoken that way. Summarizing a long and detailed story, during the times of the emir Muḥammad, there was a severe famine leading to many criminal acts and thus to many death sentences and hand amputations. The *ṣāḥib al-sūq* at the time was Ibrāhīm b. Ḥusayn b. ʿĀṣim, who was charged by the emir with being especially harsh while authorizing him to sentence quickly without elevating the cases to him, which Ibn ʿĀṣim did. One day a young boy (*fatā*) was brought to him by his neighbors, who complained about his evil deeds. They did not want him to be punished, but only taught a lesson. Yet, when the *ṣāḥib al-sūq* asked the eldest what punishment he thought the boy deserved, and the old man answered in an exaggerated way (*al-mithl wa'l-mubālagha*) that he deserved to be put in the hands of the executioners, this is precisely what the *ṣāḥib al-sūq* did. To his neighbors' dismay, the young boy was crucified.[62] Playing with words could lead to dangerous consequences and exaggeration is one of the ingredients of humor. With these and similar stories, Muslims—including judges—on alert that context should be taken into consideration when words were uttered and that this was not only common sense, but that their religion also forced them to be aware of this fact.[63]

The judge *manqué* al-Aʿshā not only liked joking, he also had a lenient view on sinful behavior such as drinking wine, and he was not alone in this: other scholars who were renowned judges are also described has having had the same attitude.[64] Al-Aʿshā eventually did not become a judge,

62 Khushanī, *Quḍāt Qurṭuba*, 177–79 (ed.)/219–22 (trans.). In the story used for illustrating the point, the official who decided according to hyperbolic testimonies was not a judge but a *ṣāḥib al-sūq* who moreover was implementing extremely severe orders given by the ruler.

63 See Ibrahim, *Assaulting with Words*. In the case of scholars, R. Kevin Jaques has shown how they were careful and deliberate in the use of words. See his "The Other Rabīʿ: Biographical Traditions and the Development of Early Shafiʿī Authority," *Islamic Law and Society* 14, no. 2 (2007): 143–79, esp. 156.

64 Ibn Ḥārith al-Khushanī has a section to deal precisely with the issue of why Andalusīs were quite open in their acceptance of wine consumption. See his *Quḍāt Qurṭuba*, 103–04 (ed.)/126–27 (trans.); see also ibid., 168 (ed.)/208 (trans.), 196 (ed.)/243 (trans.). For a funny story of how an

though he could have, despite his benevolence towards drunkards and his love for fun. Such fondness did not impair belief and morality as explicitly stated by al-Aʿshā himself, pointing to the precedent of ʿAlī b. Abī Ṭālib. The example was double-edged in an Umayyad context, given the deep anti-ʿAlid sentiment that existed then.[65] So perhaps after all al-Aʿshā's example was not the best choice to convince others that in his case, love for fun did not negate his acceptability as judge. At the same time, Ibn Ḥārith al-Khushanī came from Ifrīqiya, where, before the Fatimids, the Aghlabids had ruled in the name of the ʿAbbāsids, that is, in a context where the figure of ʿAlī b. Abī Ṭālib functioned as an exemplary model. Taking this into account, it is the reader who is invited to make a decision regarding al-Aʿshā's case: Ibn Ḥārith al-Khushanī is in control of the narrative not so much in order to bring it to a "black or white" quandary, but to alert the reader that there is not such clear demarcation between black and white, even if the colors are real and need to be known as being different one from the other.[66]

Coming now to Ibn Ḥārith al-Khushanī's two joking judges, Sulaymān b. Aswad's funny commentary happened while he was acting as judge in the mosque, but it had no direct link with any current trial. The joke, moreover, had as targets a mule and a woman, both trans-culturally and traditionally providers of material for ridiculing and laughing. Thus, his witticism—which was probably funnier in the Romance language than in the Arabic translation—affected only tangentially his office as a judge. In the case of the practical joke against Ibn Qulzum, it happened in a private setting and did not involve the *qāḍī*ship. It did reveal that Sulaymān b. Aswad did not recoil from ridiculing and mocking a fellow scholar, but on the other hand the scholar in question had put himself in jeopardy with his immoderate and publicized desire to be named director of prayer. Aslam b. ʿAbd al-ʿAzīz's funny remarks also mostly happened in a private setting except for two that took place in his court. Regarding the latter, one of them—making the venal witness realize that he had been discovered—helped the judge in putting an end to a corrupt transaction. The other also originated in the suspicion that there was something wrong in the testimony of a witness, but in this case the targeted person was offended and defended his honor, proclaiming publicly that it was unfit and unacceptable for a judge

Eastern judge supported the consumption of wine, see Szombathy, *Mujūn*, 202.

65 See Maribel Fierro, "La política religiosa de ʿAbd al-Raḥmān III," *Al-Qanṭara* 25 (2004): 119–56.

66 Ibn Ḥārith al-Khushanī is not so much providing contradictory evidence as in the case of ʿIyāḍ, according to Jonathan Brockopp, "Contradictory Evidence and the Exemplary Scholar: The Lives of Saḥnūn b. Saʿīd (d. 854)," *International Journal of Middle Eastern Studies* 43 (2011): 115–32. Brockopp shows that such cases offer the reader a variety of contextual frameworks in which individuals with their words and deeds are inscribed.

to indulge in mockery against a witness while sitting in his audience.[67] This suggests that the judges' behavior at court was not clearly regulated nor was there a consensus of what was appropriate to do and not to do on his part. Stories such as these were in fact contributions to the emergence of such consensus.

During the period considered here, the Cordoban judges had their courts in the mosque, that is, in a public space that was at the same time charged with spirituality. Mathieu Tillier has shown that some of the judges of the early ʿAbbāsid period did not consider it inappropriate to introduce profane elements into such a setting, such as reciting poetry and indulging in laughter. Reactions such as that of the scholar Muḥammad b. Musʿar regarding which attitudes were permissible or not in the mosque indicate the existence of discrepancy of opinions,[68] and it is significant that what can be called the "pro-seriousness" position is voiced not by a judge, but by a scholar: as Tillier has concluded, the early Abbāsid judges in the sources he studied do not appear as representatives of religion.[69] By Ibn Ḥārith al-Khushanī's time, a case like that of the judge of Basra, Ismāʿīl b. Ḥammād b. Abī Ḥanīfa, who recited in his *majlis* verses that fell into the *mujūn* (libertinism) category, seems to have been uncommon as he did not include any such example, but we have seen the case of a later judge in Seville who did write such poetry.[70] Hence, silence on this may be due to other reasons. In his detailed monographic study on *mujūn*, Zoltán Szombathy has pointed that among the indications of the suspect status of joking for the *ʿulamāʾ* there is the recommendation some of them make that "appointees to the position of judge (*qāḍī*) should avoid laughter and jesting."[71] On the other hand, the *ʿulamāʾ* in general were against rigidity and severity and in favor of moderation:[72] "Some celebrated savants whose dedication to Islamic norms and general propriety cannot be seriously doubted would not have serious qualms about cracking jokes themselves or sanctioning other's jesting by listening to it and showing no disapproval thereof."[73] Szombathy concludes

67 ʿAlī b. al-Ḥusayn b. Ḥarb (d. 319/931), a judge in Wāsiṭ, was also reprimanded in similar circumstances. See Tillier, "Un espace judiciaire entre public et privé," 499.

68 On this judge, see above, note 42.

69 Tillier, "Un espace judiciaire entre public et privé," 499, 503, 506.

70 See above, note 44.

71 Szombathy, *Mujūn*, 15, referring to the Andalusī jurist Ibn Juzayy's (d. 741/1340), al-*Qawānīn al-fiqhiyya,* and to the Ḥanafī al-Samarqandī (d. 375/985-6), for whom a laughing or jesting judge "destroys the solemnity of the session."

72 Asma Afsaruddin, "Exegeses of 'Moderation': Negotiating the Boundaries of Pluralism and Exclusion," *The Good Society* 16 (2007): 1–9.

73 See Szombathy, *Mujūn*, 203 and n. 130: "taken together these data do seem to imply that educated people saw no contradiction between someone's being a religious scholar and his

that more than office, it was personality which determined whether someone was in favor of or against frivolity and humor, and that there was no uniform attitude among the *ʿulamāʾ* in this field, as already indicated by Roy Mottahedeh when he pointed out that the piously minded and the *ʿulamāʾ* were not identical categories.[74] Szombathy also states that "judges were often perceived, even stereotyped, as being more lenient and perhaps more susceptible to *mujūn* than other categories of religious savants."[75] He then proceeds to give a number of examples, including a *qāḍī* of Mecca who not only did not punish a drunkard but showed sympathy for him, and the famous *qāḍī* al-Tanūkhī who indulged in wine and profligacy in the company of the vizier al-Muhallabī while maintaining proper and dignified behavior when acting as judge. Also, judges, like all others, had a past, and in their youth they could have done things that they later regretted.[76]

The fact that joking and jesting were often perceived as bordering *fisq* and *mujūn*, and that a judge would have allowed neither a *fāsiq* nor a *mājin* to act as witnesses in his court,[77] implied that a judge probably tended to be careful not to expose himself so as to be included in that category. A virtue we have already encountered, *ḥilm*,[78] was the quality with which judges would ideally be associated: it involved "a number of moral norms and attitudes, from serene justice and moderation to forbearance and leniency, touching on self-control and dignified behaviour."[79] As the scholar Muḥammad b. Musʿar reminded the judge of Basra, for God, mocking people was equal to ignorance.[80] Had He not said in the Qurʾān 49:11 "Do not let certain people scoff at others?" while a number of *ḥadīth* reports enjoined Muslims not to make fun of others.[81] While in the portrayal of the judge ʿAmr b. ʿAbd Allāh there is the suggestion that he was able to share in laughing at the jokes he was exposed to, in other cases those who were the target of joking were hurt. It is through these hurt feelings and through the dangers of exaggeration in discourse that cautionary limits—more than outright rejection—suggest an explanation for the judges' joking and to the

enjoyment of frivolous humour."

74 Roy P. Mottahedeh, *Loyalty and Leadership in an Early Islamic Society* (Princeton: Princeton University Press, 1980), 149.

75 Szombathy, *Mujūn*, 205.

76 Ibid., 206.

77 Ibid., 215–27.

78 See above, note 11.

79 Charles Pellat, "Seriousness and Humour in Early Islam," *Islamic Studies* 2 (1963): 353–62, esp. 353.

80 See above, note 42.

81 Pellat, "Seriousness and Humour in Early Islam," 354–55.

joking of those involved in court trials. At the same time, the joking reminds the audience that the court itself was an arena where human weaknesses and even foolish behavior were exposed. For those who were not rigorists and for whom humor was acceptable as just another manifestation of human behavior, it was obvious that humor could not be expelled from such an arena, especially when it reflected a character's personality, and when awareness of its dangers was necessary.

Chapter Nine

Judicial Procedure and Legal Practice on *Liʿān* (Imprecatory Oath) in al-Andalus: The Evidence from Model *Shurūṭ* Collections, 11th–12th Centuries*

Delfina Serrano

Spanish High Council for Scientific Research (CSIC)

In the last decade, the Islamic institution of *liʿān*[1] has raised a considerable level of interest among students of Islamic law given contemporary Muslim jurists' debates on how the availability of DNA fingerprinting is affecting the traditional ways to disavow paternity.[2] This has given way

* Drafts of this paper were presented at an international seminar on "Gender and Family Relationships in Pre-modern Islamic Societies" at the ILC at CCHS-CSIC in Madrid, Spain on September 25-26, 2014; at an international conference on "Writing Women's Lives" at the School of Foreign Service at Georgetown University in Doha on March 20-22, 2016; and at the international conference on "Courts and Judicial Procedure in Islamic Law" held in honor of Prof. Roy Mottahedeh at Harvard Law School in Cambridge, MA on May 6, 2016. This paper collects results from the I+D Research Project "In the footsteps of Abū ʿAlī al-Ṣadafī: tradition and devotion in al-Andalus (XIth- XIIIth centuries CE), funded by the Spanish Ministry of Economy and Competitiveness, ref. FFI2013–43172-P and from the NPRP8-1478-6-053 Grant from the Qatar National Research Fund (a member of the Qatar Foundation). I wish to thank the volume's editors and the anonymous readers of the final draft for their suggestions. The statements made herein are solely the responsibility of the author.

1 The *liʿān* procedure consists of five oaths to be sworn both by a man and his wife if he wishes to accuse her of adultery in the absence of sufficient evidence and/or to deny the paternity of her child. Swearing an oath exempts him from liability for defamation for claims of sexual impropriety (*qadhf*) and her from liability for adultery or sexual impropriety (*zinā*). Refusal to swear on her part amounts to admission to having committed *zinā* and triggers the corresponding punishment once she gives birth to her child. The completion of the procedure entails definitive and irrevocable divorce of the spouses, and the severance of filiation between the man and his ex-wife's child.

2 See, e.g., Ron Shaham, *The Expert Witness in Islamic Courts: Medicine and Crafts in the Service of Law* (Chicago: University of Chicago Press, 2010), 154–87; Ayman Shabana, "Paternity between Law and Biology: The Reconstruction of the Islamic Law of Paternity in the Wake of DNA Testing," *Zygon* 47, no. 1 (2012): 214–39; Ayman Shabana, "Negation of Paternity in Islamic Law between *Liʿān* and DNA Fingerprinting," *Islamic Law and Society* 20, no. 3 (2013): 157–201; and Ayman Shabana, "Law and Ethics in Islamic Bioethics: Nonmaleficence in Islamic Paternity Regulations,"

to thorough treatments of classical Islamic doctrines on *liʿān*.[3] In fact, the prevalence of *liʿān* in contemporary Muslim majority legal systems provides one of the best illustrations at hand of the tensions brought about in Islamic procedural and evidentiary law by both modern changes in legal and commercial culture and technological advance.[4] Although all those questions trespass on the temporal focus of this paper, the idea to look back and explore legal practice on *liʿān* in a pre-modern context like al-Andalus has been partially inspired by contemporary views regarding the institution and by reading the scholarship addressing those views.[5]

Available research on the history of Islamic law is not particularly rich in information on the means by which paternity was denied in practice; or on jurists' and judges' involvement and what they did to strike a balance between parties, avoid injustice and extreme hardship, and to prevent excessive literalism and disregard for socio-economic factors from causing harm. We thus need to observe the medieval jurists' strategies to accommodate changing circumstances, curb abuses of legal tools at people's disposal, or encourage people to use these tools to their benefit. We need to reconstruct the contents of the "*liʿān* enforcement package" from a time in which those who had the monopoly over—if not administering then at least interpreting *sharīʿa*—were the same people to whom the task used to be entrusted to construct the *liʿān* procedure. They were also the ones who would oversee the procedure and ensure its effects at a time when reaching scientific truth regarding conflicting genealogical claims was impossible and thus had to be addressed by means of legal presumptions. Ultimately, our purpose is to observe how the law was implemented to settle a man's wish to disavow his wife's child, and to reveal the role procedure played toward that goal. Justice was to correspond to that goal, a concept related, with all due precaution, to the modern concept of the rule of law.[6]

Zygon 48, no. 3 (2013): 709–31.

3 See Shabana, "Paternity between Law and Biology," and his "Negation of Paternity in Islamic Law."

4 See Mohammed Fadel and Jonathan C. Brown, "Procedure and Proof," in *The Encyclopedia of Islam and Law,* Oxford Studies Online (last accessed December 6, 2016), esp. the section on "Modern Changes in Evidentiary Standards;" Björn Bentlage, "Legislating for the Benefit of Children Born Out of Wedlock," *Die Welt des Islams* 55 (2015): 378–412, esp. 384; and Thomas Eich, "Constructing Kinship in Sunnī Islamic Legal Texts," in Marcia C. Inhorn and Soraya Tremayne, eds., *Islam and Assisted Reproductive Technologies: Sunnī and Shia Perspectives* (New York: Berghahn Books, 2012), 27–52, esp. 46–48. Both the article by Bentlage and the article by Fadel and Brown draw on Shabana's work on *liʿān*.

5 The impact of scientific means on traditional ways to establish and deny paternity in contemporary Mālikī contexts is addressed in my "*Fiqh*, Biomedicine, and Mālikī-Inspired Family Legislation: The Use of DNA Tests to Establish the Paternity of Children Born out of Wedlock" (in progress).

6 On the association between *sharīʿa* and the modern concept of the rule of law, see Noah

In what follows, I ask these questions in the context of Mālikī al-Andalus. Reconstructing legal practice on a matter like *liʿān* in al-Andalus, where the relevant legal doctrine led to extremely high levels of elaboration and refinement by the local jurists, is hampered by the well-known lack of actual legal documents and judicial archives. In the abundant *fatwā* literature of advisory opinions illustrating legal interpretation in the area, practice can at best be gleaned and reconstructed—occasionally with the help of historical chronicles and biographical dictionaries—up to the moment in which the husband must choose to either undergo the *liʿān* procedure or withdraw his accusation. For this reason, I use information about actual cases from other regions of Mālikī influence like Ifrīqiya and the central Maghrib—which were either fundamental for the development of the school doctrine in al-Andalus or were, subsequent to the fall of al-Andalus to Christian hands, projections of its legal tradition—as a complement whenever available.

LEGAL PRACTICE ON *LIʿĀN* IN ANDALUS

In her seminal work on women in al-Andalus, Manuela Marín refers to a number of Andalusī men who, according to chronicles and biographical dictionaries, resorted to swearing the *liʿān* oath to accuse their wives of adultery and/or to deny the paternity of their children.[7] Marín notes the rejection those cases produced in the authors who reported them, an attitude in line with Sunnī scholars' well-known tendency to favor concealment over publicity when the moral order was at stake. She concludes that the implementation of the *liʿān* procedure in practice must have been very scarce.

However, the attitude of one of the authorities mentioned by Marín in support of her assessment is problematic. In his famous biographical lexicon on Mālikī jurists, Qāḍī ʿIyāḍ b. Mūsā (d. 544/1149) disapproved of

Feldman, "Does *Shariah* Mean the Rule of Law?," *New York Times*, March 16, 2008. On compliance with the rule of law in classical Islamic *fiqh* see, for example, Mohammad Fadel, "Rules, Judicial Discretion and the Rule of Law in Naṣrid Granada: An Analysis of *al-Ḥadīqa al-mustaqilla al-naḍra fī al-fatāwā al-ṣādira ʿan ʿulamāʾ al-ḥaḍra*," in *Islamic Law: Theory and Practice*, ed. Robert Gleave and Eugenia Kermeli (London: I.B. Tauris, 2001), 49–86; and Chibli Mallat, "Introduction: On Islam and Democracy," in Chibli Mallat ed., *Islam and Public Law: Classical and Contemporary Studies* (London: Graham and Trotman, 1993), 1–11. On related notions of *sharīʿa* and constitutionalism in the pre-modern period see also Frank Vogel, "Tracing Nuance in Māwardī's *al-Aḥkām al-Sulṭāniyyah*: Implicit Framing of Constitutional Authority," in Kevin Reinhart and Robert Gleave, eds., *Islamic Law in Theory: Studies on Jurisprudence in Honor of Bernard Weiss* (Leiden and Boston: Brill, 2014), 331–59; and Sherman Jackson, *Islamic Law and the State: The Constitutional Jurisprudence of Shihāb al-Dīn al-Qarāfī* (Leiden: Brill, 1996).

7 Manuela Marín, "Mujeres en al-Andalus," in *Estudios Onomástico-Biográficos de al-Andalus*, 11:471–75.

the attitude of Ibn al-Hindī (d. 399/1009), a jurist who is reported to have pronounced the *liʿān* oath against his wife by order of Cordoba's chief of police—instead of the *qāḍī*. The biographer declares this instance to have been the last occasion in which such a case occurred not only in al-Andalus but in the history of Islam as a whole.[8] Yet, as Marín observes, the sources mention two other cases in which, subsequent to Ibn al-Hindī's death, Andalusī jurists instructed any man denying the paternity of a child expected by his wife to pronounce the *liʿān* oath. The latter of these cases had to be dealt with by precisely the aforementioned Qāḍī ʿIyāḍ b. Mūsā, this time in his capacity as *qāḍī* of his native Ceuta. In that case, a woman reported to him that her husband denied being the father of the child she was expecting and the Cordoban *muftīs* he consulted before issuing his judgment advised him to give the husband the option to either pronounce the *liʿān* oath or admit to the paternity of his wife's unborn child if he wanted to avoid the charge of slander.[9]

To the list of Andalusī cases provided by Marín, we might add another case presented to the Tunisian *qāḍī* ʿAbd Allāh b. Ṭālib (d. 275/880). This judge twice postponed a process concerning the daughter of his friend ʿAbd al-Raḥmān b. Muḥammad in order to avoid her husband's pronouncement of *liʿān* against her. But in the end, the *qāḍī* could not prevent that oath.[10]

That *liʿān* occurred more often than the jurists would have liked is confirmed by the Tunisian jurist al-Burzulī (d. 841/1438), who preferred to describe the social practice of his time realistically rather than overindulging in wishful thinking.[11] His treatment of *liʿān* makes clear that Ibn al-Hindī's case, which Burzulī transmits from Ibn ʿĀt's (d. 609/1212) *al-Ṭurar*, became paradigmatic of how blameworthy it was to use the law against others just

8 See Marín, *Mujeres en al-Andalus*, 473, quoting Qāḍī ʿIyāḍ b. Mūsā, *Tartīb al-madārik wa-taqrīb al-masālik li-maʿrifat aʿlām madhhab Mālik*, ed. Muhammad Bencherifa (Rabat: Wizārat al-Awqāf wa'l-Shu'ūn al-Islāmiyya, 1403/1983), 7:146–47: *bi-ḥukm ṣāḥib al-shurṭa Ibn al-Sharafī*. Qāḍī ʿIyāḍ's bold statement is reproduced without apparent objection by Wansharīsī (d. 914/1509) in *al-Miʿyār al-muʿrib wa'l-jāmiʿ al-mughrib ʿan fatāwā ahl Ifrīqiya wa'l-Andalus wa'l-Maghrib*, ed. Muḥammad Ḥajjī et al. (Rabat: Wizārat al-Awqāf wa'l-Shu'ūn al-Islāmiyya, 1401/1981), 4:76–77. On the assignment to governmental agents like the *ṣāḥib al-shurṭa* of judicial competences that were in theory exclusive to *qāḍīs* in eleventh-century al-Andalus see Christian Müller, *Gerichtspraxis im Stadtstaat Córdoba: zum Recht der Gesellschaft in einer malikitish-islamischen Rechtstradition des 5./11. Jahrhunderts* (Leiden: Brill, 1999), 247–310, esp. 289–94.

9 See Marín, *Mujeres en al-Andalus*, 473, quoting Ibn ʿIyāḍ, *Madhāhib al-ḥukkām fī nawāzil al-aḥkām*, (Beirut: Dār al-Gharb al-Islāmī, 1989), 299–300; and the Spanish translation by Delfina Serrano Ruano, *La actuación de los jueces en los procesos judiciales*, (Madrid: CSIC-AECI, 1998), 485–86.

10 See Nejmeddine Hentati, "Mais le cadi tranche-t-il?," *Islamic Law and Society* 14 (2007): 180–203, esp. 190, quoting *Fatāwā Ibn Abī Zayd al-Qayrawānī*, collected by H.M. Lahmar (Beirut: Dār al-Gharb al-Islāmī, 2004), 221.

11 See Burzulī, *Fatāwā al-Burzulī*, ed. Muḥammad al-Ḥila (Beirut: Dār al-Gharb al-Islāmī, 2002), 2:469–72.

for the sake of legalism.[12] When asked about the reason for pronouncing *liʿān* against his wife, Ibn al-Hindī replied that he "wanted to revive a dying *Sunna*: *aradtu iḥyāʾ sunna qad datharat*," and that it was only when he was reproached for having taken such an initiative and lost the reputation of being a sound religious scholar, that he stopped boasting about it.[13] Direct reproach and ostracization—and, more importantly, condemnation by one's peers—was the kind of treatment awaiting those who took interpretation of the law too freely or too literally. Another question, not mentioned by Burzulī, is whether Ibn al-Hindī would have been allowed to pronounce *liʿān* had a *qāḍī* presided over the court that ruled on his case rather than the chief of police.[14]

Subsequently, Burzulī reports that in Emir Yaḥyā's time the procedure was administered in the Zaytūna Mosque and that a similar case later occurred.[15] Unfortunately Burzulī does not provide further details about these cases. Yet he declares that he is not surprised that "factors motivating such events continue to arise given the proliferation of vicious conduct (*kathrat al-mafāsid*) in our days," whereby he seems to put the blame on married women.[16]

In Tlemcen, roughly around the same time, the grandson of Sīdī Muḥammad al-ʿUqbānī was consulted by al-Maghīlī al-Māzūnī (d. 883/1473) about the following case: A man married a woman who gave birth to a child whom he refused to recognize as his. The man had children from another wife so he ignored and rejected the newborn (*fa-ahmala hadhā al-walad wa-ramāh min nafsih*). However, all his sons died and when confronted by his solitude, he called the formerly repudiated son and told to him: "You are my son, may God forgive me for what I told you in the past." After the man's death, he left his brother and this son as the only legal heirs. Then the man's brother told the son, that is, his nephew, "You are not my brother's son," and had a document drafted collecting witnesses' testimony that the deceased did marry the boy's mother but that she gave birth to him less than six months afterwards (*wa-athbata rasm*[an] *taḍammana anna*

12 Another, still unedited, link in the rich Andalusī tradition of model *shurūṭ* works is Ibn ʿĀt's *al-Ṭurar al-mawḍūʿa ʿalā al-wathāʾiq al-majmūʿa* of which several manuscripts are extant. See the HATA [Online], an initiative directed by Maribel Fierro, section on *fiqh*. Ibn ʿĀt is one of the main sources of Ibn Salmūn's *ʿIqd*, itself one of our main references in this paper, as will be shown below. See Pedro Cano, "Algunos datos del tratado notarial de Abū al-Qāsim Ibn Salmūn (d. 767/1366)," *Philologia Hispalensis* 5, no. 1 (1990): 233–44, esp. 240.

13 See Burzulī, *Fatāwā al-Burzulī*, 2:471.

14 See above, note 8, on the assignment of government agents.

15 He may be referring to the Ḥafṣid emir, Abū Zakariyāʾ Yaḥyā, founder of the dynasty who ruled between 627/1230 and 647/1249, or to Yaḥyā (II) al-Wāthiq who ruled between 675/1277 and 678/1279.

16 See Burzulī, *Fatāwā al-Burzulī*, 2:471.

al-mayyit tazawwaja umm hadhā al-walad wa-atat bih li-aqall min sittat ashhur). However, the witnesses did not specify whether they referred to the day of the conclusion of the marriage contract or to the day the marriage was consummated, and it was difficult to ask them to clarify the issue (*wa-taʿadhdhara istifsārahum*). Is it possible then to assume, the petitioner asked, that they referred to the date the marriage contract was concluded, having taken into account that the most practiced custom in our land (*al-ʿāda al-jāriya bi-waṭaninā al-akthariyya*) is that the man consummates the marriage with his wife the night that the contract is concluded or the next day. This typically occurs by order of the bride's parents, to the point that if the husband does not respect this custom, he may be considered to have brought dishonor (*maʿarra*) to his wife and the contempt of her peers (*ḥaqrat bayna aqrānihā*)? For this reason, this custom is widespread (*muṭarrada*) and the occasions on which it is not practiced are rare. Is the boy to be deprived of the inheritance by virtue of the document, as it has been mentioned, and of the custom prevailing in practice for those cases, given the vagueness of the testimony (*ibhām al-shahāda*)?[17]

In his reply, the jurisconsult (*muftī*) stated that if the man who claimed the paternity of the boy after having rejected him did not marry his mother while she was observing the waiting period (*ʿidda*), the son must be declared legally affiliated to him (*faʾl-walad lāḥiq bih ḥukm*[an]) and cannot be disavowed except by means of *liʿān* or satisfactory evidence that she gave birth to him before six months had elapsed since the marriage contract was concluded. This is because her children become lawful from the very moment the marriage contract is concluded (*li-annahā bi-mujarrad al-ʿaqd ṣārat firāsh*[an]).[18] The *muftī* implied that the testimony presented by the deceased's brother was not satisfactory (*marḍiyya*). He did not show any interest in finding out whether withdrawal of the rejection had any of the consequences I examine below (namely, payment of the maintenance rights corresponding to the child and his mother, or liability for slander), let alone in warning the man about these consequences even if with a mere pedagogical intention. The petitioner of the *fatwā*, by contrast, did not leave any doubts about the moral regard he held for the man's action. He presented the man as cruel, selfish, and frivolous in his attempt to escape the consequences of his misconduct by merely asking God for forgiveness.

17 The Arabic text of this *fatwā* has been edited and translated into French by Elise Voguet, *Le monde rural du Maghreb central (XIVe-XVe siècles): Réalités sociales et constructions juridiques d'aprés les* Nawāzil Māzūna (Paris: Publications de la Sorbonne, 2014), 126–27.

18 See Voguet, *Le monde rural du Maghreb central (XIVe-XVe siècles)*, 127. The English translation is mine. Denial of the paternity of a child born less than six months after marriage does not require the *liʿān* procedure. See Shabana, "Negation of Paternity in Islamic Law," 179.

LEGAL PRACTICE AND PROCEDURE ON *LIʿĀN* IN THREE ANDALUSĪ MODEL *SHURŪṬ* COLLECTIONS

The existence of model legal forms specific to denial of paternity and *liʿān* was already observed by Manuela Marín.[19] Here, I will explore these forms to approach the judicial practice and procedure followed by *qāḍīs* when having to deal with denial of paternity, a scenario which, *a priori,* they are presumed to have confronted only exceptionally. In this way, I hope to expand our present knowledge on judicial practice and procedure in al-Andalus. The combined study of model *shurūṭ, fatwās*, and legal cases (*nawāzil*), along with doctrinal elaborations and historical sources from the chronicles and biographical literature, allows us to approach the actual operation of *sharīʿa* courts from the closest vantage point possible, absent judicial archives and legal documents.[20]

This paper also considers the extent to which legal doctrine on *liʿān,* and the kind of documents to which the relevant judicial procedure gave rise, were a response to a pressing need for local *qāḍī* courts to address the issue efficiently, and their involvement would provide a deterrent to violating the legal canon "*al-walad lil-firāsh*: any offspring belongs to the marital bed." This study will therefore help reveal what was meant by medieval Muslim jurists and historians who asserted that *liʿān* was hardly ever put into practice.

A number of collections of model *shurūṭ* produced in al-Andalus has been preserved and edited. In what follows I concentrate on three such collections: that of Aḥmad b. Mughīth al-Ṭulayṭulī (d. 459/1067), from Toledo, *al-Muqniʿ fī ʿilm al-shurūṭ*; that of ʿAlī b. Yaḥyā al-Jazīrī (d. 585/1189), from Algeciras, *al-Maqṣad al-maḥmūd fī talkhīṣ al-ʿuqūd*; and that of Abū al-Qāsim Salmūn b. Alī b. ʿAbd Allāh Ibn Salmūn al-Kinānī (d. 767/1366), from Granada, *al-ʿIqd al-munaẓẓam lil-ḥukkām*.[21]

These jurists cover Mālikī judicial practice over a span of three centuries, during which time important political changes took place. Some resulted from the collapse of the Umayyad caliphate of Cordoba, which led to the political fragmentation of al-Andalus into petty kingdoms (*mulūk al-*

19 See Marín, *Mujeres en al-Andalus*, 474.

20 See Wael Hallaq, "Model *Shurūṭ* Works and the Dialectic of Doctrine and Practice," *Islamic Law and Society* 2, no. 2 (1995): 109–34.

21 Aḥmad b. Mughīth al-Ṭulayṭulī (d. 459/1067), *al-Muqniʿ fī ʿilm al-shurūṭ,* ed. Francisco Javier Aguirre Sádaba (Madrid: CSIC-ICMA, 1994), 121–24; ʿAlī b. Yaḥyā al-Jazīrī, *al-Maqṣad al-maḥmūd fī talkhīṣ al-ʿuqūd*, ed. Asunción Ferreras (Madrid: CSIC-AECI, 1998), 97–103; and Ibn Salmūn, *al-ʿIqd al-munaẓẓam lil-ḥukkām fī-mā yajrī bayna aydīhim min al-ʿuqūd wa'l-aḥkām,* on the margins of Ibrāhīm b. ʿAlī Ibn Farḥūn (d. 799/1397), *Tabṣirat al-ḥukkām fī uṣūl al-aqḍiya wa-manāhij al-aḥkām* (Beirut: Dār al-Kutub al-ʿIlmiyya, 1883), 154–58. Jazīrī came from the Rif region in northern Morocco and settled in Algeciras, where he served as a *qāḍī.* Ibn Salmūn belonged to an important family of jurists and served as a chief *qāḍī* of Granada for several months.

ṭawāʾif), followed by military invasions from the other side of the Straits of Gibraltar led by the Almoravids and the Almohads. After the drastic territorial setback experienced by Andalusī Islam at the hands of northern Iberian Christians from the first quarter of the thirteenth century onwards, only the Nasrids of Granada were able to maintain power for another two centuries, though on an increasingly precarious balance with the Christians on the one hand and with the North African Banū Marīn dynasty on the other. Given the origins of their authors, the comparison between the *Muqniʿ*, the *Maqṣad*, and the *ʿIqd* allows us to observe not only temporal but also internal variations within Andalusī legal practice, that is, between Toledo, Algeciras, and Granada.[22] The relevant sections in all three collections also shed light on women's agency in an institutional context in which the Mālikī legal school viewed pregnancy outside of wedlock as valid evidence of *zinā*. As the Ẓāhirī jurist Ibn Ḥazm noted, this put women, especially the divorced and the widowed, in a situation of extreme vulnerability.[23]

al-Muqniʿ fī ʿilm al-shurūṭ by Aḥmad Ibn Mughīth from Toledo (d. 459/1067)

The material relevant to our subject in Ibn Mughīth's collection is headed by a template, or a model legal document for "denying the paternity of a fetus: *wathīqat nafy ḥaml*." The contents describe how to proceed in such an event: First, the marital bond between the involved spouses has to be established by the wife in the presence of the *qāḍī* and professional witnesses.[24] If she succeeds in demonstrating that bond, the *qāḍī* then summons the husband and inquires about his rejection of the paternity of the child she is expecting and the accusation of *zinā* against her that the denial may imply. If the man insists on accusing her and she insists on rejecting his claim, their assertions must be noted in the presence of two witnesses and dated.[25]

22 On Cordoban legal practice as reflected in model legal form collections, and how it should be compared with other Andalusī samples of the genre, see below, note 27.

23 Ibn Ḥazm's doctrine on *zinā* and *liʿān* differs from that of the Mālikīs on a number of key issues. These differences are presented by Ibn Ḥazm in the form of sharp criticisms that are instrumental to reconstructing a certain "counter-mentality" to the prevailing Mālikī point of view legitimizing Andalusī *fiqh*. See Delfina Serrano Ruano, "Paternity and Filiation According to the Jurists of Andalus: Legal Doctrines on Transgression of the Islamic Social Order," *Imago Temporis. Medium Aevum* 7 (2013): 59–75.

24 The prerequisite of establishing the existence of marriage in disputes involving paternity is mandatory because marriage is the *ratio legis* of paternity, in order to prevent "the mixing of genealogies" (*ikhtilāṭ al-ansāb*). Marriage and *firāsh* are considered the ideal ways to form a family, and family, in its turn, the ideal unit of a solidly structured society. See Shabana, "Law and Ethics in Islamic Bioethics," 713–15, 719.

25 If the man denies the woman's claim, she can still compel him to swear the *liʿān* oath by presenting two witnesses verifying her husband's accusation against her. Otherwise, she must face the consequences of slander. See Shabana, "Negation of Paternity in Islamic Law," 175–76.

In the section on *fiqh* that immediately follows the text of the template, Ibn Mughīth specifies that in the aforementioned case "the *qāḍī* has to summon the spouses in the presence of Muslim professional witnesses (*ʿudūl min al-muslimīn*) and of the *fuqahāʾ* of his advisory council" so that they can both pronounce *liʿān*. Subsequently, he describes how to pronounce the five oaths that constitute *liʿān*, conveying the seriousness of the act and the severe repercussions for perjury. As for the wife, he remarks that when swearing the fifth and final oath, she must invoke the wrath (*biʾl-ghaḍab*) of God upon herself if it turns out that her husband is actually telling the truth. The completion of the oaths entails irrevocable and irreversible dissolution of the marital bond (*ṭalāq bāʾin*).

Next, Ibn Mughīth addresses the issue of internal divergence of opinions between Saḥnūn, according to whom separation of the spouses is inherent to *liʿān* itself, and Ibn al-Qāsim, for whom separation is not inherent but must be pronounced immediately afterward by the *qāḍī* (*illā bi-ḥukm al-qāḍī fī-dhālik*).[26] Ibn Mughīth observes that Ibn al-Qāsim's argument (*ḥujja*) relies on a prophetic report (*ḥadīth*) transmitted by Aṣbagh as recorded in Abū ʿAbd Allāh Muḥammad al-ʿUtbī's (d. 255/869) *ʿUtbiyya* (a compilation of Mālikī legal opinions also known as the *Mustakhraja*). The *fiqh* section ends with the statement: "Take it into account" (*fa-ʿrifhu*), that is, the fact that there are two opinions, one of which is based on an identifiable Prophetic report. Whether Toledan practice on *liʿān* differed from its Cordoban analog is difficult to ascertain, because the chapters concerning marriage and repudiation are missing from the preserved manuscripts of the well-known earlier *shurūṭ* collection of the Cordoban Ibn al-ʿAṭṭār (d. 339/1009).[27]

The following template relates to a man's recognition of the child

---

26 Saḥnūn b. Saʿīd al-Tanūkhī (d. 240/855), from Qayrawān, was the compiler of one of the most authoritative early manuals of Mālikī doctrine, *al-Mudawwana al-kubrā*, including the answers given by Mālik b. Anas to questions posed to him by his disciples on the authority of one them, the Egyptian Ibn al-Qāsim (d. 191/806). In al-Andalus, cases of divergence—or divergent transmissions—of opinions among Mālik's disciples used to be decided in favor of Ibn al-Qāsim.

27 Ibn al-ʿAṭṭār, *Kitāb al-waṯāʾiq waʾl-siŷillāt*, ed. Pedro Chalmeta and Federico Corriente (Madrid: Fundación Matritense del Notariado e Instituto Hispano-Árabe de Cultura, 1983). Ibn al-ʿAṭṭār is said to have drawn on a series of Near Eastern sources, among which was Abū Jaʿfar Aḥmad b. Muḥammad al-Ṭaḥāwī's (d. 321/933) *Kitāb al-shurūṭ al-kabīr*, a collection that included a long chapter on marriage and repudiation. See Jeanette A. Wakin, *The Function of Documents in Islamic Law: The Chapters on Sales from Ṭaḥāwī's Kitāb al-shurūṭ al-kabīr* (Albany: State University of New York Press, 1972), 24–26. No templates relevant to *liʿān* appear in Abū Isḥāq al-Gharnāṭī's (d. 579/1183) *al-Wathāʾiq al-mukhtaṣara*, ed. Muṣṭafā Nājī (Rabat: Markaz Iḥyāʾ al-Turāth al-Maghribī, 1988), notwithstanding its inclusion of a short section on marriage and divorce; nor in ʿAbd al-Wāḥid al-Marrākushī's (d. ca. 669/1270) *Wathāʾiq al-Murābiṭīn waʾl-Muwaḥḥidīn*, ed. Ḥusayn Muʾnis (Ẓāhir: Maktabat al-Thaqāfa al-Dīniyya, 1997), which includes no section on marriage or divorce. The model *shurūṭ* collections by Abū Muḥammad al-Buntī (d. 462/1070) and ʿAlī b. ʿAbd Allāh al-Maṭṭīṭī (d. 570/1175) have not yet been edited.

expected by his wife (*wathīqat fī iqrār al-rajul bi-ḥaml jawzatih*). At first sight, this approach seems surprising because normally any child born to a man's wife is automatically attributed to him. Only the children of slaves needed the explicit recognition of their fathers. The circumstances explaining the need to produce a certification of this kind are not specified by Ibn Mughīth. In the *fiqh* section following the template, he simply remarks that making an explicit recognition like this exempts a man from producing further evidence of the paternity of the child, should the need arise in the future.

For the wife, conversely, the document is said to be useless to free her from the obligation of swearing the *liʿān* oath should her husband accuse her of adultery, although Ibn Mughīth specifies that the husband would need to present evidence contradicting the testimonies from the first acknowledgment. Otherwise, paternity would be attributed to him; and, if denial of paternity were grounded on an accusation of adultery against her, he would also incur liability for defamation. According to the legal opinions transmitted by Ibn Abī Zamanīn (d. 399/1009) in his *Muntakhab al-aḥkām,* negation of paternity of a fetus after having implicitly or explicitly recognized it was only possible if a man claimed that he had seen (*ruʾya*) his wife commit *zinā* with another man and if the child was born more than six months after the accusation.[28]

It is thus not clear whether Ibn Mughīth's remark—that rejection of a previously accepted fetus on the grounds of *zinā* amounted to slander—is a departure from the position represented by the *Muntakhab al-aḥkām*. My impression is that Ibn Mughīth's mention of the need to provide counter-evidence refers to witnesses who might testify that she had committed *zinā* or to a confession by the accused, not to the mere accusation. Interestingly, Ibn Mughīth says that this opinion—namely, that counter-evidence invalidating the first testimony of acknowledgment of the fetus is required—was held "by more than one scholar" and that it was followed in local judicial practice (*wa-bih al-ʿamal*). As a result, Ibn Mughīth's lack of precision seems to hint at a recent development less fixed in Toledan court practice than he suggests. Again it is regrettable that we cannot turn to Ibn al-ʿAṭṭār for clarification. Nevertheless, by imposing upon the husband the heavy burden of finding counter-evidence to cancel a former recognition of paternity, and leaving the interpretation of the exact meaning of that requirement for the *qāḍī*, a template that might look redundant at first sight takes a turn clearly in favor of foresighted women.

Also noteworthy is the inclusion of a template for recovering the

28 Ibn Abī Zamanīn, *Muntakhab al-aḥkām*, ed. Muḥammad Ḥammād (Rabat: Markaz al-Dirāsāt wa'l-Abḥāth wa-Iḥyāʾ al-Turāth al-Rābiṭa al-Muḥammadiyya lil-ʿUlamāʾ, 2009), 2:760–65.

paternity of a fetus or a child previously denied through *liʿān* (*wathīqat bi-istilḥāq al-mulāʿin li-mā intafā minh*).[29] In the *fiqh* section of the work, Ibn Mughīth states that such a retraction prompts the payment of maintenance for both the child and the mother from the moment she was repudiated until the moment she gave birth. Because the mother has the option to prosecute for defamation, this kind of template could be understood to have sanctioned agreements between the former spouses, so that the ex-husband could clear his conscience by admitting his mistake and redressing its consequences on condition that his ex-wife waive her right against him. Ibn Mughīth hints at the recent introduction of these practices by specifying that these *fiqh* provisions were subscribed to by "more than one jurist" and followed when issuing relevant *fatwās*.

The last type of template relating to denial of paternity in Ibn Mughīth's collection addresses the case of the slave's child (*mamlūka*), whose paternity a man can deny before witnesses during pregnancy or after the child is born. Here the slave is not required to appear before the *qāḍī* and resort to the *liʿān* procedure, nor to swear an ordinary oath, to support the claim. In the *fiqh* section of the work, Ibn Mughīth specifies that the man can retract his denial at any moment without incurring fixed-penal liability (*ḥadd*).[30] Ibn Mughīth observes again that "more than one *faqīh* held this very same opinion," and recommends spreading knowledge about it.

al-Maqṣad al-maḥmūd fī talkhīṣ al-ʿuqūd by ʿAlī b. Yaḥyā from Algeciras (d. 585/1189)

Jazīrī's treatment of *liʿān* is much more elaborate and detailed than that of Ibn Mughīth. It thereby shows the process of growth that Mālikī legal doctrine underwent during the century that separates the two collections.[31]

In Jazīrī's *Maqṣad*, the legal practices that his Toledan predecessor

29 See Ibn Mughīth, *Muqniʿ*, 121–24.

30 In this case, the template for *istilḥāq* could be used. See Ibn Mughīth, *Muqniʿ*, 358–60. The *fiqh* section includes interesting details about the work of the physiognomist (*qāʾif*).

31 Mallat, *Introduction to Middle Eastern Law*, 98–99, echoes Abū Isḥāq al-Gharnāṭī's call for at least one expert in drafting legal documents in each city. Both Gharnāṭī and Jazīrī lived during the Almohad period, which saw a significant increase in the documented number of experts and works on model *shurūṭ* documents. Jesús Zanón associates this development with changes in state structures brought about by the Almohad conquest. See Jesús Zanón, "La actividad intellectual: las ramas del saber: Centros y métodos de conocimiento," in María Jesús Viguera Molíns ed., *El retroceso territorial de al-Andalus: Almorávides y almohades* (Madrid: Espasa Calpe, 1997), 551–84, 566. Maribel Fierro further qualifies Zanón's remark with reference to the development of administrative procedure, fostered by ruling dynasties with the aim of conveying to their subjects the extension of their power and the lawfulness with which they exercised it. See Maribel Fierro, "Ulemas en las ciudades andalusíes: Religión, política y prácticas sociales," in V. Martínez Enamorado, ed., *Congreso Internacional Escenarios Urbanos de al-Andalus y el Occidente musulmán, 1º. 2010 Vélez-Málaga* (Málaga: Iniciativa Urbana 'De Toda La Villa', 2011), 137–67, esp. 144 n. 25.

had tried to shape are connected to specific legal authorities or textual sources of authority, in order to present them as in accordance with sound legal methodology. The group of relevant templates in Jazīrī's collection is preceded by an introduction to the fundamentals of Mālikī doctrine outlining the judicial procedure of *liʿān*. This text is rather specific as to the circumstances that trigger denial of paternity: either the man accuses his wife of *zinā* and claims to have seen her commit the crime with another man; or he denies the paternity of her fetus because pregnancy has become evident while she was observing the waiting period (*istibrāʾ*) or because of the absence of physical contact between them. Jazīrī also provides more detail on how to demonstrate the existence of a marital bond than did Ibn Mughīth. Regarding the treatment of the mutual allegations of sexual impropriety, Jazīrī places more emphasis on the need to repeat them several times: when presenting the claim for the first time before the *qāḍī*, after the first summons, and then, once again, before professional witnesses—something which no doubt discouraged the party with the least to lose from withdrawing.

Jazīrī's description of the *liʿān* oath-swearing procedure adds other interesting details, such as the following: The husband is required to point to his wife at the moment of swearing the oath. The right time to take the oaths is fixed at the end of the afternoon prayer (*dubr ṣalāt al-ʿaṣr*). Filiation between the man and the woman's fetus is considered broken as a consequence of the fifth oath, not before—a remark appearing to show that Saḥnūn's aforementioned opinion came to prevail over Ibn al-Qāsim's, not only in Mālikī doctrine but also in the judicial practice of *liʿān* procedures. Once the *liʿān* procedure has been completed, the *qāḍī* is to summon the ex-spouses to state any final allegations. In the absence of further arguments in their defense (*madfaʿ*), the *qāḍī* signs (*imḍāʾ*) the resulting document and makes it effective (*al-ḥukm bih*). He must include witnesses to his signature and to the veracity of the facts mentioned in the document. An additional witness is expected to attest that the *qāḍī* has followed the aforementioned instructions in the presence of witnesses on a specified date.[32] Three copies of this document are to be produced, one for each party and another for the *qāḍī*'s register.[33] The irrevocability and perpetuity of the ensuing divorce

32 This abstract description of the requisite attestation of the judicial process by witnesses can be compared to an historical example (though related to legal matters different from *liʿān*) from fourteenth-century Jerusalem in Christian Müller, "Écrire pour établir la preuve orale en Islam: la pratique d'un tribunal à Jérusalem au XIVe siècle," in *Les outils de la pensé. Étude historique et comparative des "textes,"* ed. Akira Saito and Yusuke Nakamura (Paris: Maison des Sciences de l'Homme, 2010), 63–97.

33 On judicial archives, see Wael Hallaq, "The *Qāḍī*'s *Dīwān* (*Sijill*) before the Ottomans," *Bulletin of the School of Oriental and African Studies* 61, no. 3 (1998): 415–36.

is said to be in conformity with what is "established by the *Sunna*."[34] The above-described procedure is therefore a meticulously notarized one involving close record keeping by the *qāḍī*.[35]

The introduction is followed by a template entitled "Document of Mutual Imprecation: *wathīqat al-talāʿun*." The first striking feature in this section is the shift in roles between husband and wife within the introduction. Here, it is the wife who initiates the procedure and seeks protection with the *qāḍī* (*wa-saʾalathu al-naẓar lahā*) against her husband for having falsely accused her of *zinā* (in private, it seems) or for having denied being the father of the child she is expecting. The latter sequence of events matches those described in the above-mentioned case that had come before Qāḍī ʿIyāḍ and may explain why the burden of establishing the marital bond fell to the woman rather than to her accuser. On a formal level, while Ibn Mughīth had described the steps for swearing the *liʿān* oath in his *fiqh* section, Jazīrī makes those steps part of the template itself and grounds the practice of having the husband swear in the first instance in the text of the Qurʾān.[36]

Next comes a template for the acknowledgement (*iʿtirāf*) of a child previously rejected through *liʿān*, similar to that of Ibn Mughīth's collection. Jazīrī adds the requirement that the parties must specify in the document whether the man is in his right mind (*fī jawāz amr*). The acknowledgment may take place even after the child has been born (without mention of any age limit)—in which case, the child's presence is required.

Another template consists of an attestation of a man's acknowledgment of paternity of the fetus carried by his wife. This model bears two interesting differences from the corresponding model in Ibn Mughīth's collection. First, Jazīrī refers to the form as "a document of precaution or guardedness (*istirʿāʾ*)."[37] As a precaution, witnesses declare that, on a certain date, they heard the man acknowledge his wife's

34 ʿAlī b. Yaḥyā al-Jazīrī, *al-Maqṣad al-maḥmūd fī talkhīṣ al-ʿuqūd*, 97–103.

35 On *sharīʿa* court as "a place of paperwork" and documentary practice, see Brinkley Messick, *The Calligraphic State: Textual Domination and History in a Muslim Society* (Berkeley: University of California Press, 1993), 209–10.

36 See Q. 24:2–14. For a critical reading of the traditional explanation of this passage and supporting *ḥadīths* provided by jurists, see Amira Sonbol, "Jewish and Islamic Legal Traditions: Diffusions of Law," in Firoozeh Kashani-Sabet and Beth S. Wenger, eds., *Gender in Judaism and Islam: Common Lives, Uncommon Heritage* (New York: New York University Press, 2015), 46–67, 58–61. Sonbol stresses the seriousness of *liʿān* oaths.

37 This note does not mean that the *istirʿāʾ* document, also known as a "memorial document," is absent from Ibn Mughīth's *Muqniʿ*. See, for example, his *Muqniʿ*, 187, 356. The terminology difference between Ibn Mughīth and Jazīrī implies that the former was concerned with establishing the practice of *liʿān* procedures, whereas the latter was operating in a context in which practice was well-established but compliance with sound legal methodology had to be stressed.

pregnancy in her presence, "and that this happened before he rejected being the father."[38] The application of the technicality of *istirʿāʾ* to this kind of document seems to stress the use of documentary practices to protect pregnant wives, not only by deterring husbands from negating the paternity of an unborn child, but also by anticipating that very event. That the form here is designed exclusively for the latter purpose, and not merely for men to anticipate contesting paternity, is clear from the specification that "acknowledgment of paternity took place before negating it."

The above model is followed by another one specific to denial of paternity of a slave's child (*ibn al-mamlūka*), which must occur in the presence of the child and before witnesses. The reasons for summoning the child are not explained here. Jazīrī takes it for granted that there is absolute freedom to retract this decision, provided the father declares that he has verified beyond doubt that it is his child and that he, therefore, recognizes being the father. In this case, the presence of the child is also required.

In the long *fiqh* section that closes Jazīrī's series of templates related to the *liʿān* procedure and denial of paternity, he reiterates the basic principles governing the subject. He emphasizes the conditions required for the applicability of the *liʿān* oath and, especially, the divergence of opinions regarding them.

So far, I have not been able to identify Jazīrī's sources, though, by the time he collected his templates, *liʿān* had received quite elaborate treatment in the works of other Mālikī jurists such as Ibn Abī Zamanīn, Bājī, Ibn Rushd al-Jadd, Qāḍī ʿIyāḍ, and Ibn Rushd al-Ḥafīd or Averroës (d. 595/1182), as well as in the works of the Ẓāhirī jurist Ibn Ḥazm.[39] In Jazīrī's case, he fails to establish which, among the divergent opinions regarding *liʿān* adopted by Mālikī jurists, was to be favored in practice on the grounds of its being a majority or minority opinion, or of its being the most sound.

The fact that minority views are quoted without qualification may give the impression that, despite the many restrictions outlined in the legal

38 This kind of testimony, consisting of a witness-declaration that they heard someone else say something, appears to correspond to an Islamic "hearsay" evidence (*shahādat al-khabar*—or, in the Mālikī tradition, *shahādat al-samʿ*), on the grounds of which facts pertaining to marriage, paternity, manumission, and death can be verified without requiring the originator of the statement to have been present at the moment of the testimony's production or documentation. In the latter scenario, a witness may testify to the authenticity of the document only if he or she was present when it was drawn up. See Muhammad Khalid Masud, Rudolph Peters, and David S. Powers, "Qadis and their Courts: An Historical Survey," in *Dispensing Justice in Islam: Qadis and their Judgments*, ed. Muhammad Khalid Masud, Rudolph Peters, and David S. Powers (Leiden: Brill, 2006), 1–44, esp. 25, 26; and David S. Powers, *Law, Society and Culture in the Maghrib, 1300-1500* (Cambridge: Cambridge University Press, 2002), 30–36 and n. 35.

39 Apart from the eponymous founder of the Mālikī school, the list of authorities mentioned by Jazīrī also includes Ibn al-Qāsim, Ibn Nāfiʿ, Ashhab, Ibn ʿAbd al-Ḥakam, ʿAbd al-Mālik b. Ḥabīb, Ibn Waḍḍāḥ, and Abū Isḥāq al-Baghdādī.

doctrine, men enjoyed an almost unlimited right to accuse their wives of adultery and to reject the paternity of their unborn children through the *liʿān* procedure. Yet the equal value awarded to the variant opinions—occasionally in open contradiction to each other—also means that the final decision rested with the *qāḍī* and that it could not be easily predicted. Deterrence is thus sought through uncertainty about the chances of escaping the risk of being accused of defamation.[40] Jazīrī only hints at the *liʿān* oath's capacity to restore women's social standing and good reputation, whereas the Granadan jurist Abū al-Qāsim Muḥammad b. Ahmad Ibn Juzayy al-Kalbī (d. 741/1340) asserts it quite clearly when referring to the non-Muslim (*dhimmī*) woman who is not obliged to swear the *liʿān* oath in the same circumstances as a Muslim woman, but does so nevertheless to "lift the shame from herself: *li-rafʿ al-ʿār ʿanhā*."[41]

al-ʿIqd al-munaẓẓam lil-ḥukkām by Ibn Salmūn from Granada (d. 767/1366)

In contrast to the preceding models, which, as we have seen, concentrate on the art of drafting documents designed for particular cases of *liʿān* oath procedures, Ibn Salmūn's treatise emphasizes notarization of the whole process. That is to say, he focuses on describing how to produce a written record of the process. The chapter on *liʿān* in Ibn Salmūn's *ʿIqd* is presented not as a sequence of templates preceded by an introduction and including a section on *fiqh* at the end of each template, but as a continuous narrative of the process into which different templates are inserted as the different stages of the process unfold. It traces the procedures from the moment the initiating party decides to report the facts to the *qāḍī* until the latter divorces the couple irrevocably. Excluding the calls of attention to points of doctrine affected by divergences of Mālikī opinions, Ibn Salmūn's narrative looks like a template for a complete judicial record of the *liʿān* procedure. The terminology relative to the notarization of the process is quite simple, a trait the *ʿIqd* shares with its precedents.

Again the first scenario assumed by the author is a woman taking the initiative to report her husband to the authorities for defamation and/or his negation of the paternity of her child. Worthy of mention are also some expressions qualifying the steps followed by the *qāḍī* that lend additional

40 The mere accusation of defamation on claims of sexual impropriety, without final conviction, was no minor thing, because the accusation alone could affect judgments regarding a person's integrity, potentially preventing that person from qualifying as a valid witness. See Masud, Peters, and Powers, "Qadis and their Courts," 26.

41 Ibn Juzayy, *al-Qawānīn al-fiqhiyya fī talkhīṣ madhhab al-mālikiyya* (Libya: al-Dar al-ʿArabiyya lil-Kitāb, 1982), 388–90. On the reparatory effect of *liʿān* at the social level see also Shabana, "Negation of Paternity in Islamic Law," 159.

relevance and solemnity to the procedure: "Once the declarations of the spouses and the marital bond between them (*jawziyyatuhumā*) was duly established before him, it was required, by virtue of the *qāḍī*'s discretion (*fa-iqtaḍā naẓarah*) to summon the parties to his tribunal (*majlis ḥukmih*)." The venue for swearing oaths is referred to as the place representing his [that is, the *qāḍī*'s] justice in the main congregational mosque (*mawḍiʿ ḥukmih fī al-masjid al-jāmiʿ*)."[42] The final ruling declaring the couple to be separated irrevocably after the due completion of the oath-swearing is said to be in accordance with the dictates of the *Sunna* (*ʿalā mā aḥkamathu al-Sunna*) and to have been preceded by the judge having given the parties the opportunity to present closing arguments as required (*baʿda an aʿdhara ilā wāḥid minhumā bimā awjaba an yuʿdhirah ilayh*).

When addressing questions subject to divergence of opinions, such as denial of paternity without *ruʾya* (a claim of having seen the crime with his own eyes) or *istirʿāʾ* (an assertion that the waiting period has been observed), Ibn Salmūn incorporates the views of late scholars. Those scholars include Ibn Mughīth, Bājī, Ibn Rushd al-Jadd, ʿAbd al-Ḥaqq [al-Ṣiqillī or Ibn ʿAṭiyya], and Ibn al-Jallāb. He introduces two important nuances: one is that a husband's denial of paternity with *ruʾya* can only be accepted as grounds to start the *liʿān* procedure when the claim is accompanied by a declaration made before the pregnancy has become evident not to have touched his wife. The other nuance regards a foreign couple, allowing their marriage to be established simply through the parties' acknowledgment to it. This procedure was contrary to the requirements of locals, who were to provide evidence of their marriage with witness testimony, unless their marriage was a well-known, public fact (*fāshiy*^{an}). Conversely, pregnancy of the foreign woman was to be verified by two female witnesses, but such verification was not required for a local woman.

More importantly, the capacity of the *liʿān* procedure to deter men and exonerate their wives is visibly reinforced here by mention of the requirement to imprison the husband until the moment of swearing the *liʿān* oath. It is as if the author is trying to prevent the possibility that the husband might escape at the very last moment, leaving his wife alone with the burden of bringing up a child about whom suspicion has been raised by the accusation. Ibn Salmūn bases his presentation of imprisonment as an option on the opinions of Bājī and Abū ʿUmar b. ʿAbd al-Malik, who argued that "he [the husband] is a slanderer."[43] A century later, another relevant Granadan jurist, Muḥammad b. Muḥammad Ibn ʿĀṣim (d.

42 Ibn Salmūn, *al-ʿIqd al-munaẓẓam*, 155.

43 I wonder whether the Abū ʿUmar Ibn ʿAbd al-Mālik referred by Ibn Salmūn, and whom I cannot identify, is not confused with Abū ʿUmar Ibn ʿAbd al-Barr.

829/1426) reiterated the prison requirement without leaving any scope for interpretation, saying that the husband *must* be imprisoned until he swears the oath. This assertion is made in a work considered to be a distillation of Granadan judicial practice, with which the author was well acquainted, largely through his experience as chief *qāḍī* of the Nasrid capital.[44]

In the past, imprisonment had been reserved for the man who refused the paternity of his wife's child but acknowledged that he had intercourse with her without having observed the waiting period. In the latter case, imprisonment was conceived of as a coercive measure to move the father to acknowledge the child, "lest corruption spread among the people."[45] Imprisonment had also been mentioned by Ibn Rushd al-Ḥafīd, or Averroës, in connection to a woman refusing to neutralize her husband's accusation by swearing in turn. Coercing her to swear the *liʿān* oath in this way, Averroës claimed, was better than punishing her for *zinā* absent full proof of her having committed the crime. Ḥanafīs held the position that her punishment in such circumstances was to be waived, a position that Averroës preferred, seeing it as "closer to the truth than the contrary—say, the Mālikī—position." Justifying his statement further, he added:

> Abū Ḥanīfa drew on the Prophet['s practice] when he said that "the blood of a Muslim can be shed only for having committed *zinā,* which applies only to the *muḥṣan,* for persisting in unbelief after having believed and as retaliation for killing somebody without legitimate reason." Moreover, shedding someone's blood for refusing to swear an oath goes against the principles of [Islamic] legal rulings. If a significant number of jurists does not impose financial liability when [the defendant] refuses to swear an oath [to rebuke the mere claim], it would be suitable not to impose the shedding of blood for that very same reason either. The basis of the ruling should be shedding someone's blood only when full proof or confession exist.... Indeed, Abū al-Maʿālī al-Juwaynī, notwithstanding the fact that he was a Shāfiʿī, was also convinced by Abū Ḥanīfa's persuasive argument, as stated in his *Burhān*.[46]

44 Ibn ʿĀṣim, *Matn al-ʿĀṣimiyya al-musammā bi-Tuḥfat al-ḥukkām fī nukat al-ʿuqūd waʾl-aḥkām*, ed. M. Amīn ʿImrān (Cairo: Maṭbaʿa Muṣṭafā al-Bābī al-Ḥalabī, 1930), 34.

45 Burzulī, *Nawāzil*, 3:469, quoting ʿAbd al-Raḥmān b. Qāsim al-Shaʿbī (d. 499/1106), who had it from al-Ishbīlī, in *al-Aḥkām* (Beirut: Dār al-Gharb al-Islāmī, 1992), 34. See Delfina Serrano Ruano, "La lapidación como castigo legal de las relaciones sexuales no legales (*zinā*) en el seno de la escuela malikí: doctrina, práctica legal y actitudes individuales frente al delito (ss. XI y XII)," *Al-Qanṭara* 26, no. 2 (2005): 449–73, at 463. See also Wansharīsī, *Miʿyār*, 4:72–73.

46 Ibn Rushd, *Bidāyat al-mujtahid wa-nihāyat al-muqtaṣid*, 6th ed. (Beirut: Dār al-Maʿrifa, 1982), 2:119–20; and Imran Ahsan Khan Nyazee, trans., *The Distinguished Jurist's Primer: A Translation of Bidāyat al-mujtahid* (London: Centre for Muslim Contribution to Civilization-Garnet Publishing Limited, 1996), 2:146–47.

Borrowing from divergent opinions (*talfīq*, or *murāʿāt al-khilāf*) is adopted here on the grounds of logic, cogency, and ethics, as well as for the benefit of the weakest party toward avoiding shedding her blood by locking her up temporarily if need be. Averroës, whose many scholarly specializations included medicine,[47] further alludes to the opinion of some Muslim jurists that denial of paternity is possible only during the waiting period, and that subsequent to it, rejection of her child is tantamount to defamation.[48] Moreover, Averroës notes that Mālik stipulated that paternity could be denied only during pregnancy, not after the child was born.[49]

Another remarkable piece of doctrine collected by Ibn Salmūn refers to a husband who claims to have seen his wife commit *zinā* with another man, but resumes marital relations with her subsequently. It is the husband who is to be punished with a *ḥadd* penalty and assigned the paternity of the child, obviously on the assumption that no man in his right mind would want to touch his wife after having seen her commit *zinā* with another man, or that men without good reputations must take responsibility for children born to their wives irrespective of their biological origins.

Ibn Salmūn also extended the right to have a child's paternity explicitly recognized before or after its birth to the slave mother. As in the cases mentioned above, this rule served as an impediment to the negation of paternity in the future without a valid excuse. Ibn Salmūn's predecessors likely would not have disagreed with this protection, but they do not appear to have felt the need to mention it explicitly.

FINAL CONSIDERATIONS AND CONCLUSIONS

Closer scrutiny of the templates relevant to *liʿān* procedures from select Andalusī model *shurūṭ* collections invites reconsideration of the idea that the *liʿān* procedure was hardly ever put into practice. The very facts of special templates designed to address the contingencies of *liʿān* oaths, the gradual design of a sophisticated procedure, the *qāḍī*'s role in following and monitoring it, and the solemnity associated with the act of swearing the oaths is telling. These facts show that publicity was better

47 A fact adding to his prestige in the eyes of contemporary Muslim scholars like Yūsuf al-Qaraḍāwī. See Mohammed Ghaly, "Biomedical Scientists as Co-Muftis: Their Contribution to Contemporary Islamic Bioethics," *Die Welt des Islams* 55 (2015): 286–311, 302.

48 Shabana, "Negation of Paternity in Islamic Law," 178 and n. 57. This opinion seems to be in line with what Ibn Salmūn attributed to Bājī and "Ibn ʿAbd al-Mālik," with some doubt (on which, see above, note 43). It is pertinent to remember that Hina Azam has found that, in contrast to mainstream Mālikī doctrine, Bājī and Ibn ʿAbd al-Barr were reluctant to accept pregnancy as valid evidence of *zinā*. See Hina Azam, *Sexual Violation in Islamic Law: Substance, Evidence, and Procedure* (Cambridge: Cambridge University Press, 2015), 141–42.

49 Shabana, "Negation of Paternity in Islamic Law," 180, n. 62.

than concealment when the latter threatened to end in honor crimes, violent extra-judicial outcomes, and injustice being done to women and their offspring. Indeed, we can assume that the occasions on which *liʿān* oaths were actually pronounced were very rare. This fact may have been the result of the high level of sophistication reached by the relevant legal doctrines and procedures, both designed to limit the procedure to those absolutely convinced of their righteousness. Thus, the relevance of the *liʿān* procedure should not be assessed on the basis of the frequency with which the procedure was actually enacted, but rather on the basis of the procedure's effectiveness at preventing initial accusations, which must have been relatively frequent, from ending up in the mosque-court.

An accusation of adultery against a woman did not have to be proved when the accuser was her husband. Refusing to swear an oath on her part was considered tantamount to confession of the crime. Further, her child could be rejected with the argument that he or she was born less than six months after she got married, based on the difference between the date of the marriage contract and the day the union was consummated. These facts minimized the weight of the legal canon stipulating that "any offspring belongs to the marital bed: *al-walad lil-firāsh*," and inclined the balance towards its sequel, "and for the adulterer is the stone: *wa-lil-ʿāhir al-ḥajar*." Jurists were well aware of the gap and strived to fill it by elaborating and refining the relevant judicial procedure and documentary practice. Accordingly, they encouraged women to take advantage of the earliest opportunity to obtain explicit recognition of their pregnancy from their husbands before witnesses. Should problems arise, they were then encouraged to report them to the *qāḍī*. Should the husband resist all the pressure of the legal and social systems and still decide to reject his paternity, jurists offered the possibility of withdrawing his decision with quite satisfactory terms to all the concerned parties.

The social practice visible through these templates on *liʿān* procedures does not suggest vulnerable men, torn between assuming the paternity of unwanted children and facing rejection from their social milieu. Nor does it suggest men who were threatened with being deprived of the children born to their wives by their former husbands as was and continues to be frequent in tribal societies.[50]

Rather, the concerns revealed by the templates have more to do with *de facto* situations which may have never reached the *qāḍī*'s court or experts in the art of drafting legal documents: men rejecting their children with whatever pretense, such as claims that the child had been born less

50 For a recent illustration of this practice see Aref Abu-Rabia, "Paternity Suits in Tribal Society in the Middle East," *US-China Law Review* 9, no. 29 (2012): 29–44.

than six months after the conclusion of the marriage—a very handy excuse except when it had to be proved before the *qāḍī*—or that the mother was an adulterer. Should a man see fit to recognize the son he had previously rejected, he could do so without responding to claims of defamation of the mother. Even when a case was reported to the authorities, many men seem to have managed to escape the *liʿān* proper, such as by fleeing away to the frontier, or to postpone it *sine die,* on the basis of taking a long trip. If this were not the case, Granadan jurists would not have introduced the requirement to imprison men until the date fixed for the swearing. Moreover, even as they preserved *liʿān* procedure as a means to deal with a very sensitive issue challenging patriarchy in the family institution, some of the most influential jurists reached the point of almost criminalizing rejection of paternity because, even though the man always kept the option of escaping punishment by swearing a *liʿān* oath, from an ethical point of view he was seen as a slanderer. The other jurists did not question a man's right to reject his wife's child but strived to make its exercise increasingly risky and difficult, even when the mother was a slave.

Through documentary practice on the *liʿān* procedure, the relevance of both *qāḍī* courts and judicial procedure for the fulfillment of the ideal of justice in Islamic law and the protection of individual rights is also made evident. This aspect of the study of model *shurūṭ* collections is all the more interesting given that the role played by procedure in bringing about the rule of law, though assumed, is not particularly well elaborated in Islamic legal studies on procedure and evidence.[51]

Classical Islamic law can be said to uphold the requisite of representation by counsel at court hearings inasmuch as litigants are allowed to seek the advice of a *muftī*. But Islamic courts were not held responsible for providing that service, which was rather left up to the parties' own initiative. Queries on whether everyone in al-Andalus—man or woman, rich or poor, urban settler or rural inhabitant—had equal access to documents and courts of justice, and whether justice reached all corners of the territory under a ruler's control, are questions to which no conclusive answer can be given with the present state of research.[52] However, the sources well document sensitivity to each question on the part of both the

51 This shortcoming finds parallel in western legal philosophy where the need to consider the relationship between procedure and the rule of law has been emphasized only recently. See Jeremy Waldron, "The Rule of Law and the Importance of Procedure," in James E. Fleming, *Getting to the Rule of Law* (New York: New York University Press, 2011), 3–31; and Jeremy Waldron, "The Rule of Law," *Stanford Encyclopedia of Philosophy* [Online] (last accessed December 13, 2016), esp. section 5.2 on "Procedural Aspects."

52 On representation by counsel and generality as procedural requisites, see Waldron, "The Rule of Law," sections 5.2 and 9; and Waldron, "The Rule of Law and the Importance of Procedure," 5–7.

jurists and the executive authorities from the period under study, together with their overall readiness to solve it.[53] Certainly men belonging to the upper social and economic levels are those best represented in the legal sources at our disposal. Women, whether upper class, slaves, peasants, cattle breeders, or the practitioners of "métiers viles," are less conspicuous. The occasions on which we can observe them interacting with some form of Islamic justice have to be dug out from the sources with much effort and methodological subtlety, and, even so, they are found in no representative proportions. But they are not totally absent.

When the claim is made that *sharīʿa* in the pre-modern period represented an ideal that may be compared to the modern concept of the rule of law,[54] it cannot be thus taken to refer to an earthly paradise of widespread respect for the law by both ordinary people and judges. In practice, people did not behave according to manuals of legal doctrine and ethical standards reflected therein. But that fact does not mean that the corresponding rules and norms were not enforced by the courts. A *qāḍī* or any other authority over the subjects of the law may have been corrupt, acted unprofessionally, or have been appointed by an unjust ruler. Still, this does not mean that Islamic law was not efficient in regulating social relationships. Moreover, the ruler or legal authorities committing unlawful acts had many risks as deterrents, such as the withdrawal of popular or military support, loss of political legitimacy, rebellion, dismissal, ostracization, or condemnation to perpetual ignominy in literary and historical works.

Thus, although the hand that drafted them was not female, the templates relevant to *liʿān* procedures examined here transmit the echo of the voices of a particular group in society. They provide a platform for voices of married women and concubine mothers under threat of being abandoned in the care of their children, and for their expressions of fear and concern, complaints of vulnerability while being blamed for societal ills, and their demands for justice and balance. We do not only glimpse the jurists' readiness to put a series of legal instruments in their hands but also the women's agency and readiness to use the tools provided by the templates if need be, especially for situations wherein a *qāḍī* was within reach.

The templates show unique relationships between justice and

53 On the increase of judicial seats during the Almohad period, see Mustafa Benouis, "L'Organisation du *Qaḍā'* sous les Almohades," in Patrice Cressier, Maribel Fierro, Luis Molina, eds., *Los almohades: problemas y perspectivas* (Madrid: Consejo Superior de Investigaciones Científicas, 2005), 1:505–24. On the increase in the number of experts in the art of drafting legal documents registered during the same period, see above, note 31, where sources there echo Abū Isḥāq al-Gharnāṭī's call for at least one expert in drafting legal documents in each city.

54 See above, note 6, on the association between *sharīʿa* and the rule of law.

procedure. Within the *qāḍī*'s jurisdiction, the templates show that justice was administered by means of a sophisticated procedure that safeguarded the parties' rights at the same time that it encouraged them to reflect on and reconsider their initial claims in view of severe repercussions in this life and the next. Another, more novel, relationship between procedure and justice revealed by the templates consists of the need for a written record of the procedure duly attested to by professional witnesses, to be stored in an archive under the *qāḍī*'s custody and to be handed to the parties. This aspect highlights provisions for the rule of law by enhancing the enforceability of a final decision according to the principle of *res judicata* (claim preclusion), reviewability, and accountability of judicial agents. These agents could be held accountable through the acquisition of written documents and through procedural notarization.

The need for *qāḍī* courts for the application of procedures for *liʿān* described with so much detail in the relevant legal literature does not necessarily mean that the procedure became useless in the absence of that kind of court. Warnings by means of advisory opinions (*fatwās*) were also a powerful regulator of social conduct.

The authors of model *shurūṭ* collections cited divergent opinions on *liʿān* procedures, often without qualification. This practice was designed to assist the litigants, the authorities in charge of deciding their disputes, and the legal "profession" as a whole. The practice was a reflection of the author's erudition but also a pointer to possible strategies, leaving Andalusī *qāḍīs* wide scope for flexibility in their reasoning. Apparently minor or isolated opinions echo alternative states of mind that may not have shaped mainstream legal doctrine but that give us an idea of the pressures for coherence within a certain legal school or system. These pressures could end with new opinions making their way into judicial practice and creating new forms of consensus. Explicit recognition within the legal literature may have taken longer, but the history of *liʿān* procedures shows that neither the doctrine nor the system lost its distinctiveness of identity and integrity through judicial practice.

READING WITH ROY: THE SCHOLARLY OUTPUT OF ROY MOTTAHEDEH

An Essay on Roy Mottahedeh's Career and Publications

Cemal Kafadar
Harvard University

Reading primary sources with Professor Mottahedeh, with Roy, has been one of the greatest pleasures of my life, and the same is true for several generations of Harvard students and colleagues who have been fortunate enough to join him in seminars with some lame excuse, such as "co-teaching." I had the privilege of "co-teaching" with him a seminar on Seljuk history, for instance, offering it three times over the course of nine or ten years. In that course, we read chronicles from medieval Iran and Anatolia. The most memorable and sustained aspect of following Roy's reading and interpretation of medieval Persian prose of the high register is that one learns to share his great joy in encountering these often dense texts and in facing their challenges. He recognizes, appreciates, and helps you understand their intricacies and delights that otherwise seem too well hidden or unfathomable. At the same time, his deep respect for and sympathetic reading of the texts does not ever get so overwhelming as to turn a blind eye to the not-so-rare instances of vacuousness or shallowness. You learn that you can laugh with the sources but also laugh at them, and begin to gauge the line between eloquence and pretense, between rhetoric and pompousness.

In that respect, I always felt that Roy has made the best of his background in being a New Yorker and a son of a Kashani mercantile family—from two places known for their intellectual sophistication and down-to-earth worldliness at the same time. It may be that mercantile background of his family that gives him a particular perspective on the world of scholars, poets, and scribes—all of whom he knows how to appreciate but also to observe with an ethnographer's eye to see into all their bizarre ways and follies, their accomplishments and pretensions.

This makes it easier for me to understand how he managed to shape the field of Middle East studies and Islamic studies quite broadly but particularly at Harvard, to begin at the local level. While he strikes many who do not know him well as the perfect unworldly professor, Roy has made a profound impact on the field of both an intellectual and a practical, institutional nature. During the last three decades, everything one says about Islam or the Middle East has acquired a heavy political-ideological and emotional charge, which makes it exceedingly difficult to maintain a humanistic vision for the study of Islamic societies. But Roy has shaped the field along precisely those lines, at least in Islamic studies at Harvard for sure, but even beyond, in a most positive, most creative, most imaginary and even visionary manner. It is his vision and his initiatives and his strategizing that took the field from a relatively small position here on campus, and a problematic one in the early 1980s, to a growing, flourishing network of fields and disciplines speaking to one another within the larger framework of Middle Eastern and Islamic studies. In that time, the field has produced two generations or more, if one thinks of them as scholarly generations, of scholars out there in many different corners of the world as former students of Roy's: shaping the world of scholarship in his field and beyond. In my own field of Ottoman history, students frequently remind me how indebted they are to Roy even if they did work on much later periods than his area of expertise, having had their eyes opened to the riches of medieval history by maybe taking one course with Roy or, better yet, by doing a field with him and having had the benefit of his presence on their dissertation committee.

In short, Roy's impact is really tremendous in the ways an instructor and an adviser makes an impact. In terms of new positions at Harvard, in terms of the way centers and programs related to Middle Eastern and Islamic studies do their business on campus—all is a world way beyond what it was three decades ago. And we owe much of that to Roy's intellectual vision as well as his success at the practical level, which seems contradictory given that reputation of unworldliness. All Harvard colleagues, I am certain, have been witness to some aspect of that practical success, be it in raising funds, or in being convincing to the administration, or in creating positions, etc., etc., etc.

This is, in some measure, due to his principled position that the greatest social capital of an academic is intellectual stature and scholarly accomplishments. We never talked about this with Roy, but we did not need to. You often learn from Roy simply because he's Roy. You don't have to get aphorisms; you don't have to get specific, pedagogical, and didactic comments; but by observing what he does and how he does it, one learns a good deal.

So rather than work on administrative efficiency and managerialism, Roy chose to build on vision and intellectual depth.He could not have realized any of his projects, and he could not have developed Middle Eastern and Islamic studies at Harvard the way he did and have made an impact on the rest of the academic world the way he did, had he not acquired worldwide recognition as a leading historian and a great mind. Period.

Roy did not scare people, but inspired respect, and even some awe maybe with his mind and with his learning. He achieved all this early on—the MacArthur award that is generally called the genius award was bestowed on him in 1981 soon after he published his first book. Let us note that 1981 was a very early moment in the history of those awards. So he acquired his reputation early on, but accomplished something just as difficult thereafter—namely he maintained and improved upon that reputation for a long and productive career.

Obviously, the reputation was built and sustained through deep interpretive studies and field-shaping books and articles. The promise of serious and imaginative scholarship is already there in Roy's senior thesis, "Shaykh Abu Ishaq al-Kazaruni and the Persian Renaissance," completed in 1960 at Harvard. From that, he moved to another degree at Cambridge, and returned to Harvard for a Ph.D. He submitted his dissertation in 1970. It was not published as such but is well known, widely read, and meaningfully utilized by many; and it is partly used also in some of his later publications on "Administration in the Būyid Kingdom of Rayy."

Then came his early masterpiece, *Loyalty and Leadership in Early Islamic Society*, published in 1980. There is no doubt that this book played a major role in reorienting the field, at first only in medieval Islamic studies perhaps, but eventually its influence grew in other areas of Middle Eastern and Islamic studies. It developed one of the most effective strategies against the orientalist tradition even if it did not explicitly take part in that debate at a time when polemical and overtly political concerns had taken center stage. In a decided manner, the book foregrounded the mental map of the social order within the emic categories of medieval Islamic courtly-military society itself. To look at the social order of Islamic societies through the meaning-making categories of those who wrote and peopled our sources was a truly unprecedented step. In *Loyalty and Leadership*, Roy elaborated an approach that took the modes and means of analysis used by Muslim authors seriously as instruments for our own understanding of those societies rather than dismissing them as cliches of some medieval Muslim mind. Over time the influence of his approach moved far beyond medieval Islamic studies, as a major source of inspiration in Ottoman studies, for instance.

Then came *The Mantle of the Prophet*, published in 1985, which I admire for many reasons but above all for being one of the most accomplished and elegant examples of my (and, I suspect, many other readers') favorites among the rhetorical arts: studied ease, or studied simplicity (*sahl al-mumtaniʿ*). It is well known that the book reached not only an *academic* audience but also a huge *public* audience worldwide, and it has been translated into many languages. Its almost legendary reputation has inspired many others to attempt similar projects, but the *Mantle* remains brightest in its constellation as it manages to maintain the highest academic standards and rigors in speaking about the long durée of Iranian history while remaining consistently friendly to non-academic readers.

Roy has also published on Islamic law, an area in which he has more projects in preparation. A significant study in its own right was his 2003 book, styled as a translation of an important work of *uṣūl al-fiqh: Lessons in Islamic Jurisprudence*, by Muḥammad Bāqir al-Ṣadr. Roy translated this work with a lengthy introduction on the framework of the history of Islamic law.

Along the way, there are many seminal articles, of course, as well. Roy's early article on the *shuʿūbiyya* movement is still a point of departure if one wants to read about social movements or for any kinds of discussion about national consciousness before the modern era, even if it is simply to deny the existence of such consciousness. "The Idea of *Jihād* in Islam Before the Crusades," appeared in a volume that he co-edited with the late Angeliki E. Laiou at a very critical moment, namely soon after 9/11 when the idea of *jihād* was attracting attention, mostly for the worst of reasons and within reductionist categories. This was a very important scholarly piece, which had the advantage at the same time of making a very important intellectual intervention in public debate. To give an example of his life-long interest in market norms and ethics, Roy also published, with Kristen Stilt, "Public and Private as Viewed through the Work of the *Muḥtasib*." His "*ʿAjāʾib* in *The Thousand and One Nights*," is merely an example of several studies in which he explored the medieval Arabic and Persian literature on marvels. It is famously entertaining, famously informative, and famously learned. I am sure each of Roy's readers has his or her favorites. I just named a few of my own favorites among them.

Let me conclude by pointing out how appropriate it is that we should celebrate Roy's career at a moment when he has decided to retire from the routine responsibilities of a regular academic position and thus to be at more liberty to conclude some of his ongoing projects and to move on to new ones. May he be able to do all that as he pleases, and have fun. What a good idea (of the editors and all who contributed to this volume) that it should get started with an intellectual feast in his honor, namely with papers on courts and judicial procedure in Islamic law, inspired by and in conversation with his work.

A list of Roy's publications from over the course of his career to date follows.

LIST OF ROY MOTTAHEDEH'S PUBLICATIONS

1960

1 "Shaykh Abu Ishaq al-Kazaruni and the Persian Renaissance." A.B. Honors Thesis, Harvard University, 1960.

1967

2 "Sources for the Study of Iran." *Iranian Studies* 1, no. 1 (Winter 1967): 4–7.

3 "Na'ím: A Bahá'í Poet." *World Order* (Winter 1967): 47–53.

1968

4 A Century of Administration in Iraq and Iran. n.p.: 1968.

1970

5 "Administration in the Būyid Kingdom of Rayy." PhD Diss., Harvard University, 1970.

1973

6 "Administration in Būyid Qazwīn." In *Islamic Civilisation 950–1150: A Colloquium Published under the Auspices of the Near Eastern History Group, Oxford, the Near East Center, University of Pennsylvania.* Edited by D. S. Richards. Oxford: Cassirer, 1973: 33–45.

1975

7 "The ʿAbbāsid Caliphate in Iran." In *The Cambridge History of Iran.* Edited by R. N. Frye. Cambridge: Cambridge University Press, 1975: 4:57–89.

1976

8 "The Shuʿûbîyah Controversy and the Social History of Early Islamic Iran." *International Journal of Middle East Studies* 7, no. 2 (April 1976): 161–82.

1980

9 *Loyalty and Leadership in an Early Islamic Society.* Princeton: Princeton University Press, 1980.

10 "Some Attitudes towards Monarchy and Absolutism in the Eastern Islamic World of the Eleventh and Twelfth Centuries A.D." *Israel Oriental Studies* 10 (1980): 85–91.

11 "Iran's Foreign Devils." *Foreign Policy* 38 (Spring 1980): 19–34.

12 The *Shuʿūbīyah* controversy and the social history of early Islamic Iran. Vol. 28 of *Princeton Near East Papers.* Princeton, NJ: Program in Near Eastern Studies, Princeton University, 1980. (Reprint of 8.)

1981

13 "A Note on the 'Tasbib'." In *Studia Arabica et Islamica: Festschrift for Ihsān ʿAbbās on His Sixtieth Birthday.* Edited by Wadad al-Qadi. Beirut: American University of Beirut, 1981: 347–51.

1983

14 "Bureaucracy and the Patrimonial State in Early Islamic Iran and Iraq." *al-Abhath* 29 (1983): 25–36.

1984

15 "The Foundations of State and Society." In *Islam: The Religious and Political Life of a World Community.* Edited by Marjorie Kelly. New York: Praeger, 1984: 55–72.

1985

16 *The Mantle of the Prophet: Religion and Politics in Iran*. New York: Pantheon, 1985.

1987

17 *Der Mantel des Propheten oder das Leben eines persischen Mullah zwischen Religion und Politik*. Translation by Klaus Krieger. Munich: Beck, 1985. (German translation of 16.)

1989

18 "Consultation and the Political Process in the Islamic Middle East of the 9th, 10th, and 11th Centuries." In *Arabian Studies in Honour of Mahmoud Ghul*: Symposium at Yarmouk University, December 8-10, 1984. Edited by Moawiyah M. Ibrahim. Wiesbaden: Harrassowitz, 1989: 83–88.

19 "ʿAzod-al-Dawla." In *Encyclopaedia Iranica*. London and New York: Routledge and Kegan Paul, 1989: 3:265–69.

1991

20 With Antonia Chayes. "Security Diplomacy for the Middle East." *The Aspen Quarterly* (1991): 74–97.

1992

21 "Afkār hawl taswiya mā baʿd al-azma fī al-Sharq al-Awsaṭ." In *Azmat al-Khalīj wa-mustaqbal al-Sharq al-Awsaṭ: Ruʾā ʿArabiyya wa-Amrīkiyya.* Edited by Saʿd al-Dīn Ibrāhīm and Ḥasan Wajīh. Kuwait: Dār Suʿād al-Ṣabāḥ; Cairo: Markaz Ibn Khaldūn lil-Dirāsāt al-Inmāʾiyya, 1992: 51–65.

1993

22 "Toward an Islamic Theology of Toleration." In *Islamic Law Reform and Human Rights: Challenges and Rejoinders.* Edited by Tore Lindholm and Kari Vogt. Oslo: Nordic Human Rights Publications,

1993: 25–36.

23 "Consultation and the Political Process in the Islamic Middle East of the 9th, 10th, and 11th Centuries." In *Islam and Public Law: Classical and Contemporary Studies*. Edited by Chibli Mallat. London: Graham and Totman, 1993: 19–28. (Reprint of **18**.)

1994

24 Foreword to *The Muslims of Bosnia-Herzegovina: Their Historic Development from the Middle Ages to the Dissolution of Yugoslavia*. Edited by Mark Pinson. Cambridge, MA: Center for Middle Eastern Studies of Harvard University; Distributed by Harvard University Press, 1994: vii–viii.

25 "Some Islamic Views of the Pre-Islamic Past." *Harvard Middle Eastern and Islamic Review* 1, no. 1 (1994): 17–26.

1995

26 "Traditional Shiʿite Education in Qom." *Harvard Middle Eastern and Islamic Review* 2, no. 1 (1995): 89–98.

27 "The Islamic World 1400–1700." In *Societies and Cultures in World History*. Edited by Mark Kishlansky et al.. New York: Harper Collins, 1995: 440–71.

28 "The Islamic Movement: The Case for Democratic Inclusion." *Contention* 4 (Spring 1995): 107–27.

29 "The Clash of Civilizations: An Islamicist's Critique." *Harvard Middle Eastern and Islamic Review* 2, no. 2 (1995): 1–26.

1996

30 "Shiʿite Political Thought and The Destiny of the Iranian Revolution." In *Iran and the Gulf: A Search for Stability*. Edited by Jamal S. Suwaidi. London: I.B. Tauris, 1996: 70–80.

31 "al-Fikr al-siyāsī al-Shīʿī wa-maṣīr al-thawra al-Īrāniyya." In *Īrān wa'l-Khalīj: al-baḥth ʿan al-istiqrār*. Edited and translated by Jamāl Sanad al-Suwaydī. Abu Dhabi: Markaz al-Imārāt lil-Dirāsāt wa'l-Buḥūth al-Istirātījiyya, 1996: 103–15. (Arabic translation of **30**.)

32 "Astonishment in the *1001 Nights.*" *Ḥadīth al-Dār* 4 (1996): 21–24.

1997

33 "*Aja'ib* in *The Thousand and One Nights.*" In *The Thousand and One Nights in Arabic Literature and Society*. Edited by Richard C. Hovannisian and Georges Sabagh. Cambridge: Cambridge University Press, 1997: 29–39.

34 "The Transmission of Learning: The Role of the Islamic Northeast." In *Madrasa: la transmission du savoir dans le monde musulman*. Edited by Nicole Grandin and Marc Gaborieau. Paris: Editions Arguments, 1997: 63–72.

35 With Mamoun Fandy. "The Islamic Movement: The Case for Democratic Inclusion." In *The Persian Gulf at the Millennium: Essays in Politics, Economy, Security, and Religion*. Edited by Gary G. Sick and Lawrence G. Potter. New York: St. Martin's Press, 1997: 297–318.

1998

36 "Traditional Shiʿite Education in Qom." In *Philosophers on Education: Historical Perspectives*. Edited by Amélie Oksenberg Rorty. London: Routledge, 1998: 449–54. (Reprint of **26**.)

37 "In memoriam: Jeanette Ann Wakin (1928–1998)." *Middle East Studies Association Bulletin* 32, no. 1 (1998): 141–42.

2000

38 *The Mantle of the Prophet: Religion and Politics in Iran*. Oxford: Oneworld, 2000. (Reprint with a new introduction of **16**.)

2001

39 *Loyalty and Leadership in an Early Islamic Society*. London: I.B. Tauris, 2001. (Reprint with a new introduction of **9**.)

40 With Angeliki E. Laiou, eds. *The Crusades from the Perspective of Byzantium and the Muslim World*. Washington, D.C.: Dumbarton Oaks Research Library and Collection, 2001.

41 "The Idea of Jihād in Islam before the Crusades." In *The Crusades from the Perspective of Byzantium and the Muslim World*. Edited by Angeliki E. Laiou and Roy Parviz Mottahedeh. Washington, D.C.: Dumbarton Oaks Research Library and Collection, 2001: 23–29.

42 "A Just War? Judeo-Christian and Islamic Perspectives: A Conversation with J. Bryan Hehir and Roy Mottahedeh." Panel hosted by the American Academy of Arts and Sciences, Cambridge, MA, December 10, 2001: 1–29.

43 "Brother and Brotherhood." In *Encyclopaedia of the Qur'ān*. Edited by Jane Dammen McAuliffe. Leiden: Brill, 2001: 1:259–63.

2003

44 aṣ-Ṣadr, Muhammad Bāqir. *Lessons in Islamic Jurisprudence*. Translated and edited by Roy Parviz Mottahedeh. Oxford: Oneworld, 2003.

45 "Keeping the Shiʿites Straight." *Religion in the News* 6, no. 2 (2003): 4–6.

46 With Kristen Stilt. "Public and Private as Viewed Through the Work of the *Muhtasib*." *Social Research: An International Quarterly of the Social Sciences* 70, no. 3 (2003): 735–48.

47 "The Clash of Civilizations: An Islamicist's Critique." In *The New Crusades: Constructing the Muslim Enemy*. Edited by Emran Qureshi and Michael A. Sells. New York: Columbia University Press, 2003: 131–51. (Reprint of **29**.)

2004

48 Foreword to *Globalization and the Muslim World: Culture, Religion, and Modernity*. Edited by Birgit Schaebler and Leif Stenberg. Syracuse, NY: Syracuse University Press, 2004: vii–ix.

2005

49 *Profetens kappe: laerdom og magt i Iran*. Translation by Claus Bech. Copenhagen: Forlaget Vandkunsten 2005. (Danish translation of **16**.)

50 Foreword to *Modern Islamic Political Thought: the Response of the Shīʿī and the Sunnī Muslims to the Twentieth Century*. By Hamid Enayat. London: I.B. Tauris, 2005: ix–x.

51 With Jay Tolson. "Islam: A Primer." In *Religion, Culture, and International Conflict: A Conversation*. Edited by Michael Cromartie. Lanham, MD: Rowman and Littlefield Publishers, 2005: 53–72.

2006

52 "Pluralism and Islamic Traditions of Sectarian Divisions." *Svensk Teologisk Kvartzalskrift* 82 (2006): 155–61.

2007

53 Afterword to *Shariʿa: Islamic Law in the Contemporary Context*. Edited by Abbas Amanat and Frank Griffel. Stanford, CA: Stanford University Press, 2007: 178–82.

54 *Burdat al-Nabī: al-dīn wa'l-siyāsa fī Irān*. Translation by Ridwān al-Sayyid. Beirut: Dār al-Madār al-Islāmī, 2007. (Arabic translation of **16**.)

2008

55 "Oaths and Public Vows in the Middle East of the Tenth and Eleventh Centuries." In *Oralité et lien social au moyen âge (Occident, Byzance, Islam): parole donnée, foi jurée, serment*. Edited by Marie-France Auzépy and Guillaume Saint-Guillain. Paris: ACHCByz, 2008: 117–22.

2009

56 *Awzāʿ-i ijtemāʿī-yi dawreh-yi Āl-i Būyeh*. Mashhad: n.p., 2009. (Persian translation of **9**.)

2010

57 "Faith and Practice: Muslims in Historic Cairo." In *Living in Historic Cairo: Past and Present in an Islamic City*. Edited by Farhad Daftary,

Elizabeth Fernea, and Azim Nanji. Seattle: University of Washington Press, 2010: 104–16.

58 "Pluralism and Islamic Traditions of Sectarian Divisions." In *Diversity and Pluralism in Islam: Historical and Contemporary Discourses amongst Muslims*. Edited by Zulfikar Hirji. London: I.B. Tauris, 2010: 3–42.

2012

59 "The Idea of Iran in the Buyid Dominions." In *Early Islamic Iran*. Edited by Edmund Herzig and Sarah Stewart. London: I.B. Tauris, 2012: 153–60.

60 "Qurʾānic commentary on the verse of *khums* (*al-Anfāl* VIII: 41)." In *Sayyids and Sharifs in Muslim Societies: The Living Links to the Prophet*. Edited by Morimoto Kazuo. New York: Routledge, 2012: 3–48.

2013

61 "The Eastern Travels of Solomon: Re-imagining Persepolis and the Iranian Past." In *Law and Tradition in Classical Islamic Thought: Studies in Honor of Professor Hossein Modarressi*. Edited by Michael Cook, Najam Haider, Intisar Rabb, and Asma Sayeed. New York: Palgrave Macmillan, 2013: 247–67.

62 With Michael Cook et al. Introduction, to *Law and Tradition in Classical Islamic Thought: Studies in Honor of Professor Hossein Modarressi*. Edited by Michael Cook, Najam Haider, Intisar Rabb, and Asma Sayeed. New York: Palgrave Macmillan, 2013.

2014

63 *The Quandaries of Emulation: The Theory and Politics of Shi'i Manuals of Practice. The 2011 Farhat J. Ziadeh Distinguished Lecture in Arab and Islamic Studies*. Seattle: Department of Near Eastern Languages and Civilization, University of Washington, 2014.

64 "The Islamic Foundation for Citizenship and Pluralism." *Kufa Review* 7 (2014): 9–15.

2015

65 "Finding Iran in the Panegyrics of the Ghaznavid Court." In *Medieval Central Asia and the Persianate World: Iranian Tradition and Civilisation*. Edited by A.C.S. Peacock and D.G. Tor. London: I.B. Tauris, 2015: 129–42.

2016

66 With Alireza Korangy, Wheeler M. Thackston, and William Granara, eds. *Essays in Islamic Philology, History, and Philosophy*. Vol. 31 of *Studies in the History and Culture of the Middle East*. Berlin: De Gruyter, 2016.

67 "Friendship in Islamic Ethical Philosophy." In *Essays in Islamic Philology, History, and Philosophy*. Edited by Alireza Korangy, Wheeler M. Thackston, Roy P. Mottahedeh, and William Granara. Vol. 31 of *Studies in the History and Culture of the Middle East*. Berlin: De Gruyter, 2016: 229–39.

68 "The Najaf Ḥawzah Curriculum." *Journal of the Royal Asiatic Society* 26, nos. 1–2 (2016): 341–51.

Forthcoming

69 "Caliphate." In *The Wiley-Blackwell Encyclopedia of Social Theory*. Edited by Bryan S. Turner. Forthcoming 2017.

70 With David Durand-Guédy, eds. *Cities of Medieval Iran: Sites, Society, Politics, and Culture*. Forthcoming 2018.

TABULA GRATULATORIA

The following notes were authored by students, colleagues, and friends of Roy Mottahedeh as part of an event called *Law, Loyalty and Leadership*, organized by Sarah Bowen Savant and Kristen Stilt at Harvard University in 2012, in honor of Roy's seventieth birthday. Of the dozens of notes submitted on themes as disparate as his life as a teacher and mentor, his generosity as a scholar and friend, and more, we selected some twenty notes primarily related to his scholarship and reflections on his scholarly trajectory by colleagues often there at the start. Each reflection is reproduced, with slight modifications, with the express permission of each author (or of their estate, in the case of those no longer with us).

The full list of contributors is available below, and their full notes are available online, at scholar.harvard.edu/mottahedeh/tabula-gratulatoria-0.

Select Contributors

Jane McAuliffe
William O. Beeman
Richard W. Bulliet
Juan Cole
Michael Cook
Farhad Daftary
Carl W. Ernst
William A. Graham
Wolfhart P. Heinrichs
Louise Marlow
Susan Miller
David Morgan
Erez Naaman
Afsaneh Najmabadi
Abdulaziz Sachedina
Sarah Bowen Savant
Leif Stenberg
Maria Subtelny
Christopher S. Taylor
Ehsan Yarshater

There is an abiding kindness in Roy that warms all who approach him. In his honor, I would like to offer the following vignette: I found [a] response written by [a] Seminar participant who was tasked with presenting a response to *The Mantle*. Quickly admitting to ignorance of both Islam and Persian history, he nevertheless found the "sweep over two millennia of Iranian history combined with a treatise on Islam in a single volume of 400 pages" to be a "*tour de force* indeed!" His reaction was shared by all the other participants, providing yet another testimony to the broad impact and enduring value of Roy's scholarship.

~ Jane McAuliffe
Director, John W. Kluge Center Office of Scholarly Programs
Library of Congress, USA

Of course, his monumental *The Mantle of the Prophet* has become familiar to legions of students and mature scholars as the most comprehensible introduction to Shiʿa Islam, and to Iranian religious traditions.... Though the general public may not appreciate it as much, his more scholarly writings have advanced the field of Islamic Studies and the History of the Middle East in remarkable ways. I single out his astonishing "translation" of *Lessons in Islamic Jurisprudence* by Muḥammad Bāqir al-Ṣadr. This is far, far more than a translation. It is an exegesis of a major Islamic legal work. Reading the text one realizes what a fantastically important job Roy has done. The most confusing issues suddenly become clear, and the light breaks out on the shadowy world of Islamic legal thought. Not only the words, but the logic behind them emerge as a kind of epiphany. We are grateful to Roy for so many things, but above all, his generous role as a gentle teacher for all of us.

~ William O. Beeman
Professor and Chair, Department of Anthropology
University of Minnesota, USA

In 1977 Roy and I attended a conference in Hamadan, Iran. An excursion by bus to a monumental Parthian remain stopped short of its goal when the bus bogged down in a muddy ditch. With Nush-i Jan in sight atop a lofty mound a mile or two away, Professor Anne Lambton, the doyenne of Iranian historians, decided to walk the remaining distance. Roy and I accompanied her while the other conferees stewed about. Halfway to our destination, Professor Lambton announced that we should cut across the muddy fields to shorten our trek. I disagreed saying that if we proceeded as we were going, we would come to a proper driveway to the site. Professor Lambton said there was no driveway; I replied that I could see one. This left Roy with a choice, to proceed on with his old friend or leave the venerable (and formidable) professor—Professor Lambton was then about sixty-five—to traverse the muddy fields by herself. Ever the diplomat, Roy set off through the mud with Professor Lambton. I continued on to the driveway and met them at Nush-i Jan, but as I recall, there was just about as much mud on the driveway as in the fields.

~ Richard W. Bulliet
Professor (emeritus) & Special Lecturer, Department of History
Columbia University, USA

Roy's amazingly subtle, and yet accessible, *The Mantle of the Prophet* had an enormous impact on me—I think I wrote him a gushing fan letter from Bahrain or Yemen after reading it hungrily on a long plane journey.

~ Juan Cole
Richard P. Mitchell Collegiate Professor of History
University of Michigan, USA

My first memory of Roy is of him standing in the stairwell at Laundress Lane, the building in Cambridge (the real Cambridge) where Peter Avery had his office and would hold court when he was not doing so at his home. Roy was holding a Persian text and puzzling over the question whether a word written b-m-b could really something as vulgar and alien to the heritage of Hafez and Saʿdī as "bomb." I joined in his puzzlement. Maybe we were a little naïve, but given the number of bombs that have gone off in the Middle East since then, it's hard not to look back on our innocence with a certain nostalgia.

The next two times I saw him were in Oxford. One was at a conference organized by Albert Hourani, a pleasant occasion when we had dinner together. The other was a working lunch that marked a turning-point in my life: Roy was briefing me on the courses I would be teaching during my visit to Princeton in the spring of 1984. He was my host throughout that spring semester, and my guide in the crucial initial stages of my adaption to the manners and customs of the American academy. Between then and my return to Princeton in a permanent role I must have seen him several times. My only regret, but a real one, was that after playing so crucial a part in the process that brought me to Princeton, both on stage and behind the scenes, he left for Harvard the very summer that I arrived.

~ ***Michael Cook***
Class of 1943 University Professor of Near Eastern Studies
Princeton University, USA

I first heard Roy's name when I came across his contribution on the ʿAbbāsid Caliphate to the fourth volume of *The Cambridge History of Iran*, published in 1973. Subsequently, I became more aware, and much more impressed, by both the depth and width of his scholarship in Iranian and Islamic studies.

~ ***Farhad Daftary***
Co-Director & Head of Academic and Research Publications
The Institute of Ismaili Studies, UK

I have always admired his distinctive contributions to Islamic and Iranian studies. *The Mantle the Prophet* remains one of the most original and accessible treatments ever written of the intellectual heritage of Iran. All students of Islamic history owe a debt of gratitude to Roy both for his immense scholarship and his willingness to communicate it.

~ ***Carl W. Ernst***
William R. Kenan Jr. Distinguished Professor of Religious Studies
University of North Carolina at Chapel Hill, USA

Roy Parviz Mottahedeh is among the foremost scholars of his generation in the study of the Islamic world, and the Persian- and Arab-Islamic world in particular. The range of his command of the sources, history, arts, and languages of the Islamic Middle East and Western Asia is exceptional and his critical sensibilities and insights stunning. I need only cite his *Loyalty and Leadership* and [*The*] *Mantle of the Prophet* as double evidence of his creative approach and the rock-solid scholarship that mark all his work. It has been my immense privilege to be his Harvard colleague and friend for over a quarter-century. I value greatly having shared in the work of the Center for Middle Eastern Studies during his directorship, then my own, and ever since. Our joint, repeated efforts over numerous years to find support for an Islamic-studies program at Harvard finally bore fruit when our last proposal of many was accepted and issued ultimately in Harvard's Prince Alwaleed bin Talal Islamic Studies Program, which Roy so ably chaired during its first years. I cherish the doctoral students we have shared, the Arabic-reading course we jointly taught, the many evening telephone consultations about Islamic studies we have had, the travel we have done together, and the many evenings of friendship and breaking of bread, not to mention the growth of our respective sons from infancy to adulthood, that Barbara and I have shared with Roy and Pat. No one could ask for a better colleague or more constant friend.

~ ***William A. Graham***
Murray A. Albertson Professor of Middle Eastern Studies
Harvard University, USA

When I was first exposed to Roy's scholarship (*The Mantle of the Prophet* and works of approximately the same time), I was very impressed by what I, as an approximation, called "living" scholarship. My own type of scholarly existence was the traditional philologist. Life, if any, was instilled in the congealed texts by listening to the reconstructed re-animated voices hidden in them. Our curves of interest came closer together somewhat later, when I ventured into Islamic legal theory (dealing with two outliers of same, *qawāʿid* and *furūq*) and Roy translated Muḥammad Bāqir al-Ṣadr's *Durūs fī ʿilm al-uṣūl*: *Lessons in Islamic Jurisprudence*, a masterpiece of expert translation. I am really happy to have him as a friend, a supporter in need and—last but not least—as a representative of Islamic legal studies (to name but one of his specialties) at the same university.

~ Wolfhart P. Heinrichs
James Richard Jewett Professor of Arabic (emeritus) [deceased]
Harvard University, USA

Martin Hinds and Peter Avery gave me the newly published *Loyalty and Leadership in an Early Islamic Society*. I devoured Roy's book with a combination of pleasure, excitement and a certain relief, and it was *Loyalty and Leadership*, more than any other reading, that inspired me to continue my studies at the postgraduate level.

~ Louise Marlow
Professor of Religion
Wellesley College, USA

I worked with Roy in the early 1990s when he was CMES Director. His motto was "Let a thousand flowers bloom," and he made a place for everyone at the Center. The parade of people who went through CMES in the old Coolidge Hall was stunning: Palestinians and Zionists, Sunnis and Shi'is, Copts and Kurds, communists and capitalists, Berbers and Arabs, Zoroastrians and Baha'is. His vision, courage, and good sense energized CMES and made it a home for all sorts of creativity. Under his leadership, we revived the Moroccan Studies program and returned North Africa to the CMES firmament, adding Maghribi studies to the teaching curriculum, and enabling CMES to help produce some of the finest young scholars of North African history, literature, and anthropology around today. Another of his mottoes—one that will stay with me always—was "Onward and upward!"—a simple declaration of historical inevitability, I suppose, but one that has served me well over the years. Salve, Roy, you are among the immortals! "... And the future lies ahead!"

~ ***Susan Miller***
Professor of History
University of California at Davis, USA

Roy's great book *The Mantle of the Prophet*, still in my estimation the best book yet written about the Iranian mullas—among much else—has long been a prescribed text on my "Islam in Iran" course in Madison. I once said to him, rather cheekily, "Roy, you know how much I admire *The Mantle of the Prophet*. But I have to say that I think it's a profoundly misleading book." He looked very worried. "What do you mean? What do you mean?" "Well," I said, "I think the problem is that people read it, and then sometimes tend to imagine that Ali Hashemi is a typical example of what the mullas are actually like. If only that were indeed true!" "Ah, yes," he said, "I see what you mean, yes."

~ ***David O. Morgan***
Professor Emeritus of History and Religious Studies
University of Wisconsin-Madison, USA
Professorial Research Associate
School of Oriental and African Studies, University of London, UK

In the preface to the second edition of *Loyalty and Leadership in an Early Islamic Society*, Roy shares an anecdote with the reader. What encouraged him to write this book, the reader learns, was "a kindly academic colleague who had the slightly annoying habit of beginning many of his conversations by saying: 'You owe me a favor.'" He suddenly realized that the meaning of this sentence, when applied to Iraq and Western Iran of the tenth and eleventh centuries, is the key to understanding the bonds underlying their government and societies. Roy's encounter with this slightly annoying habit yielded a true masterpiece of social history that unveiled the fundamental rules behind the functioning of the Buyid state.

When I read this anecdote and tried to picture the colleague, his habit, and Roy's response, I could not help laughing. A couple of years later, when I was working on my dissertation focusing on the court of the Buyid vizier al-Ṣāḥib Ibn ʿAbbād, I realized how much I owe Roy for his masterpiece. Among the social bonds he described and analyzed brilliantly in his book was the one based on benefit (*niʿma*) in exchange for gratitude. ...

~ Erez Naaman
Associate Professor, World Languages and Cultures
American University, USA

Back in the early 1980s, I was obsessed with understanding (and explaining to others, to make sure everyone understood) this phenomenon that I referred to as "the Revolution," not [to] name it "the Islamic Revolution." Like so many Iranians of my time, I had participated in the Revolution that, as Shaul Bakhash aptly put it, we loved but it didn't love us back. Back in the United States in 1983, I read widely, about any revolution I thought would help me to understand mine, and about earlier historical periods of Iran as far back as the Safavids. Then a book was published. I had heard Roy present a talk about it at CMES (when he was still at Princeton). I read *The Mantle of the Prophet* with a speed unusual for me. I put it down with a deep sense of envy and an even deeper sense of relief. Relief: I no longer had to explain; here was a lucid powerful narrative that explained it all beautifully, thoughtfully, skillfully. Envy: Don't I wish I could have written that book? I feel the same envy and relief all these years later. I have always wanted to thank Roy for writing that book; but I also want to thank Roy for at least one more thing ...: more than anyone else in academia that I know, at a critical and difficult time, he helped numerous uprooted Iranian scholars to find new homes here. Thank you, Roy, for your persistent generosity.

~ Afsaneh Najmabadi
Francis Lee Higgonson Professor of History of Studies of Women, Gender, and Sexuality
Harvard University, USA

I will always cherish that morning when I heard from Roy Mottahedeh for the first time. His earlier work on *Loyalty and Leadership* was the beginning of my interest in the evolution of Shiite religious leadership. I was aware that Roy had been awarded a prestigious MacArthur Fellowship in 1982 to pursue his interest in the emergence of Iranian religious leadership. It was sometime in 1983 that one Saturday morning I received a call from Roy Mottahedeh in Charlottesville, who wanted to speak to me about Iranian clerics. He might have been under the impression that I was one of the clerics because of my interest in Shiite messianic thought and the development of juridical authority during the absence of the theological Imam of the Shiites. The telephone interview, as I realized, lasted for almost an hour. The main topic of the interview was the innovative juridical thinking among the Iranian Shiite jurists. This professor, as I thought to myself, knew his subject very well. He was probably exploring the possibility of whether I could be his clerical interlocutor for his forthcoming research. When *The Mantle of the Prophet* appeared in 1985, I realized that Professor Mottahedeh was looking for a "turbaned" molla who could explain the process of becoming a "Khomeini-like imam" whose religious leadership had shaken the confidence of the social scientists engaged in elaborating the paradigm shift in Weber's categories of "charismatic" leadership in traditional Shiite society. *The Mantle of the Prophet* remains, to this day, a classic in understanding [the] "Khomeini-concept" both academically and politically.

~ ***Abdulaziz Sachedina***
Professor and IIIT Chair of Islamic Studies
George Mason University, USA

Many of Roy's interests have become my own, especially early Islamic Iran and historiography, but I am at least as grateful to him for showing me ways to read history. I appreciate his perceptive and modest style, his ability to choose just the right anecdote, and his empathy with the people whose works he studies, and with the subjects of the stories they tell. In assigning many different treatments of the same periods in history, Roy taught us about perspective, periodisation, and the ways that historians shape their material, but this was no free-for-all, as he offered answers to big questions. My debts to him extend now well beyond Harvard, as I work in an Institute in which Roy's ideas played a seminal role in its foundation.

~ ***Sarah Bowen Savant***
Associate Professor, Institute for the Study of Muslim Civilisations
Aga Khan University, London, UK

To me, *The Mantle and Prophet* is an extraordinary scholarly work, written in a truly unique, elegant and refreshing style—a dimension to the book that reveals the humble and humorous personality of the author. Later, as a means of showing my appreciation and admiration for Roy's outstanding scholarship I invited him to Sweden to receive an honorary Doctorate at Lund University. Roy accepted the invitation and his and Pat's visit at Lund University is still a cherished memory, not only to me but also to many of my colleagues who enjoyed his presence at our university.

~ ***Leif Stenberg***
Professor in Islamology & Director, Center for Middle Eastern Studies
Lund University, Sweden

Roy's insightful scholarship has been a constant presence in my life over the years. I have consulted his brilliant *Loyalty and Leadership in an Early Islamic Society* countless times for everything from technical Islamic terms to abstract notions of justice. It is one of those books whose usefulness is seemingly inexhaustible. Recently, it again proved invaluable when I was exploring the möchälgä, or binding pledge, in Ilkhanid, Timurid, and Safavid political culture....

~ ***Maria Subtelny***
University of Toronto, Canada

In the summer of 1993 the journal *Foreign Affairs* published a provocative article by the Eaton Professor of the Science of Government at Harvard. I don't think anyone reading that article in the summer of 1993 could have imagined the global influence or impact that Sam Huntington's "The Clash of Civilizations" would have. Among the flood of responses to Huntington there remains one that stands out for me as the most sensible and important. It was authored by Roy Mottahedeh and published in the *Harvard Middle Eastern and Islamic Review*. Unfortunately, as we all know, authors rarely have much control over how widely their work is read or disseminated, and Roy Mottahedeh's "The Clash of Civilizations: An Islamicist's Critique," did not get a fraction of the attention or coverage that Huntington's original piece did.

Over the intervening two decades I have often wondered if the course of relations between the Islamic world and "the West" might not have been profoundly different had many more people had the opportunity to read Roy's wonderful response to Huntington. What Roy did is correct the fundamental and fatal flaw in Huntington's argument by contextualizing the reality of clash within the complex totality of relations between the Islamic Middle East and the West over the past 1,500 years. His conclusion, sadly missed by so many, was that Huntington's thesis was misinformed by its lack of critical appreciation for the broad range of interactions between the Islamic world and the West over the past millennium and a half, the vast majority of which were peaceful and benign.

~ *Christopher S. Taylor*
Professor & Director, Drew University Center on Religion, Culture, and Conflict
Drew University, USA

The first memoir, which comes to my mind about Roy is when he told me what his father had written in his notes about my father. I have felt closer to him ever since. I also cannot forget the enjoyment that I had by reading his *Loyalty and Leadership in an Early Islamic Society* and how enlightening it was about the Buyids, and his *The Mantle of the Prophet: Religion and Politics in Iran*, which depicted sympathetically the life and career of an Islamic seminarian.

~ *Ehsan Yarshater*
Hagop Kevorkian Professor Emeritus of Iranian Studies,
Director, Center for Iranian Studies
Columbia University, USA

Tabula Gratulatoria: Full List of Contributors

Asma Afsaruddin
Abbas Amanat
Zayde Antrim
Ali Asani
William O. Beeman
Annabelle Boettcher
Mehrzad Boroujerdi
Sarah Bowen Savant
L. Carl Brown
Richard W. Bulliet
Jocelyne Cesari
Cosroe Chaqueri
Mark R. Cohen
Juan Cole
Michael Cook
Farhad Daftary
Terri DeYoung
Fred M. Donner
Ahmed El Shamsy
Carl W. Ernst
Richard N. Frye
Bruce Fudge
Gene R. Garthwaite
Irene Gendzier
Kambiz GhaneaBassiri
Ellis Goldberg
Arthur Goldschmidt
William A. Graham
Vartan Gregorian
Beatrice Gruendler
Leor Halevi
Wolfhart P. Heinrichs
Baber Johansen
Jere L. Bacharah
Meir Litvak
Ahmad Mahdavi-Damghani
Beatrice Manz
Louise Marlow
Lenore G. Martin
Ann Elizabeth Mayer
Jane McAuliffe
Christopher Melchert
Susan Miller
David Morgan
Erez Naaman
Afsaneh Najmabadi
Bernard O'Kane
Aida Othman
András Riedlmayer
Chase Robinson
Sara Roy
Adam Sabra
Abdulaziz Sachedina
Nina Safran
George Saliba
Biancamaria Scarcia Amoretti
Boaz Shoshan
Amy Singer
Peter Sluglett
Leif Stenberg
Maria Subtelny
Christopher S. Taylor
Deborah Tor
Eve Troutt Powell
Nargis Virani
John Voll
Richard Wilson
Ehsan Yarshater
Travis Zadeh

CONTRIBUTORS

Abigail K. Balbale, Bard Graduate Center. Assistant Professor at Bard Graduate Center, where her research and teaching focus on the cultural history of the Islamic world. She is the co-author, with Jerrilynn Dodds and María Rosa Menocal, of the award-winning book, *The Arts of Intimacy: Christians, Jews and Muslims in the Making of Castilian Culture* (Yale University Press, 2008), and co-editor of *Spanning the Strait: Studies in Unity in the Western Mediterranean* (Brill, 2013). Her research has been supported by grants from the Fulbright Foundation, the National Endowment for the Humanities, the American Council of Learned Societies, the Mellon Foundation and the Medieval Academy of America. She received an undergraduate degree in Arabic and Islamic Studies and Humanities from Yale University and earned a PhD in History and Middle Eastern Studies from Harvard University.

Michael Cook, Princeton University. Class of 1943 University Professor of Near Eastern Studies at Princeton University. He is the recipient of a Distinguished Achievement Award by the Andrew W. Mellon Foundation. His publications include *Early Muslim Dogma* (Cambridge, 1981), *The Koran: A Very Short Introduction* (Oxford, 2000), and *Commanding Right and Forbidding Wrong in Islam* (Cambridge 2001), which won the Albert Hourani Book Award as the year's most notable book in Middle Eastern and Islamic Studies. He was educated at Cambridge University in England.

Maribel Fierro, Consejo Superior de Investigaciones Científicas (Spanish National Research Council). Research Professor in the history of Islam and Islamic Law at the Humanities branch of the Spanish National Research Council (CSIC) in Madrid, Spain. She has held fellowships and research positions at the Islamic Legal Studies Program at Harvard Law School, at the Institute for Advanced Studies at The Hebrew University of Jerusalem, at the University of Chicago, and at the Institute for Advanced Study at Princeton. She has published works on *The Almohad Revolution: Politics and Religion in the Islamic West during the Twelfth-Thirteenth Centuries* (Variorum, 2012), *Abd al-Rahman III: The First Cordoban Caliph* (Oneworld, 2005), and dozens of other books, articles, and translations of early Islamic historical and legal works. Fierro received a doctorate degree at the Complutense University of Madrid, Spain.

William Graham, Harvard University. Professor of Middle Eastern Studies in the Harvard Faculty of Arts and Sciences and a member of the Faculty of Divinity. He has served as director of the Center for Middle Eastern Studies, and chair of the Department of Near Eastern Languages and Civilizations, the Committee on the Study of Religion, and the Core Curriculum Committee on Foreign Cultures at Harvard. He has received a Lifetime Achievement Award from the *Journal of Law and Religion*, has held John Simon Guggenheim and Alexander von Humboldt research fellowships, and is a fellow at the American Academy of Arts and Sciences. His book *Divine Word and Prophetic Word in Early Islam* was awarded the American Council of Learned Societies History of Religions Prize, and he is the author of numerous books and articles on the history of religion, *ḥadīth*, and law. He received a BA from the University of North Carolina and an AM and PhD from Harvard University.

Cemal Kafadar, Harvard University. Vehbi Koç Professor of Turkish Studies in the Department of History at Harvard University, and the Director of Doctoral Studies at the Center for Middle Eastern Studies. He is interested in the social and cultural history of the Middle East and Southeastern Europe in the early modern era. He teaches courses on Ottoman history, urban space, travel, popular culture, history, and cinema. His latest publications include an article on "The Ottomans and Europe, 1400-1600" and a book on the rise of the Ottoman state. He obtained a PhD in Islamic Studies from McGill University.

Mahmood Kooria, Leiden University. Researcher who recently completed a doctoral dissertation on the historical circulation of Islamic legal ideas and texts across the Indian Ocean and eastern Mediterranean worlds between the thirteenth and nineteenth centuries. He is the translator, with others, of the book *Tahrid: Ahl al-Iman—An Indigenous Account against Early Modern European Interventions in the Indian Ocean World* by Sheikh Zainuddin b. 'Ali (Other Books, 2012). He received an MA and MPhil in History from the Centre for Historical Studies at Jawaharlal Nehru University in New Delhi, and a PhD from Leiden University.

Christian Lange, Utrecht University. Professor of Arabic and Islamic Studies at Utrecht University. He has taught Islamic Studies at Harvard University and Edinburgh University, and has published books on *Paradise and Hell in Islamic Traditions* (Cambridge University Press, 2015) (an edited volume), *Locating Hell in Islamic Traditions* (Brill, 2015), and *Justice, Punishment and the Medieval Muslim Imagination* (Cambridge University Press, 2008), together with articles on medieval Islamic history and eschatology. He received a PhD from Harvard University.

Louise Marlow, Wellesley College. Professor and Program Director of Middle Eastern Studies at Wellesley College. She is the author of, among other publications, *Counsel for Kings: Wisdom and Politics in Tenth-Century Iran: The Naṣīḥat al-mulūk of Pseudo-Māwardī* (Edinburgh University Press, 2016), *Writers and Rulers: Perspectives on Their Relationships from Abbasid to Safavid Times*, co-edited with Beatrice Gruendler (Reichert Verlag, 2004), and *Hierarchy and Egalitarianism in Islamic Thought* (Cambridge University Press, 1997). She received an MA from Cambridge University and a PhD from Princeton University.

Hossein Modarressi, Princeton University. Bayard Dodge Professor of Near Eastern Studies at Princeton University. He teaches courses in Islamic law and Islamic thought, and has published numerous books and articles on Islamic law, philosophy, and history—including: *Tradition and Survival: A Bibliographical Survey of Early Shīʿite Literature* (Oneworld, 2003); *Crisis and Consolidation in the Formative Period of Shīʿite Islam* (Darwin Press, 1993), and *An Introduction to Shīʿī Law* (Ithaca Press, 1984). He first attended the Islamic seminary at Qum (Iran) where he received a complete traditional Islamic education in Arabic language and literature; Qurʾān and *ḥadith*; and Islamic philosophy, theology, and law. He then received degrees from secular institutions, culminating in a PhD in Islamic law from Oxford University.

Intisar A. Rabb, Harvard Law School. Professor of Law at Harvard Law School, Professor of History at Harvard University, Susan S. and Kenneth L. Wallach Professor at the Radcliffe Institute for Advanced Studies at Harvard University. She also serves as Director of the Islamic Legal Studies Program at Harvard Law School and founding editor-in-chief of SHARIAsource, an online repository for content and context on Islamic law. She is the author of *Doubt in Islamic Law: A History of Legal Maxims, Interpretation, and Islamic Criminal Law* (Cambridge University Press, 2015), and several articles on Islamic history and law. She holds a Bachelor's degree from Georgetown University, an MA and PhD from Princeton University, and a JD from Yale Law School.

Nahed Samour, Helsinki University. Post-Doctoral Research Fellow at the Erik Castrén Institute of International Law and Human Rights at the University of Helsinki. She was a doctoral fellow at the International Max Planck Research School for Comparative Legal History in Frankfurt am Main, clerked at the Higher Court of Appeals in Berlin, and was a Junior Faculty for Islamic Law and Policy at Harvard Law School's Institute for Global Policy and Law. Her work focuses on Islamic law, public law, and the history of international law. Her publications include articles on "Al-Shāfiʿī und Kelsen: Über die formale Rechtsordnung," in *Die Normativität formaler Ordnungen und Prozeduren in der Antike – Mathematische und rechtliche Regelsysteme im Vergleich*, ed. A. Warner, G. Pfeifer, D. Bawanypeck (forthcoming), and "Is There a Role for Islamic International Law in the History of International Law?," *European Journal of International Law* 25, no. 1 (2014): 313–19. She has studied law and Islamic studies at universities in Berlin, Bonn, Birzeit, Cambridge (Harvard), Damascus, Humboldt, and London (SOAS).

Delfina Serrano, Consejo Superior de Investigaciones Científicas (Spanish National Research Council). Tenured Researcher at the Spanish National Research Council (CSIC) in Madrid, Spain. She is a member of the research group "Islamology: Past and Present of the *Shari`a* through its Textual Tradition" She focuses on Islamic law and the intellectual history of the pre-modern Islamic west, including the relationship between *fiqh* and other Islamic sciences like *kalām* and Sufism, as well as the relevance of theory and practice of classical Islamic jurisprudence to contemporary Muslim societies. She is currently the chief editor of the CSIC series Estudios Árabes e Islámicos. Her publications include: "Explicit Cruelty, Implicit Compassion: Judaism, Forced Conversions and the Genealogy of the Banū

Rushd," *Journal of Medieval Iberian Studies* 2, no. 2 (2010): 217–33; al-Qāḍī ʿIyāḍ, *Madhāhib al-ḥukkām fī nawāzil al-aḥkām = La actuación de los jueces en los procesos judiciales*, trans. Delfina Serrano (CSIC, 1998); and *Crueldad y compasión en la literatura árabe e islámica* (Cruelty and Compassion in Arabic and Islamic Literature), ed. Delfina Serrano (CSIC, 2011). She received a PhD from the University of Seville.

Ahmed El Shamsy, University of Chicago. Associate Professor of Islamic Thought at the University of Chicago. He studies the intellectual history of Islam, focusing on the classical Islamic disciplines and their interplay with the media of orality, literacy, and print. He holds a fellowship at the Islamic Legal Studies Program at Harvard Law School and is the recipient of several national and international awards, including grants from the Volkswagen Foundation, the American Council of Learned Societies/Mellon Foundation, and the Middle East Studies Association (Malcolm H. Kerr Dissertation Award (2009)). He is the author of *The Canonization of Islamic Law: A Social and Intellectual History* (Cambridge University Press, 2013), and numerous articles on the early history of Islamic law. He obtained a PhD in History and Middle Eastern Studies from Harvard University.

BIBLIOGRAPHY

Notes on Citation, Transliteration, and Style

For citations and punctuation, we generally follow the *Chicago Manual of Style (CMOS)*, 15th edition. We also adopt the following conventions: we use one digit for alternative years given as date ranges, that is, successive CE years representing the span of possible years for a definitive Hijrī year, and vice-versa. Multiple works by the same author(s) are listed in reverse chronological order from the first date of publication. For Arabic and Persian translations, we follow the *International Journal of Middle East Studies* (*IJMES*), with the following exceptions: we omit the initial definite article from proper names or places when mentioned alone except when that article is a commonly known part of the proper name (thus, al-Mutawakkil, but Balādhurī); we retain the definite article al- in transliterated passages unless preceded by the conjunctions *wa-* and *fa-*, in which case the *alif* is assimilated and represented by a *hamza* preceded by a hyphen, or unless preceded by the prepositions *bi*, *ka*, or *li*, in which case the *alif* is assimilated without a *hamza* and no preceding hyphen. We use a lower case "b." for ibn ("son of") and "bt." for bint ("daughter of"), but write out each when beginning a name or when a part of the name by which a figure is best known (thus, Ibn Ḥanbal or Aḥmad Ibn Ḥanbal, but Muḥammad b. Aḥmad al-Dhahabī). Only Qurʾānic verses are fully vowelled. We have attempted to provide After Hijra (*hijrī*) and Common Era death dates upon first mention in each chapter in the format AH/CE, and typically refer to CE whenever dates appear alone. *SHARIAsource at Harvard Law School* will publish an online companion book, housing the primary sources that accompany each printed chapter.

ENCYCLOPEDIAS, ONLINE SOURCES, & OTHER REFERENCE MATERIAL

Barrasī-hā-yi tārīkhī. Directed by Hassan Ansari. http://ansari.kateban.com/entryprint1951.html.

Prosopografía de los ulemas de al-Andalus (= PUA). Directed by María Luisa Avila. http://www.eea.csic.es/pua.

Biblioteca de al-Andalus. Edited by Jorge Lirola Delgado and José Miguel Puerta Vílchez. Almería: Fundación Ibn Tufayl de Estudios Árabes, 2004–13. Online Edition: http://www.ibntufayl.org/index.php?option=com_glossary&Itemid=81.

Encyclopaedia Iranica. Edited by Ehsan Yarshater. London: Routledge and Kegan Paul, 1982–. Online Edition: http://www.iranicaonline.org/

Encyclopaedia of Islam. 2nd edition (*EI*²). Edited by P. Bearman, Th. Bianquis, C.E. Bosworth, E. van Donzel, and W.P. Heinrichs. Leiden: Brill, 1960–2009. Online Edition: http://referenceworks.brillonline.com/browse/encyclopaedia-of-islam-2.

Encyclopaedia of Islam. 3rd edition (*EI-THREE*). Edited by G. Krämer, D. Matringe, J. Nawas, and E. Rowson. Leiden: Brill, 2007–. Online Edition: http://referenceworks.brillonline.com/browse/encyclopaedia-of-islam-3.

The Encyclopaedia of the Qurʾān (EQ). Edited by Jane Dammen McAuliffe. Leiden: Brill, 2001–6. Online Edition: http://referenceworks.brillonline.com/browse/encyclopaedia-of-the-quran.

The Encyclopedia of Islam and Law. Edited by John Esposito. In Oxford Islamic Studies Online: http://www.oxfordislamicstudies.com.

Historia de los Autores y Transmisores de al-Andalus (HATA). Edited by Maribel Fierro: http://kohepocu.cchs.csic.es/.

al-Mawsūʿa al-fiqhiyya (MF). Kuwait: Wizārat al-Awqāf waʾl-Shuʾūn al-Islamiyya, 1984–2006.

The Princeton Encyclopedia of Islamic Political Thought. Edited by Gerhard Böwering. Princeton: Princeton University Press, 2013.

SHARIAsource. A Project of the Islamic Legal Studies Program at Harvard Law School. Edited by Intisar A. Rabb: https://beta.shariasource.com.

The Stanford Encyclopedia of Philosophy. Edited by Edward N. Zalta. Stanford: Stanford University, 1997–. Online Edition: https://plato.stanford.edu.

CASES (U.S.)

Bond v. United States. 529 U.S. 334 (2000).

Brown v. Plata. 563 U.S. 493 (2011).

PRIMARY SOURCES

Ābī (d. 421/1030), Abū Saʿd Manṣūr b. al-Ḥusayn al-. *Nathr al-durr fī al-muḥāḍarāt*. Edited by Muḥammad ʿAlī Qurna. Cairo: al-Hayʾa al-Miṣriyya al-ʿĀmma lil- Kitāb, 1980.

Abū Nuwās (d. between 198/813 and 200/815). *Dīwān Abī Nuwās*. Edited by al-Ḥasan b. Hāniʾ. Beirut: Dār al-Kitāb al-ʿArabī, 1982.

Abū Yūsuf (d. 182/798). *Kitāb al-Kharāj*. Edited by Iḥsān ʿAbbās. Beirut: Dār al-Shurūq, 1975.

______. *Kitāb al-Āthār*. Edited by Abū al-Wafāʾ al-Afghānī. Hyderabad: Lajnat Iḥyāʾ al-Maʿārif al-Nuʿmāniyya, 1355/1936.

ʿĀmilī (d. 1226/1811), Muḥammad Jawād b. Muḥammad al-. *Miftāḥ al-karāma fī sharḥ Qawāʿid al-ʿAllāma*. Qum: Muʾassasat al-Nashr al-Islāmī, 1999.

Baghawī (d. 516/11122), al-Ḥusayn b. Masʿūd al-. *Maʿālim al-tanzīl*. Edited by Muḥammad ʿAbd Allāh al-Nimr et al. Riyadh: Dār al-Ṭība, 1997.

Baghdādī (d. 463/1071), al-Khaṭīb al-. *Taʾrīkh Madīnat al-Salām wa-akhbār muḥaddithīhā = Taʾrīkh Baghdād*. Beirut: Dār al-Gharb al-Islāmī, 2001.

Bakrī al-Andalusī (d. 487/1094), Abū ʿUbayd al-. *Muʿjam mā ʾstuʿjim min asmāʾ al-bilād waʾl-mawāḍiʿ*. Edited by Jamāl Ṭulba. Beirut: Dār al-Kutub al-ʿIlmiyya, 1998.

Balādhurī (d. 279/896), Aḥmad b. Yaḥyā al-. *Jumal min Ansāb al-ashrāf*. Edited by Suhayl Zakkār and Riyāḍ Ziriklī. Beirut: Dār al-Fikr, 1996.

_______. *Futūḥ al-buldān*. Edited by ʿAbd Allāh Anīs al-Ṭabbāʿ. Beirut: Muʾassasat al-Maʿārif, 1987.

_______. *Ansāb al-Ashrāf*. Edited by Shelomo Dov F. Goitein. Jerusalem: Azriel Press, 1936.

Bayhaqī (d. 470/1077), Abū al-Faḍl al-. *Tārīkh-i Bayhaqī = Tārīkh-i Masʿūdī*. Edited by Q. Ghanī and A. A. Fayyāḍ. Tehran, 1945–6.

Bayhaqī (d. 458/1066), Abū Bakr al-. *Maʿrifat al-sunan waʾl-āthār*. Edited by ʿAbd al-Muʿṭī Amīn Qalʿahjī. Aleppo: Dār al-Waʿī, 1991.

_______. *al-Sunan al-kubrā*. Edited by ʿAbd al-Raḥmān al-Muʿallimī. Hyderabad: Majlis Dāʾirat al-Maʿārif al-Niẓāmiyya, 1925–37.

Bīdpāʾī, al-. *Kalīla wa-Dimna*. Beirut: al-Maktabāt al-Thaqāfiyya, n.d.

_______. *Fables of Bidapai*. Translated by Thomas North. Edinburgh: Ballantyne, Hanson and Co., n.d.

Bukhārī (d. 256/870), Muḥammad b. Ismāʿīl al-. *Jāmiʿ al-ṣaḥīḥ*. Edited by Muḥammad Zuhayr al-Nāṣir. Beirut: Dār Ṭawq al-Najāt, 2001.

Bunnāhī al-Andalusī (d. circa 794/1391) = Nubāhī [*sic*], ʿAlī b. ʿAbd Allāh al-. *al-Marqaba al-ʿulyā fī man yastaḥiqqu al-qaḍāʾ waʾl-futyā: La Atalaya Suprema sobre el Cadiazgo y el muftiazgo*. Edited and translated by Cuellas Marqués and Celia del Moral. Granada: Universidad de Granada, 2005.

Burzulī (d. 841/1438), Abū al-Qāsim Aḥmad b. Muḥammad al-. *Fatāwā al-Burzulī*. Edited by M. al-Ḥīla. Beirut: Dār al-Gharb al-Islāmī, 2002.

Dawānī (d. 908/1502-3), Jalāl al-Dīn al-. *Dīwān-i Maẓālim*. Edited by Hossein Modarressi in *Farhang-i Irānzamīn* 27 (1987): 98–119.

Dhahabī (d. 748/1348), Muḥammad b. Aḥmad al-. *Siyar aʿlām al-nubalāʾ*. Edited by Bashshār ʿAwwād Maʿrūf and Shuʿayb al-Arnaʾūṭ. Beirut: Muʾassasat al-Risāla, 2001.

Fīrūzābādī (d. 823/1415), Muḥammad b. Yaʿqūb al-. *al-Maghānim al-Muṭāba fī maʿālim Ṭāba*. Edited by Ḥamad al-Jāsir. Riyadh: Dār al-Yamāma, 1969.

Gharnāṭī (d. 579/1183), Abū Isḥāq al-. *al-Wathāʾiq al-mukhtaṣara*. Edited by Muṣṭafā Nājī. Rabat: Markaz Iḥyāʾ al-Turāth al-Maghribī, 1988.

Ghazālī (d. 505/1111), Abū Ḥāmid al-. *al-Wajīz fī fiqh al-Imām al-Shāfiʿī*. Edited by ʿAlī Muʿawwaḍ and ʿĀdil ʿAbd al-Mawjūd. Beirut: Dār al-Arqam, 1997.

———. *al-Wasīṭ fī al-madhhab*. Edited by Muḥammad Muḥammad Tāmir and Aḥmad Maḥmūd Ibrāhīm. Cairo: Dār al-Salām, 1997.

———. *Naṣīḥat al-mulūk*. Edited by Jalāl al-Dīn Humāʾī. Tehran: Kitābkhāna-yi Millī, 1972.

Ḥimyarī (d. circa 9th/15th c.), Muḥammad b. Muḥammad b. ʿAbd Allāh al-. *al-Rawḍ al-miʿṭār fī khabar al-aqṭār*. Edited by Iḥsān ʿAbbās. Beirut: Maktabat Lubnān, 1975.

Ibn ʿAbbād (d. 385/995), al-Ṣāḥib. *al-Muḥīṭ fī al-lugha*. Edited by Muḥammad Ḥasan Āl Yāsīn. Beirut: ʿĀlam al-Kutub, 1994.

Ibn Abī Zamanīn (d. 399/1009). *Muntakhab al-aḥkām*. Edited by Muḥammad Ḥammād. Rabat: Markaz al-Dirāsāt waʾl-Abḥāth wa-Iḥyāʾ al-Turāth al-Rābiṭa al-Muḥammadiyya lil-ʿUlamāʾ, 2009.

Ibn Abī Zayd al-Qayrawānī (d. 386/996), Abū Muḥammad ʿAbd Allāh. *Fatāwā Ibn Abī Zayd al-Qayrawānī*. Collected by H.M. Lahmar. Beirut: Dār al-Gharb al-Islāmī, 2004.

———. *al-Nawādir waʾl-ziyādāt ʿalā mā fī al-Mudawwana min ghayrihā min al-ummahāt*. Edited by ʿAbd al-Fattāḥ al-Ḥulw et al. Beirut: Dār al-Gharb al-Islāmī, 1999.

Ibn ʿAsākir (d. 571/1176). *Taʾrīkh madīnat Dimashq*. Beirut: Dār al-Fikr, 1995.

Ibn ʿĀṣim (d. 829/1426), Muḥammad b. Muḥammad. *Matn al-ʿĀṣimiyya al-musammā bi-Tuḥfat al-ḥukkām fī nukat al-ʿuqūd wa'l-aḥkām*. Edited by M. Amīn ʿImrān. Cairo: Maṭbaʿat Muṣṭafā al-Bābī al-Ḥalabī, 1930.

Ibn al-Athīr (d. 630/1233), ʿIzz al-Dīn. *al-Kāmil fī al-ta'rīkh*. Edited by ʿUmar ʿAbd al-Salām Tadmurī. Beirut: Dār al-Kitāb al-ʿArabī, 1997.

_______. *al-Kāmil fī al-ta'rīkh = Ibn-el-Athiri Chronicon quod perfectissimum inscribitur*. Edited by C. J. Tornberg. Leiden: E. J. Brill, 1862. Reprinted Beirut: Dār Ṣādir, 1965–1967.

Ibn al-ʿAṭṭār (d. 339/1009). *Kitāb al-wathā'iq wa'l-sijillāt*. Edited by Pedro Chalmeta and Federico Corriente. Madrid: Fundación Matritense del Notariado e Instituto Hispano-Árabe de Cultura, 1983.

Ibn Bābawayh (d. 381/991-2). *Kitāb man lā yaḥduruh al-faqīh*. 2nd ed. Qum: Daftar-i Intishārāt-i Islāmī, 1992.

Ibn Ḥazm (d. 456/1064), ʿAlī b. Aḥmad. *al-Sīra al-Nabawiyya*. Edited by Aḥmad Farīd al-Mazīdī. Beirut: Dār al-Kutub al-ʿIlmiyya, 2004.

_______. *al-Muḥallā bi'l-āthār*. Edited by ʿAbd al-Ghaffār Sulaymān al-Bandārī. Beirut: Dār al-Kutub al-ʿIlmiyya, 1988. Cairo Edition: Cairo: Idārat al-Ṭibāʿa al-Munīriyya, 1929–1934.

_______. *al-Iḥkām fī uṣūl al-aḥkām*. Cairo: Dār al-Ḥadīth, 1984.

Ibn Ḥajar al-ʿAsqalānī (d. 852/1449), Aḥmad b. ʿAlī, *Rafʿ al-ʿiṣr ʿan quḍāt Miṣr*. Edited by ʿAlī Muḥammad ʿUmar. Cairo: Maktabat al-Khānjī, 1998.

Ibn ʿIyāḍ (d. 576/1180), Muḥammad. *La actuación de los jueces en los procesos judiciales*. Translated by Delfina Serrano Ruano. Madrid: Consejo Superior de Investigaciones Científicas—Agencia Española de Cooperación Internacional, 1998.

_______. *Madhāhib al-ḥukkām fī nawāzil al-aḥkām*. Beirut: Dār al-Gharb al-Islāmī, 1989.

Ibn al-Jawzī (d. 597/1201), Abū al-Faraj ʿAbd al-Raḥmān b. ʿAlī. *al-Muntaẓam fī ta'rīkh al-umam wa'l-mulūk*. Edited by Muḥammad ʿAbd al-Qādir ʿAṭā' et al. Beirut: Dār al-Kutub al-ʿIlmiyya, 1412/1992.

_______. *al-Adhkiyā'*. Beirut: al-Maktab al-Tijārī, 1966.

Ibn Juzayy (d. 741/1340), Muḥammad b. Aḥmad. *al-Qawānīn al-fiqhiyya fī talkhīṣ madhhab al-Mālikiyya*. Libya: al-Dār al-ʿArabiyya lil-Kitāb, 1982.

Ibn Kathīr (d. 774/1373), Ismāʿīl b. ʿUmar. *Musnad al-Fārūq*. Manṣūra: Dār al-Wafā', 1991.

Ibn Khallikān (d. 681/1282). *Wafayāt al-aʿyān wa-anbāʾ abnāʾ al-zamān*. Edited by Iḥsān ʿAbbās. Beirut: Dār Ṣādir, 1977.

Ibn Mājah (d. 273/887). *al-Sunan*. Edited by Muḥammad Fuʾād ʿAbd al-Bāqī. Cairo: ʿĪsā al-Bābī al-Ḥalabī, 1952.

Ibn Manẓūr (d. 711/1311). *Lisān al-ʿArab*. Beirut: Dār Ṣādir, 1997.

Ibn Māzah (d. 536/1141), al-Ṣadr al-Shahīd. *Sharḥ Adab al-qāḍī* [by Aḥmad b. ʿUmar Khaṣṣāf (d. 261/ 874)]. Edited by Muḥyī Hilāl al-Sarḥān. Baghdad: Maṭbaʿat al-Irshād, 1977.

Ibn al-Muqaffaʿ (d. circa 139/757). *Āthār Ibn al-Muqaffaʿ*. Edited by ʿUmar Abū al-Naṣr. Beirut: Dār Maktabat al-Ḥayāt, 1966.

Ibn Mughīth al-Ṭulayṭulī (d. 459/1067), Aḥmad. *al-Muqniʿ fī ʿilm al-shurūṭ*. Edited by Francisco Javier Aguirre Sádaba. Madrid: Consejo Superior de Investigaciones Científicas—Instituto de Ciencia de Materiales de Aragón, 1994.

Ibn al-Nadīm (d. ca. 380/990), Muḥammad b. Isḥāq. *Kitāb al-Fihrist*. Edited by Ayman Fuʾād Sayyid. London: Al-Furqan Islamic Heritage Foundation, 2009.

Ibn Qayyim al-Jawziyya (d. 751/1350), Muḥammad b. Abī Bakr. *al-Ṭuruq al-ḥukmiyya fī al-siyāsa al-sharʿiyya*. Edited by Nāyif b. Aḥmad al-Ḥamad. Mecca: Dār ʿĀlam al-Fawāʾid, 2007.

________. *Badāʾiʿ al-fawāʾid*. Mecca: Dār ʿĀlam al-Fawāʾid, 2004.

________. *Iʿlām al-muwaqqiʿīn ʿan Rabb al-ʿĀlamīn*. Beirut: Dār al-Kutub al-ʿIlmiyya, 1991.

Ibn Qudāma (d. 620/1223), Muwaffaq al-Dīn. *al-Mughnī ʿalā Mukhtaṣar Abī al-Qāsim al-Khiraqī*. Edited by ʿAbd Allāh b. ʿAbd al-Muḥsin al-Turkī and ʿAbd al-Fattāḥ Muḥammad al-Ḥulw. Cairo: Dār Hajar, 1986–1990.

Ibn Qutayba (d. 276/889). *Kitāb ʿUyūn al-akhbār*. Cairo: Maṭbaʿat Dār al-Kutub al-Miṣriyya, 1925.

Ibn Rāhawayh (d. 238/853), Isḥāq. *Masāʾil al-Imām Aḥmad b. Ḥanbal wa-Isḥāq b. Rāhawayh*. Medina: Islamic University, 2002.

Ibn Rushd I (d. 520/1126), Abū al-Walīd Muḥammad b. Aḥmad. *al-Bayān wa'l-taḥṣīl wa'l-sharḥ wa'l-tawjīh wa'l-taʿlīl fī masāʾil al-mustakhraja*. Beirut: Dār al-Gharb al-Islāmī, 1984.

Ibn Rushd al-Hafīd/II (d. 595/1198). *The Distinguished Jurist's Primer: A Translation of Bidāyat al-mujtahid*. Translated by Imran Ahsan Khan Nyazee. London: Centre for Muslim Contribution to Civilization—Garnet Publishing Limited, 1996.

_______. *Bidāyat al-mujtahid wa-nihāyat al-muqtaṣid*. 6th ed. Beirut: Dār al-Maʿrifa, 1982. 2000 Beirut Edition: Edited by ʿAlī Muḥammad Muʿawwaḍ and ʿĀdil Aḥmad ʿAbd al-Mawjūd. Beirut: Dār al-Kutub al-ʿIlmiyya, 2000.

Ibn Saʿd (d. 230/844-5). *al-Ṭabaqāt al-kubrā*. Edited by ʿAlī Muḥammad ʿUmar. Cairo: Maktabat al-Khānjī, 2001.

Ibn Salmūn (d. 767/1366), Abū al-Qāsim Salmūn b. Alī b. ʿAbd Allāh. *al-ʿIqd al-munaẓẓam lil-ḥukkām fī-mā yajrī bayna aydīhim min al-ʿuqūd waʾl-aḥkām*. Published on the margins of Ibrāhīm b. ʿAlī Ibn Farḥūn (d. 799/1397). *Tabṣirat al-ḥukkām fī uṣūl al-aqḍiya wa-manāhij al-aḥkām*. Beirut: Dār al-Kutub al-ʿIlmiyya, 1883.

Ibn Shabba (d. 262/876), ʿUmar. *Taʾrīkh al-Madīna al-Munawwara*. Edited by Fahīm Muḥammad Shaltūt. Beirut: Dār al-Turāth, 1990.

Ibn Shahrāshūb (d. 588/1192). *Manāqib Āl Abī Ṭālib*. Qum: n.p., 1959.

Iṣbahānī (d. 356/967), Abū al-Faraj al-. *Maqātil al-Ṭālibiyyīn*. Najaf: Maktabat al-Ḥaydariyya, 2002-3.

Jāḥiẓ (d. 255/868-9), al-. *Rasāʾil al-Jāḥiẓ*. Edited by ʿAbd al-Salām Muḥammad Hārūn. Cairo: Maktabat al-Khānjī, 1964–79.

_______. *al-Bayān waʾl-tabyīn*. Edited by ʿAbd al-Salām Muḥammad Hārūn. Cairo: Maktabat al- Khānjī, 1960.

_______. *Le livre de la couronne: Kitāb at-tāǧ*. Translated by Charles Pellat. Paris: Société d'Édition Les Belles Lettres, 1954.

_______. *Kitāb al-Tāj fī akhlāq al-mulūk = Le livre de la couronne*. Edited by Ahmed Zeki Pacha. Cairo: Imprimerie nationale, 1914.

Jaṣṣāṣ (d. 370/980), Abū Bakr Ahmad b. ʿAlī al-, *Sharḥ Adab al-qāḍī*. Edited by Farhat Ziadeh. Cairo: American University Press, 1978.

_______. *Kitāb Aḥkām al-Qurʾān*. Cairo: Salafiyya, 1335/1916-7.

Jaṣṣāṣ (d. 370/980), Abū Bakr al-, and Abū Jaʿfar al-Ṭaḥāwī (d. 321/933). *Mukhtaṣar Ikhtilāf al-ʿulamāʾ*. Edited by ʿAbd Allāh Nadhīr. Beirut: Dār al-Bashāʾir al-Islāmiyya, 1996.

Jazīrī (d. 585/1189-90), ʿAlī b. Yaḥyā al-. *al-Maqṣad al-maḥmūd fī talkhīṣ al-ʿuqūd*. Edited by Asunción Ferreras. Madrid: Consejo Superior de Investigaciones Científicas—Agencia Española de Cooperación Internacional, 1998.

Juwaynī (d. 478/1085), Imām al-Ḥaramayn al-. *Nihāyat al-maṭlab fī dirāyat al-madhhab*. Edited by ʿAbd al-ʿAẓīm Maḥmūd al-Dayyib. Jedda: Dār al-Minhāj, 2007.

Jūzjānī/Minhāj-i Sirāj (d. between 664/1265 and 686/1287), Abū ʿAmr Minhāj al-Dīn ʿUthmān b. Sirāj al-Dīn al-. *Ṭabaqāt-i Nāṣirī*. Edited by W. Nassau Lees, Mawlawī Khadim Hosain, and ʿAbd al-Ḥayy. Calcutta: College Press, 1864.

_______. *Ṭabakāt-i-Nāṣirī: A general history of the Muhammadan dynasties of Asia, including Hindustan, from A.H. 194 (810 A.D.) to A.H. 658 (1260 A.D.) and the irruption of the infidel Mughals into Islam*. Translated by Henry George Raverty. London: Gilbert and Rivington, 1881.

Kāsānī (d. 587/1191), Abū Bakr al-. *Badāʾiʿ al-ṣanāʾiʿ fī tartīb al-sharāʾiʿ*. Edited by Aḥmad Mukhtār ʿUthmān. Cairo: Zakariyyā ʿAlī Yūsuf, 1968.

Khalīl b. Aḥmad (d. between 160/776 and 175/791). *Kitāb al-ʿAyn*. Qum: Hijrat, 1989.

Khallāl (d. 311/923), Aḥmad b. Muḥammad al-. *Aḥkām ahl al-milal min al-jāmiʿ li-masāʾil al-Imām Aḥmad b. Ḥanbal*. Edited by Sayyid Kasrawī Ḥasan. Beirut: Dār al-Kutub al-ʿIlmiyya, 1994.

Khushanī (d. 361/971), Ibn Ḥārith al-. *Quḍāt Qurṭuba*. Edited and translated by Julián Ribera. Madrid: Iberica, 1914.

Khuzāʿī (d. 1387-8), ʿAlī b. Muḥammad al-. *Takhrīj al-dalālāt al-samʿiyya*. Edited by Iḥsān ʿAbbās, 2nd ed. Beirut: Dār al-Gharb al-Islāmī, 1999.

Kindī (d. 350/961), Muḥammad b. Yūsuf al-. *Histoire des cadis égyptiens = Akhbār qudāt Misr*. Translated and edited by Mathieu Tillier. Cairo: Institut Français d'Archéologie Orientale, 2012.

_______. *The Governors and Judges of Egypt, or Kitāb el umarāʾ (el wulāh) wa Kitāb el quḍāh of el Kindī*. Edited by Rhuvon Guest. Leiden: Brill, 1912.

_______. *Akhbār quḍāt Miṣr*. Edited by Richard J. H. Gottheil. Paris: P. Geuthner, 1908.

Kulaynī (d. 329/940-1), Muḥammad b. Yaʿqūb al-. *al-Kāfī*. 4th ed. Tehran: Dār al-Kutub al-Islāmiyya, 1999.

Majlisī (d. 1110/1698), Muḥammad Bāqir al-. *Biḥār al-anwār*. Edited by Jawād al-ʿAlawī. Tehran: Dār al-Kutub al-Islāmiyya, 1957–1973.

Marrākushī (d. circa 669/1270), ʿAbd al-Wāḥid al-. *Wathāʾiq al-Murābiṭīn waʾl-Muwaḥḥidīn*. Edited by Ḥusayn Muʾnis. Ẓāhir: Maktabat al-Thaqāfa al-Dīniyya, 1997.

Māwardī (d. 450/1058), Abū al-Ḥasan al-. *al-Nukat waʾl-ʿuyūn*. Edited by Ibn ʿAbd al-Maqṣūd b. ʿAbd al-Raḥīm. Beirut: Dār al-Kutub al-ʿIlmiyya, 1992.

_______. *Naṣīḥat al-mulūk al-mansūb ilā Abī al-Ḥasan al-Māwardī*. Edited by Fuʾād ʿAbd al- Munʿim Aḥmad. Alexandria: Muʾassasat Shabāb al-Jāmiʿa, 1988.

_______. *Tashīl al-naẓar wa-taʿjīl al-ẓafar*. Edited by R. al-Sayyid. Beirut: Dār al-ʿUlūm al-ʿArabiyya, 1987.

_______. *al-Aḥkām al-sulṭāniyya waʾl-wilāyāt al-dīniyya*. Cairo: Muṣṭafā al-Bābī al-Ḥalabī, 1966. 1978 Cairo Edition: Cairo: al-Maktaba al-Tawfīqiyya, 1978.

_______. *Adab al-dunyā waʾl-dīn*. Edited by Muṣṭafā Saqqā. Cairo: Maṭbaʿat Muṣṭafā al-Bābī al-Ḥalabī, 1973.

_______. *Adab al-qāḍī*. Edited by Muḥyī Hilāl al-Sarḥān. Baghdad: Maṭbaʿat al-Irshād/ Maṭbaʿat al-ʿĀnī/Dīwān al-Awqāf, 1971-2.

Marwazī, Isḥāq b. Manṣūr al-Kawsaj al- (comp.). *Masāʾil al-Imām Aḥmad b. Ḥanbal wa-Isḥāq b. Rāhawayh*. Medina: Islamic University, 2002.

Mīrkhwānd/Mīr Khvānd (d. 903/1498), Muḥammad b. Khāvandshāh. *Tarīkh-i Rawẓat al-ṣafāʾ*. Tehran: Markazī-yi Khayyām Pīrūz, 1959–60.

Maʿmar b. Rāshid (d. 153/770), Abū ʿUrwa al-Baṣrī. *The Expeditions: An Early Biography of Muḥammad*. Translated by Sean Anthony. New York: New York University Press, 2014.

Mubarrad (d. 286/900), Abū al-ʿAbbās Muḥammad b. Yazīd al-. *al-Kāmil fī ʾl-lugha waʾl-adab*. Edited by Muḥammad Abū al-Faḍl Ibrāhīm. 3rd ed. Cairo: Dār al-Fikr al-ʿArabī, 1997.

Muḥāsibī (d. 243/857), al-Ḥārith b. Asad al-. *al-Baʿth waʾl-nushūr*. Edited by Muḥammad ʿĪd Riḍwān. Beirut: Dār al-Kutub al-ʿIlmiyya, 1406/1987.

_______. *Kitāb al-Tawahhum*. Edited and translated by André Roman. Paris: Librairie Klincksieck, 1978.

Muzanī (d. 264/878), Abū Ibrāhīm Ismāʿīl b. Yaḥyā al-. *Mukhtaṣar al-Muzanī fī furūʿ al-Shāfiʿiyya*. Edited by Muḥammad ʿAbd al-Qādir al-Shāhīn. Beirut: Dār al-Kutub al-ʿIlmiyya, 1998.

Narshakhī (d. 348/959), Abū Bakr Muḥammad b. Jaʿfar al-. *Tārīkh-i Bukhārā*. Translated by Abū Naṣr Aḥmad b. Muḥammad b. Naṣr al-Qubāwī. Edited by Mudarris Raẓavī. Tehran: Kitābfurūshī-yi Sanāʾī, 1984.

Nasāʾī (d. 303/915), Aḥmad b. ʿAlī al-. *Sunan al-Nasāʾī bi-sharḥ al-Ḥāfiẓ Jalāl al-Dīn al-Suyūṭī*. Beirut: Dār al-Fikr, 1930.

Nasafī (d. 537/1142), Najm al-Dīn ʿUmar b. Muḥammad b. Aḥmad al-. *al-Qand fī dhikr ʿulamāʾ Samarqand*. Edited by Yūsuf al-Hādī. Tehran: Āʾīna-yi Mīrāth (Mirʾāt al-Turāth), 1999.

Nawawī (d. 676/1271), Yaḥyā b. Sharaf al-. *Minhāj al-ṭālibīn wa-ʿumdat al-muftīn*. Edited by Muḥammad Ṭāhir Shaʿban. Beirut: Dār al-Minhāj, 2005.

Niẓām al-Mulk (d. 485/1092). *The Book of Government or Rules for Kings*. Translated by Hubert Darke. London: Routledge and Kegan Paul, 1978.

________. *Siyar al-mulūk = Siyāsatnāma*. Edited by Hubert Darke. Tehran: Bungāh-i Tarjama va Nashr-i Kitāb, 1962.

Nuwayrī (d. 733/1333), Shihāb al-Dīn al-. *Nihāyat al-arab fī funūn al-adab*. Cairo: al-Muʾassasa al-Miṣriyya al-ʿĀmma, 1923–.

Qāḍī ʿIyāḍ b. Mūsā (d. 544/1149). *Tartīb al-madārik wa-taqrīb al-masālik li-maʿrifat aʿlām madhhab Mālik*. Edited by M. Bencherifa. Rabat: Wizārat al-Awqāf wa'l-Shuʾūn al-Islāmiyya, 1403/1983.

Qalqashandī (d. 821/1418), Aḥmad b. ʿAlī al-. *Ṣubḥ al-aʿshā*. Cairo: Dār al-Kutub al-Khidīwiyya, 1913–1922.

Qudūrī (d. 428/1037), Abū al-Ḥusayn al-. *Tajrīd (al-Mawsūʿa al-fiqhiyya al-muqārana)*. Edited by Muḥammad Aḥmad al-Sirāj and ʿAlī Jumuʿa Muḥammad. Cairo: Dār al-Salām, 2004.

Qurṭubī (d. 671/1272), Muḥammad b. Aḥmad al-. *Tanbīh al-ghāfilīn*. Edited by Haytham Khalīfa al-Ṭuʿaymī. Beirut: al-Maktaba al-ʿAṣriyya, 1427/2006.

________. *al-Tadhkira fī aḥwāl al-mawtā wa-umūr al-ākhira*. Edited by Yūsuf ʿAlī Badīwī. Damascus: Dār Ibn Kathīr, 1999.

Rāfiʿī (623/1226), ʿAbd al-Karīm al-. *al-Muḥarrar fī al-fiqh al-Shāfiʿī*. Edited by Muḥammad Ḥasan Ismāʿīl. Beirut: Dār al-Kutub al-ʿIlmiyya, 2005.

________. *al-Fatḥ al-ʿazīz fī sharḥ al-Wajīz*. Edited by ʿAlī Muʿawwaḍ and ʿĀdil ʿAbd al-Mawjūd. Beirut: Dār al-Kutub al-ʿIlmiyya, 1997.

Rūyānī (d. 502/1108), ʿAbd al-Wāḥid b. Ismāʿīl al-. *Baḥr al-madhhab fī furūʿ madhhab al-Imām al-Shāfiʿī*. Edited by Aḥmad ʿIzzū ʿInāya al-Dimashqī. Beirut: Dār Iḥyāʾ al-Turāth al-ʿArabī, 2002.

Saḥnūn (d. 240/854), ʿAbd al-Salām b. Saʿīd al-, comp. *al-Mudawwana*. Riyadh: Wizārat al-Awqāf, n.d. Reprint of Cairo: Maṭbaʿat al-Saʿāda, 1906.

Samʿānī (d. 534/1140), Aḥmad b. Manṣūr al-. *al-Ansāb*. Hyderabad: Maṭbaʿat Majlis Dāʾirat al-Maʿārif al-ʿUthmāniyya, 1962–82.

Samarqandī (d. 373/983), Abū al-Layth Naṣr b. Muḥammad al-. *Baḥr al-ʿulūm*. Edited by Maḥmūd Maṭrajī. Beirut: Dār al-Fikr, n.d.

Samhūdī (d. 911/1506), ʿAlī b. ʿAbd Allāh al-. *Wafāʾ al-wafā bi-akhbār dār al-Muṣṭafā*. Edited by Qāsim al-Sāmmarāʾī. London: Muʾassasat al-Furqān, 2001.

Ṣanʿānī (d. 211/827), ʿAbd al-Razzāq al-. *al-Muṣannaf*. Edited by Ḥabīb al-Raḥmān Aʿẓamī. Beirut: al-Majlis al-ʿIlmī, 1970.

Sarakhsī (d. 483/1090), Shams al-Aʾimma al-. *al-Mabsūṭ*. Edited by Khalīl al-Mays. Beirut: Dār al-Fikr, 2000.

Shaʿbī (d. 499/1106), ʿAbd al-Raḥmān b. Qāsim al-. *al-Aḥkām*. Beirut: Dār al-Gharb al-Islāmī, 1992.

Shāfiʿī (d. 204/820), Muḥammad b. Idrīs al-. *al-Umm*. Edited by Rifʿat Fawzī ʿAbd al-Muṭṭalib, al-Manṣūra: Dār al-Wafāʾ, 2001.

Shirbīnī (d. 922/1560), Muḥammad b. Aḥmad al-Khaṭīb al-. *Mughnī al-muḥtāj ilā maʿrifat maʿānī alfāẓ al-Minhāj*. Edited by Muḥammad Khalīl ʿAytanī. Beirut: Dār al-Maʿrifa, 1997.

Sharīf al-Murtaḍā (d. 436/1044), ʿAlam al-Hudā ʿAlī b. al-Ḥusayn al-. *al-Intiṣār*. Najaf: Manshūrāt al-Maṭbaʿa al-Ḥaydariyya, 1971.

Shaybānī (d. 189/804-5), Muḥammad b. al-Ḥasan al-. *al-Aṣl*. Edited by Mehmet Boynukalın. Qatar: Wizārat al-Awqāf and Beirut: Dār Ibn Ḥazm, 2012.

Sijistānī (d. 275/888), Abū Dāwūd al-. *Sunan Abī Dāwūd*. Edited by Muḥammad Muḥyī al-Dīn ʿAbd al-Ḥamīd. Beirut: al-Maktaba al-ʿAṣriyya, n.d.

Subkī (d. 771/1370), Tāj al-Dīn al-. *Ṭabaqāt al-Shāfiʿiyya al-kubrā*. Edited by Maḥmūd al-Ṭanāḥī and ʿAbd al-Fattāḥ al-Ḥulw. Cairo: Maṭbaʿat ʿĪsā al-Ḥalabī, 1964.

________. *Ṭabaqāt al-Shāfiʿīyya al-kubrā*. Edited by Maḥmūd Muḥammad al-Ṭanāḥī and ʿAbd al-Fattāḥ Muḥammad al-Ḥulw. Cairo: Maṭbaʿat ʿĪsā al-Bābī al-Ḥalabī, n.d.

Suhaylī (d. 581/1185), ʿAbd al-Raḥmān b. ʿAbd Allāh al-. *Al-Rawḍ al-unuf fī sharḥ al-Sīra al-Nabawiyya li-Ibn Hishām*. Edited by ʿAbd al-Raḥmān al-Wakīl. Cairo: Dār al-Kutub al-Ḥadītha, 1967–1970.

Ṭabarī (d. 310/923), Abū Jaʿfar Muḥammad b. Jarīr al-. *Jāmiʿ al-bayān ʿan taʾwīl āy al-Qurʾān*. Edited by ʿAlī ʿĀshūr. Beirut: Dār Iḥyāʾ al-Turāth al-ʿArabī, 2011.

________. *Taʾrīkh al-Ṭabarī = Taʾrīkh al-rusul waʾl-mulūk*. Edited by M. Faḍl Ibrāhīm. Cairo: Dār al-Maʿārif, 1960–1977.

Thaʿlabī (d. 427/1035), Aḥmad b. Muḥammad al-. *al-Kashf waʾl-bayān ʿan tafsīr al-Qurʾān*. Edited by Abū Muḥammad b. ʿĀshūr. Beirut: Dār Iḥyāʾ al-Turāth al-ʿArabī, 2002.

Tirmidhī (d. 279/892), Muḥammad b. ʿĪsā al-. *al-Jāmiʿ al-Ṣaḥīḥ wa-huwa Sunan al-Tirmidhī*. Edited by Muḥammad Fuʾād ʿAbd al- Bāqī. Beirut: Dār Iḥyāʾ al-Turāth al-ʿArabī, n.d.

Ṭūsī (d. 460/1067), Shaykh al-Ṭāʾifa Muḥammad b. al-Ḥasan al-. *Kitāb al-Khilāf*. Qum: Muʾassasat al-Nashr al-Islāmī, 1987–1996.

Ṭurayḥī (d. 1085/1674), Fakhr al-Dīn al-. *Majmaʿ al-baḥrayn*. Tehran: Murtaḍā, 1960.

Wakīʿ (d. 306/917), Muḥammad b. Khalaf. *Akhbār al-quḍāt*. Edited by ʿAbd al-ʿAzīz al-Marāghī. Cairo: al-Maktaba al-Tijāriyya al-Kubrā, 1947–1950. 1980 Beirut edition: Beirut: ʿĀlam al-Kutub, 1980. 2001 Beirut Edition: Edited by Saʿīd Muḥammad al-Laḥḥām. Beirut: ʿĀlam al-Kutub, 2001.

Wansharīsī (d. 914/1508), Aḥmad b. Yaḥyā al-. *al-Miʿyār al-muʿrib waʾl-jāmiʿ al-mughrib ʿan fatāwā ahl Ifrīqiya waʾl-Andalus waʾl-Maghrib*. Edited by Muḥammad Ḥajjī et al. Rabat: Wizārat al-Awqāf waʾl-Shuʾūn al-Islāmiyya, 1401/1981.

Yaḥyā b. Ādam al-Qurashī (d. 203/818). *Kitāb al-Kharāj*. Edited by Aḥmad Muḥammad Shākir. Cairo: al-Maṭbaʿa al-Salafiyya, 1929.

Yāqūt b. ʿAbd Allāh al-Ḥamawī (d. 626/1229). *Muʿjam al-buldān*. Beirut: Dār Ṣādir, 1955. Cairo Edition: Edited by Muḥammad Amīn al-Khānjī. Cairo: Maṭbaʿat al-Saʿāda, 1906.

________. *Marāṣid al-iṭṭilāʿ fī maʿrifat asmāʾ al-amkina waʾl-biqāʿ*. Edited by Muḥammad al-Bajāwī. Cairo: Dār Iḥyāʾ al-Kutub al-ʿArabiyya, 1954.

________. *Kitāb al-Mushtarak waḍʿan waʾl-muftaraq ṣuqʿan*. Published as *Jacut's Moschtarik, das ist: Lexicon geographischer Homonyme*. Bremen, Germany: Druck und Verlag der Dieterichschen Buchhandlung, 1846.

Zabīdī (d. 1206/1791), Muḥammad b. Muḥammad al-Murtaḍā al-. *al-Tāj al-ʿarūs min jawāhir al-Qāmūs*. Edited by ʿAlī Shīrī. Beirut: Dār al-Fikr, 1994.

Zamakhsharī (d. 538/1144), Abū al-Qāsim al-. *Rabīʿ al-abrār wa-nuṣūṣ al-akhyār*. Baghdad: Wizārat al-Awqāf, 1976–1982.

SECONDARY SOURCES

Abbès, Makram. *Al-Māwardī: De l'éthique du prince et du gouvernement de l'état*. Paris: Les Belles Lettres, 2015.

Ābidī, ʿAlī Ḥājī. *al-Waqf wa 'l-mawqūfāt Amīr al-Mu'minīn*. Mashhad: Majmaʿ al-Buḥūth al-Islāmiyya, 1435: 78–92.

Abou El Fadl, Khaled. *Rebellion and Violence in Islamic Law*. Cambridge: Cambridge University Press, 2001.

Abu-Rabia, Aref. "Paternity Suits in Tribal Society in the Middle East." *US-China Law Review* 9, no. 29 (2012): 29–44.

Adang, Camilla, Hassan Ansari, Maribel Fierro, and Sabine Schmidtke, eds. *Accusations of Unbelief in Islam: A Diachronic Perspective on* Takfīr. Leiden: Brill, 2016.

Aḥmad, Fuʾād ʿAbd al-Munʿim. "Muqaddimat al-dirāsa waʾl-taḥqīq." In *Kitāb Durar al-sulūk fī siyāsat al-mulūk*. Edited by Fuʾād ʿAbd al-Munʿim Aḥmad. Riyadh: Dār al-Waṭan, 1997: 7–52.

______. "Muqaddimat al-taḥqīq waʾl-dirāsa." In *Naṣīḥat al-mulūk al-mansūb ilā Abī 'l-Ḥasan al-Māwardī*. Alexandria: Muʾassasat Shabāb al-Jāmiʿa, 1988: 5–33.

______. *Abū l-Ḥasan al-Māwardī wa-kitāb Naṣīḥat al-mulūk*. Alexandria: Muʾassasat Shabāb al-Jāmiʿa, n.d.

Ahmed, Asad. *The Religious Elite of the Early Islamic Ḥijāz: Five Prosopographical Case Studies*. Oxford: Unit for Prosopographical Research, 2011.

Ahmed, Shahab. *What Is Islam? The Importance of Being Islamic*. Princeton: Princeton University Press, 2015.

ʿAjlān, ʿAbd Allāh al-. *al-Qaḍāʾ biʾl-qarāʾin al-muʿāṣira*. Riyadh: Jāmiʿat al-Imām Muḥammad b. Saʿūd al-Islāmiyya, 2006.

Akbar, Ilhām Sirāj ʿUmar. *Bilād Yanbuʿ: Dirāsa taʾrīkhiyya ḥiḍāriyya (363–923/973–1517)*. Medina: al-Ḥumayḍī, 2015

Albānī, Muḥammad Nāṣir al-Dīn al-. *Irwāʾ al-ghalīl*. 2nd ed. Beirut: al-Maktab al-Islāmī, 1985.

Ali, Saleh E. el-. "Muslim Estates in the Hidjaz in the First Century AH." *Journal of the Economic and Social History of the Orient* 2 (1959): 247–61.

Arkoun, Mohammed. *Essais sur la pensée islamique.* 3rd ed. Volume 23 of *Islam d'hier et d'aujourd'hui*. Paris: Éditions Maisonneuve et Larose, 1984.

_______."L'Éthique musulmane d'après Māwardī." *Revue des études islamiques* 31 (1964): 1–31. Reprinted in *Essais sur la pensée islamique.* 3rd ed. Volume 23 of *Islam d'hier et d'aujourd'hui*. Paris: Éditions Maisonneuve et Larose, 1984: 251–81.

_______. "Contribution à l'étude du lexique de l'éthique musulmane." *Bulletin d'études orientales* 22 (1969): 205–39.

_______. "Éthique et histoire d'après les Tajarib al-Umam." *Atti del terzo Congresso di studi arabi e islamici.* Naples: Instituto Universitario Orientale, 1967: 83–112.

Afsaruddin, Asma. "Exegeses of 'Moderation': Negotiating the Boundaries of Pluralism and Exclusion." *The Good Society* 16 (2007): 1–9.

Asif, Manan Ahmed. *A Book of Conquest: The* Chachnama *and Muslim Origins in South Asia*. Cambridge: Harvard University Press, 2016.

_______. "The Long Thirteenth Century of the *Chachnama*." *The Indian Economic and Social History Review* 49, no. 4 (2012): 467–70.

Azam, Hina. *Sexual Violation in Islamic Law: Substance, Evidence, and Procedure.* Cambridge York: Cambridge University Press, 2015.

Bagley, F. R. C. *Ghazālī's Book of Counsel for Kings.* London: Oxford University Press, 1964.

Bahrami, Mehdi. "A Gold Medal in the Freer Gallery of Art." In *Archaeologica Orientalia in Memoriam Ernst Herzfeld.* Edited by George C. Miles. Locust Valley, New York: J.J. Augustin, 1952: 5–20.

Bahri, Fethi. "Abū l-ʿArabet al-Khuchanī, deux auteurs et une oeuvre." *IBLA* 190 (2002): 187–202.

Basanta, Fernando N. Velázquez. "Retrato jaṭibiano del poeta y Qāḍī l-ŷamāʿa de Granada Abū Ŷaʿfar Aḥmad b. Furkūn (el abuelo)." *Revista del Centro de Estudios Históricos de Granada y su Reino* 5 (1991): 47–53.

Bell, Abraham and Gideon Parchomovsky. "Givings." *The Yale Law Journal* 111, no. 3 (2001): 547–618.

Benouis, Mustafa. "L'Organisation du *Qaḍā'* sous les Almohades." In *Los almohades: problemas y perspectivas*. Edited by Patrice Cressier, Maribel Fierro, and Luis Molina. Madrid: Consejo Superior de Investigaciones Científicas, 2005. 1:505–24.

Bentlage, Björn. "Legislating for the Benefit of Children Born Out of Wedlock." *Die Welt des Islams* 55 (2015): 378–412.

Bernards, Monique and John Nawas. "The Geographical Distribution of Muslim Jurists during the First Four Centuries AH." *Islamic Law and Society* 10, no. 2 (2003): 168–81.

Bosworth, C. E. "An Early Arabic Mirror for Princes: Ṭāhir Dhū l-Yamīnain's Epistle to His Son ʿAbdallāh (206/821)." *Journal of Near Eastern Studies* 29 (1970): 25–41.

_______. "The Tahirids and Arabic Culture." *Journal of Semitic Studies* 14 (1969): 45–79.

_______. "The Rise of the Karamiyyah in Khurasan." *The Muslim World* 50, no. 1 (1960): 5–14.

Bravmann, M. M. "Allah's Liberty to Punish or Forgive." *Der Islam* 47 (1971): 236–37.

Bray, Julia. "Literary Approaches to Medieval and Early Modern Arabic Biography." *Journal of the Royal Asiatic Society* 20 (2010): 237–53.

Brockopp, Jonathan. "Contradictory Evidence and the Exemplary Scholar: The Lives of Saḥnūn b. Saʿīd (d. 854)." *International Journal of Middle Eastern Studies* 43 (2011): 115–32.

Bujnūrdī, Muḥammad Ḥasan al-. *al-Qawāʿid al-fiqhiyya*. Edited by Mahdī al-Mihrīzī and Muḥammad Ḥusayn al-Dirāyatī. Qum: Dalīl-i Mā, 1424/2003-4.

Būrnū, Muḥammad Ṣidqī b. Aḥmad al-. *Mawsūʿat al-qawāʿid al-fiqhiyya*. 3rd ed. Beirut: Dār al-Risāla al-ʿĀlamiyya, 2015.

Cano, Pedro. "Algunos datos del tratado notarial de Abū al-Qāsim Ibn Salmūn (d. 767/1366)." *Philologia Hispalensis* 5, no. 1 (1990): 233–44.

Carmona, Alfonso. "Le malékisme et les conditions requises pour l'exercice de la judicature." *Islamic Law and Society* 7, no. 2 (2000): 122–58.

_______. "Los *ādāb al-quḍāt* o normas de conducta del juezislámico." In *Homenaje al Profesor Juan Torres Fontes*. Murcia: Universidad de Murcia, 1987.

Cheikh-Moussa, Abdallah. "L'historien et la littérature arabe médiévale." *Arabica* 43 (1996): 152–88.

Cheneb, Mohammed Ben, ed. and trans. *Classes des savants de l'Ifrīqīya par Abu' l-ʿArab Moḥammed ben Aḥmed ben Tamīm et Moḥammed ben al-Ḥāriṯ ben Asad al-Ḫošanī*. Paris: E. Leroux, 1915. Reprinted Alger: E. Leroux, 1920.

Coope, Jessica A. *The Martyrs of Córdoba: Community and Family Conflict in an Age of Massive Conversion*. Lincoln: Nebraska University Press, 1995.

Cooperson, Michael. "Images Without Illustrations: The Visual Imagination in Classical Arabic Biography." In *Islamic Art and Arabic Literature: Textuality and Visuality in the Islamic World*. Edited by Oleg Grabar and Cynthia Robinson. Princeton: Mark Wiener Publishers, 2001: 7–20.

Coulson, Noel J. "Doctrine and Practice in Islamic law: One Aspect of the Problem." *Bulletin of the School of Oriental and African Studies* 18 (1956): 211–26.

Crone, Patricia. *Roman, Provincial and Islamic Law: The Origins of the Islamic Patronate*. Cambridge: Cambridge University Press, 1987.

Crone, Patricia and Martin Hinds. *God's Caliph: Religious Authority in the First Centuries of Islam*. Cambridge: Cambridge University Press, 1986.

Darke, Hubert. *The Book of Government or Rules for Kings*. London: Routledge and Kegan Paul, 1978.

Darling, Linda T. *A History of Social Justice and Political Power in the Middle East: The Circle of Justice from Mesopotamia to Globalization*. London: Routledge, 2013.

________. "Social Cohesion (*ʿAsabiyya*) and Justice in the Late Medieval Middle East." *Comparative Studies in Society and History* 49 (2007): 329–57.

________. "'Do Justice, Do Justice, For That Is Paradise': Middle Eastern Advice for Indian Muslim Rulers." *Comparative Studies of South Asia, Africa and the Middle East* 22 (2002): 3–19.

Doutté, Edmond. *Missions au Maroc: En tribu*. Paris: P. Geuthner, 1914.

Eich, Thomas. "Constructing Kinship in Sunni Islamic Legal Texts." In *Islam and Assisted Reproductive Technologies: Sunni and Shia Perspectives*. Edited by M.C. Inhorn and S. Tremayne. New York: Berghahn Books, 2012: 27–52.

Elad, Amikam. *The Rebellion of Muḥammad al-Nafs al-Zakiyya in 145/762: Ṭālibids and Early ʿAbbāsids in Conflict*. Leiden: Brill, 2015.

El Shamsy, Ahmed. *The Canonization of Islamic Law: A Social and Intellectual History*. New York: Cambridge University Press, 2013.

Eskridge, Jr., William N. *Interpreting Law: A Primer on How to Read Statutes and the Constitution*. St. Paul, MN: Foundation Press, 2016.

Ess, Josef van. *Chiliastische Erwartungen und die Versuchung der Göttlichkeit: Der Kalif al-Ḥākim (386–411 H.)*. Heidelberg: Carl Winter, 1977.

_______. *Theologie und Geschichte im 2. und 3. Jahrhundert Hidschra: Eine Geschichte des religiösen Denkens im Islam*. Berlin: de Gruyter, 1991–1997.

_______. *Die Erkenntnislehre des ʿAḍudaddīn al-Īcī: Übersetzung und Kommentar des ersten Buches seiner Mawāqif*. Wiesbaden: Franz Steiner Verlag, 1966.

Fadel, Mohammad. "Rules, Judicial Discretion and the Rule of Law in Naṣrid Granada: An Analysis of *al-Ḥadīqa al-mustaqilla al-naḍra fī al-fatāwā al-ṣādira ʿan ʿulamāʾ al-ḥaḍra*." In *Islamic Law: Theory and Practice*. Edited by Robert Gleave and Eugenia Kermeli. London: I.B. Tauris, 2001. 49–86.

_______. "Two Women, One Man: Knowledge, Power, and Gender in Medieval Sunni Legal Thought." *International Journal of Middle East Studies* 29, no. 2 (1997): 185–204.

Feldman, Noah. "Does *Shariah* Mean the Rule of Law?" *The New York Times*. March 16, 2008.

Fierro, Maribel. "Los cadíes de Córdoba de ʿAbd al-Raḥmān III (r. 300/912-350/961)." In *Cadíes y cadiazgo en al-Andalus y el Magreb medieval*. In *Estudios Onomástico-Biográficos de al-Andalus*. Edited by Rachid El Hour. Madrid: Consejo Superior de Investigaciones Científicas, 2012: 18:65–98.

_______. "Plants, Mary the Copt, Abraham, Donkeys and Knowledge: Again on Batinism During the Umayyad Caliphate in al-Andalus." In *Differenz und Dynamikim Islam: Festschrift für Heinz Halm zum 70. Geburtstag*. Würzburg: Ergon, 2012. 125–44.

_______. "Ulemas en las ciudades andalusíes: Religión, política y prácticas sociales." In *Congreso Internacional Escenarios Urbanos de al-Andalus y el Occidente musulmán, 1º. 2010 Vélez-Málaga*. Ed. Virgilio Martínez Enamorado. Málaga: Iniciativa Urbana 'De Toda La Villa', 2011: 137–67.

_______. "Idraʾū al-Ḥudūd bi-al-Shubuhāt: When Lawful Violence Meets Doubt." *Hawwa* 5, nos. 2–3 (2007): 208–38.

———. "La política religiosa de ʿAbd al-Raḥmān III." *Al-Qanṭara* 25 (2004): 119–56.

———. "Tres familias andalusíes de época omeya apodadas Banū Ziyād." In *Estudios Onomástico-Biográficos de al-Andalus* 5. Edited by M. Marín and J. Zanón. Madrid, 1992. 85–141.

———. *La Heterodoxia en al-Andalus durante el periodo omeya*. Madrid: Instituto Hispano-Árabe de Cultura, 1987.

Franz-Murphy, Gladys. "The Reinstitution of Courts in Early Islamic Egypt." *Bulletin de la société archéologique d'Alexandrie* 47 (2003): 71–84.

———. "A Comparison of Arabic and Earlier Egyptian Contract Formularies, Part I: The Arabic Contracts from Egypt (3rd/9th–5th/11th Centuries)." *Journal of Near Eastern Studies* 40, no. 3 (1981): 203–25.

Frye, Richard N. *The History of Bukhara: Translated from the Persian Abridgment of the Arabic Original by Narshakhi.* Princeton: Markus Wiener, 2007.

Garulo, Teresa. "Notas sobre *muŷūn* en al-Andalus: El capítulo VII del *Nafḥ al-ṭīb* de al-Maqqarī." *Anaquel de Estudios Árabes* 26 (2015): 93–120.

Ghaly, Mohammed. "Biomedical Scientists as Co-Muftis: Their Contribution to Contemporary Islamic Bioethics." *Die Welt des Islams* 55 (2015): 286–311.

Goitein, Shelomo Dov "A Turning Point in the History of the Muslim State (Apropos of the *Kitāb al-ṣaḥāba* of Ibn al-Muqaffaʿ)." In *Studies in Islamic History and Institutions.* Leiden: Brill, 1968: 149–67

Griffel, Frank. "Review Picken, *Spiritual Purification.*" *Ilahiyat Studies* 2, no. 1 (2011): 126–32.

———. *Apostasie und Toleranz im Islam: Die Entwicklung zu al-Ġazālī's Urteil gegen die Philosophie und die Reaktionen der Philosophen.* Leiden: Brill, 2000.

Grignaschi, Mario. "La «*Siyâsatu-l-ʿâmmiyya*» et l'influence iranienne sur la pensée politique islamique." In *Acta Iranica.* Vol. 3 of *Hommages et Opera Minora Monumentum H. S. Nyberg.* Leiden: Brill, 1975: 33–286.

Hallaq, Wael. *The Origins and Evolution of Islamic Law.* Cambridge: Cambridge University Press, 2005.

———. "The *Qāḍī's Dīwān* (*Sijill*) before the Ottomans." *Bulletin of the School of Oriental and African Studies* 61, no. 3 (1998): 415–36.

_______. "Model *Shurūṭ* Works and the Dialectic of Doctrine and Practice." *Islamic Law and Society* 2, no. 2 (1995): 109–34.

Hāshimī, Maḥmūd al-. "Ḥukm al-qāḍī bi-ʿilmih." *Fiqh Ahl al-Bayt* 16 (1420/2000): 11–84.

Heck, P. L. "Law in ʿAbbasid Political Thought from Ibn al-Muqaffaʿ (d. 139/756) to Qudāma b. Jaʿfar (d. 337/948)." In *ʿAbbasid Studies: Occasional Papers of the School of ʿAbbasid Studies, Cambridge, 6-10 July, 2002*. Edited by James Montgomery. Leuven: Peeters, 2004. 83–109.

Hentati, Nejmeddine. "Mais le cadi tranche-t-il?" *Islamic Law and Society* 14 (2007): 180–203.

Huitema, Taede. *De voorspraak (shafaʿa) in den Islam*. Leiden: Brill, 1936.

Ibrahim, Abdullahi Ali. *Assaulting with Words. Popular Discourse and the Bridle of Sharīʿah*. Evanston, IL: Northwestern University Press, 1994.

Jaques, R. Kevin. "The Other Rabīʿ: Biographical Traditions and the Development of Early Shafiʿī Authority." *Islamic Law and Society* 14, no. 2 (2007): 143–79.

János, Jany. "The Origins of the Kalīlah wa-Dimnah: Reconsideration in the Light of Sasanian Legal History." *Journal of the Royal Asiatic Society* 22, nos. 3–4 (2012): 505–18.

Jāsir, Ḥamad al-. *Bilād Yanbuʿ: Lamaḥāt ta'rīkhiyya jughrāfiyya wa-inṭibāʿāt khāṣṣa*. Riyadh: Dār al-Yamāma, 1967.

Johansen, Baber. "The Muslim *Fiqh* as a Sacred Law." In *Contingency in a Sacred Law: Legal and Ethical Norms in the Muslim Fiqh*. Leiden: Brill, 1998. 1–76.

_______. "Formes de langage et fonctions publiques: stéréotypes, témoins et offices dans la preuve par écrit en droit musulman." *Arabica* 44, no. 3 (1997): 333–76.

_______. "Wahrheit und Geltungsanspruch: Zur Begründung und Begrenzung der Autorität des Qadi-Urteils im islamischen Recht." In *La Giustizia nell'Alto Medieoevo (Secoli IX-XI)*. Edited by the Centro Italiano di Studi sull'Alto Medioevo. Spoleto: Presso la Sede del Centro, 1997: 975–1065.

_______. "Zum Prozessrecht der *ʿuqūbāt*." *ZDMG*, Supplement 3:1, XIX. Deutscher Orientalistentag (1977): 429. Reprinted in *Contingency in a Sacred Law: Legal and Ethical Norms in the Muslim* Fiqh. Leiden: Brill, 1999: 421–33.

Ju-kua, Chau. *Chu-fan-chï*. Translated by Friedrich Hirth and W.W. Rockhill. St. Petersberg: Printing Office of the Imperial Academy of Sciences, 1911.

Juynboll, G. H. A. *Encyclopedia of Canonical Ḥadīth*. Leiden: Brill, 2007.

Khaṭīb, ʿAbd al-Karīm Maḥmūd al-. *al-Yanbuʿ*. Riyadh: Jāmiʿat al-Malik Saʿūd: 1993.

Khomeini, Ayatollah Ruhollah. *Taḥrīr al-wasīla*. Najaf: Maṭbaʿat al-Ādāb, 1967.

Kister, M.J. "The Battle of the Ḥarra: Some Socio-Economic Aspects." In *Studies in Memory of Gaston Wiet*. Edited by Myriam Rosen Ayalon. Jerusalem: Hebrew University of Jerusalem, 1977: 33–49.

________. "Land Property and Jihād." *Journal of the Economic and Social History of the Orient* 34, no. 3 (1991): 270–311.

Knatchbull, Wyndham. *Kalila and Dimna or the Fables of Bidpai*. Oxford: W. Baxter, 1819.

Kristó-Nagy, István T. *La pensée d'Ibn al-Muqaffaʿ: Un «agent double» dans le monde persan et arabe*. Paris: Éditions de Paris, 2013.

Kūfī, ʿAlī b. Ḥāmid b. Abī Bakr al-. *Fatḥnāma-i Sind al-maʿrūf bi Chachnāma*. Edited by ʿUmar b. Muḥammad Dāʾūdpota. Hyderabad: Majlis Makhṭūṭāt-i Fārsiya, 1939.

________. *The Chachnamah: An Ancient History of Sind, Giving the Hindu period down to the Arab Conquest*. Translated by Mirza Kalichbeg Fredunbeg. Delhi: Idara-i Adabiyat-i Delli, 1979 [Orig. publication year 1900].

Lagardère, Vincent. *Histoire et société en Occident Musulman au Moyen Âge: Analyse du Miʿyārd'al-Wanšarīsī*. Madrid, Casa de Velázquez, 1995.

Lambton, A. K. S. "Justice in the Medieval Persian Theory of Kingship." *Studia Islamica* 17 (1962): 91–119.

Landau-Tasseron, Ella. "Arabia." In *The New Cambridge History of Islam*. Edited by Chase F. Robinson. Cambridge: Cambridge University Press, 2010. 1:397–447.

Lane, Edward William. *Arabic-English Dictionary*. Edinburgh: Williams and Norgate, 1863.

Lange, Christian. *Paradise and Hell in Islamic Traditions*. Cambridge: Cambridge University Press, 2016.

________. *Locating Hell in Islamic Traditions*. Leiden: Brill, 2015.

________. *Justice, Punishment and the Medieval Muslim Imagination.* Cambridge: Cambridge University Press, 2008.

Lawson, Todd. *The Crucifixion and the Qur'an: A Study in the History of Muslim Thought.* Oxford: Oneworld, 2009.

Leder, Stefan. "Aspekte arabischer und persischer Fürstenspiegel: Legitimation, Fürstenethik, politische Vernunft." In *Specula principum.* Edited by Angela de Benedictis. Frankfurt: Vittorio Klostermann, 1999: 21–50.

Le Goff, Jacques. "Introduction." In *The Medieval Imagination.* Translated by Arthur Goldhammer. Chicago: University of Chicago Press, 1988.

Løkkegaard, Frede. *Islamic Taxation in the Classical Period.* Copenhagen: Branner and Korch, 1950.

Lowry, Joseph E. "The First Islamic Legal Theory: Ibn al-Muqaffaʿ on Interpretation, Authority, and the Structure of the Law." *Journal of the American Oriental Society* 128 (2008): 25–40.

M'hamed, Ahda. "Le droit coutumier des Ait Attad'Aoufous (Sud-Est Marocain)." *Awal. Cahiers d'Études Berbères* 24 (2001): 87–117.

Madelung, Wilferd. *The Succession to Muḥammad: A Study of the Early Caliphate.* Cambridge: Cambridge University Press, 1996.

Mallat, Chibli. "Introduction: On Islam and Democracy." In *Islam and Public Law: Classical and Contemporary Studies.* Edited by Chibli Mallat. London: Graham and Trotman, 1993: 1–11.

Marín, Manuela. "Signos visuales de la identidad andalusí." In *Tejer y vestir: de la antigüedad al islam.* Madrid: Consejo Superior de Investigaciones Científicas, 2001: 137–180.

________. *Mujeres en al-Andalus.* Estudios Onomástico-Biográficos de al-Andalus, vol. 11. Madrid: Consejo Superior de Investigaciones Científicas, 2000.

________. "*Šūrā* et *ahl al-šūrā* dans al-Andalus." *Studia Islamica* 62 (1985): 25–52.

Marlow, Louise. *Counsel for Kings: Wisdom and Politics in Tenth-Century Iran.* Edinburgh: Edinburgh University Press, 2016.

________. *Hierarchy and Egalitarianism in Islamic Thought.* New York: Cambridge University Press, 1997.

Maróth, Miklós. *The Correspondence between Aristotle and Alexander the Great: An Anonymous Greek Novel in Letters in Arabic Translation.* Piliscsaba: The Avicenna Institute of Middle Eastern Studies, 2006.

Masud, Muhammad Khālid. "A Study of Wakīʿ's (d. 306/917) *Akhbār al-quḍāt*." In *The Law Applied: Contextualizing the Islamic Sharīʿa*. Edited by Wolfhart Heinrichs et al. London: I.B. Tauris, 2008: 116–27.

Masud, Muhammad Khalid, Rudolph Peters, and David S. Powers. "Qadis and Their Courts: An Historical survey." In *Dispensing Justice in Islam: Qadis and their Judgments*. Edited by Muhammad Khalid Masud, Rudolph Peters, and David S. Powers. Leiden: Brill, 2006: 1–44.

Mermelstein, Arie and Shalom E. Holtz. "Introduction: The Divine Courtroom in Comparative Perspective." In *The Divine Courtroom in Comparative Perspective*. Edited by Ari Mermelstein et al. Leiden: Brill, 2014: 1–5.

Messick, Brinkley. *The Calligraphic State: Textual Domination and History in a Muslim Society*. Berkeley: University of California Press, 1993.

Mitter, Ulrike. "Problemen van het onderzoek naar ontleningen aan niet-Arabische rechtsstelsels in het ontstaan en de ontwikkeling van het Islamitisch recht." *Sharqiyyat* 9, no. 2 (1997): 107–23.

Mnookin, Robert and Lewis Kornhauser. "Bargaining in the Shadow of the Law: The Case of Divorce." *Yale Law Journal* 88, no. 5 (1979): 950–97.

Modarressi, Hossein. "Essential Islam: The Minimum that a Muslim is Required to Acknowledge." In *Accusations of Unbelief in Islam: A Diachronic Perspective on Takfīr*. Edited by Camilla Adang, Hassan Ansari, Maribel Fierro, and Sabine Schmidtke. Leiden: Brill, 2016: 395–412.

________. *Tradition and Survival: A Bibliographical Survey of Early Shīʿite Literature*. Oxford: Oneworld, 2003.

________. *Kharāj in Islamic Law*. London: Anchor, 1983.

________. "Facts or Fables: Muslims' Evaluation of Historical Memory" (forthcoming).

Mottahedeh, Roy P. "The Eastern Travels of Solomon: Reimagining Persepolis and the Iranian Past." In *Law and Tradition in Classical Islamic Thought: Studies in Honor of Professor Hossein Modarressi*. Edited by Michael Cook, Najam Haider, Intisar A. Rabb, and Asma Sayeed. New York: Palgrave Macmillan, 2013: 247–67.

________. *Loyalty and Leadership in an Early Islamic Society*. Princeton: Princeton University Press, 1980. 2nd ed. London: I. B. Tauris, 2001.

______. *The Mantle of the Prophet: Religion and Politics in Iran*. New York: Simon and Schuster/Pantheon, 1985, 1986. Reprinted Oxford: Oneworld, 2000.

______. "The Transmission of Learning: The Role of the Islamic Northeast." In *Madrasa: La transmission du savoir dans le monde musulman*. Edited by Nicole Grandin and Marc Gaborieau. Paris: Éditions Arguments, 1997: 61–70.

Motzki, Harold. "The Role of Non-Arab Converts in the Development of Early Islamic Law." *Islamic Law and Society* 6, no. 3 (1999): 293–317.

Müller, Christian. "Écrire por établir la preuve orale en Islam: la pratique d'un tribunal à Jérusalem au XIVe siècle." In *Les outils de la pensé: Étude historique et comparative des "textes."* Edited by Akira Saito and Yusuke Nakamura. Paris: Maison des Sciences de l'homme, 2010: 63–97.

______. *Gerichtspraxis im Stadtstaat Córdoba: zum Recht der Gesellschaft in einer malikitish-islamischen Rechtstradition des 5./11. Jahrhunderts*. Leiden: Brill, 1999.

Nawas, John. "The Emergence of Fiqh as a Distinct Discipline and the Ethnic Identity of the Fuqahā' in Early and Classical Islam." In *Studies in Arabic and Islam: Proceedings of the 19th Congress, Halle 1998*. Edited by S. Leder, H. Kilpatrick, B. Martel-Thoumian, and H. Schonig. Leuven: Peters, 2002: 491–99.

Otto-Dorn, Katharina. "Das seldschukische Thronbild." In *Die islamische Welt zwischen Mittelalter und Neuzeit: Festschrift für Hans Robert Roemer zum 65. Geburtstag*. Edited by Ulrich Haarmann et al. Wiesbaden: Steiner, 1979. 503–22.

Paul, Jürgen. *Lokale und imperiale Herrschaft im Iran des 12. Jahrhunderts. Herrschaftspraxis und Konzepte*. Wiesbaden: Reichert Verlag, 2016.

______. *Herrscher, Gemeinwesen, Vermittler: Ostiran und Transoxanien in vormongolischer Zeit*. Beirut: Franz Steiner Verlag, Stuttgart, 1996.

______. "The Histories of Samarqand." *Studia Iranica* 22 (1993): 69–92.

Pellat, Charles. *Ibn al-Muqaffaʿ 'conseilleur' du calife*. Paris: G.P. Maisonneuve et Larose, 1976.

______. "Seriousness and Humour in Early Islam." *Islamic Studies* 2 (1963): 353–62.

Posner, Richard A. "Statutory Interpretation—In the Classroom and in the Courtroom." *University of Chicago Law Review* 50 (1983): 800–22.

Powers, David S. "*Kadijustiz* or *Qāḍī* Justice? A Paternity Suit from Fourteenth-Century Morocco," *Islamic Law and Society* 1 (1994): 332–66.

Powers, David. *Law, Society and Culture in the Maghrib, 1300–1500*. Cambridge: Cambridge University Press, 2002.

Rabb, Intisar A. "Society and Propriety: The Cultural Construction of Defamation and Blasphemy as Crimes in Islamic Law." In *Accusations of Unbelief in Islam: A Diachronic Perspective on Takfīr*. Edited by Camilla Adang, et al. Leiden: Brill, 2016: 434–64.

________. *Doubt in Islamic Law: A History of Legal Maxims, Interpretation, and Islamic Criminal Law*. New York: Cambridge University Press, 2015.

________. "Against *Kadijustiz*: On the Negative Citation of Foreign Law." *Suffolk University Law Review* 48 (2015): 343–78.

Renaudot, Eusèbe. *Ancient Accounts of India and China by Two Mohammedan Travellers who Went to those Parts in the 9th Century*. London: S. Harding, 1733.

Rosenthal, Franz. *Humor in Early Islam*. Philadelphia: Brill, 1956.

Ruano, Delfina Serrano. "Paternity and Filiation According to the Jurists of Andalus: Legal Doctrines on Transgression of the Islamic Social Order." *Imago Temporis. Medium Aevum* 7 (2013): 59–75.

________. "La lapidación como castigo de las relaciones sexuales no legales (*zinā*) en el seno de la escuela malikí: doctrina, práctica legal y actitudes individuales frente al delito (ss. XI y XII)." *Al-Qanṭara* 26, no. 2 (2005): 449–73.

Sauvaget, Jean. *Aḥbār aṣ-Ṣīn wa l-Hind: Relation de la Chine et de l'Inde, rédigée en 851*. Paris: Belles Lettres, 1948.

Sayyid, Riḍwān al-. "Tamhīd: al-Ijtimāʿ al-basharī: Dirāsa fī ru'yat al-Māwardī al- ijtimāʿiyya." In *Tashīl al-naẓar wa-taʿjīl al-ẓafar*. Edited by Riḍwān al-Sayyid. Beirut: Dār al-ʿUlūm al-ʿArabiyya, 1987: 7–93.

Scalia, Antonin and Bryan A. Garner. *Reading Law*. St. Paul: Thompson/West, 2012.

Schacht, Joseph. "On the title of the *Fatāwā al-ʿĀlamgīriyya*." In *Iran and Islam: In Memory of the Late Vladimir Minorsky*, edited by C.E. Bosworth. Edinburgh: Edinburgh University Press, 1971: 475–78.

________. "Foreign Elements in Islamic Law." *Journal of Comparative Legislation and International Law* 32, nos. 3–4 (1950): 9–17.

Schimmel, Annemarie. *Mystical Dimensions of Islam.* Chapel Hill: North Carolina University Press, 1975.

Schneider, Irene. *Das Bild des Richters in der "adab al-qāḍī"-Literatur.* Frankfurt: Peter Lang, 1990.

Shabana, Ayman. "Law and Ethics in Islamic Bioethics: Nonmaleficence in Islamic Paternity Regulations." *Zygon* 48, no. 3 (2013): 709–31.

________. "Negation of Paternity in Islamic Law between *Liʿān* and DNA Fingerprinting." *Islamic Law and Society* 20, no. 3 (2013): 157–201.

________. "Paternity between Law and Biology: The Reconstruction of the Islamic Law of Paternity in the Wake of DNA Testing." *Zygon* 47, no. 1 (2012): 214–39.

Shaham, Ron. *The Expert Witness in Islamic Courts: Medicine and Crafts in the Service of Law.* Chicago: Chicago University Press, 2010.

Shaykha, Jumʿa. "Abū ʿAbd Allāh Muḥammad b. Ḥārith b. Asad al-Khushanī al-Ifrīqī al-Andalusī." *Cahiers de Tunisie* 26 (1978): 33–60.

Shurrāb, Muḥammad b. Muḥammad Ḥasan. *al-Maʿālim al-athīra fī al-sunna wa'l-sīra.* Damascus: Dār al-Qalam, 1991.

Smith, Jane Idleman and Yvonne Yazbeck Haddad. *The Islamic Understanding of Death and Resurrection.* New York: Oxford University Press, 2002.

Sonbol, Amira. "Jewish and Islamic Legal Traditions: Diffusions of Law." In *Gender in Judaism and Islam: Common Lives, Uncommon Heritage.* Edited by Firoozeh Kashani-Sabet and Beth S. Wenger. New York: New York University Press, 2015: 46–67.

Straface, Antonella. "An Ismāʿīlī interpretation of *šubbihalahum* (Qur. IV, 157) in the *Kitāb šağarat al-yaqīn.*" In *Authority, privacy and public order in Islam: Proceedings of the 22nd Congress of L'Union Européenne des Arabisants et Islamisants.* Edited by B. Michalak-Pikulska and A. Pikulski. Leuven: Peeters, 2006. 95–100.

Szombathy, Zoltár. *Mujūn: Libertinism in Mediaeval Muslim society and literature.* Warminster: Gibb Memorial Trust, 2013.

Tafazzoli, A. "Iranian Languages." In *History of Civilizations of Central Asia.* Edited by C.E. Bosworth and M.S. Asimov. Paris: United Nations Educational, 2000: 321–31.

Tillier, Mathieu. *L'invention du cadi. La justice des musulmans, des juifs et des chrétiens aux premiers siècles de l'Islam.* Paris: Publications de la Sorbonne, 2017.

_______. "The Qāḍī before the Judge: The Social Use of Eschatology in Muslim Courts." In *The Divine Courtroom in Comparative Perspective*. Edited by Ari Mermelstein et al. Leiden: Brill, 2014: 260–75.

_______. "Legal Knowledge and Local Practices under the Early ʿ Mathieu." In *History and Identity in the Eastern Mediterranean*. Edited by Philip Wood. New York: Oxford University Press, 2013: 187–204.

_______. *Les cadis d'Iraq et l'État abbasside (132/750–334/945)*. Damascus: IFPO, 2009.

_______. "L'exemplarité chez al-Tanūḫī: les cadis dans le *Niśwār al-muḥāḍara*." *Arabica* 54 (2007): 1–24.

_______. "Un espace judiciaire entre public et privé. Audiences de cadis à l'époque abbaside." *Annales Islamologiques* 38 (2004): 491–512.

Treadwell, W. L. "The Political History of the Sāmānid State." Unpublished PhD Diss., University of Oxford, 1991.

Tyan, Émile. *Histoire de l'organisation judiciaire en pays d'Islam*. Leiden: Brill, 1960.

_______. *Le notariat et le régime de la preuve par écrit dans la pratique du droit musulman*, 2nd ed. Harissa, Lebanon: Saint Paul, 1959.

ʿUthmān, Muḥammad Raʾfat. *al-Niẓām al-qaḍāʾī fī al-fiqh al-islāmī*. Beirut: Dār al-Bayrūt, 1994.

Vogel, Frank. "Tracing Nuance in Māwardī's al-Aḥkām al-Sulṭāniyyah: Implicit Framing of Constitutional Authority." In *Islamic Law in Theory: Studies on Jurisprudence in Honor of Bernard Weiss*. Edited by A. Kevin Reinhart and Robert Gleave. Leiden: Brill, 2014: 331–59.

Voguet, Elise. *Le monde rural du Maghreb central (XIVe–XVe siècles): Réalités sociales et constructions juridiques d'aprés les* Nawāzil Māzūna. Vol. 5 of *Bibliothèque Historique des pays d'Islam*. Paris: Publications de la Sorbonne, 2014.

Volz, Paul. *Jüdische Eschatologie von Daniel bis Akiba*. Tübingen: J.C.B. Mohr, 1903.

Wahba, Wafaa H. *Al-Māwardī: The Ordinances of Government*. Reading: Garnet Publishing, 1996.

Wakin, Jeanette A. *The Function of Documents in Islamic Law: The Chapters on Sales from Ṭaḥāwī's Kitāb al-shurūṭ al-kabīr*. Albany: State University of New York Press, 1972.

Waldron, Jeremy. "The Rule of Law and the Importance of Procedure." In *Getting to the Rule of Law*. Edited by James E. Fleming. New York: New York University Press, 2011: 3–31.

Weber, Max. *Economy and Society*. Edited by Guenther Roth and Claus Wittich. Translated by Ephraim Fischoh et al. New York: Bedminster Press, 1968.

Wensinck, Arent Jan. *Concordance et indices de la tradition musulmane*. Leiden: Brill, 1992.

Wolf, Kenneth B. *Christian martyrs in Muslim Spain*. Cambridge University Press, 1988.

Yarbrough, Luke. "Did ʿUmar b. ʿAbd al-ʿAzīz Issue an Edict Concerning Non-Muslim Officials?" In *Christians and Others in the Umayyad State*. Edited by Antoine Borrut and Fred M. Donner. Chicago: Oriental Institute, 2016: 173–206.

Young, M.J.L. "Abū l-ʿArab al-Qayrawānī and his biographical dictionary of the scholars of Qayrawān and Tunis." *Al-Masāq* 6 (1993): 57–75.

Zanón, Jesús. "La actividad intellectual: las ramas del saber: Centros y métodos de conocimiento." In *El retroceso territorial de al-Andalus: Almorávides y almohades*. Edited by María Jesús Viguera Molíns. Madrid: Espasa Calpe, 1997: 551–84.

Zaydān, ʿAbd al-Karīm. *Niẓām al-qaḍāʾ fī al-sharīʿa al-Islāmiyya*. Baghdad: Maṭbaʿat al-ʿĀnī, 1984.

GENERAL INDEX

Index of Qurʾānic Verses